INTELLECTUAL FREEDOM MANUAL

Sixth Edition

OIF ALA

Compiled by the
Office for Intellectual Freedom
of the
American Library Association

AMERICAN LIBRARY ASSOCIATION
Chicago and London
2002

Composition by ALA Editions in Britannic and Palatino using QuarkXpress 4.1 on a PC platform

Printed on 50-pound white offset, a pH-neutral stock, and bound in 10-point cover stock by McNaughton & Gunn

The paper used in this publication meets the minimum requirements of American National Standard for Information Sciences—Permanence of Paper for Printed Library Materials, ANSI Z39.48-1992. ∞

Library of Congress Cataloging-in-Publication Data

Intellectual freedom manual / compiled by the Office for Intellectual Freedom of the American Library Association. — 6th ed.
     p.   cm.
    Includes bibliographical references and index.
    ISBN 0-8389-3519-2 (alk. paper)
    1. Libraries—Censorship—United States—Handbooks, manuals, etc.
  2. Freedom of information—United States—Handbooks, manuals, etc.
  I. American Library Association. Office for Intellectual Freedom.

Z711.4 .I57 2002
025.2'13—dc21   2001026684

Printed in the United States of America.

06   05   04   5   4   3   2

CONTENTS

PREFACE   ix

ACKNOWLEDGMENTS   xi

INTRODUCTION   xiii

CONTRIBUTORS   xix

PART I

Intellectual Freedom and Libraries: An Overview

1. ALA and Intellectual Freedom: A Historical Overview   3
      JUDITH F. KRUG

2. Challenges and Issues Today   33
      EVELYN SHAEVEL and BEVERLEY BECKER

3. Intellectual Freedom: An All-Embracing Concept   41
      EVELYN SHAEVEL and BEVERLEY BECKER

PART II

Library Bill of Rights

1. *Library Bill of Rights:* The Policy   57
          History   59

2. *Library Bill of Rights:* Interpretations   72
      2.1   Access for Children and Young People to
            Videotapes and Other Nonprint Formats
                Interpretation   75
                History   78

2.2   Access to Electronic Information, Services,
      and Networks
            Interpretation   80
            Questions and Answers   84
            History   94

2.3   Access to Library Resources and Services
      regardless of Gender or Sexual Orientation
            Interpretation   97
            History   100

2.4   Access to Resources and Services in the School
      Library Media Program
            Interpretation   105
            History   107

2.5   Challenged Materials
            Interpretation   112
            History   113

2.6   Diversity in Collection Development
            Interpretation   118
            History   120

2.7   Economic Barriers to Information Access
            Interpretation   128
            History   132

2.8   Evaluating Library Collections
            Interpretation   136
            History   138

2.9   Exhibit Spaces and Bulletin Boards
            Interpretation   140
            History   142

2.10 Expurgation of Library Materials
            Interpretation   147
            History   149

2.11 Free Access to Libraries for Minors

        Interpretation   152

        History   154

2.12 Intellectual Freedom Principles for Academic
      Libraries

        Interpretation   163

        History   166

2.13 Library-Initiated Programs as a Resource

        Interpretation   168

        History   170

2.14 Meeting Rooms

        Interpretation   173

        History   175

2.15 Restricted Access to Library Materials

        Interpretation   176

        History   178

2.16 Statement on Labeling

        Interpretation   184

        History   186

2.17 The Universal Right to Free Expression

        Interpretation   193

        History   196

PART III

Protecting the Freedom to Read

1. The Freedom to Read

        Policy Statement   201

        History   207

2. Libraries: An American Value
    Policy Statement   228
    History   230

3. Policy on Confidentiality of Library Records
    Policy Statement   232
    Suggested Procedures for Implementing
        "Policy on Confidentiality of Library
        Records"   234
    History   236

4. Policy concerning Confidentiality of Personally
   Identifiable Information about Library Users
    Policy Statement   241
    History   243

5. Resolution and Statement on the Use of Filtering
   Software in Libraries
    Resolution on the Use of Filtering
        Software in Libraries   245
    Statement on Library Use of Filtering
        Software   247
    History   252

6. Policy on Governmental Intimidation
    Policy Statement   255
    History   256

7. Resolution on Access to the Use of Libraries and
   Information by Individuals with Physical or
   Mental Impairment
    Resolution   260
    History   262

8. Guidelines for the Development and Implementation
   of Policies, Regulations and Procedures Affecting Access
   to Library Materials, Services and Facilities
    Guidelines   263
    History   267

9. Guidelines for the Development of Policies and
   Procedures regarding User Behavior and Library Usage
             Guidelines   271
             History   275

10. Dealing with Concerns about Library Resources
             Procedural Statement   278
             History   282

11. Guidelines and Considerations for Developing
   a Public Library Internet Use Policy
             Guidelines   287
             History   296

PART IV

Intellectual Freedom and the Law

1. ALA Intellectual Freedom Policies and the First
   Amendment   301
      BRUCE J. ENNIS

2. Libraries and the Internet   305
      JUDITH F. KRUG

3. School Libraries and the Courts   311
      THERESA CHMARA

4. The Buckley Amendment: Student Privacy versus
   Parents' Right to Know   319
      ANNE LEVINSON PENWAY

5. Public Libraries as Limited Public Fora for Access
   to Information   323
      ANNE LEVINSON PENWAY

PART V

Before the Censor Comes: Essential Preparations

1. Before the Censor Comes: Essential Preparation   331
       BEVERLEY BECKER

2. Developing a Confidentiality Policy   347

3. Communicating the Intellectual Freedom Message   356
       LINDA K. WALLACE

4. The Censor: Motives and Tactics   366

5. Responding to Religious Right Censorship Attempts   370
       ROB BOSTON

PART VI

Working for Intellectual Freedom

1. Combating Censorship: Where to Go for Help   385
       DON WOOD

2. Lobbying for Intellectual Freedom   399
       CAROL C. HENDERSON and the
       ALA WASHINGTON OFFICE

APPENDIXES

1. Code of Ethics   407

2. Selected Bibliography   409

INDEX   411

PREFACE

This manual is designed to answer practical questions that confront librarians in applying the principles of intellectual freedom to library service. It is our hope that every librarian will keep this volume close at hand as a convenient reference work. If, for example, a librarian wants to know what the American Library Association can do to help resist censorship of library materials, how to handle complaints, or how to write an appropriate letter to legislators, help can be found in this volume. If the problem is complex— for example, the development of a materials selection program— practical guidelines on how to tackle the problem are offered.

Part I of the manual explains the meaning of intellectual freedom in library service and how today's broad concept of intellectual freedom evolved from opposition to book censorship. It also includes an overview of today's issues and the challenges they present, ranging from the Internet to privacy and confidentiality. Part II, Library Bill of Rights, and part III, Protecting the Freedom to Read, present the texts and historical development of the ALA's intellectual freedom policies and guidelines (the Interpretations of the *Library Bill of Rights* are arranged in alphabetical order, for convenient reference), and give concrete examples of problems librarians can expect to encounter or should anticipate in formulating policy for their own institutions.

New to this edition of the manual is material specifically relating to libraries and the Internet, including "Resolution and Statement on Library Use of Filtering Software" (part III) and an article on "Libraries and the Internet" (part IV). To accommodate this new material, several articles from the previous edition, as well as some original new material prepared in conjunction with this sixth edition, can now be found on the ALA Web site (www.ala. org/alaorg/oif). It is suggested that you check the Web site regularly to find the latest news on these evolving issues, as well as to monitor changes in ALA policies.

Applying the principles and guidelines in this manual cannot ensure that the rights of librarians and users will never be challenged or that difficulties will not arise. But adhering to these principles in every library is absolutely essential if librarians and users are to enjoy the full benefit of freedom of expression under the First Amendment.

JUDITH F. KRUG, Director
Office for Intellectual Freedom

ACKNOWLEDGMENTS

S pecial thanks and appreciation are due Evelyn Shaevel, a former longtime ALA staff member now working at the Medical Library Association, who served as project director for this sixth edition. Besides updating, editing, and rewriting portions of the manual, Evelyn revised the overall arrangement of the sixth edition to provide better access to both the existing and new information it provides. Beverley Becker and Don Wood, staff members of the Office for Intellectual Freedom, contributed articles and provided valuable support throughout the revision process. All of their work over the past year brought this sixth edition into existence.

INTRODUCTION

Censorship reflects a society's lack of confidence in itself. It is a hallmark of an authoritarian regime . . .

—Justice Potter Stewart, dissenting
Ginzberg v. *United States*, 383 U.S. 463
(1966)

Intellectual freedom can exist only where two essential conditions are met: first, that all individuals have the right to hold any belief on any subject and to convey their ideas in any form they deem appropriate; and second, that society makes an equal commitment to the right of unrestricted access to information and ideas regardless of the communication medium used, the content of the work, and the viewpoints of both the author and receiver of information. Freedom to express oneself through a chosen mode of communication, including the Internet, becomes virtually meaningless if access to that information is not protected. Intellectual freedom implies a circle, and that circle is broken if either freedom of expression or access to ideas is stifled.

Intellectual freedom is freedom of the mind, and as such, it is both a personal liberty and a prerequisite for all freedoms leading to action. Moreover, intellectual freedom, protected by the guarantees of freedoms of speech and press in the First Amendment, forms the bulwark of our constitutional republic. It is an essential part of government by the people. The right to vote is alone not sufficient to give citizens effective control of official actions and policies. They also must be able to take part in the formation of public opinion by engaging in vigorous and wide-ranging debate on controversial matters. Censorship can only stifle this debate, thus weakening government by the people. In the words of Thomas Paine:

> He that would make his own liberty secure must guard even his enemy from opposition; for if he violates this duty he establishes a precedent that will reach to himself.[1]

Intellectual freedom is not only the bulwark of our constitutional republic but also the rallying cry of those who struggle for democracy worldwide. The metaphorical circle of intellectual freedom has expanded to global proportions over the past two decades with the advent of potent new communications technologies and the growing international recognition of the Universal Declaration of Human Rights, Article 19 of which declares the right of all people to freedom of expression. As the free flow of information transcends national boundaries, it becomes increasingly clear that prohibitions on freedom of expression in one country will inhibit the freedom of those in many other countries around the world. In an age of multinational media corporations, international computer links, global telecommunications, and the World Wide Web, we can no longer think simply in local terms. Promoting and defending intellectual freedom requires "thinking globally, and acting locally."

The ALA has recognized the importance of global thinking in an Interpretation of the *Library Bill of Rights,* titled "The Universal Right to Free Expression." Recognizing the crucial role that free access to information plays in the international arena, and the international effects of restrictions imposed on the creation, distribution, and receipt of information and expression, this Interpretation acknowledges free expression as a basic human right. The ALA has also recognized for many years the right of individuals to be free from governmental intimidation in the exercise of their right to free expression. The "Policy on Government Intimidation" was adopted February 2, 1973, and amended July 1, 1981.

Since that time, a multitude of new challenges to intellectual freedom have arisen in the United States. Significant changes in political, social, and economic conditions in the 1980s and 1990s have had a powerful effect on librarians' ability to defend intellectual freedom.

Intellectual freedom is challenged by groups across the political spectrum—from conservatives to liberals—and both old-fashioned political organizing and newer, nontraditional methods are being used to silence critics or suppress materials deemed objectionable for a variety of reasons. In the politically conservative climate that prevailed following the November 1994 congressional elections, free expression came under intensified attack; conservative religious organizations made headway in their demands for restrictions on the availability of information their members find offensive, often using the excuse of "protecting the children" to advance a broader social agenda of a "return" to more conservative times when all supposedly adhered to one view of "family values" and one type of fundamentalist Christian belief. Although such organized groups—including the Christian Coalition, Focus on the Family, Citizens for Excellence in Education/National Association of Christian Educators, Concerned Women for America, and local, ad hoc groups that often spring up around specific controversies— have been around for some time, through careful planning and dogged grassroots organizing, their political clout has grown substantially. Through their efforts and influence, virtually every session of Congress, as well as state legislatures, now features the introduction of sweeping antipornography, antigay, or parental rights legislation designed to limit the availability of constitutionally protected information in schools, libraries, and bookstores.

Conservative religious organizations have alleged that schools and libraries are "promoting" occult or satanic religions in violation of the Establishment Clause of the First Amendment by making available materials on witchcraft, mythology, or fantasy—with the most recent attacks by these groups directed against the *Harry Potter* books. Other approaches to censorship used by individuals and groups across the political spectrum include labeling campaigns— voluntary or not—to "warn" consumers about the content of books, videos, television programs, or musical lyrics; "political correctness" campaigns to purge library collections of works deemed offensive because of racist, sexist, homophobic, ethnic, or religious stereotyping or themes; the proposal of legislation to force providers of Internet access to label or screen material that is posted or accessible; "protect the children" campaigns designed to stifle the availability for adults of sexually explicit information, using potential access by children as the mechanism; attempts by law enforcement officials and others to gain access to confidential patron records; the use of the federal Racketeer Influenced and Corrupt Organizations (RICO) Act and state statutes on "harmful material" to prosecute booksellers, newspaper editors, and others for selling allegedly obscene materials (and sometimes resulting in the confiscation of inventories composed largely of nonobscene, constitutionally protected material); the use of Strategic Lawsuits Against

Public Participation (SLAPPs) by developers, businesses, or public officials to intimidate critics and quell locally organized opposition to their projects or public policies; the use of zoning laws to restrict booksellers or movie theaters that allegedly sell obscene materials or show obscene films; and perhaps the most insidious and difficult to combat, the trend toward self-censorship to avoid legal battles, emotional duress, or any number of other deleterious consequences that may befall the purveyor of a controversial work.

Computer and communications technologies have revolutionized global information flow—making information on breaking events instantly accessible worldwide. The Internet has opened new avenues for communication about a virtually unlimited array of subjects on a scale never before heard of between people of differing backgrounds and means. This has inevitably created tensions—over the equitable allocation of costly computer services to library patrons and over access to an amazing breadth of electronic information, much of which some people consider inappropriate, especially for minors.

In 1996 the Communications Decency Act (CDA) was signed into law as a way to keep "indecent" material from anyone under the age of 18. The ALA and the American Civil Liberties Union (ACLU) combined to challenge the constitutionality of the CDA because it put librarians and libraries at risk since the term "indecent" was not defined in the legislation. In June 1996 a lower court declared the CDA unconstitutional, and ultimately, in June 1997, by a 9-0 vote, the United States Supreme Court agreed. (See part IV, section 2, "Libraries and the Internet.")

The ALA Intellectual Freedom Committee addressed these issues in an Interpretation of the *Library Bill of Rights* titled "Access to Electronic Information, Services, and Networks," which explains how long-standing principles of intellectual freedom apply in the arena of electronic information access. A question-and-answer sheet and an "Internet Toolkit" have also been developed to assist librarians with this issue. Also relevant to the discussion of intellectual freedom and electronic information is the Interpretation entitled "Economic Barriers to Information Access." Providing information via electronic means is costly—libraries must find strategies for providing access without discriminating against patrons of limited economic means.

At the same time the Internet and other computer networks have expanded global information access, social tensions continue among different racial, ethnic, religious, and class-based groups. These tensions have engendered calls for restrictions on speech in a misguided effort to curb the harassment or violence that can erupt as a result of real or perceived inequities and unaddressed frustrations. Although the economy is expanding, budget cuts continue for libraries, schools, and academic institutions, making it easier to eliminate controversial materials and limit the diversity of collections under the guise of economic necessity. This further limits access to information for those who are least able to afford it.

Now more than ever, librarians need to be mindful of the special role libraries play as centers for uninhibited intellectual inquiry. Librarians have taken upon themselves the responsibility to provide, through their institutions, all points of view on all questions and issues of our times, and to make these ideas and opinions available to anyone who needs or wants them, regardless of age, background, or views. These statements should sound familiar; they are basic principles outlined in the *Library Bill of Rights,* which serves as the library profession's interpretation of the First Amendment to the United States Constitution.

The freedom of expression guaranteed by the First Amendment and Article 19, and the corollary to that freedom, the freedom to read, are uniquely fulfilled by the library. Any person, regardless of station, can have access to materials and information. Although libraries are widely recognized as the repositories of civilization, in order to guarantee that the freedom to read has substance, libraries must also acquire and provide information without prejudice or restriction. It is this latter point that gives the *Library Bill of Rights* and its guidance for professional librarianship special importance.

Intellectual freedom cannot bring itself into existence. Librarians must apply the principles of intellectual freedom to activities undertaken daily—materials selection, reference service, reevaluation, protection of confidential patron information, and most important, collection building. It is in acquisition and its product, the collection, that intellectual freedom must be reflected.

The role of the library as governed by the *Library Bill of Rights* cannot be filled by any other societal institution. Newspapers provide information, but it is perforce abridged and can reflect the prejudices of an editor or publisher. Schools educate but according to a program designed to fit the many; one attends school under conditions devised and imposed by administrators and educators. It is in the library, and in the library alone, that self-directed learning, to the limits of one's abilities and to the limits of what is known, can take place.

No one—least of all the librarian—should underestimate the importance of this role. If its significance has been overlooked by many, including librarians, perhaps it is because some librarians have been neither vigorous in the application of these principles nor imaginative in the provision of library services. With the application of the principles of intellectual freedom, with vision and imagination, librarians can—and do—measure up to their unique task.

NOTE

1. Thomas Paine, *Dissertation on First Principles of Government.*

CONTRIBUTORS

Beverley Becker is associate director of the ALA Office for Intellectual Freedom.

Rob Boston is assistant director of communications for Americans United for Separation of Church and State in Washington, D.C., and the author of *Close Encounters with the Religious Right: Journeys into the Twilight Zone of Religion and Politics.*

Theresa Chmara is a partner in the Washington, D.C., office of Jenner & Block. She has served as a counsel to the Freedom to Read Foundation for 12 years. Chmara was an instructor for both Lawyers for Libraries I and Lawyers for Libraries II. She frequently speaks to library groups around the country. She is a current member of the board of the American Booksellers Foundation for Free Expression.

Bruce Ennis served as general counsel for the Freedom to Read Foundation from 1985 until his death in July 2000.

Carol C. Henderson was the executive director of the American Library Association's Washington Office from 1994 to 1999.

Judith F. Krug is the director of the ALA Office for Intellectual Freedom and is executive director of the Freedom to Read Foundation, a First Amendment legal defense organization.

Anne Levinson Penway served as assistant director of the Office for Intellectual Freedom and deputy executive director of the Freedom to Read Foundation from 1988 to 1995.

Evelyn Shaevel, currently assistant to the executive director of the Medical Library Association, has served as executive director of the ALA's Young Adult Services Division, as director of marketing for ALA Publishing, and has worked in both a school library and a public library.

Linda K. Wallace, a communications consultant based in Chicago, is a former journalist and director of the American Library Association's Public Information Office.

Don Wood is the program officer/communications for the ALA Office for Intellectual Freedom.

PART I

Intellectual Freedom
and Libraries
An Overview

I

ALA and Intellectual Freedom
A *Historical Overview*

JUDITH F. KRUG

A t the outset, two myths can be dispelled; namely, that intellectual freedom in libraries is a tradition and that intellectual freedom has always been a major, if not the major, part of the foundation of library service in the United States. Both myths, assumed by
many librarians, are grounded in the belief that librarians support a
static concept of intellectual freedom. Nothing, however, could be
further from the truth.

The attitude of librarians toward intellectual freedom has
undergone continual change since the late 19th century when,
through the American Library Association (ALA), the profession
first began to approach such issues with the semblance of a unified
voice. The ALA, however, has never endorsed a uniform definition
of "intellectual freedom." Instead, through the Council (the ALA's
governing body), the Intellectual Freedom Committee (IFC), and
the Office for Intellectual Freedom (OIF), the ALA has promoted a
variety of principles aimed at fostering a favorable climate for intellectual freedom, but without the limits imposed by a rigid definition. This approach has permitted a broad definition capable of
meeting the needs of librarians as they arise.

The seeds of the general definition of intellectual freedom were
sown in the movement against censorship of published materials
and grew into a strong, central trunk from which many branches of
ALA and intellectual freedom have continued to spring. One branch

---

Updated by Evelyn Shaevel

concerns the library user's access to all the materials in a library collection. Another pertains to the librarian's professional practice, particularly selecting and making available all published materials to all library users, and protecting the confidentiality of patron records to ensure that every individual may use the library freely and without fear of reprisal. At stake also is the librarian's personal intellectual freedom: participation in the democratic process, the right to free expression, and the right to pursue a chosen lifestyle without fear of negative professional repercussions. Yet another aspect of intellectual freedom encompasses the library as an institution and its role in social change and education. Of particular importance is the question of "advocacy" versus "neutrality." Can a library committed to intellectual freedom and to providing materials that represent all points of view also support one point of view?

Each of these branches in turn has sprouted a plethora of twigs and, viewed in its entirety, the tree makes anything other than an issue-oriented approach nearly impossible. Consequently, the profession's stance on intellectual freedom has sometimes lagged behind that of society at large; most often it has paralleled public opinion; and, occasionally, it has anticipated changes in taste, mores, and social issues, and has taken positions in advance of the rest of the citizenry.

Censorship of Published Materials

The catalyst spurring librarians to take the initial steps toward supporting intellectual freedom was the censorship of specific publications. "Censorship" in this context means not only deletion or excision of parts of published materials but also efforts to ban, prohibit, suppress, proscribe, remove, label, or restrict materials. Opposition to these activities emanated from the belief that freedom of the mind is basic to the functioning and maintenance of democracy as practiced in the United States. Such democracy assumes that educated, free individuals possess powers of discrimination and are to be trusted to determine their own actions. It assumes further that the best guarantee of effective and continuing self-government is a thoroughly informed electorate capable of making real choices. Denying the opportunity of choice, for fear it may be used unwisely, destroys freedom itself. Opposition to censorship derives naturally from the library's historical role as an educational institution providing materials that develop individuals' abilities, interests, and knowledge. Censorship denies the opportunity to choose from all possible alternatives and thereby violates intellectual freedom. The library profession has aimed to ensure every individual's freedom of the mind so that society as a whole benefits. Even in this central area, however, the professional position has fluctuated, being influenced by such factors as taste, quality, responsibility, morality, legality, and purpose.

One early incident concerning censorship, involving a substantial number of librarians, occurred in 1924 when the Librarians' Union of the American Federation of Labor reported that the Carnegie Libraries fostered "a system under which only books approved in a certain manner may be placed on Carnegie Library shelves and that amounts to censorship and is so intended."[1] The ALA Executive Board considered the union's charges and offered to enlist volunteers to investigate the claims. Apparently, however, the union did not act upon the offer, and the matter was not considered further by the Executive Board.

In 1929, the Association indicated its future approach to censorship when the ALA Executive Board studied a proposed federal tariff bill and opposed prohibiting the import of materials "advocating or urging treason, insurrection, or forcible resistance to any law of the U.S. . . . or any obscene book, paper, etc."

The Board's opposition was based

> on the grounds that this clause creates an effective censorship over foreign literature, will ban many of the classics on modern economics, will keep out material relating to revolution in foreign countries, will indirectly stop the reprinting of such books by our own publishers, and is a reflection upon the intelligence of the American people by implying that they are so stupid and untrustworthy that they cannot read about revolutions without immediately becoming traitors and revolutionaries themselves; and because the question of social policy is withdrawn from the ordinary courts and placed in the hands of officials primarily chosen for their special qualifications in dealing with the administrative details of tariff laws.[2]

Ironically, just four years later, when the Executive Board received a letter requesting that the Association "take some action in regard to the burning of books in Germany by the Hitler regime, the matter was "considered briefly but it was the sense of the meeting that no action should be taken."[3]

In 1934, the Association recorded its first protest against the banning of a specific publication, *You and Machines*, a pamphlet by William Ogburn. Prepared for use in Civilian Conservation Corps camps under a grant from the American Council on Education, the pamphlet was denied circulation by the camps' director, who believed it would induce a philosophy of despair and a desire to destroy existing economic and political structures. Initially, the ALA president and executive secretary wrote a joint letter to President Franklin D. Roosevelt, stating that "[governmental] censorship on a publication of this character written by a man of recognized authority is unthinkable."[4] Later the board discussed the banning further and appointed a committee to draft another letter for approval by the ALA Council. The result was a formal request that President Roosevelt "make it possible for the U.S. Commissioner of Education and the Education Director of the Civilian Conservation Corps to direct the educational policies to be operative in these camps and to make available the reading matter essential in a modern program of education."[5]

These examples illustrate the Association's wavering position and reflect the ambivalent attitude of the profession as a whole regarding censorship. A review of library literature reveals relatively few articles on intellectual freedom prior to the 1930s, and many of the articles that did appear supported censorship and only quibbled over the degree and nature of it. Typical was the opinion of ALA president Arthur E. Bostwick, whose inaugural address at the 1908 Annual Conference included these remarks:

> "Some are born great; some achieve greatness; some have greatness thrust upon them." It is in this way that the librarian has become a censor of literature. . . . Books that distinctly commend what is wrong, that teach how to sin and how pleasant sin is, sometimes with and sometimes without the added sauce of impropriety, are increasingly popular, tempting the author to imitate them, the publishers to produce, the bookseller to exploit. Thank Heaven they do not tempt the librarian.[6]

Given the multiplicity of professional attitudes toward censorship of print materials, it is not surprising that censorship of nonprint media was once viewed as completely outside the concerns of the profession. For example, as late as 1938, the ALA Executive Board believed it was inappropriate to protest when the Federal Communications Commission forced a radio station to defend its broadcast of Eugene O'Neill's *Beyond the Horizon.*[7]

The Association's basic position in opposition to censorship finally emerged in the late 1930s, when John Steinbeck's *The Grapes of Wrath* became the target of censorship pressures around the country. It was banned from libraries in East St. Louis, Illinois; Camden, New Jersey; Bakersfield, California; and other localities. While some objected to the "immorality" of the work, most opposed the social views advanced by the author.

The ALA's initial response to the pressures against *The Grapes of Wrath* was the adoption in 1939 of the *Library's Bill of Rights,* the precursor of the present *Library Bill of Rights,* the profession's basic policy statement on intellectual freedom involving library materials. (See *Library Bill of Rights,* in part II.)

In 1940, one year after adoption of the *Library's Bill of Rights,* the Association established the Intellectual Freedom Committee, or IFC. (Originally called the Committee on Intellectual Freedom to Safeguard the Rights of Library Users to Freedom of Inquiry, the Committee's name was shortened by Council action in 1948 to Committee on Intellectual Freedom and inverted through usage to Intellectual Freedom Committee.) The 1940 charge to the IFC was "to recommend such steps as may be necessary to safeguard the rights of library users in accordance with the Bill of Rights and the *Library's Bill of Rights,* as adopted by Council."[8] Although the IFC's role has varied, its main function has been to recommend policies concerning intellectual freedom, especially—but not limited to— matters involving violations of the *Library Bill of Rights.* Although its original statement of authority referred only to library users, in reality the IFC became active in promoting intellectual freedom for librarians and patrons as well. Its diversified role was recognized and formalized in 1970 when the Council approved a revised statement of authority:

> To recommend such steps as may be necessary to safeguard the rights of library users, libraries, and librarians, in accordance with the First Amendment to the United States Constitution and the *Library Bill of Rights* as adopted by the ALA Council. To work

closely with the Office for Intellectual Freedom and with other units and officers of the Association in matters touching intellectual freedom and censorship.[9]

The original *Library's Bill of Rights* focused on unbiased book selection, a balanced collection, and open meeting rooms. It did not mention censorship or removal of materials at the behest of groups or individuals. Over the years, however, the document has been revised, amended, and interpreted, often in response to specific situations with general implications. The first change, a 1944 amendment against banning materials considered "factually correct," was occasioned by attacks on *Under Cover,* an exposé of Nazi organizations in the United States, and *Strange Fruit,* a novel about interracial love. The reference to "factually correct" was later dropped, but the directive against removal of materials remained. Opposition to censorship of nonprint media was amended to the document in 1951 because of attacks on films alleged to promote communism. To combat the suppression of communist materials or other allegedly "subversive" publications, the Association issued its "Statement on Labeling" (see part II, section 2.16), which stated that designating materials "subversive" is subtle censorship, because such a label predisposes readers against the materials. Responding to pressures against materials about civil rights activities, a 1967 amendment to the *Library Bill of Rights* warned against excluding materials because of the social views of the authors. In its 1971 "Resolution on Challenged Materials," the Association counseled libraries not to remove challenged materials unless, after an adversary hearing in a court of law, the materials were judged to be outside the protection of the First Amendment. (See "Challenged Materials," part II, section 2.5.)

Changing circumstances necessitate constant review of the *Library Bill of Rights* and often result in position statements to clarify the document's application. (See "*Library Bill of Rights:* Interpretations" in part II, section 2.) The present *Library Bill of Rights* was last revised in 1980. Its interpretive documents were systematically reviewed and updated in 1980, 1981, 1982, 1989, 1991, 1994, and most recently in 1999–2000. The newest interpretations are "Access to Electronic Information, Services, and Networks," adopted by the ALA Council in January 1996; and "Intellectual Freedom Principles for Academic Libraries," approved by the Association of College and Research Libraries' Board of Directors in June 1999 and adopted by the ALA Council in July 2000.

Taken together, these documents recognize and explain that censorship of any materials, in any guise, eventually affects the library. The *Library Bill of Rights,* therefore, provides principles upon which libraries may stand to oppose censorship and promote intellectual freedom. Referring directly to censorship practices, the *Library Bill of Rights* states that no library materials should be "excluded because of the origin, background, or views of those contributing to their creation," and that materials should not be "proscribed or removed because of partisan or doctrinal disapproval."

On its face, the profession's view of intellectual freedom is a pure one, based on a strict reading of the First Amendment to the U.S. Constitution, which states, "Congress shall make no law . . . abridging freedom of speech, or of the press." Within the limits defined by the United States Supreme Court (for example, the legal doctrines governing obscenity, defamation, or "fighting words"), the position relies on the extension of First Amendment principles via the Fourteenth Amendment to the states and their agencies, including publicly supported libraries. (Some state constitutions actually provide greater protection for free speech than does the First Amendment as interpreted by the United States Supreme Court, but no state is permitted to provide less protection for these fundamental rights.) In actual practice, the purist position sometimes gives way to compromises by individual librarians, resulting in the removal, labeling, or covert nonselection of certain materials.

If followed by librarians and governing bodies, however, the Association's policy statements provide an effective means of helping to prevent library censorship. Ideally, application of these policies to materials selection, circulation practices, and complaint handling establishes the library as an indispensable information source for individuals exercising their freedom of inquiry.

Free Access to Library Materials

Access to library collections and services is another concern of the profession. For intellectual freedom to flourish, opposition to censorship of materials is not enough. Free access to materials for every member of the community must also be ensured. The ALA first recognized this in the 1939 *Library's Bill of Rights*, which included a proviso that library meeting rooms be available on equal terms to all groups in the community regardless of the beliefs and affiliations of their members.

Another policy on free access emerged from a study of segregation made by the Association's Special Committee on Civil Liberties during the late 1950s. One result of the study was a 1961 amendment to the *Library Bill of Rights*, stating that "the rights of an individual to the use of a library should not be denied or abridged because of his race, religion, national origins, or political views." This amendment was broadened in 1967, when "social views" and "age" were incorporated to emphasize other areas of potential discrimination. "Age" was included to resolve a long-standing debate on the right of minors to have access to libraries on the same basis as adults. It should be noted that the addition of "age" illustrates one instance in which the library profession acted well in advance of public opinion.

In 1971, at the urging of the Task Force on Gay Liberation of the Social Responsibilities Round Table, the Association recommended that libraries and ALA members strenuously combat discrimination in serving any individual from a minority, whether it be an ethnic, sexual, religious, or any other kind of minority. In 1980, the *Library Bill of Rights* was revised to encompass all discrimination based on "origin, age, background, or views." Interpretations of the *Library Bill of Rights* addressing specific issues that fall under these deliberately broad categories include "Access for Children and Young People to Videotapes and Other Nonprint Formats," "Access to Resources and Services in the School Library Media Program," "Free Access to Libraries for Minors," "Economic Barriers to Information Access," and "Access to Library Resources and Services regardless of Gender or Sexual Orientation." (See the relevant sections in part II.)

Another aspect of the library patron's access to materials was broached in 1970 when the Internal Revenue Service requested permission from several libraries to examine circulation records to determine the names of persons reading materials about explosives and guerrilla warfare. The Association responded by developing its "Policy on Confidentiality of Library Records," urging libraries to designate such records as confidential and accessible only "pursuant to such process, order, or subpoena as may be authorized under the authority of, and pursuant to, federal, state, or local law relating to civil, criminal, or administrative discovery procedures or legislative investigatory power." (See part III, section 3.) The rationale of the policy was that circulation records are purely circumstantial evidence that a patron has read a book and that fear of persecution or prosecution may restrain users from borrowing any conceivably controversial materials, for whatever purpose.

The question of library records and the confidentiality of relationships between librarians and library users arose again in 1971 regarding the "use of grand jury procedure to intimidate anti-Vietnam War activists and people seeking justice for minority communities." In response, the Association asserted "the confidentiality of the professional relationships of librarians to the people they serve, that these relationships be respected in the same manner as medical doctors to their patients, lawyers to their clients, priests to the people they serve," and that "no librarian would lend himself to a role as informant, whether of voluntarily revealing circulation records or identifying patrons and their reading habits." (See part III, section 6, "Policy on Governmental Intimidation.")

In late 1987 it was disclosed that Federal Bureau of Investigation (FBI) agents were visiting libraries in what are best described as "fishing expeditions." Agents generally first approached library clerks and solicited information on the use of various library services (e.g., interlibrary loan, database searches) by "suspicious looking foreigners" and, in some instances, asked to see the library's circulation records.

A public confrontation between the IFC and the FBI eventually ensued. The IFC stressed the inextricability of First Amendment and privacy rights, as well as the fact that the FBI was requesting that librarians violate not only a professional ethic but also the law in thirty-eight states and the District of Columbia. (As of this writing, there are confidentiality laws in forty-seven states and an attorney general's opinion supporting confidentiality in one state.) The FBI refused to back away from what it characterized as a program (the "Library Awareness Program") to alert librarians to the possibility that libraries were being used by foreign agents as a place to recruit operatives, that librarians themselves were sometimes targeted for approach by foreign agents, and that valuable material was being stolen by these agents and their operatives. The IFC emphasized, in congressional testimony and in the media, the principle of open access to publicly available information and the central role of libraries in this society as providers of that access.

In the fall of 1989, through a Freedom of Information Act (FOIA) request, the ALA obtained documents from the FBI in which 266 individuals, all of whom had in some way criticized the Library Awareness Program, were identified as subjects of FBI "index checks." These documents also suggested that the Library Awareness Program covered parts of the country other than New York City alone, as previously claimed by the FBI.

Early in 1990, the ALA wrote to President George Bush, then to FBI director William Sessions, and to the relevant House and Senate committees, urging that the Library Awareness Program be discontinued and that the files of the 266 individuals be released to them and expunged from FBI records. Director Sessions responded in March 1990, defending the program and denying that any investigation of the 266 had taken place, claiming that "index checks" were administrative and not investigative in nature. Subsequently, individuals were urged to make their own FOIA requests, but only one person who filed such a request later reported receiving any information from the FBI.

In addition, the ALA filed yet another FOIA request, which was denied, as was the appeal of that denial, on the grounds that the FBI was in litigation with the National Security Archive (NSA) over the same issue. The FBI promised to give the ALA any information released to the NSA and eventually did so. Nevertheless, the ALA reserved the right to bring suit against the FBI for denying its right of appeal and obstructing a legitimate attempt to gain information under the Freedom of Information Act.

The FBI has never publicly abandoned the Library Awareness Program, and may still be conducting it.

Federal agencies are not alone in attempting to make use of library patron records. Local law enforcement officials, journalists, students, parents, fund-raisers, marketing professionals, civil litigants, and politicians have been known to seek borrowing records, registration data, mailing lists, and other information about library patrons. In 1990 a library director in Decatur, Texas, challenged one

such attempt in court and won an important victory for library confidentiality policies. In *Decatur Public Library* v. *District Attorney's
Office of Wise County*,[10] the district attorney, investigating a
child-abandonment case, subpoenaed the records of all libraries in
Wise County, requesting the names, addresses, and telephone numbers of all individuals who had checked out books on childbirth
within the previous nine months, the titles they borrowed, and the
dates the materials were checked out and returned. The police had
no evidence indicating that the person who abandoned the child
might have borrowed library books or otherwise used the library.
They were simply conducting a "fishing expedition."

The director of the Decatur Public Library refused to comply
with the subpoena and, with the help of the city attorney, filed a
motion to quash it on behalf of the library's patrons. On May 9,
1990, Judge John R. Lindsey ruled in favor of the library and
quashed the subpoena. His decision recognized the library's standing to assert a constitutional privilege on behalf of its unnamed
patrons and clients, affirmed a constitutional right of privacy available to patrons, and held that the State was unable to demonstrate
a compelling governmental objective under its police powers or
other legitimate function of government to warrant intrusion of
those rights.

In 1995, the issue of library user confidentiality again reached
the courts in connection with a lawsuit brought by a tobacco company, Brown and Williamson, against the University of California.
The company alleged that the University of California at San
Francisco library possessed in its collection documents stolen from
the company that purportedly showed that the tobacco industry had
known of a link between smoking and cancer for many years and
had failed to disclose it. The documents had previously been leaked
to the press and discussed in congressional hearings at the time the
lawsuit was filed. The lawsuit sought not only return of the documents but a list of all library patrons who had access to them and a
description of the nature of those users' research and publications.

The ALA's sister organization, the Freedom to Read Foundation
(see below and part VI, section 1, "Combating Censorship: Where to
Go for Help"), identified the case as one of extreme importance,
with the potential to set a positive precedent in favor of First
Amendment protection for library-user privacy, and filed an amicus

brief explaining the crucial link between library confidentiality and First Amendment rights. Although the case ultimately was resolved without reaching the confidentiality issue, the fact that a request for library-user records was made as part of the lawsuit indicates the breadth of circumstances in which a threat to confidentiality may arise.

Through the Association's various position statements, the profession has established a code of free access to services and materials for all library users. Opposed to using the library as a means of intimidating patrons, the profession strives to enhance the intellectual freedom of the library user by providing not only all materials requested, but also free and equal access to all materials without fear of recrimination for pursuing one's interests.

The Librarian and Intellectual Freedom

Although the profession, through the ALA, formulates policies to help ensure a climate favorable to intellectual freedom, the individual librarian is the key to achieving the end result. Adherence to the *Library Bill of Rights* by individual librarians is the only means of effecting the profession's goals. Consequently, the concept of intellectual freedom also considers the individual librarian's intellectual freedom, both in pursuit of professional responsibilities and in personal life. Several agencies within or closely affiliated with the ALA, accordingly, encourage and protect the librarian's commitment to the principles of intellectual freedom. In relation to support for intellectual freedom, the "Code of Ethics" of the American Library Association (see appendix 1), passed by the ALA Council in June 1995, specifically states: "We uphold the principles of intellectual freedom and resist all efforts to censor library materials."

From 1940 until 1967, most such activities were centered in the Intellectual Freedom Committee. For many years, it not only recommended policies but also directed a variety of educational efforts, including collecting and publicizing information about censorship incidents, sponsoring censorship exhibits at conferences, conducting preconferences on intellectual freedom themes, and planning complementary programs to further the Association's goals regarding intellectual freedom.

One of these complementary programs is the Office for Intellectual Freedom (OIF), established in December 1967. The OIF evolved finally from a 1965 preconference on intellectual freedom held in Washington, D.C. That meeting recommended establishing an ALA headquarters unit to conduct and coordinate the Association's intellectual freedom activities and to provide continuity for the total program. The goal of the OIF is to educate librarians and the general public on the importance of intellectual freedom, relieving the IFC of this task and allowing it to concentrate on developing policy. The OIF serves as the administrative arm of the Intellectual Freedom Committee and bears the responsibility for implementing ALA policies on intellectual freedom, as approved by the Council. The philosophy of the Office for Intellectual Freedom is based on the premise that if librarians are to appreciate the importance of intellectual freedom they must first understand the concept as it relates to the individual, the institution, and the functioning of society. Believing that with understanding comes the ability to teach others, the OIF maintains a broad program of informational publications, projects, and services.

The regular OIF publication is the bimonthly *Newsletter on Intellectual Freedom.* The OIF prepares special educational materials, for instance, the *Banned Books Week Resource Kit* and others as need dictates. In addition, the OIF works closely with ALA Editions (part of Publishing) to develop books. Recent titles have included *Libraries, Access, and Intellectual Freedom: Developing Policies for Public and Academic Libraries,* by Barbara M. Jones (ALA, 1999); *Libraries, the First Amendment, and Cyberspace: What You Need to Know,* by Robert S. Peck (ALA, 2000); and *Speaking Out! Voices in Celebration of Intellectual Freedom,* by Ann K. Symons and Sally Gardner Reed (ALA, 1999). The OIF also distributes documents, articles, brochures, and all ALA policy statements concerning intellectual freedom in print and on the Web. As part of its information program, the OIF maintains and distributes a banned books exhibit. The exhibit is available for display at national, state, and local conferences, workshops, seminars, and other meetings.

The Office for Intellectual Freedom advises and consults with librarians confronting potential or actual censorship problems. Telephone and letter requests about materials that have drawn the censorial efforts of an individual or group in the community prompt efforts to give appropriate assistance. Another means of assistance established in 1994 is the Intellectual Freedom Action

Network (see part VI, section 1, "Combating Censorship: Where to Go for Help"), a group of concerned volunteers who have identified themselves as willing to stand up in support of intellectual freedom when controversy comes to their area, and to alert the OIF to the activities of censorship pressure groups in their communities. The OIF coordinates the Action Network, calling upon its members when necessary to write letters, attend meetings, or provide moral support to librarians fighting censorship in their localities.

The OIF also coordinates the Intellectual Freedom Committee's relations with other organizations having similar concerns. These include the intellectual freedom committees of the ALA divisions and the state library associations' intellectual freedom committees. Close contact with nonlibrary organizations—such as the Association of American Publishers, the American Booksellers Association, the American Civil Liberties Union, the National Coalition against Censorship, and others—is also maintained.

As the ALA's intellectual freedom program developed, the need for an organizational forum through which individual ALA members could participate in intellectual freedom activities according to their varying levels of interest began to be felt. At the 1973 Annual Conference in Las Vegas, the Intellectual Freedom Round Table (IFRT) was organized as the Association's membership-activity program for intellectual freedom. The activities of the Round Table supplement the OIF's education program and offer opportunities for ALA members to become active in the Association's intellectual freedom efforts.

The IFRT sponsors three intellectual freedom awards. The annual State and Regional Achievement Award, given by the IFRT since 1984, was revised in 1991. Formerly presented to a state intellectual freedom committee, the award has been expanded to include "state educational media association intellectual freedom committee[s], state intellectual freedom coalition[s], legal defense fund[s] or other such group that has implemented the most successful and creative state intellectual freedom project during the calendar year. The award also may be presented for on-going or multiyear projects." The IFRT established the John Phillip Immroth Memorial Award for Intellectual Freedom, given annually in memory of the cofounder and first chairperson of the Round Table, "to honor notable contributions to intellectual freedom and demonstrations of personal courage in defense of freedom of expression." Biennially, the IFRT sponsors the Eli M. Oboler Memorial Award, presented for the best published work in the area of intellectual freedom.

Soon after adoption of the *Library Bill of Rights* and establishment of the Intellectual Freedom Committee, the profession realized that more than just information sources were needed to foster the practice of intellectual freedom in libraries. Some members called for a "policing" effort to publicize censorship problems and bring pressure upon authorities to correct conditions conducive to censorship. As early as the 1948 ALA Annual Conference in Atlantic City, Robert D. Leigh, director of the Public Library Inquiry, addressed the Council and recommended that "some responsible group" be created to investigate reports of library censorship, make public reports of investigations, give possible aid to professionals who become victims of censorship, and in extreme cases, exercise "a professional boycott against the libraries of censoring authorities."[11] Some of Leigh's recommendations were debated for nearly 20 years before a national resolution of the problems began to emerge. As a first substantive step, in 1969 the Association adopted its Program of Action in Support of the *Library Bill of Rights.*

The first Program of Action, developed by the IFC and approved by the Council, created a mechanism whereby complaints about censorship incidents were reported to the Office for Intellectual Freedom and acted upon by the Intellectual Freedom Committee. Such complaints were studied by the OIF and the IFC to determine whether they involved intellectual freedom problems within the scope of the *Library Bill of Rights.* If the complaint fell under the Program of Action, the Office for Intellectual Freedom and the Intellectual Freedom Committee attempted to mediate, arbitrate, or provide appropriate assistance to effect a just resolution of the problem. If these means failed, one prerogative of the Committee was to establish a fact-finding team to investigate further. After such an investigation, the team reported its findings to the IFC for review. Further substantive action required a recommendation by the IFC to the ALA Executive Board. Under a sanctions policy adopted in 1971, the IFC could recommend publication of a summary of the report, publication of the entire report, or various other sanctions against groups or individuals violating the spirit of the *Library Bill of Rights.* The ALA Executive Board made the final disposition of the Intellectual Freedom Committee's recommendations.

From 1969 to 1971, in response to requests for action, three fact-finding projects were undertaken by the IFC. The first major case was brought by Joan Bodger. An extensive investigation explored Bodger's charge that she had been fired from the Missouri State Library because of her public support of intellectual freedom. She had written a letter to a local newspaper protesting the suppression of an underground newspaper. The IFC concluded that her allegations were correct and recommended publication of the complete report in *American Libraries*, vindicating Bodger and deploring the Missouri State Library Commission's actions, which resulted in her firing.

The other two requests for action also entailed fact-finding studies, after which the Intellectual Freedom Committee found it could not support charges contained in the complaints. Reports summarizing the two cases were published in *American Libraries*.[12]

The three complaints investigated under the Program of Action made it clear that cases involving intellectual freedom also might raise issues of tenure, academic status, ethical practices, and a variety of other matters. The difficulty of focusing only on intellectual freedom increased in late 1970 when a complaint was received from J. Michael McConnell, who was denied a position at the University of Minnesota library shortly after his well-publicized application for a marriage license to marry another male. Charging the university discriminated against him because of his homosexuality, McConnell appealed to the IFC, claiming his case fell under the Program of Action. To support his claim, he cited the 1946 ALA "Statement of Principles of Intellectual Freedom and Tenure for Librarians," which states, "Intellectual freedom precludes partisan political control of appointments and makes it possible for librarians to devote themselves to the practice of their profession without fear of interference or of dismissal for political, religious, racial, marital or other unjust reasons."

The IFC did not dispute McConnell's claim that his case fell under the scope of the 1946 policy statement. It disagreed, however, that the case came within the jurisdiction of the Program of Action, because that mechanism dealt only with violations of the *Library Bill of Rights*. The Committee attempted to resolve the problem by rewriting the Program of Action to allow jurisdiction over all ALA policies on intellectual freedom. The revision, completed during a special December 1970 meeting of the IFC, was to come before the

Council for approval in January 1971. At its Midwinter Meeting, however, the Committee again revised the document to include all ALA policies on intellectual freedom and tenure. It was then pointed out that both the Library Administration Division (LAD) and the Association of College and Research Libraries (ACRL) claimed vested interests in investigations, particularly those involving tenure of academic librarians. The complex jurisdictional problems resulted in an appeal to ALA president Lillian Bradshaw to take steps immediately to develop a central investigatory agency for the entire Association. Moving swiftly, President Bradshaw appointed a membership group representing various interests. In June 1971, the group presented the Program of Action for Mediation, Arbitration, and Inquiry to the Council, which adopted it and rescinded the first Program of Action.

The new Program of Action established a Staff Committee on Mediation, Arbitration, and Inquiry (SCMAI), which functioned somewhat as the IFC had under the old document. In addition to intellectual freedom problems, however, the new committee handled cases involving tenure, professional status, fair employment practices, ethical practices, and due process as set forth in ALA policies. In June 1990, the SCMAI was replaced by the Standing Committee on Review, Inquiry, and Mediation (SCRIM). Lack of funding caused the SCRIM to cease operation on September 1, 1992.

The Intellectual Freedom Committee, the Office for Intellectual Freedom, and the Intellectual Freedom Round Table are the primary agencies for establishing and promoting the Association's positions on questions involving intellectual freedom. In addition, the Intellectual Freedom Action Network supports these positions and responds to controversies on the local level. The element in the Association's program in support and defense of intellectual freedom that takes the most aggressive, proactive role, however, is the Freedom to Read Foundation.

Incorporated in November 1969, the Freedom to Read Foundation was the ALA's response to librarians who increasingly wanted defense machinery to protect their jobs from jeopardy when they undertook to challenge violations of intellectual freedom. Another primary objective in establishing the Foundation was to have a means through which librarians and other concerned individuals and groups could begin to set legal precedents for the freedom to read. The Foundation was created outside the structure of the ALA and, to ensure its full freedom to act with vigor in the legal arena, it remains legally and financially independent. But the Foundation is closely affiliated with the ALA through the ex officio membership of ALA officers on its board of trustees. The Foundation's executive director also serves as director of the ALA Office for Intellectual Freedom.

A program of education on the importance of, and the necessity for a commitment to, the principles of intellectual freedom requires assurance that such commitment will not result in reprisals, such as legal prosecution, financial loss, or personal damage. The Freedom to Read Foundation attempts to provide that assurance through financial and legal assistance and legal challenges to restrictive legislation, thereby helping to create a favorable climate for intellectual freedom. Through the provision of financial and legal assistance, the Foundation attempts to negate the necessity for librarians to make the difficult choice between practical expediency (that is, keeping a job) and upholding principles, such as in selecting materials for library collections. Through its various projects and grants, the Foundation hopes to establish those principles enunciated in the *Library Bill of Rights* as legal precedents rather than mere paper policies.

Established by the Freedom to Read Foundation, but now formally independent, the LeRoy C. Merritt Humanitarian Fund was created in 1970. The Merritt Fund was established by the Foundation's board of trustees in recognition of individuals' need for subsistence and other support when their positions are jeopardized or lost as a result of defending intellectual freedom. This special fund offers short-term, immediate assistance even prior to the development of all pertinent facts in a particular case, whether or not legal action has been taken.

In the combined forces of the Intellectual Freedom Committee, the Office for Intellectual Freedom, the Intellectual Freedom Round Table, the Intellectual Freedom Action Network, and the Freedom to Read Foundation, along with the LeRoy C. Merritt Humanitarian Fund, the library profession has available a complete program to support the practice of intellectual freedom. The profession, however, has not yet achieved the same success in a closely related area, that of the librarian's personal rather than professional intellectual freedom. The question of what support should be given to librarians who suffer professionally because of personal beliefs and actions has been approached in individual cases but has not been fully resolved.

One of the first instances involving potential recriminations in a professional capacity as a result of personal beliefs occurred in the late 1940s, with the advent of "loyalty oaths" and "loyalty programs" designed to ferret out communists and "subversives." The Intellectual Freedom Committee faced the loyalty issue with its "Policy on Loyalty Programs," first adopted by the Council in 1948 and revised in 1951. When another case arose in Florida in 1969, the "Policy on Loyalty Programs" was reexamined and again revised. The last revision, adopted by the Council in January 1971, states in part the following:

> The American Library Association strongly protests loyalty programs which inquire into a library employee's thoughts, reading matter, associates, or membership in organizations, unless a particular person's definite actions warrant such investigation. We condemn loyalty oaths as a condition of employment and investigations which permit the discharge of an individual without a fair hearing.[13]

In 1969, another incident arose involving a librarian who lost his position because of actions, based on personal beliefs, taken in his capacity as a private citizen. T. Ellis Hodgin was fired as city librarian of Martinsville, Virginia, shortly after he joined a lawsuit challenging the constitutionality of a religious education course taught in the city school his daughter attended. He had also been active in civil rights efforts. Hodgin's situation sparked a controversy among librarians, resulting in a recommendation from the Intellectual Freedom Subcommittee of the Activities Committee on New Directions for ALA (ACONDA):

> The scope of intellectual freedom encompasses considerably more than just the freedom to read. Support must also be rendered to the librarian who is fired for sporting a beard, for engaging in civil rights activities, etc., etc. And he should not have to claim "poverty" in order to receive it.[14]

The recommendation, however, was not approved as part of the final ACONDA report.

Some concerned librarians responded to Hodgin's plight by organizing the National Freedom Fund for Librarians (NFFL), which collected several thousand dollars to aid him. (When the NFFL disbanded in 1971, its cash balance was sent to the LeRoy C. Merritt Humanitarian Fund.)

Hodgin also appealed to the Freedom to Read Foundation for assistance to defray the financial hardship he suffered when he lost his position. In June 1970, the Foundation's executive committee awarded him $500

> for having suffered in his defense of freedom of speech as a result of which he lost his position as a librarian. Inasmuch as it is the obligation of the librarian to protect free speech and a free press through his work as a librarian, it is then particularly appropriate that, when he is deprived of his job because of his own exercise of free speech, the Freedom to Read Foundation assist him in the defense of his freedom.[15]

A second grant of $500 was made to Hodgin in January 1971 for the specific purpose of perfecting an appeal of his suit for reinstatement to the U.S. Supreme Court.

The limits of intellectual freedom were again debated by the profession when the previously mentioned case of J. Michael McConnell arose in 1970. The Intellectual Freedom Committee found that McConnell's rights "under the First Amendment have been violated" because he met reprisals for freely expressing his sexual preference.[16] On that basis the LeRoy C. Merritt Humanitarian Fund granted $500 to help defray financial hardship occasioned by his inability to find another job.

The question of how far librarians are willing to extend the scope of intellectual freedom for the benefit of their colleagues was raised anew in 1979 by the case of Utah librarian Jeanne Layton. In September 1979, Layton was dismissed from her position as library director in Davis County after she refused to comply with requests to remove the novel *Americana,* by Don DeLillo, from library shelves. The following month she filed suit to regain her job.

The suit was supported from the beginning by the Freedom to Read Foundation, but it soon became clear that the legal battle would be a lengthy and very costly one. Both the Intellectual Freedom Committee and the Freedom to Read Foundation designated the case a priority for 1980. The Utah Library Association rallied librarians and others statewide in support. At the 1980 ALA Annual Conference in New York, the Freedom to Read Foundation announced that it would match two dollars for every dollar contributed to Jeanne Layton's defense from June 27, 1980, to December 31, 1980, up to a limit of $10,000 in matching funds. The response was, in the words of Foundation president Florence McMullin, "nothing short of overwhelming." When the challenge expired, $6,024 had been received, of which $5,000 was matched "two for one" by the Foundation. Moreover, Jeanne Layton won her suit and regained her job, and one of her main antagonists was defeated for reelection to the county commission.

Although the question of how far librarians will go to support colleagues in defense of intellectual freedom will always be resolvable only on a case-by-case and issue-by-issue basis, the response to Layton's courageous stand surely indicates that in general the library profession takes its responsibilities on this front seriously indeed.

The Library and Intellectual Freedom

Each aspect of intellectual freedom in libraries that has been discussed to this point has involved library users and their access to all published materials, as well as librarians and their practice of professional or personal intellectual freedom.

One last branch of intellectual freedom remains to be examined, that being the library as an institution and the nature of its role in social change and education. Continually debated within the profession and the American Library Association, the issue has been summarized as "neutrality versus advocacy." In essence, the question is, can libraries, as institutions, advocate social or political causes and still maintain their image as providers of views representing all sides of all questions?

Whenever the question is raised, it initiates further queries. For example, what constitutes advocating a cause-biased book selection, biased displays, or a prejudicial assignment of library meeting rooms? For that matter, what constitutes a cause—peace, ecology, democracy? If a library sponsors a display of books on peace, in order to maintain neutrality must it also sponsor a display on war? The questions are complex, and the answers have shown no uniformity whatsoever. The American Library Association itself has vacillated on the main issue, reaching only a partial resolution in the late 1960s and the early 1970s.

At the 1969 Annual Conference in Atlantic City, the membership and the Council debated whether or not the Association should take a public stand opposing the war in Vietnam or opposing deployment of an antiballistic missile system (ABM). It was argued that because political and moral issues are so deeply entangled with education and library issues, institutions such as the ALA and libraries are obligated to take such positions. Those who opposed such positions argued in favor of neutrality on questions not directly related to libraries. They argued that intellectual freedom for those librarians opposed to the majority view would be violated if the Association attempted to take stands on social and political issues. They further maintained that they had tradition on their side, since the Association had always declined to take a stand on issues not directly related to libraries. That argument, of course, was incorrect. The Association had previously taken stands in some instances and refused to do so in others.

In June 1921, for example, the ALA Council espoused a very decided position on the question of disarmament after the First World War. In a strong resolution, the Council stated the following:

WHEREAS, The members of the American Library Association had full demonstration of the pain and pinch that belongs to war and the increased cost of all necessities, both personal and professional, caused thereby; and

WHEREAS, The exigencies of international conditions brought about by the cost of war is appalling from every standpoint; and

WHEREAS, We believe the example of the United States in this matter will be followed by the other nations;

THEREFORE BE IT RESOLVED, That the American Library Association urge upon the president of the United States and Congress the initiative of a movement leading to a reduction of armament at the earliest possible moment; and be it further

RESOLVED, That a request be made by the members of the American Library Association to their individual congressman for such action and that a record be made of the replies.[17]

However, in 1928, when faced by a request from the American Civil Liberties Union that the ALA adopt "one or more resolutions on civil liberty," the ALA Executive Board declined, saying the Association "does not take actions on questions outside the library and bibliographic field."[18] That was similar to the philosophy that prevailed in 1969, when the Vietnam and ABM resolutions failed to pass the Council. The question arose again, though, at the 1970 and 1971 Midwinter Meetings and Annual Conferences. After a great deal of debate, the Council voted at its 1970 Annual Conference in Detroit to "define the broad social responsibilities of ALA in terms of the willingness of ALA to take a position on current critical issues with the relationship to libraries and library service clearly set forth in the position statements."[19]

In line with this policy, a carefully reworded resolution opposing the war in Vietnam was adopted by the Council one year later:

WHEREAS, The stated objective of the American Library Association is the promotion and improvement of library service and librarianship; and

WHEREAS, Continued and improved library service to the American public requires sustained support from the public monies; and

WHEREAS, The continuing U.S. involvement in the conflict in Southeast Asia has so distorted our national priorities as to reduce substantially the funds appropriated for educational purposes, including support for library services to the American people; and

WHEREAS, Continued commitment of U.S. arms, troops, and other military support has not contributed to the solution of this conflict;

BE IT THEREFORE RESOLVED, That the American Library Association calls upon the president of the United States to take immediately those steps necessary to terminate all U.S. military involvement in the present conflict in Southeast Asia by December 31, 1971, and to insure the reallocation of national resources to meet pressing domestic needs.[20]

With approval of the Vietnam resolution, the Association seemed to give broader interpretation to the old "library and bibliographic field." However, this more permissive interpretation still did not resolve the more basic question of whether libraries themselves should follow the course of neutrality or advocacy.

The contradiction was further focused in July 1974, when the ALA endorsed the Equal Rights Amendment (ERA). The ALA's support for ERA went much further than its opposition to U.S. military involvement in Southeast Asia. In 1977, the Council voted not to hold conferences in states that had not ratified the amendment. In June 1978, the Council endorsed the ERA Extension Resolution and, at the 1979 Midwinter Meeting, established an ERA task force charged with assisting and consulting with "ALA Chapters in carrying out the commitment to passage of the Equal Rights Amendment in ways best suited to the individual states."[21]

The Association justified this active support of the proposed amendment, first, by noting the support already expressed by other professional associations "by reason of its beneficial implications for all persons in the American society," and, more specifically, as an outgrowth of the ALA's policy requiring equal employment opportunity in libraries, adopted at the 1974 Midwinter Meeting. The resolution in support of ERA noted that "women constitute 82 percent of the library profession." Hence, it was argued, "equal employment required support of equal rights for women."[22] None of the operative resolutions on ERA addressed themselves to the content of library collections. Opponents of the amendment and pro-ERA advocates of ALA neutrality, however, were quick to argue that library users "have a right to expect the library to furnish them with uncensored information on both sides of this and all other issues. Adoption of advocacy positions and participation in boycotts cannot help but strike a blow at the public's confidence in the fair-mindedness and even-handedness of librarians."[23]

Yet another aspect of the "advocacy versus neutrality" conundrum was addressed by the Association in 1987 at its Annual Conference in San Francisco. David Henington, director of the Houston Public Library, brought to the IFC for its response and assistance an anti-apartheid ordinance passed and implemented by the city of Houston. This ordinance required that all city agencies obtain certification from suppliers of goods and services that they had no affiliates in, and did no business with, the Republic of South Africa.[24] Henington asserted that this requirement was causing serious acquisition problems for the library. Major information services such as the New York Times Company, the *Wall Street Journal*, and leading publishers refused to sign such certificates. Some refused because they had reporters in South Africa, one religious group because it had missionaries there, and others on principle, in the belief that the free flow of information both into and out of South Africa must be defended and enlarged for the sake of those struggling to dismantle the apartheid system there. Because it did not have a copy of the ordinance in hand and because it had received reports of similar ordinances elsewhere, the IFC voted to explore the matter further.

Two ALA members decided that the issue should be taken to the membership at that Conference, and they presented a resolution at the Membership Meeting. The resolution stressed the intellectual freedom implications of this policy and asked that ideas and information be exempted from the laudable goal of enforcing economic sanctions against South Africa for its abhorrent apartheid system. A heated encounter ensued between the presenters and other supporters of the resolution and those who saw it as supportive of apartheid and, therefore, racist. The resolution was resoundingly defeated.

At the 1988 Annual Conference in New Orleans, the membership adopted a resolution reaffirming its commitment to Article 19 of the Universal Declaration of Human Rights: "Everyone has the right to freedom of opinion and expression; this right includes freedom to hold opinions without interference and to seek, receive and impart information and ideas through any media regardless of frontiers."

Measuring the Profession's Response

The foregoing discussion illustrates that anything other than an issue-oriented definition of intellectual freedom is impossible. At the present time, the profession uniformly disdains censorship of published materials, print or nonprint. The attitude toward user access is somewhat uniform but contains a great deal of dissent on the question of access for minors to all the materials in a library collection. On the question of the librarian's professional practice of intellectual freedom, there is near agreement that every effort should be made to encourage and protect this aspect of librarianship. The librarian's personal intellectual freedom, on and off the job, presents some points of agreement, but major areas of dissent still exist. The same is true in the area of institutional neutrality versus advocacy.

One conclusion from a review of the history, status, and future of intellectual freedom in libraries is that the American Library Association's positions and programs provide one of the few gauges for measuring the profession's response to the problems of defining, promoting, and defending the concept. The ALA's evolving position reflects the steady emergence of a philosophy within the entire library community. Although that philosophy exhibits some loose ends, its core grows firmer, based on a history of trial and error and forced response to a continually changing social climate. The philosophy is young, too young to be rooted in tradition, but gradually it has gained recognition as the substance of the total philosophy shaping library service in the United States.

At the 1990 Midwinter Meeting, the ALA was asked to review and support an Association of American Publishers (AAP) report on the effect of book boycotts in South Africa titled "The Starvation of Young Black Minds: The Effect of Book Boycotts in South Africa," which recommended that the boycott on books and other educational materials be discontinued. The Intellectual Freedom Committee reported no existing ALA policy upon which to base recommendations regarding the AAP report, and at the 1990 Annual Conference proposed a new Interpretation of the *Library Bill of Rights,* initially called "The Free Flow of Information," to address free expression issues raised in the global arena. The resolution was adopted by the Council at the 1991 Midwinter Meeting as "The Universal Right to Free Expression, An Interpretation of the *Library Bill of Rights.*" (See part II, section 2.17.) At the same time, the Council adopted Article 19 of the Universal Declaration of Human Rights as official ALA policy. This action superseded a 1988 ALA membership resolution, reaffirming its commitment to Article 19, which read: "Everyone has the right to freedom of opinion and expression; this right includes freedom to hold opinions without interference and to seek, receive and impart information and ideas through any media regardless of frontiers."

Simultaneously with the 1990 AAP request, the Social Responsibilities Round Table (SRRT) proposed "Guidelines for Librarians Interacting with South Africa." The Intellectual Freedom Committee responded with a memorandum on guidelines for librarians interacting with South Africa in which the Committee recommended that the guidelines be rewritten to address, among other matters, the intellectual freedom concerns absent from the text. The ALA Council declined to adopt the guidelines as written, following which a motion carried to refer the guidelines back to the IFC, the International Relations Committee (IRC), and the Committee on Professional Ethics. At the 1991 Midwinter Meeting, these committees returned a joint recommendation that no further action be taken until the guidelines were rewritten. The Council then referred the document to the Executive Board.

The subject of including books and informational materials in the sanctions against South Africa was never revisited in light of the new policy, "'The Universal Right to Free Expression.'" Subsequently, with the elimination of apartheid in South Africa and progress toward democratic majority rule, the issue was diffused.

Another issue to raise the advocacy versus neutrality controversy was the war in the Persian Gulf. At the 1991 Midwinter Meeting, the Council passed a resolution condemning the war. This action provoked strong protest from parts of the ALA membership, many of whom believe the Association should not involve itself in matters of public policy not directly related to library interests and concerns. Many members had loved ones serving in the armed forces in the Persian Gulf region at the time. Also at the 1991 Midwinter Meeting, the new policy "The Universal Right to Free Expression" was inaugurated with the passage of two resolutions calling for the "exemption of publications and other informational materials from sanctions" levied by the United States and by the United Nations against Iraq and Kuwait.

The passage of "The Universal Right to Free Expression" opens new vistas to librarians concerned about intellectual freedom. With the exponential growth in global communications and publications, it will be possible for American librarians to act in support of their colleagues and counterparts in countries where intellectual freedom principles are under fire—China, Turkey, Israel, Syria, Saudi Arabia, Guatemala, El Salvador, Kenya, and many others. Conversely, librarians facing censorship attempts in the United States may benefit from the experience and support of those in other countries who have endured far greater challenges.

The Association revisited the debate over advocacy versus neutrality, or "library related" and "non-library related" matters, with its decision to withdraw the 1995 Midwinter Meeting from the city of Cincinnati, where voters had repealed a gay rights ordinance. Many ALA members felt it would be outrageous to sponsor a meeting in a city that had withdrawn legal protection from discrimination for their gay colleagues. Others felt that the ALA was compromising its intellectual freedom principles by taking a political position that implied official disapproval of the opinions of Cincinnati's voters and could have the effect of jeopardizing, in the mind of the library-using public, librarians' neutrality in the provision of information from all points of view on homosexuality and other controversial subjects.

Challenges and Issues Today

The major issues facing libraries today continue to focus on free and open access to information. The ALA continues to support a commitment to the right of unrestricted access to information and ideas, regardless of the communications medium. This commitment was confirmed most recently in regard to the Internet.

In February 1996, the Communications Decency Act (CDA) was signed into law by President William Clinton as a way to keep "indecent" material from anyone under the age of eighteen. It said that if anyone under eighteen was allowed to view "indecent" material, the provider was subject to a fine of up to $250,000 and/or up to two years in prison. The CDA placed librarians and libraries at risk because the term "indecent" was not defined, providing no guidelines for librarians. The ALA filed a lawsuit (*American Library Association v. U.S. Department of Justice*) in February 1996 challenging the CDA's constitutionality. This lawsuit was later consolidated with, and decided under, a separate suit brought by the ACLU (*Reno v. ACLU*). (See part IV, section 2, "Libraries and the Internet.") The lawsuit argued three points: (1) prohibiting material as "indecent" was unconstitutional because the term was vague and undefined, and, in addition, the act did not distinguish between the information needs of a five-year-old child and a seventeen-year-old in college; (2) Congress had not considered alternative ways that parents might protect their own children in their own home, for instance, by using filtering software; and (3) the Internet is not a broadcast medium but is more like the print medium in that each person controls what they access. In June 1996, a lower court declared the CDA unconstitutional. The government appealed, and in June 1997, the U.S. Supreme Court, by a 9-0 vote, held the CDA unconstitutional.

In addition to the ongoing debate over the Internet and filtering, there are a number of other issues facing libraries and librarians today. These include:

- harassment, or a hostile work environment, produced by open access to the Internet;
- First Amendment rights of minors and their free access to information, as well as the attempt by some to mandate protection for minors from materials that may be "harmful to minors"; and
- continued requests to libraries for patron records under the Freedom of Information Act. This has been of great concern to librarians in relation to new technology which can track a specific patron's Internet use.

The ALA continues to regularly develop resources to aid librarians in managing and communicating about the Internet. These include "Libraries & the Internet Toolkit." For the most current resources and the latest information, see the ALA Web site, which is updated and revised regularly (www.ala.org/alaorg/oif/internet toolkit.html).

Undoubtedly, as threats to free expression at home and abroad become more complex and interwoven, the line separating advocacy from neutrality will be crossed many times. Following the best of democratic traditions, a healthy debate on the library's role in the issues of the moment must be encouraged.

NOTES

1. American Library Association, "Minutes of Executive Board Meetings," mimeographed, 3:20 (Sept. 29, 1924).

2. Ibid., 5:11 (Jan. 1, 1930).

3. Ibid., 6:214 (Oct. 15, 1933).

4. Ibid., 7:89 (Dec. 27, 1934).

5. Ibid., 7:48–49 (Dec. 27, 1934).

6. Arthur E. Bostwick, "The Librarian as Censor," *ALA Bulletin* 2:113 (September 1908).

7. American Library Association, "Minutes of Executive Board Meetings," mimeographed, 10:48 (Oct. 5, 1938).

8. "Cincinnati Proceedings—Council," *ALA Bulletin* 34:P-37 (August 1940).

9. American Library Association, *Handbook of Organization, 1971–1972* (Chicago: American Library Association, n.d.), p. 13.

10. No. 90-05-192, 271st Judicial District Court; Wise and Jack Counties, Texas; (Letter Opinion) Judge John R. Lindsey.

11. Robert D. Leigh, "Intellectual Freedom," *ALA Bulletin* 42:369 (September 1948).

12. Rosichan summary, *American Libraries* 1:433 (May 1970); and Scott summary, *American Libraries* 2:316–17 (March 1971).

13. "Resolution on Loyalty Investigations," *American Libraries* 2:270 (March 1971).

14. American Library Association Activities Committee on New Directions for ALA, "Final Report and Subcommittee Reports, June 1970," mimeographed, p. 53.

15. "Hodgin Appeal Rests with U.S. Supreme Court," *Freedom to Read Foundation News* 1:5 (Fall 1971).

16. David K. Berninghausen, "Report of the Intellectual Freedom Committee to Council, Dallas, June 25, 1971," *American Libraries* 2:891 (September 1971).

17. *ALA Bulletin* 15:169 (July 1921).

18. American Library Association, "Minutes of Executive Board Meetings," 4:142 (May 29, 1928).

19. *American Libraries* 1:674 (July–August 1970).

20. "Resolution on Southeast Asia Conflict," *American Libraries* 2:826 (September 1971).

21. News release, American Library Association (September 1979).

22. *ALA Council Minutes*, 1974, p. 335.

23. Terence L. Day, Chairman, Neill Public Library Board of Trustees, Letter to the Editor, *Chicago Tribune*, January 21, 1979.

24. The Houston City Council subsequently voted to exempt both the public library and the city zoo from the requirements of the ordinance.

2
Challenges and Issues Today

EVELYN SHAEVEL
and
BEVERLEY BECKER

In a democratic society which operates best when information flows freely and is freely available, it is the library's unique responsibility to provide open and unfettered access to that information. With information available and accessible, citizens have the tools necessary for self-improvement and participation in the political process. An essential part of this responsibility is assuring that the information is not limited because of the format in which it is found, be it of a book, a video, a compact disc, or a Web site contained on the Internet.

Unfortunately, libraries must frequently confront and deal with objections to free access to library materials, most often raised by those who believe that unlimited access to information and ideas causes harm to the individual or society, and sometimes both. These objections currently center upon five major issues: (1) access to the Internet; (2) harassment; (3) the right of youth to access library materials; (4) the privacy of library patrons and the confidentiality of patrons' records; and (5) the use of Freedom of Information Act requests to access library records. As will be seen, the issues raised by these objections share a common thread: the impact of the new Internet technologies on the production and delivery of information.

Because the challenges these issues present to libraries and librarians are continually evolving, it is important to know about the issues and to be aware of the laws and court decisions which govern the library's provision of materials and services to its patrons, as well as those patrons' rights. Frequently updated sources of information about challenges and legal issues can be found on the Web sites maintained by the Freedom to Read Foundation (www.ftrf.org) and the American Library Association's Office for Intellectual Freedom (www.ala.org/alaorg/oif). It is also important to regularly consult with your library's legal counsel, who will be able to provide detailed information about any state or local laws that affect your provision of library services.

The Internet

The Internet may well be the most significant technological innovation of this century, rivaling the printing press for the changes it is bringing to communications, commerce, and the availability of information. Through the Internet, one may find a vast array of news, ideas, opinions, and entertainment, all easily accessible to anyone with a computer and a modem. By supplying access to the World Wide Web, libraries can now provide their patrons with information resources unimagined only a few decades ago. With just a click of a mouse, each patron is free to choose among the thousands of Web sites, newsgroups, and databases, selecting for herself the materials that best suit her desire for information or entertainment.

But the Internet's wealth of information and the ease with which it is accessed raise concern for some persons, who argue that the Internet provides *too much* access, especially for children. These parties fear that children may find or look for Web sites that contain sexually explicit material, or that children may come across information and ideas deemed objectionable by a particular religious or political community. Some even believe that such unlimited access is harmful for adults as well. Acting on these fears, they campaign for the use of filtering software in public libraries, believing the harms that arise from censorship to be minor in comparison to the harm they believe will arise when patrons view material they deem "inappropriate."

The American Library Association does not recommend the use of filters on computers located in public libraries, however. In its groundbreaking opinion in *Reno* v. *ACLU,* the Supreme Court declared that the Internet, as a medium of communication, deserves the First Amendment's highest protection, and that persons using the Internet enjoy the same right to publish information and receive information as do those who use the print media. These rights extend to minors, who enjoy the same right to receive information as do adults. The use of filters compromises not only these constitutional freedoms, but also the core values of librarianship, which esteem a person's right to read and hear ideas without limitation, and regardless of income, status, or age.

Filters also compromise a community's right to govern its own library and that library's selection policies, especially when such filtering is imposed by state or federal authorities through the operation of law. The mandated use of filters forces the community to conform its library's selection policies to the biases and beliefs of the corporate entities which design filtering software, while disregarding the community's right to operate its library according to its own norms and values.

Moreover, filtering software does not work. Along with the "objectionable" material, filters block access to valuable information that is often important for education and self-fulfillment. Among the Web sites that have been blocked by filtering software are the sites for Amnesty International, the Chicago Public Library, the American Family Association, and the Mars Exploration site. Filters also can fail to fulfill their primary task, permitting access to sexually explicit material when the software has not been designed or updated to identify a site or its contents as "objectionable."

Rather than relying on an imperfect and robotic technology, the ALA believes that education offers the best means of addressing the issue of Internet safety, for both children and adults. Libraries that offer classes to teach children how to play and learn on the Internet safely and effectively not only ensure a positive experience for their young patrons, but also equip them with lifelong learning tools with which to evaluate and deal with the wide range of material found on the World Wide Web. Similar classes for parents and other adult patrons on "netiquette," search engines, and the use of the Internet as a means of communicating with others about special interests such as genealogy, cooking, and travel familiarize adult patrons with the utility and worth of this new technology and assist them to become online guides and resources for their children.

Additionally, libraries that develop Internet use policies can address the fears of those who dread even inadvertent exposure to material they deem inappropriate, while effectively protecting their patrons' right to access information and right to privacy. Written policies can emphasize the library's support for the principles of intellectual freedom and its respect for the diversity of its community, while at the same time establishing that the library does not condone the use of its computers to access materials that are obscene or otherwise illegal. The use of time limits, terminal placement, privacy screens, and education classes can further support the library's mission while addressing community needs.

More detailed information on the Internet and filtering in public libraries can be found at http://www.ala.org/alaorg/oif/filtersandfiltering.html and at http://www.ala.org/pio/internettoolkit/index.html. Information on the legal issues raised by the use of filters in public libraries is available on the Web at http://www.ftrf.org/internetfilteringmemo.html.

Harassment

When the Loudoun County (Virginia) Library's Board of Trustees voted to install filters on its terminals, several members justified their decision to censor the Internet by arguing that the display of sexually explicit materials on library terminals could constitute "sexual harassment" or create a "hostile work environment" under federal anti-discrimination statutes. Pro-filtering proponents continue to advance this argument as a "pro-civil rights" basis to block library patrons' full access to the Internet. A few public librarians, personally offended by occasions when patrons accessed sexually explicit materials by chance or on purpose, have initiated legal action against their employers in support of their campaign to have filters installed on the library's computers.

These attempts to deny patrons of a public library unfettered access to the Internet based upon the offended sensibilities of the library's employees deny the core values of libraries and librarianship, which call on library professionals to oppose both censorship and the invasion of patrons' privacy rights. The public library belongs to its community and the citizens who make use of its resources. As a matter of ethics, those resources should not be curtailed merely because a library employee finds a particular resource or item objectionable.

As a matter of law, no court has yet decided whether a library's decision to install filters to avoid liability for sexual harassment or employment discrimination claims would pass muster under the First Amendment. Prior decisions of the Supreme Court, however, consistently state that the Constitution protects the right to receive information, including the right to receive material that may be offensive to others. Moreover, because a library is a limited public forum governed by the First Amendment, it cannot implement a content-based regulation restricting access to any form of constitutionally protected speech unless the rule or policy is justified by a compelling government interest, and no other, less restrictive means exists to achieve that interest.

It is also important to note that harassment consists of purposeful, ongoing conduct that intimidates, ridicules, or insults a person based upon their gender, race, or religion. Such conduct must be directed at the employee and must be sufficiently severe or pervasive so as to change the conditions of the employee's working environment. Isolated or sporadic conduct that is merely offensive to the employee does not rise to the type of harassment actionable under the law. Present case law suggests that the presence of temporary visual images on a computer screen, unaccompanied by any discriminatory verbal or physical conduct, would not qualify as actionable workplace harassment. However, the context in which the offensive conduct takes place will determine whether harassment exists, and in each case, the court will examine the specific facts and circumstances before deciding whether the conduct is sufficiently harassing, pervasive, and severe to impose liability on the employer.

The first step for any library confronting this issue is to develop, with the advice of counsel, a harassment policy which makes clear that the library does not condone, encourage, or tolerate the harassment of its employees by other employees or patrons by use of any means, as well as to develop procedures to address complaints of a hostile work environment from employees. Practical methods to address employees' exposure to Internet materials include the relocation of computer terminals and the use of privacy screens.

It is important, however, that libraries consult with their legal counsel on this issue when developing policies or when responding to complaints, as the law in this area is still evolving and may differ depending on state or local law. A more detailed legal discussion may be found at http://www.ftrf.org/work_jb.html.

Rights of Youth

Whether it's *Harry Potter* books, R-rated videos, or "porn" on the Internet, most efforts to censor or remove materials from libraries arise when some citizens seek to limit young people's access to information in order to "protect" their moral and emotional development. Such campaigns to "save the children" can focus on information about sex, the occult, or alternative religions or lifestyles, or they can center on classic works that are perceived as racist, sexist, homophobic, or hostile to certain ethnic or religious groups.

Yet, subject to some exceptions concerning illegal materials and curriculum development, young persons patronizing a library enjoy the same rights to read and receive information as do adult patrons. In *Tinker* v. *Des Moines Independent School District*, the Supreme Court held that students "do not shed their constitutional rights at the schoolhouse gate" and that the First Amendment protects public school students' rights to express political and social views. In another landmark Supreme Court decision, *Board of Education, Island Trees Union Free School District No. 26* v. *Pico*, Justice William J. Brennan Jr. declared that "[l]ocal school boards may not remove books from school library shelves simply because they dislike the ideas contained in those books and seek by their removal to prescribe what shall be orthodox in politics, nationalism, religion or other matters of opinion." In these decisions, the Supreme Court made clear that First Amendment freedoms are not conditional on reaching the age of majority. As the Court noted in its opinion in *Erznoznik* v. *City of Jacksonville*, "[S]peech . . . cannot be suppressed solely to protect the young from ideas or images that a legislative body thinks unsuitable for them."

Accordingly, the American Library Association believes strongly that young people are entitled to freely access ideas and information, subject only to limitations imposed by their parents or guardians. Indeed, in "Free Access to Libraries for Minors: An Interpretation of the *Library Bill of Rights*," it specifically states "The American Library Association opposes all attempts to restrict access to library services, materials, and facilities based on the age of library users." Limiting access to books, videos, compact discs, or the Internet does not protect the young from the complex and challenging world that confronts them, but can deprive them of information that is important to them or even vital for their learning and development as maturing persons. The ALA believes, therefore, that teaching young people how to evaluate information, how to think critically about the information they do receive, and how to make decisions about the materials they view offers the best protection for them. Fostering the individual youth's discernment and curiosity assures that we are preparing future citizens who are able to participate fully in our democracy and think for themselves. Ultimately, the role of the librarian is to guide and advise young people on how to find and use the best available material for their information needs. Any decisions on whether to limit a youth's access to materials are most appropriately made by the child's parents, who are best equipped to know and understand their child's intellectual and emotional development.

For a detailed discussion of minors' First Amendment rights, see the resources located on the Internet at http://www.ftrf.org/minor_jb.html.

Privacy and Confidentiality

Privacy is the bedrock foundation for the individual's constitutional right to freely read and receive ideas, information, and points of view. Only when the individual is assured that her choice of reading material does not subject her to reprisals or punishment can the individual enjoy fully her freedom to explore ideas, weigh arguments, and decide for herself what she believes.

In order to give meaning to this core principle of intellectual freedom, libraries must protect each library user's right to privacy by providing for the confidentiality of library records. Such confidentiality extends not only to the patron's personal information, but also to database search records, circulation records, and other materials that identify a person's use of library materials, activities, or facilities.

The advent of the Internet raises new concerns about the privacy of library patrons. Sophisticated software designed to track Internet usage and identify visitors to particular Web sites pose an ongoing threat to patrons' confidential use of the Internet and other library resources contained on library computers. For this reason, libraries must keep abreast of advances in software designed to identify Internet users, and adopt any necessary measures to protect the privacy of their patrons. Written log-in sheets for Internet access should be destroyed regularly, the cache on public Internet terminals should be cleared as soon as possible, and any circulation records should be kept confidential under all circumstances.

Recent federal legislation, the Children's Online Privacy Protection Act, provides special safeguards for confidential information belonging to children aged twelve and under. Under this act, commercial online content providers with actual knowledge that they are dealing with children twelve or under, or who design and market their content for an audience of children, must obtain verifiable parental consent before they can collect, archive, use, or resell any personal information pertaining to a particular child.

To learn more about the Children's Online Protection Act and its effect on libraries, see http://www.ala.org/oitp/privacy.html. To review ALA policies on confidentiality and learn more about privacy, visit http://www.ala.org/alaorg/oif/privacy.html.

Freedom of Information Act Requests

In the past few years, libraries across the country have been receiving Freedom of Information Act (FOIA) requests seeking information on "patron and staff complaints about persons accessing inappropriate material on public Internet terminals," and other information on libraries' practices concerning the use of the Internet. While libraries support free and open access to information, and support the Freedom of Information Act, they must also defend their patrons' right to privacy. For this reason, FOIA requests must be carefully reviewed to assure that the request complies with applicable state and federal laws.

Such laws are complex and can contain exemptions from FOIA disclosure requirements. For example, forty-seven states and the District of Columbia provide a specific exemption protecting certain library records from disclosure. Because these exemptions vary from state to state, and because each state's FOIA contains differing disclosure requirements, librarians are strongly urged to have legal counsel review any FOIA request the library may receive.

For more detailed information on Freedom of Information Act requests, go to http://www.ftrf.org/foia.html.

3

Intellectual Freedom
An All-Embracing Concept

EVELYN SHAEVEL
and
BEVERLEY BECKER

*A popular government, without popular information, or
the mean(s) of acquiring it, is but a prologue to a farce or
a tragedy; or perhaps both. Knowledge will forever govern ignorance; and a people who mean to be their own
governors must arm themselves with the power which
knowledge gives.*

—JAMES MADISON

The First Amendment is integral to American librarianship. It is
the basis of the concept librarians call intellectual freedom. In
turn, intellectual freedom accords to citizens the right to both seek
and receive information from all points of view without restriction
in their libraries. Intellectual freedom allows us to be well informed
by exploring any and all sides of a question, cause, or movement. It
is the mechanism which allows us to be effective self-governors, a
necessity in our constitutional republic.

To help librarians promote and defend the principles of intellectual freedom, the American Library Association provides guidance and assistance to librarians confronting challenges to intellectual freedom in their libraries.

Although those challenges may vary according to the type of
library—academic, school, public, special, etc.—intellectual freedom

is the foundation of library service. The sections below address some of the issues that may affect the various types of publicly supported libraries, including public, school, academic, federal, and state. They are excerpted from articles (in some instances, slightly edited for readability), the full texts of which are available on the Web at www.ala.org/alaorg/oif/.

Public Libraries and Intellectual Freedom

(Excerpted from an article by Gordon Conable.
Full text available at www.ala.org/alaorg/oif/.)

At the time the public library movement began, books and education were scarce commodities. Today, the quantity of information that is generated and distributed is increasing exponentially. The issue of scarcity is superseded now by new problems of access. But the essential function of the public library is unchanged: to offer knowledge and information to the average citizen. In this way, public libraries provide tangible commitment to free speech, self-government, and self-education by collecting, organizing, preserving, disseminating, and protecting everyone's rights of access to the richness of human expression in all its recorded forms.

In order to fulfill this responsibility, public libraries must serve as neutral ground for opposing positions. In doing so, they may become targets for censors who seek to have particular items removed from the library collection, restricted as to access, expurgated, labeled, or otherwise censored. They should also consider carefully fees, formats, facilities, political agendas, and user confidentiality and privacy, all of which may have serious implications for intellectual freedom.

Censorship pressure can come from both sources external to the library and sources within the library itself. When the occasional controversy does erupt, the process can provide a healthy demonstration of democracy and free speech in action. It should be approached in this manner, and the library should utilize the experience as a means of making its point about the importance of the underlying issues of free expression.

It is important to note that people who complain about materials are not themselves censors, unless they are in a position actually to limit access to material or censor it by their own actions. Complaints and protests are not censorship, and those who object to material in libraries are exercising their own free-speech rights. It is those very rights that librarians defend when they protect challenged material. Censorship only occurs when libraries and librarians respond to complaints about, and challenges to, collection materials by removing or restricting books or other items. Such actions, carried out by librarians or by their governing bodies or institutions, are the censorship, and it is the public officials or employees who engage in such activities who are the censors, not the original protesters.

The issues with which public libraries must deal relating to intellectual freedom are varied and complex. Public libraries need to remember that with proper groundwork, preparation, and training, censorship attacks can be withstood and that individuals and groups exist in the community who will defend the library.

The active advocacy of intellectual freedom is a challenge that all librarians accept when they join the profession. It lies at the heart of the public's trust, and it is the librarian's highest duty.

School Library Media Centers and Intellectual Freedom

(Excerpted from an article by Dianne McAfee Hopkins. Full text available at www.ala.org/alaorg/oif/.)

Intellectual freedom issues arise in many broad areas of school library administration and operation. School library media specialists should consider the intellectual freedom implications of their role as resource specialists; how they provide intellectual and physical access for students; how their collection development policies address intellectual freedom; procedures for handling challenges to school library resources and services, including student access to the Internet; professional practice; and how they might appropriately promote intellectual freedom as an aspect of a free and democratic society.

Access

The school library media specialist promotes access to a wide variety of resources, including materials in the school's library media center, as well as nearby schools, public libraries, academic libraries, and networks. In the school, the library media specialist should work closely with classroom teachers to make school library media center (LMC) resources an integral part of daily instruction. In so doing, intellectual freedom is promoted for students.

Collection Development Policy

Public school districts are governed by school boards that are legally responsible for the materials available to students. They delegate selection of materials to certified library media specialists and administrators under whom the library media specialist works. A written collection development policy, approved by the school board, establishes the climate in which, and the criteria by which, library media collections are developed. The collection development policy should promote intellectual freedom through a recognition of the value of information in a variety of formats. Materials should reflect the cultural diversity and pluralistic nature of contemporary American society. The policy should include the American Library Association's *Library Bill of Rights* and other appropriate intellectual freedom statements from professional associations such as the Association for Educational Communications and Technology, International Reading Association, National Council of Teachers of English, and the National Council for the Social Studies.

Library media specialists should give careful attention to the section of the collection development policy dealing with the procedures for the reconsideration of materials. Such procedures must be clearly written and thoughtfully considered with a view toward promoting intellectual freedom on behalf of students and teachers. It is critical that the established procedures be followed systematically in dealing with each question.

Once developed, the collection development policy should be used regularly as the basis for the evaluation and selection of materials. It should be reviewed and revised at least every three years.

School policies and guidelines also should evaluate the electronic resources available to teachers and students through the library media center.

Procedures

Professional practice, in terms of rules and regulations that govern student access to school library media centers, should be scrutinized to ascertain the promotion of intellectual freedom. The overriding question is whether rules encourage or inhibit intellectual freedom for students.

Questions about school library media materials can be expected. While many may view with alarm any question that arises, every question is not necessarily an effort to censor. Parents of students have the right to query public school officials regarding the materials that are made available for student use. Providing an understanding of the selection process and the principles upon which libraries exist may go far in answering questions that may be asked. Letting a questioner know that a concern is respectfully received is another way to respond constructively.

Electronic access to information, especially to the Internet, offers particular concern for potential challenges. Unlike materials physically located in the LMC, the Internet, by its very nature, carries the potential for exposing students to information that may be controversial or possibly deemed unsuitable for students. Here, the communication of the school with its students and parents is important, in addition to the development of appropriate guidelines and policies. (See part I, section 2, "Challenges and Issues Today," for discussion of the Internet and school libraries.)

Promotion of Intellectual Freedom

Intellectual freedom must be promoted within the school as well as in the community. Selection of library media center materials, although coordinated by the library media specialist, should actively involve teachers, administrators, and students. Discussions and in-service programs about the philosophy of libraries in general, the purpose and objectives of the library media center, and the criteria used in selection should be ongoing, not only for new faculty but for all faculty, as well as school staff. School board members also should actively participate. In addition, up-to-date information on a continuing basis is valuable to the community.

Conclusion

Intellectual freedom requires that all who are responsible for the education of the young—school board members, administrators, teachers, and library media specialists—work together continuously to ensure that First Amendment rights and intellectual freedom are a reality for children and young adults.

Academic Libraries and Intellectual Freedom

(Excerpted from an article by Barbara M. Jones. Full text available at www.ala.org/alaorg/oif/.)

In the twenty-first-century academic library, the concept of intellectual freedom has broadened to include such library issues as fee-based services, donor restrictions on manuscript collections, reference interviews, and purchasing "politically incorrect" materials, not to mention the Internet's impact. This major vehicle for scholarly communication has raised important First Amendment issues on college campuses—including the problem of explicit content offensive to some, and campus network-use policies that sometimes conflict with the *Library Bill of Rights.*

Many academic libraries depend on the American Association of University Professors' academic freedom principles as sufficient backup in case of a First Amendment problem. Library intellectual freedom issues, however, have become so complex that complementary statements, based on the ALA's intellectual freedom principles, need to be part of any campus's comprehensive policies on academic freedom.

For publicly funded academic institutions and the libraries therein, the obligation for upholding the First Amendment is particularly important. The legal concept covering all publicly funded libraries—and that includes publicly funded academic libraries—is that of a "limited public forum." In such a forum, users have a right to receive information, and librarians have a right to provide it. Yet, this forum can set limits; it need not be as "freewheeling" as a soapbox in a public park, for example. As a "limited" public space—which extends to cyberspace—libraries are free to set reasonable regulations in order to achieve their mission of providing information and other services. Such regulations might include the establishment of hours and definitions of appropriate patron conduct.

Any regulations, however, must be applied equitably to all users. If, as in some academic libraries, there are different levels of borrowers and access, care must be taken that these levels don't discriminate on the basis of physical disabilities, race, gender, or other categories recognized in U. S. civil rights legislation.

Academic libraries must devote the time to discuss, develop, write, and update good written policies. Written policies help assure staff consistency in handling intellectual freedom issues and display a library's professionalism and managerial excellence. Policies are best written by groups within the library who share common interests but bring different perspectives to the table.

While written regulations and policies are necessary in all academic libraries, they are only part of promoting and protecting intellectual freedom. It is equally important that librarians and staff be well trained and knowledgeable about the principles of intellectual freedom. It is important that prospective library employees understand that academic libraries can be "uncomfortable" in terms of the ideas contained in much of the information that is purchased, cataloged, or exhibited on computer terminals. Staff should always be protected from any illegal workplace activity, but the library's contents are most likely constitutionally protected.

The Library Collections

Content-based censorship is one of the primary barriers to intellectual freedom. Written collection development policies should describe an academic library's subject specialties and priorities. These are an essential component to assure balanced coverage of a particular topic. The policies should follow the *Library Bill of Rights*

Interpretations, especially "Diversity in Collection Development" and "Evaluating Library Collections."

While in most cases, academic libraries must make collection decisions based, to a certain extent, on the quality and importance of the scholarship, this rationale should never be used as a way of avoiding the purchase of a book in great demand by the users. Consortia or interlibrary loan partnerships also should not be used as a way to avoid buying a controversial book. Librarians need to be sure to provide contextual materials, representing many points of view, so that the collections are balanced on any particular topic.

Services

Librarians should be very sensitive to letting personal biases about particular topics or reference sources act as a "filter" between librarian and researcher. Librarians are uniquely qualified to teach users how to think critically in evaluating information resources. Thus the student can conduct research independently and with a certain modicum of privacy.

Fee-based information services are too expensive for many students. Library administrators should review the budget and try to keep such information as low cost as possible, or provide low-cost alternatives of the same quality. Licensing agreements also can erect economic barriers, and should be negotiated if at all possible.

Cataloging records can introduce cultural bias into scholarly inquiry. Because research libraries often do original cataloging and thus assign subject headings, it is important to understand the "power" of a subject heading in providing access and index points, especially in an electronic environment where browsing depends so much on language of the headings.

Privacy

Circulation policies should include the state confidentiality statute. Library records can't be turned over to officials without a court-ordered subpoena. Alert student workers to this fact, since they are often on the front line. Investigations of plagiarism also require a subpoena before librarians can reveal the circulation records of a student.

Many privacy-related situations relate to use of the campus computer network. Most campuses keep transaction logs far longer than libraries keep automated circulation records. Care should be taken to protect the privacy of students on campus networks, in regard to library records, reference questions, and other communications via the Internet.

Make sure when negotiating the public access catalog contract that the vendor spells out the various levels of security. Libraries should be very careful, when assigning security clearance to personnel, that there has been thorough training in privacy issues.

Special collections libraries face particularly difficult situations with intellectual freedom. When negotiating donor agreements, librarians should try to achieve as little restriction as possible, in the interest of comprehensive access. Another difficult conflict arises over the retention of circulation records. On the one hand, special collections libraries want to be able to trace the users of a particular book, if it later turns up stolen or mutilated. On the other hand, this kind of information could be used in ways that invade a scholar's personal and research privacy.

Campus Civility

In recent years, administrators have tried to implement "hate speech codes" to prevent verbal and written attacks on various groups on increasingly diverse campuses. Most of these have been overturned on First Amendment grounds. Libraries are often accused of promoting this problem when they buy materials criticizing certain groups. As a public forum, the library plays an important role in promoting civil campus discourse through its collections and services. This can be achieved by providing information and holding exhibits and programs about controversial issues from all points of view.

Federal Libraries
and Intellectual Freedom

Bernadine Abbott Hoduski
(Text also available at www.ala.org/alaorg/oif/.)

The federal library community is composed of a variety of libraries comparable in type to those in the library community as a whole. Federal libraries range from the one-of-a-kind Library of Congress to small school libraries on Native American reservations and to specialized libraries serving executive agencies.

Federal libraries have censorship problems just like other libraries, but these are seldom brought to the attention of the library profession or the public. Many federal librarians feel there is no problem with censorship in government libraries. Others do not agree. Most of them do agree that positive steps should be taken to help prevent possible censorship situations.

Even though federal libraries differ in many respects, they do have some things in common: (1) they must function according to a number of federal laws and regulations; (2) their mission is usually dictated by the agency to which they belong; and (3) because they are supported by federal taxes, they are answerable, directly or indirectly, to all U.S. citizens. Many federal libraries are contracted out to private vendors, so it is important that the federal official legally responsible for seeing that the library function as a federal entity be involved in developing the library's policies.

Federal libraries can prevent many problems, including censorship, by following some simple procedures:

1. With the assistance of the agency's lawyer, it should be determined which laws and regulations govern the agency and the library, because regulations differ from one agency to the next.

2. An order describing the purpose, functions, and policies of the library should be written, thus officially establishing and protecting the existence of the library. This order should be signed and distributed by the secretary of a department or the administrator of an agency.

3. Librarians should take every opportunity to educate the secretary of a department, the agency administrator, the staff, and the public as to the policies of the library.

4. Federal libraries should cooperate with each other, comparing policies on materials selection, access to the collection, and other issues, including policies about information in electronic and audiovisual formats. Such comparisons can be used as examples in establishing policies and educating the agency's staff.

5. Library directors should determine whether and how the Freedom of Information Act affects the library. Some federal libraries serve as the agency's public reading room in order to fulfill the

requirements of the law, which states that the public must have reasonable access to documents issued by an agency. If the library is the official repository for agency documents, these have to be accessible to the public. If the library keeps classified and unclassified documents, some provision will have to be made to keep these separate. The library also should have an agreed-upon plan for providing documents once they are declassified. This should be done in consultation with the agency's attorney.

6. Library directors should determine what policies they should follow if they are a federal depository library. If the agency requires secrecy or denies access to the public, the library will be in direct conflict with the laws governing depository libraries. The agency will have to explore ways of complying with both requirements or risk losing its status.

7. If possible, a library committee representing all elements of the agency should be established so that materials selection, access policies, and other practices will be fair to all. In turn, the library committee can help educate the rest of the agency employees and support library policies.

8. The library should have a written access policy not favoring one group in an agency over another. If the library circulates material to the public, it should do so for everyone, not just for a select few. Libraries may decide to lend through another library rather than to individuals. If so, this decision should be publicized. Some agencies have regulations that do not allow those outside the agency to use their libraries.

9. The library should maintain a written materials selection policy. Even though the subject area is often determined by the mission of the agency, the diversity of views in that subject area must be guarded. An obvious example of censorship would be refusal to buy publications critical of an agency.

10. Finally, the library should develop and implement a policy protecting the confidentiality of library users. Records associating individuals with the materials they borrow should never be released to others– whether requested by employers or colleagues– without the written consent of the individual in question.

Because federal libraries are important information links in the decision-making process of the U.S. government, and because citizen access to information about that process is crucial to the preservation of a free society, federal libraries must be protected from censorship.

State Library Agencies and Intellectual Freedom

(Excerpted from an article by Diana Young.
Full text available at www.ala.org/alorg/oif/.)

The state library agency, as an institution, varies from state to state. Most state library agencies have responsibility for promoting library development and coordinating interlibrary cooperation. In some states, the agency is responsible for maintaining a collection, either to serve state government or to serve the residents of the state. Whatever the state library structure may be, it usually assumes the responsibility of fostering the free exchange of information and ideas.

State libraries help local libraries prepare to handle challenges in many ways. First, all libraries are encouraged to have policies and procedures in place and adopted by library boards, delineating what to do and when to do it. Sample policies are often collected and made available, and libraries that have recently updated or developed new policies are encouraged to submit them to the state library. Second, many state libraries maintain a relationship with active and supportive intellectual freedom committees of their state's library association, which can provide assistance and a link to a statewide network of supporters of intellectual freedom willing to come forward in a crisis.

State libraries develop library standards or performance measures as a means by which libraries may be evaluated and held accountable. The state library should develop such standards or measures upon the philosophy that every individual should have equal access to information and that the citizens of the state should have access to library services as envisioned in the *Library Bill of Rights*.

In its leadership capacity, the state library agency also must assume legislative leadership and coordination roles at both the state and federal levels. It is critical for the state library agency to monitor state and federal legislation and case law. Librarians, trustees, and other interested individuals need to be kept informed about legislative efforts and new court rulings that have an impact on intellectual freedom.

As a component of state government, the state library agencies are in a unique position to influence state law and policy. State library administrators are informed about the philosophies of government leaders and are knowledgeable about the decision-making processes of government. Of particular importance is the state library agency's leadership role in guaranteeing the citizens' "'right to know." First and foremost, the general public and government officials need to be kept aware of the importance of the free flow of government information. The state library agency needs to monitor the development and implementation of policy and procedure relating to the flow of both state and federal government information. If policies and procedures adverse to the free flow of information are promulgated, the state library agency needs to exert its leadership in changing them.

The state library agency in any state plays a pivotal role in the development of library services. A significant part of that role is to ensure that citizens have the best possible access to information. This access, in turn, will help preserve our democratic society as we now know it and will allow citizens to participate fully in the society.

PART II

Library Bill of Rights

I

Library Bill of Rights
The Policy

The American Library Association affirms that all libraries are forums for information and ideas, and that the following basic policies should guide their services.

I. Books and other library resources should be provided for the interest, information, and enlightenment of all people of the community the library serves. Materials should not be excluded because of the origin, background, or views of those contributing to their creation.

II. Libraries should provide materials and information presenting all points of view on current and historical issues. Materials should not be proscribed or removed because of partisan or doctrinal disapproval.

III. Libraries should challenge censorship in the fulfillment of their responsibility to provide information and enlightenment.

IV. Libraries should cooperate with all persons and groups concerned with resisting abridgment of free expression and free access to ideas.

V. A person's right to use a library should not be denied or abridged because of origin, age, background, or views.

VI. Libraries which make exhibit spaces and meeting rooms available to the public they serve should make such facilities available on an equitable basis, regardless of the beliefs or affiliations of individuals or groups requesting their use.

Adopted June 18, 1948. Amended by the ALA Council February 2, 1961; June 27, 1967; and January 23, 1980, inclusion of "age" reaffirmed January 23, 1996.

HISTORY

Library Bill of Rights

The *Library Bill of Rights* constitutes the American Library Association's basic policy on intellectual freedom. The document derives from a statement originally developed by Forrest Spaulding, librarian of the Des Moines Public Library, and adopted by that library on November 21, 1938, as the *Library's Bill of Rights:*

> Now when indications in many parts of the world point to growing intolerance, suppression of free speech, and censorship, affecting the rights of minorities and individuals, the Board of Trustees of the Des Moines Public Library reaffirms these basic policies governing a free public library to serve the best interests of Des Moines and its citizens.
>
> I. Books and other reading matter selected for purchase from public funds shall be chosen from the standpoint of value and interest to the people of Des Moines, and in no case shall selection be based on the race or nationality, political, or religious views of the writers.
>
> II. As far as available material permits, all sides of controversial questions shall be represented equally in the selection of books on subjects about which differences of opinion exist.
>
> III. Official publications and/or propaganda of organized religious, political, fraternal, class, or regional sects, societies, or similar groups, and of institutions controlled by such, are solicited as gifts and will be made available to library users without discrimination. This policy is made necessary because of the meager funds

available for the purchase of books and reading matter. It is obviously impossible to purchase the publications of all such groups and it would be unjust discrimination to purchase those of some and not of others.

IV. Library meeting rooms shall be available on equal terms to all organized nonprofit groups for open meetings to which no admission fee is charged and from which no one is excluded.

The document approved by the ALA Council at the 1939 Annual Conference in San Francisco as the *Library's Bill of Rights* retained the spirit of the Des Moines Public Library policy but differed from the original in several respects. The principal differences concerned Articles II, III, and IV of the Des Moines policy. In Article II, reference to equal representation "in the selection of books on subjects about which differences of opinion exist" was changed to "fair and adequate" representation. This change recognized the impossibility of equal representation in terms of numbers of volumes on a particular subject. Article III of the Des Moines policy was completely deleted because it dealt with the individual budget, needs, and purposes of a specific library. As such, it was inappropriate for a document to be applied nationwide.

Article IV of the Des Moines policy, concerning the use of library meeting rooms, was revised extensively before approval by the Council. An introductory phrase establishing the library as "an institution to educate for democratic living" was added, and references to "nonprofit groups" and "admission fee" were deleted. The resulting article broadened the sense of the original by stating that library meeting rooms be available "on equal terms to all groups in the community regardless of their beliefs or affiliations." As adopted by the ALA Council, the revised *Library's Bill of Rights* read as follows:

Today indications in many parts of the world point to growing intolerance, suppression of free speech, and censorship affecting the rights of minorities and individuals. Mindful of this, the Council of the American Library Association publicly affirms its belief in the following basic policies which should govern the services of free public libraries.

I. Books and other reading matter selected for purchase from the public funds should be chosen because of value and interest to people of the community, and in no case should the selection be influenced by the race or nationality or the political or religious views of the writers.

II. As far as available material permits, all sides of questions on which differences of opinion exist should be represented fairly and adequately in the books and other reading matter purchased for public use.

III. The library as an institution to educate for democratic living should especially welcome the use of its meeting rooms for socially useful and cultural activities and the discussion of current public questions. Library meeting rooms should be available on equal terms to all groups in the community regardless of their beliefs or affiliations.

The three-point declaration approved by the Council was recommended by the Association to governing boards of individual libraries for adoption. The ALA could not force individual librarians and boards to take specific action, but this policy statement, as all other Association recommendations and statements, provided a guide.

For five years, the *Library's Bill of Rights* stood without change. In 1944, the Intellectual Freedom Committee, chaired by Leon Carnovsky, recommended that Article I of the document be amended to include the statement, "Further, books believed to be factually correct should not be banned or removed from the library simply because they are disapproved of by some people." Approved by the ALA Council on October 14, 1944, the amendment proclaimed for the first time the Association's position regarding the banning or removal of materials. The addition, however, also introduced the phrase "factually correct," which was later to be a source of controversy, debate, and change.

Four years later, with David K. Berninghausen as chair, the Intellectual Freedom Committee recommended a broad revision of the *Library's Bill of Rights* and called for a considerable expansion of the document's scope. Its introductory passage was pared to a precise statement of the Association's purpose: "The Council of the American Library Association reaffirms its belief in the following basic policies which should govern the services of all libraries." By 1948, there was no longer the pre-World War II need to point out "growing intolerance, suppression of free speech, and censorship affecting the rights of minorities and individuals." In the developing Cold War, those factors justifying the 1939 policy were even more evident, and it was recognized that the remedies stated in the *Library's Bill of Rights* were necessary to protect free library service in times of peace as well as of crisis.

Article I was prefaced by the phrase "As a responsibility of library service." Intellectual freedom was thus clearly related to the process of materials selection and, moreover, highlighted by being designated a "responsibility." Reference to purchase from the public funds was deleted, thereby extending application of the policy to all library materials, not just those acquired through purchase. Whereas the 1939 document stated that selection should not be influenced by the race, nationality, or political or religious views of writers, the revision more explicitly said that no materials by any authors should be excluded on those grounds.

The first part of Article II was changed to effect a smoother reading, but there were no substantive alterations. However, the 1944 amendment concerning "books believed to be factually correct" was changed to "books . . . of sound factual authority" and the word "banned" was replaced by "proscribed." Despite their seeming slightness, these subtle changes in the second part of the Article actually enlarged the scope of the policy.

A totally new Article III recognized the need of libraries to challenge "censorship of books urged or practiced by volunteer arbiters of morals or political opinion or by organizations that would establish a coercive concept of Americanism." A new Article IV recognized the libraries' responsibility to cooperate with "allied groups . . . in science, education, and book publishing in resisting all abridgment of the free access to ideas and full freedom of expression." Article III of the 1939 document, concerning the use of library meeting rooms, became Article V of the new policy. Although the wording was altered, no change was made in the intent.

The entire recommended revision was adopted by the ALA Council on June 18, 1948. In effect, it was a completely different document from its predecessor, the 1939 bill. The new bill's scope and possible applications were broadly expanded, establishing its national significance. For the first time, the policy mentioned censorship, and also for the first time, the Association declared the responsibility of libraries to challenge censorship—alone and with allied organizations. As adopted by the Council, the newly entitled *Library Bill of Rights* read as follows:

> The Council of the American Library Association reaffirms its belief in the following basic policies which should govern the services of all libraries.

> I. As a responsibility of library service, books and other reading matter selected should be chosen for values of interest, information and enlightenment of all the people of the community. In no case should any material be excluded because of race or nationality, or the political or religious views of the writer.

> II. There should be the fullest practicable provision of material presenting all points of view concerning the problems and issues of our times, international, national, and local; and books or other reading matter of sound factual authority should not be proscribed or removed from library shelves because of partisan or doctrinal disapproval.

> III. Censorship of books, urged or practiced by volunteer arbiters of morals or political opinion or by organizations that would establish a coercive concept of Americanism, must be challenged by libraries in maintenance of their responsibility to provide public information and enlightenment through the printed word.

> IV. Libraries should enlist the cooperation of allied groups in the fields of science, of education, and of book publishing in resisting all abridgment of the free access to ideas and full freedom of expression that are the tradition and heritage of Americans.

> V. As an institution of education for democratic living, the library should welcome the use of its meeting rooms for socially useful and cultural activities and discussion of current public questions. Such meeting places should be available on equal terms to all groups in the community regardless of the beliefs and affiliations of their members.

Although the text of the 1948 document remained unchanged until 1961, its application was broadened in 1951. On the recommendation of the Intellectual Freedom Committee, with the endorsement of the Audio-Visual Board, the Council unanimously resolved that "the *Library Bill of Rights* shall be interpreted as applying to all materials and media of communication used or collected by libraries." The statement, appended as a footnote to all printings of the *Library Bill of Rights* until June 27, 1967, resulted from a Peoria, Illinois, case of attempted censorship by the American Legion and a local newspaper. The Peoria Public Library was pressured to remove the films *The Brotherhood of Man*, *Boundary Lines*, and *Peoples of the U.S.S.R.* All three films appeared on the ALA Audio-Visual Committee's 1947 list of films suggested for purchase by small libraries. The Educational Film Library Association urged the ALA to combat censorship of library film collections, but some librarians contended that the *Library Bill of Rights* applied only to print on paper. The Council resolved the problem by its action of February 3, 1951. That same year, in response to efforts to suppress allegedly "subversive" publications, the Council also adopted the first interpretive statement on the *Library Bill of Rights*, the "Statement on Labeling." Additional Interpretations on a wide variety of issues were to follow in subsequent years. (See part II, section 2.)

In 1961, another major addition to the *Library Bill of Rights* was approved by the Council. From 1948 through February 1961, the library profession had studied the problem of segregation in libraries. A study made by the Association's Special Committee on Civil Liberties recommended that a new Article be added to the *Library Bill of Rights* stating that "the rights of an individual to the use of a library should not be denied or abridged because of his race, religion, national origins, or political views." The recommendation was approved by the Council on February 2, 1961. The new statement became Article V; and the old Article V, concerning use of meeting rooms, became Article VI. The revised *Library Bill of Rights* read as follows:

> The Council of the American Library Association reaffirms its belief in the following basic policies which should govern the services of all libraries.
>
> I. As a responsibility of library service, books and other reading matter selected should be chosen for values of interest, information and enlightenment of all the people of the community. In no case should any book be excluded because of the race or nationality or the political or religious views of the writer.
>
> II. There should be the fullest practicable provision of material presenting all points of view concerning the problems and issues

of our times, international, national, and local; and books or other reading matter of sound factual authority should not be proscribed or removed from library shelves because of partisan or doctrinal disapproval.

III. Censorship of books, urged or practiced by volunteer arbiters of morals or political opinion or by organizations that would establish a coercive concept of Americanism, must be challenged by libraries in maintenance of their responsibility to provide public information and enlightenment through the printed word.

IV. Libraries should enlist the cooperation of allied groups in the fields of science, of education, and of book publishing in resisting all abridgment of the free access to ideas and full freedom of expression that are the tradition and heritage of Americans.

V. The rights of an individual to the use of a library should not be denied or abridged because of his race, religion, national origins or political views.

VI. As an institution of education for democratic living, the library should welcome the use of its meeting rooms for socially useful and cultural activities and discussion of current public questions. Such meeting places should be available on equal terms to all groups in the community regardless of the beliefs and affiliations of their members.

By official action of the Council on February 3, 1951, the "Library Bill of Rights" shall be interpreted to apply to all materials and media of communication used or collected by libraries.

On June 27, 1967, almost thirty years after its origin, the *Library Bill of Rights* underwent its second thorough revision. The need for change was made explicit during a special preconference, sponsored by the Intellectual Freedom Committee with Ervin Gaines as chair, held prior to the 1965 Midwinter Meeting in Washington, D.C. The primary target in the text was the phrase "of sound factual authority," introduced into Article I in 1944, and revised and transferred to Article II in 1948. Criticism of the phrase arose when a librarian in Belleville, Illinois, used it to exclude a Protestant publication that he, being Catholic, described as lacking "sound factual authority."

In their discussion of the Belleville situation, the preconference participants determined that some of the most profound and influential publications in our culture lack the element of "sound factual authority," and the phrase itself could easily be abused to thwart the intent and purpose of the *Library Bill of Rights*. It was apparent that the phrase also could effectively hold the Association from defending fiction or any of those great works that start from philosophical premises but have nothing to do with fact.

Along with a recommendation that the troublesome phrase be dropped, the Intellectual Freedom Committee also asked that several other textual changes be made. In Articles I and V, the word "social" was a suggested addition because of far-reaching results of the civil rights movement. In Article IV, the Committee recommended eliminating the phrase "that are the tradition and heritage of Americans" because it was both redundant and nationalistic. The Committee further recommended that the reference in Article IV be expanded beyond the groups in science, education, and book publishing to reflect the wider context in which librarians and the Association actually operated.

It was also recommended that Article VI, concerning the use of meeting rooms, be amended to include the phrase, "provided that the meetings be open to the public." This amendment clarified the Association's position regarding the use of library meeting rooms by private groups with restricted attendance. The enlarged scope of the text led the IFC to recommend that "library materials" be substituted for "reading matter," thus making the footnote of 1951 regarding nonprint materials unnecessary.

By the time the Intellectual Freedom Committee's proposed changes came before the Council in 1967, a preconference on Intellectual Freedom and the Teenager had recommended that young people be given free access to all books in a library collection. Accordingly, the Committee included with its previous suggestions the recommendation that Article V include the word "age."

On June 28, 1967, the Council adopted all of the Intellectual Freedom Committee's recommendations. The revision was a statement very different from its 1939 progenitor. Whereas the original document concerned itself primarily with unbiased book selection, a balanced collection, and *open* meeting rooms, the new version went much further. It recognized that censorship of any materials and in any guise eventually *affects* the library. It therefore provided libraries with principles for opposing censorship and promoting intellectual freedom, in the broadest sense. The 1967 revision of the *Library Bill of Rights* read as follows:

> The Council of the American Library Association reaffirms its belief in the following basic policies which should govern the services of all libraries.
>
> I. As a responsibility of library service, books and other library materials selected should be chosen for values of interest, information and enlightenment of all the people of the community. In no case should library materials be excluded because of the race or nationality or the social, political, or religious views of the authors.
>
> II. Libraries should provide books and other materials presenting all points of view concerning the problems and issues of our times; no library materials should be proscribed or removed from libraries because of partisan or doctrinal disapproval.
>
> III. Censorship should be challenged by libraries in the maintenance of their responsibility to provide public information and enlightenment.
>
> IV. Libraries should cooperate with all persons and groups concerned with resisting abridgment of free expression and free access to ideas.
>
> V. The rights of an individual to the use of a library should not be denied or abridged because of his age, race, religion, national origins or social or political views.
>
> VI. As an institution of education for democratic living, the library should welcome the use of its meeting rooms for socially useful and cultural activities and discussion of current public questions. Such meeting places should be available on equal terms to all groups in the community regardless of the beliefs and affiliations of their members, provided that the meetings be open to the public.

Yet the document, though thoroughly refined, was still not above criticism. During the following decade, questions were raised about its silence with respect to sex discrimination and institutional censorship in college and research libraries, while its unqualified references to "the community" and to "public" meeting rooms made it appear as a document for public libraries only. Moreover, the profound changes in American society that took place in the late 1960s and early 1970s virtually mandated further changes. Hence, in January 1980, the *Library Bill of Rights* underwent a third major revision, the product of nearly three years of careful review.

The initial impetus for revision came in 1977 with a request from the Committee on the Status of Women in Librarianship that the *Library Bill of Rights* be revised to reject sex discrimination in library services and to eliminate sex-linked pronoun usage from the document itself, which the Intellectual Freedom Committee agreed to act upon as part of an overall reassessment of the document. The subsequent review process involved unprecedentedly broad participation from all sectors of the library community.

At the 1978 Midwinter Meeting, the Intellectual Freedom Committee asked a subcommittee of its own members to prepare a new draft. At the 1978 Annual Conference, the Committee received a report from the subcommittee and conducted a membership hearing on the revision process. At the 1979 Midwinter Meeting, a draft *Library Bill of Rights* was approved for distribution and sent for comment to all ALA councilors, divisions, round tables, and committees, and to all chapter intellectual freedom committees, journals, and bulletins. The draft was also published in the national library press. Comments received were then reviewed at the 1979 Annual Conference, where the Committee also held another open hearing. Shortly after the close of this conference, a new draft was approved by mail and circulated by the IFC to all councilors and ALA units and the library press. Final comments were reviewed by the Committee at the 1980 Midwinter Meeting, where Frances C. Dean, its chair, submitted the final revision to the Council.

In addition to eliminating the use of sex-linked pronouns, the Committee recommended revision of the preamble to state explicitly the role of libraries in maintaining intellectual freedom. Libraries are described in the revision as "forums for information and ideas," employing the word "forum" to indicate that the library should be open to any opinion or view. During discussion of this revision, it was suggested that the library be defined as in Article VI, as "an institution of education for democratic living." This formulation was rejected because it could imply support for the idea that libraries should censor all materials that it deems antidemocratic.

"Democracy," strictly speaking, means "rule by the majority." From the standpoint of intellectual freedom, the library's role in our society is not based on the principle of majority rule but on the principle embodied in the First Amendment, that minority points of view have a right to be heard, no matter how unpopular with, or even detested by, the majority.

In Article I, the Intellectual Freedom Committee recommended the elimination of verbiage that seemed to detract from clarity and simplicity of expression, and the modification of the word "community" to read "the community the library serves," inasmuch as many libraries serve a special public, such as a specific academic or school community. The Committee further recommended replacing the word "author" with the phrase "those contributing to their creation" because the originators of many library materials are today referred to by other terms.

In Article II, the Committee recommended adding that libraries have an obligation to provide information and diverse points of view on historical as well as current issues. In Article III, stylistic changes, as well as elimination of the modifier "public," were suggested. The meaning of that word in the Article's context placed an obligation on nonpublic libraries that such libraries insist they do not have.

The revision of Article V was marked by considerable debate about whether a general statement affirming the rights of all individuals to library use could serve the same function as a more detailed list of all those specific conditions or factors that might lead to infringement of this right. Considering that explicitly designating one or more factors as discriminatory might risk excluding other grounds not specifically mentioned, either by oversight or inability to predict the future; and judging the so-called laundry list approach to be stylistically unwieldy, the Committee recommended instead a general statement condemning discrimination according to origin, background, or views. The Committee recommended, however, retaining specific reference to age, because a suitable generic term that would readily be recognized as inclusive of this factor could not be found.

Finally, Article VI was revised to take into account differences among types of libraries and to eliminate any implication that libraries might censor materials and exclude programs on the grounds that they contain antidemocratic ideas or are not socially useful. The revision laid firm emphasis on the principle of equitable and nondiscriminatory application of rules and regulations governing meeting rooms and exhibit space, while permitting libraries broad flexibility in formulating these according to the dictates of their widely varied situations.

On January 23, 1980, the Council adopted the recommendations of the Intellectual Freedom Committee. The resulting document constitutes the present *Library Bill of Rights*.

At the 1988 Annual Conference, the Minority Concerns Committee recommended, and the Council approved, that "the *Library Bill of Rights* be reviewed to include the concepts of freedom of access to information and libraries without limitation by language or economic status." During its initial review of this Council action at the 1989 Midwinter Meeting, the Intellectual Freedom Committee suggested that a revision of the Interpretations be undertaken first to address explicitly and immediately the issues raised by the Minority Concerns Committee. The *Library Bill of Rights* would then be reassessed in light of the revised Interpretations. Thus began a review process that resulted in the reworking of all but one of the then-extant Interpretations and the addition of new Interpretations: "The Universal Right to Free Expression"' and "Economic Barriers to Information Access." (See part II, section 2.)

During the process of reviewing the Interpretations, other concerns regarding gender and sexual orientation were also brought to the attention of the Committee. When review of the existing Interpretations was complete, the Intellectual Freedom Committee considered the *Library Bill of Rights* itself in light of the revised Interpretations and the request of the Minority Concerns Committee. The IFC concluded that revision of the basic document not only was unnecessary but that it would be unwise to open a document that had stood the test of time to the "laundry list" approach. To address concerns relating to economic status and fees for library service, the Committee recommended adoption of a new Interpretation, "Economic Barriers to Information Access." To address the issues of equity of service and access and representation in the collection for gays, bisexuals, and lesbians, which had been raised during the process of review, the Committee recommended adoption of another new Interpretation, "Access to Library Resources and Services Regardless of Gender or Sexual Orientation." The new Interpretations were adopted by the ALA Council in 1993.

In 1994, in response to a rapidly changing information environment and the need for guidance expressed by many librarians about how to apply the *Library Bill of Rights* to electronic access to information, the Committee began work on a new Interpretation called "Access to Electronic Information, Services, and Networks." As part of the development process, the Committee sponsored a hearing at the 1995 Midwinter Meeting in Philadelphia to receive testimony and observations from librarians working in different library settings on the issue of access to information via electronic means. Meeting in Chicago in March 1995, the IFC prepared a draft Interpretation, which was circulated to all ALA units for comments. A further draft was presented to the ALA Council at the 1995 Annual Conference in Chicago. After concerns were raised on the floor of Council about the effect of some of the language relating to fees and nondiscriminatory access, particularly in academic library settings, the draft was sent back to the IFC for further consideration. A new version of the Interpretation was distributed prior to the 1996 Midwinter Meeting. Further refinements in the document were made at the 1996 Midwinter Meeting, and the Council adopted it on January 24, 1996. At that time it became clear that, although there was general agreement that the *Library Bill of Rights* and its Interpretations apply to the provision of access to electronic information, it is extremely difficult to produce a document that directly addresses each type of library and library service. As a result, the Office for Intellectual Freedom developed "Questions and Answers: Access to Electronic Information, Services, and Networks: An Interpretation of the *Library Bill of Rights*," which was finalized in June 1997. (See part II, section 2.2.)

At the 1996 ALA Midwinter Meeting, the Board of Directors of the American Library Trustee Association (ALTA) voted to reaffirm the inclusion of "age" in the *Library Bill of Rights* because of challenges which might result in restricting access to libraries and library materials to children and young adults. ALTA brought a request to the Council to reaffirm the inclusion of "age." The motion was passed by the ALA Council on January 24, 1996, by acclamation.

Although there is little doubt that future developments will mandate yet further revision or the development of additional interpretive statements, the *Library Bill of Rights* is by no means a product of hasty work, and as its history proves, it remains a vibrant statement of principle and a useful guide to action for librarians in all library settings.

2
Library Bill of Rights
Interpretations

Although the Articles of the *Library Bill of Rights* are unambiguous statements of basic principles that should govern the service of all libraries, questions do arise concerning application of these principles to specific library practices. For example, a 1951 Peoria, Illinois, case involving certain films in the public library required the Association to clarify the application of the *Library Bill of Rights* to nonprint materials. A recommendation by the Intellectual Freedom Committee and the Audio-Visual Board resulted in the ALA Council's adding an interpretive footnote explaining that the *Library Bill of Rights* applies to all materials and media of communication used or collected by libraries.

During the 1971 Annual Conference in Dallas, the Intellectual Freedom Committee considered censorship cases that clearly called for Interpretations of the *Library Bill of Rights* to define its application to certain practices. Believing that frequent revisions, amendments, or additions of footnotes weaken the document's effectiveness, the Committee resolved instead to develop statements to be called Interpretations of the *Library Bill of Rights*. The Committee said further that certain documents already in existence should be designated Interpretations of the *Library Bill of Rights*.

After the Council adopted the 1980 revision of the *Library Bill of Rights*, the Intellectual Freedom Committee undertook the first systematic review of all the Interpretations. The initial purpose of this review was to make all policies consistent with both the letter and the spirit of the revised *Library Bill of Rights*. As the process developed, however, the goals became more sweeping. Important gaps in policy were filled, and, taken as a group, the Interpretations were remolded into a unified general guide to application of the *Library Bill of Rights.* Not only were most policies thoroughly rewritten or amended, but new Interpretations were also formulated and outdated or inadequate material eliminated. As with the 1980 revision of the *Library Bill of Rights,* the IFC sought and received extensive comments from ALA councilors, units, and chapters to whom all drafts were circulated in advance. The process of revision was completed at the 1982 Annual Conference in Philadelphia.

In response to a 1988 Minority Concerns Committee report, recommending a revision of the *Library Bill of Rights* to ensure protection against discrimination in library services based on language or economic status, the Intellectual Freedom Committee began the second comprehensive review of the Interpretations. The IFC agreed that each Interpretation would be considered separately and recommended to the Council for adoption upon completion of any necessary revisions. The process resulted in the revision of all but one Interpretation, the addition of two new Interpretations, "The Universal Right to Free Expression" and "Economic Barriers to Information Access," and the rescission of an Interpretation no longer deemed relevant. Indirectly, the process spurred the development of two other new Interpretations, "Access to Library Resources and Services regardless of Gender or Sexual Orientation" and "Access to Electronic Information, Services, and Networks."

In line with the ongoing practice of periodic review, the IFC carefully reviewed *all* of the Interpretations during 1999–2000, especially in regard to the applicability to the Internet. Changes were recommended in the following Interpretations.

- "Access to Library Resources and Services regardless of Gender or Sexual Orientation." The changes removed references to terms of sexual orientation in the belief that terms can become dated or offensive, or both; affirmed that all materials —regardless of format or services—are protected by the *Library Bill of Rights;* and referenced ALA policy 52.5.2, "Sex Education Materials in Libraries," in the Interpretation.
- "Library-Initiated Programs as a Resource" was changed by the addition of "should," in some instances, and the substitution of "that cross" for "across."

- "Access to Resources and Services in the School Library Media Program" was changed for grammar and inclusion.
- "Restricted Access to Library Materials" was changed with additional words to emphasize meaning or intention, and the addition of the following sentence: "More recently, some libraries have applied filtering software to their Internet stations that prevent users from finding targeted categories of information, much of which is constitutionally protected."

Following are those documents designated by the Intellectual Freedom Committee as Interpretations of the *Library Bill of Rights*, along with background statements detailing the philosophy and history of each. For convenience and easy reference, the documents are presented in alphabetical order. These documents are policies of the American Library Association, having been adopted by the ALA Council.

2.1

Access for Children and Young People to Videotapes and Other Nonprint Formats

An Interpretation of the *Library Bill of Rights*

Library collections of videotapes, motion pictures, and other nonprint formats raise a number of intellectual freedom issues, especially regarding minors.

The interests of young people, like those of adults, are not limited by subject, theme, or level of sophistication. Librarians have a responsibility to ensure young people have access to materials and services that reflect diversity sufficient to meet their needs.

To guide librarians and others in resolving these issues, the American Library Association provides the following guidelines.

Article V of the *Library Bill of Rights* says, "A person's right to use a library should not be denied or abridged because of origin, age, background, or views."

ALA's "Free Access to Libraries for Minors: An Interpretation of the *Library Bill of Rights*" states:

> The "right to use a library" includes free access to, and unrestricted use of, all the services, materials, and facilities the library has to offer. Every restriction on access to, and use of, library resources, based solely on the chronological age, educational level, or legal emancipation of users violates Article V.

> . . . [P]arents—and only parents—have the right and the responsibility to restrict the access of their children—and only their children—to library resources. Parents or legal guardians who

do not want their children to have access to certain library services, materials or facilities, should so advise their children. Librarians and governing bodies cannot assume the role of parents or the functions of parental authority in the private relationship between parent and child. Librarians and governing bodies have a public and professional obligation to provide equal access to all library resources for all library users.

Policies which set minimum age limits for access to videotapes and/or other audiovisual materials and equipment, with or without parental permission, abridge library use for minors. Further, age limits based on the cost of the materials are unacceptable. Unless directly and specifically prohibited by law from circulating certain motion pictures and video productions to minors, librarians should apply the same standards to circulation of these materials as are applied to books and other materials.

Recognizing that libraries cannot act in loco parentis, ALA acknowledges and supports the exercise by parents of their responsibility to guide their own children's reading and viewing. Published reviews of films and videotapes and/or reference works which provide information about the content, subject matter, and recommended audiences can be made available in conjunction with nonprint collections to assist parents in guiding their children without implicating the library in censorship. This material may include information provided by video producers and distributors, promotional material on videotape packaging, and Motion Picture Association of America (MPAA) ratings *if they are included on the tape or in the packaging by the original publisher* and/or if they appear in review sources or reference works included in the library's collection. Marking out or removing ratings information from videotape packages constitutes expurgation or censorship.

MPAA and other rating services are private advisory codes and have no legal standing.* For the library to add such ratings to the materials if they are not already there, to post a list of such

---

*For information on case law, please contact the ALA Office for Intellectual Freedom. *See also* "Statement on Labeling" and "Expurgation of Library Materials," Interpretations of the *Library Bill of Rights*.

ratings with a collection, or to attempt to enforce such ratings through circulation policies or other procedures constitutes labeling, "an attempt to prejudice attitudes" about the material, and is unacceptable. The application of locally generated ratings schemes intended to provide content warnings to library users is also inconsistent with the *Library Bill of Rights*.

Adopted June 28, 1989, by the ALA Council; the quotation from "Free Access to Libraries for Minors" was changed after Council adopted the July 3, 1991, revision of that Interpretation.

HISTORY

Access for Children and Young People to Videotapes and Other Nonprint Formats

In January 1989, the IFC examined the Interpretation "Circulation of Motion Pictures and Video Productions" in response to urgings from the ALA youth divisions and to the Minority Concerns Committee's request for a review of the *Library Bill of Rights* to ensure that it provided for equitable access without regard to language or economic status. The IFC concluded that a new Interpretation was necessary to address fully the issue of minors' access to videos and to provide similar guarantees for nonprint materials resulting from new technologies.

The Committee also sought to provide clearer guidelines for librarians, emphasizing the importance of parent—not librarian—responsibility for guiding a child's viewing or choice of other library materials, opposing the use of cost-based restrictions to inhibit minors' access to materials, and rejecting the imposition of private rating systems and the unapproved editing of films or other copyright materials, for classroom use.

The new draft Interpretation was presented to the Committee at the June 1989 ALA Annual Conference. After discussion with representatives from the youth divisions and the Professional Ethics Committee, which resulted in minor editorial changes, the Interpretation was adopted and recommended to the Council. On June 28, 1989, the Council adopted the new Interpretation in place of the former "Circulation of Motion Pictures and Video Productions." The latter was then rescinded by the Council.

As part of the periodic review of all of the Interpretations, "Access for Children and Young People to Videotapes and Other Nonprint Formats" was reviewed by the IFC in 1999–2000. No changes were recommended.

2.2

Access to Electronic Information, Services, and Networks

An Interpretation of the
Library Bill of Rights

The world is in the midst of an electronic communications revolution. Based on its constitutional, ethical, and historical heritage, American librarianship is uniquely positioned to address the broad range of information issues being raised in this revolution. In particular, librarians address intellectual freedom from a strong ethical base and an abiding commitment to the preservation of the individual's rights.

Freedom of expression is an inalienable human right and the foundation for self-government. Freedom of expression encompasses the freedom of speech and the corollary right to receive information. These rights extend to minors as well as adults. Libraries and librarians exist to facilitate the exercise of these rights by selecting, producing, providing access to, identifying, retrieving, organizing, providing instruction in the use of, and preserving recorded expression regardless of the format or technology.

The American Library Association expresses these basic principles of librarianship in its "Code of Ethics" and in the *Library Bill of Rights* and its Interpretations. These serve to guide librarians and library governing bodies in addressing issues of intellectual freedom that arise when the library provides access to electronic information, services, and networks.

Issues arising from the still-developing technology of computer-mediated information generation, distribution, and retrieval need to be approached and regularly reviewed from a context of constitutional principles and ALA policies so that fundamental and traditional tenets of librarianship are not swept away.

Electronic information flows across boundaries and barriers despite attempts by individuals, governments, and private entities to channel or control it. Even so, many people, for reasons of technology, infrastructure, or socio-economic status do not have access to electronic information.

In making decisions about how to offer access to electronic information, each library should consider its mission, goals, objectives, cooperative agreements, and the needs of the entire community it serves.

The Rights of Users

All library system and network policies, procedures or regulations relating to electronic resources and services should be scrutinized for potential violation of user rights.

User policies should be developed according to the policies and guidelines established by the American Library Association, including "Guidelines for the Development and Implementation of Policies, Regulations, and Procedures Affecting Access to Library Materials, Services and Facilities."

Users should not be restricted or denied access for expressing or receiving constitutionally protected speech. Users' access should not be changed without due process, including, but not limited to, formal notice and a means of appeal.

Although electronic systems may include distinct property rights and security concerns, such elements may not be employed as a subterfuge to deny users' access to information. Users have the right to be free of unreasonable limitations or conditions set by libraries, librarians, system administrators, vendors, network service providers, or others. Contracts, agreements, and licenses entered into by libraries on behalf of their users should not violate this right. Users also have a right to information, training and assistance necessary to operate the hardware and software provided by the library.

Users have both the right of confidentiality and the right of privacy. The library should uphold these rights by policy, procedure, and practice. Users should be advised, however, that because security is technically difficult to achieve, electronic transactions and files could become public.

The rights of users who are minors shall in no way be abridged.*

Equity of Access

Electronic information, services, and networks provided directly or indirectly by the library should be equally, readily and equitably accessible to all library users. American Library Association policies oppose the charging of user fees for the provision of information services by all libraries and information services that receive their major support from public funds (50.3; 53.1.14; 60.1; 61.1). It should be the goal of all libraries to develop policies concerning access to electronic resources in light of "Economic Barriers to Information Access: An Interpretation of the *Library Bill of Rights*" and "Guidelines for the Development and Implementation of Policies, Regulations and Procedures Affecting Access to Library Materials, Services and Facilities."

Information Resources and Access

Providing connections to global information, services, and networks is not the same as selecting and purchasing material for a library collection. Determining the accuracy or authenticity of electronic information may present special problems. Some information accessed electronically may not meet a library's selection or collection development policy. It is, therefore, left to each user to determine what is appropriate. Parents and legal guardians who are concerned about their children's use of electronic resources should provide guidance to their own children.

---

*See "Free Access to Libraries for Minors"; "Access to Resources and Services in the School Library Media Program"; and "Access for Children and Young People to Videotapes and Other Nonprint Formats."

Libraries and librarians should not deny or limit access to information available via electronic resources because of its allegedly controversial content or because of the librarian's personal beliefs or fear of confrontation. Information retrieved or utilized electronically should be considered constitutionally protected unless determined otherwise by a court with appropriate jurisdiction.

Libraries, acting within their mission and objectives, must support access to information on all subjects that serve the needs or interests of each user, regardless of the user's age or the content of the material. Libraries have an obligation to provide access to government information available in electronic format. Libraries and librarians should not deny access to information solely on the grounds that it is perceived to lack value.

In order to prevent the loss of information, and to preserve the cultural record, libraries may need to expand their selection or collection development policies to ensure preservation, in appropriate formats, of information obtained electronically.

Electronic resources provide unprecedented opportunities to expand the scope of information available to users. Libraries and librarians should provide access to information presenting all points of view. The provision of access does not imply sponsorship or endorsement. These principles pertain to electronic resources no less than they do to the more traditional sources of information in libraries.*

Adopted by the ALA Council, January 24, 1996.
*See "Diversity in Collection Development."

QUESTIONS AND ANSWERS

Access to Electronic Information, Services, and Networks

An Interpretation of the
Library Bill of Rights

Following the initial adoption by the ALA Council of "Access to Electronic Information, Services, and Networks: An Interpretation of the *Library Bill of Rights*" in January 1996, the ALA Intellectual Freedom Committee produced a sample set of questions and answers to clarify this Interpretation's implications and applications.

As librarians, we have a professional obligation to strive for free access to all information resources. However, many of the questions concerning electronic information will not have a single answer. ALA recognizes that each library needs to develop policies in keeping with its mission, objectives, and users. Librarians also need to be cognizant of local legislation and judicial decisions that may affect implementation of their policies.

Introduction

1. *What are the factors that uniquely position American librarianship to provide access to electronic information?*

   Electronic media offer an unprecedented forum for the sharing of information and ideas envisioned by the Founding Fathers in the U.S. Constitution. Their vision cannot be realized unless libraries provide free access to electronic information, services, and networks.

   Thomas Jefferson, James Madison, and others laid the basis for a government that made education, access to information, and toleration for dissent cornerstones of a great democratic experiment. With geographic expansion and the rise of a mass press, American government facilitated these constitutional principles through the creation of such innovative institutions as the public school, land grant colleges, and the public library. By the close of the 19th century, professionally trained librarians developed specialized techniques in support of their democratic mission. In the 1930s, the *Library Bill of Rights* acknowledged librarians' professional and ethical responsibilities to the Constitution's promise of access to information in all formats to all people.

2. *What is the library's role in facilitating freedom of expression in an electronic arena?*

    Libraries are an essential part of the national information infrastructure, providing people with access and participation in the electronic arena. They are fundamental to the informed debate demanded by the Constitution and for the provision of access to electronic information resources to those who might otherwise be excluded.

3. *Why should libraries extend access to electronic information resources to minors?*

    Those libraries with a mission that includes service to minors should make available to them a full range of information necessary to become thinking adults and the informed electorate envisioned in the Constitution. The opportunity to participate responsibly in the electronic arena is also vital for nurturing the information literacy skills demanded by the Information Age. Librarians need to remember that minors also possess First Amendment rights. Only parents and legal guardians have the right and responsibility to restrict their children's—and only their own children's—access to any electronic resource.

4. *Do the policies of ALA regarding intellectual freedom and ethics apply to electronic information, services, and networks in libraries?*

    Yes, because information is information regardless of format. Library resources in electronic form are increasingly recognized as vital to the provision of information that is the core of the library's role in society.

5. *Does the ALA require that libraries adopt the* Library Bill of Rights *or the ALA "Code of Ethics"?*

No. ALA has no authority to govern or regulate libraries. ALA's policies are voluntary and serve only as guidelines for local policy development.

6. *Does ALA censure libraries or librarians who do not adhere to or adopt the* Library Bill of Rights *or the ALA "Code of Ethics"?*

No, ALA does not.

7. *Do libraries need to develop policies about access to electronic information, services, and networks?*

In view of the complex issues associated with access to electronic information, the ALA strongly recommends that libraries formally adopt and periodically reexamine policies that develop from the missions and goals specific to their institutions.

Rights of Users

8. *How can libraries impact vendors/network providers/licensors when they attempt to limit or edit access to electronic information?*

Librarians have a mandate to be strong advocates of open access to information. Therefore, when purchasing electronic information resources, librarians should conduct contract negotiations with vendors/network providers/licensors to ensure the least restrictive access in current and future products.

Libraries, themselves, along with any parent institution and consortia partners, should also communicate their intellectual freedom concerns and public responsibilities in the production of their own electronic information resources.

9. *How can libraries help to ensure library user confidentiality in regard to electronic information access?*

Librarians must be aware of patron confidentiality laws on library records for their particular state and community. In accordance with such laws and professional and ethical responsibilities, librarians should ensure and routinely review policies and procedures for maintaining confidentiality of personally identifiable use of library materials, facilities, or services. These especially include electronic circulation and online use records.

Electronic records on individual use patterns should also be strictly safeguarded. Software and protocols should be designed for the automatic and timely deletion of personal identifiers from the tracking elements within electronic databases. System access to computer terminals or other stations also should be designed to eliminate indicators of the research strategy or use patterns of any identifiable patron. For example, the efforts of the last user of a terminal or program should not remain on the monitor or be easily retrievable from a buffer or cache by subsequent users. Methods used by libraries or institutions to monitor reserving computer time and the amount of time spent in electronic information resources also must protect the confidentiality rights of patrons.

Libraries and their institutions should provide physical environments that facilitate user privacy for accessing electronic information. For instance, libraries should consider placing terminals, printers, and access stations so that user privacy is enhanced. Computer accessories, such as privacy screens, offer additional protection. Where resources are limited, libraries should consider time, place, and manner restrictions.

Finally, libraries must be sensitive to the special needs for confidential access to electronic information sources of physically challenged patrons.

10. *Our library is just one of many autonomous institutions in a consortium. How can we be sure that our cooperating partners honor the confidentiality of our library users in a shared network environment?*

This is a contractual and legal matter. The importance of confidentiality of personally identifiable information about library users transcends individual institutional and type of library boundaries. Libraries should establish and regularly review interlibrary and interagency cooperative agreements to ensure clear confidentiality policies and procedures, which obligate all members of a cooperative, or all departments and branches within a parent institution.

11. *Do libraries need a use policy for electronic information access? If so, what elements should be considered for inclusion?*

Access questions are rooted in constitutional mandates and a *Library Bill of Rights* that reach across all media. These should be professionally interpreted through general service policies that also relate to the specific mission and objectives of the institution. Such general policies can benefit from the legacy and precedents within the ALA's *Intellectual Freedom Manual,* including new interpretations for electronic resources.

Reasonable restrictions placed on the time, place, and manner of library access should be used only when necessary to achieve substantial library managerial objectives and only in the least restrictive manner possible. Libraries should focus on developing policies that ensure broad access to information resources of all kinds. Policies should not limit the kinds of information accessed by which patrons and in what manner.

12. *Why shouldn't parental permission be required for minor access to electronic information?*

As with any other information format, parents are responsible for determining what they wish their own children to access electronically. Libraries may need to help parents understand their options during the evolving information revolution, but should not be in the policing position of enforcing parental restrictions within the library. In addition, libraries cannot use children as an excuse to violate their constitutional duty to help provide for an educated adult electorate.

The *Library Bill of Rights*—its various Interpretations (especially "Free Access to Libraries for Minors; Access for Children and Young People to Videotapes and Other Nonprint Formats"), and ALA's "Guidelines for the Development and Implementation of Policies, Regulations and Procedures Affecting Access to Library Materials, Services and Facilities"— also endorse the rights of youth to library resources and information as part of their inalienable rights and the passage to informed adulthood. Electronic information access is no different in these regards.

13. *Does our library have to make provisions for patrons with disabilities to access electronic information?*

    Yes. The Americans with Disabilities Act and other federal and state laws forbid providers of public services, whether publicly or privately governed, from discriminating against individuals with disabilities. All library information services, including access to electronic information, should be accessible to patrons regardless of disability.

    Many methods are available and under development to make electronic information universally accessible, including adaptive devices, software, and human assistance. Libraries must consider such tools in trying to meet the needs of persons with disabilities in the design or provision of electronic information services.

Equity of Access

14. *My library recognizes different classes of users. Is this a problem?*

    The mission and objectives of some libraries recognize distinctions between classes of users. For example, academic libraries may have different categories of users (e.g., faculty, students, others). Public libraries may distinguish between residents and nonresidents. School library media centers embrace curricular support as their primary mission; some have further expanded access to their collections. Special libraries vary their access policies, depending on their definition of primary clientele. Establishing different levels of users should not automatically assume the need for different levels of access.

15. *Does the statement that "electronic information, services, and networks provided directly or indirectly by the library should be equally, readily and equitably accessible to all library users" mean that exactly the same service must be available to anyone who wants to use the library?*

    No. It means that access to services should not be denied on the basis of an arbitrary classification; for example, age or physical ability to use the equipment. This phrase, from "Economic Barriers to Information Access: An Interpretation of the *Library Bill of Rights*," clarifies that simply making printed information sources available to those unable to pay while charging for electronic information sources abridges the principles of equality and equity.

16. *Which is a higher priority: To offer more information or not to charge fees? Does this mean my library cannot charge fees?*

    The higher priority is free services. Charging fees creates barriers to access. That is why ALA has urged librarians, in "Economic Barriers to Information Access," to "resist the temptation to impose user fees to alleviate financial pressures, at long-term cost to institutional integrity and public confidence in libraries."

17. *Does "provision of information services" include printouts?*

    Whenever possible, all services should be without fees. In any case, fees should not create a barrier to access. Translated to the electronic environment, this means that some libraries will provide the text on the screen at no charge, but might charge for printouts.

18. *If my library has no "major support from public funds," can we then charge fees?*

    Yes, but ALA advocates achieving equitable access and avoiding and eliminating barriers to information and ideas whenever possible.

19. *What do you do if one person monopolizes the equipment?*

    Libraries should address this issue in their use policies. Time, place, and manner restrictions should be applied equitably to all users.

Information Resources and Access

20. *How does providing connections to "global information, services, and networks" differ from selecting and purchasing material for an individual library?*

Selection begins with the institution's mission and objectives. The librarian performs an initial selection from available resources, and then the user makes a choice from that collection. Many electronic resources, such as CDs, are acquired for the library's collection in this traditional manner. Collections consist of fixed discrete items.

When libraries provide Internet access, they provide a means for people to use the wealth of information stored on computers throughout the world, whose ever-changing contents are created, maintained and made available beyond the library. The library also provides a means for the individual user to choose for him- or herself the resources accessed and to interact electronically with other computer users throughout the world.

21. *How can libraries use their selection expertise to help patrons use the Internet?*

Libraries should play a proactive role in guiding users, especially parents and their children, to the most effective locations and answers. Library Web sites are one starting place to the vast resources of the Internet. All libraries are encouraged to develop Web sites, including links, to Internet resources to meet the information needs of their users. These links should be made within the existing mission, collection development policy, and selection criteria of the library.

22. *Should the library deny access to constitutionally protected speech on the Internet in order to protect its users or reflect community values?*

No. The library should not deny access to constitutionally protected speech. People have a right to receive constitutionally protected speech, and any restriction of those rights imposed by a library violates the U.S. Constitution. Only a court of law can judge speech to be outside of the protection of the First Amendment.

23. *Does using software that filters or blocks access to electronic information resources on the Internet violate "Access to Electronic Information, Services, and Networks: An Interpretation of the* Library Bill of Rights?"

This interpretation states that libraries and librarians should not deny access to constitutionally protected information. The use of filters presents a number of complex legal, technical, and ethical issues. For a discussion of these problems, librarians need to review information located on the Office for Intellectual Freedom Web page, "Filters and Filtering," at http://www.ala.org/alaorg/oif/filtersandfiltering.html.

24. *Why do libraries have an obligation to provide government information in electronic format?*

The role of libraries is to provide ideas and information across the spectrum of social and political thought and to make these ideas and this information available to anyone who needs or wants it. In a democracy, libraries have a particular obligation to provide library users with information necessary for participation in self-governance. Because access to government information is rapidly shifting to electronic format only, libraries should plan to continue to provide access to information in this format, as well.

25. *What is the library's role in the preservation of information in electronic formats?*

The online electronic medium is ephemeral and information may disappear without efforts to save it. Libraries may need to preserve and archive electronic information critical to their mission.

26. *Does "must support access to information on all subjects" mean a library must provide material on all subjects for all users, even if those users are not part of the library's community of users or the material is not appropriate for the library?*

The institution's mission and objectives will drive these decisions.

27. *The Interpretation states that libraries should not deny access to resources, solely because they are perceived to lack value. Does this mean the library must buy or obtain every electronic resource available?*

No. The institution's mission and objectives will drive these decisions.

28. *How can the library avoid becoming a game room and still provide access to this material?*

   Libraries need to develop policies that address time, place, or manner restrictions when determining the use of electronic equipment and resources. Such restrictions should not be based on content.

29. *Do copyright laws apply to electronic information?*

   Yes. Librarians have professional and ethical responsibilities to keep abreast of copyright and fair use rights. This responsibility applies to the library's own online publications, contractual obligations with authors and publishers, and informing library users of copyright laws that apply to their use of electronic information.

Adopted by the ALA Intellectual Freedom Committee, June 5, 1997; revised November 17, 2000.

HISTORY

Access to Electronic Information, Services, and Networks

At the 1994 Annual Conference meeting in Miami Beach, the Intellectual Freedom Committee discussed its response to a document titled "Principles for the Development of the National Information Infrastructure," which had been developed by several ALA divisions and other library organizations as a unified statement of the library community's hopes with regard to development of the national "information superhighway." The Committee endorsed the concept of the draft but found many areas of concern, including wording that suggested an acceptance of fees for access to electronic information and distinctions between library service based upon the type or the format of information to be provided. An atmosphere of urgency about issuing a statement on the subject of the national information infrastructure pervaded the 1994 conference. Bills on the subject were pending before Congress. Nevertheless, the Intellectual Freedom Committee felt that the ALA's basic intellectual freedom policies were being swept aside, at least to some degree, in the rush by many library organizations to become "players" in the discussions taking place in Washington on the structure of the national information superhighway. It was the compound effect of these concerns, coupled with an increasing volume of requests for guidance from librarians in the field, that solidified the Intellectual Freedom Committee's determination to develop a new Interpretation of the *Library Bill of Rights*, "Access to Electronic Information, Services, and Networks." An IFC subcommittee was appointed at the 1994 Annual Conference to prepare a first draft; at the same time, the Committee agreed to sponsor open hearings on the subject at the 1995 Midwinter Meeting in Philadelphia.

Both before and during the hearing, the Committee received comment and testimony from librarians, representing a broad variety of types of libraries and library services, expressing their concerns and questions about access to electronic information. The Committee itself also identified several areas of concern, not the least of which was the definition of "electronic communication." For example, is the Internet a public forum, or is it not? Are parts of it public fora and parts of it not? Other areas of concern included privacy and confidentiality; attribution or lack thereof of articles and information appearing on the Internet; "flaming" and hate speech; punishment by cutting off information or user accounts; fees; children's access; content and diversity; collection development; language; disability; and restriction of news groups. Recognizing the breadth of issues that needed to be addressed and the urgency of the need, the Committee decided to hold a special meeting to work on and produce a draft Interpretation for circulation prior to the 1995 Annual Conference.

The Committee met in Chicago on March 3–5, 1995. An intensive weekend of work resulted in a draft document composed of four sections: an introductory section placing electronic information, services, and networks squarely within the realm of First Amendment rights, freedom of expression, and public forum concepts; a section on the rights of users; a section on equity of access; and a section on information resources and access issues. The draft was circulated broadly to the ALA's Council and Executive Board, all of the divisions and round tables, chapter intellectual freedom committees, and all other interested librarians. It also was posted on the Office for Intellectual Freedom's list, ALAOIF, and comments were invited from all participants.

At the 1995 Annual Conference in Chicago, discussions of additional comments received resulted in editorial changes and rearrangement of some of the language of the draft. The sections on equity of access and the rights of users were changed to clarify the Committee's intent that fees not be charged for electronic information services and that services be provided in a nondiscriminatory manner.

The revised draft was circulated to all ALA units meeting at the conference for additional comments and was endorsed by the Public Library Association and the American Association of School Librarians. Other units, particularly the Association of College and Research Libraries, expressed strong reservations about the draft, especially about its principles on fees and equity of access. In light of these concerns, the draft was sent back to the IFC for additional work. At the 1996 Midwinter Meeting, the IFC presented a revised Interpretation to the Council which was adopted on January 24, 1996.

As part of the ongoing review in 1999–2000, the Interpretation was again reviewed. No changes were recommended.

2.3

Access to Library Resources and Services regardless of Gender or Sexual Orientation

An Interpretation of the
Library Bill of Rights

American libraries exist and function within the context of a body of laws derived from the United States Constitution and the First Amendment. The *Library Bill of Rights* embodies the basic policies which guide libraries in the provision of services, materials, and programs.

In the preamble to its *Library Bill of Rights*, the American Library Association affirms that *all* [emphasis added] libraries are forums for information and ideas. This concept of *forum* and its accompanying principle of *inclusiveness* pervade all six Articles of the *Library Bill of Rights*.

The American Library Association stringently and unequivocally maintains that libraries and librarians have an obligation to resist efforts that systematically exclude materials dealing with any subject matter, including gender or sexual orientation:

- Article I of the *Library Bill of Rights* states that "Materials should not be excluded because of the origin, background, or views of those contributing to their creation." The Association affirms that books and other materials coming from gay presses, gay, lesbian, or bisexual authors or other creators, and materials regardless of format or services dealing with gay lifestyles are protected by the *Library Bill of Rights*. Librarians are obligated by the *Library Bill of Rights* to endeavor to select materials without regard to the gender or sexual orientation of their creators by using the criteria identified in their written, approved selection policies (ALA policy 53.1.5).

- Article II maintains that "Libraries should provide materials and information presenting all points of view on current and historical issues. Materials should not be proscribed or removed because of partisan or doctrinal disapproval." Library services, materials, and programs representing diverse points of view on gender or sexual orientation should be considered for purchase and inclusion in library collections and programs (ALA policies 53.1.1; 53.1.9; and 53.1.11). The Association affirms that attempts to proscribe or remove materials dealing with gay or lesbian life without regard to the written, approved selection policy violate this tenet and constitute censorship.

- Articles III and IV mandate that libraries "challenge censorship" and cooperate with those "resisting abridgment of free expression and free access to ideas."

- Article V holds that "A person's right to use a library should not be denied or abridged because of origin, age, background, or views." In the *Library Bill of Rights* and all its Interpretations, it is intended that: "origin" encompasses all the characteristics of individuals that are inherent in the circumstances of their birth; "age" encompasses all the characteristics of individuals that are inherent in their levels of development and maturity; "background" encompasses all the characteristics of individuals that are a result of their life experiences; and "views" encompasses all the opinions and beliefs held and expressed by individuals.

   Therefore, Article V of the *Library Bill of Rights* mandates that library services, materials, and programs be available to all members of the community the library serves, without regard to gender or sexual orientation. This includes providing youth with comprehensive sex education literature (ALA policy 52.5.2).

- Article VI maintains that "Libraries which make exhibit spaces and meeting rooms available to the public they serve should make such facilities available on an equitable basis, regardless of the beliefs or affiliations of individuals or groups requesting their use." This protection extends to all groups and members of the community the library serves, without regard to gender or sexual orientation.

  The American Library Association holds that any attempt, be it legal or extra-legal, to regulate or suppress library services, materials, or programs must be resisted in order that protected expression is not abridged. Librarians have a professional obligation to ensure that all library users have free and equal access to the entire range of library services, materials, and programs. Therefore, the Association strongly opposes any effort to limit access to information and ideas. The Association also encourages librarians to proactively support the First Amendment rights of all library users, regardless of gender or sexual orientation.

Adopted June 30, 1993; amended July 12, 2000, by the ALA Council.

HISTORY

Access to Library Resources and Services regardless of Gender or Sexual Orientation

The American Library Association held its 1993 Midwinter Meeting in Denver, Colorado, two months after that state had adopted a constitutional amendment repealing legislation protecting the civil rights of gays and lesbians. The amendment, Colorado Constitutional Amendment 2, was one of several such initiatives that sprang up in Western and Pacific Northwestern states in 1992 and reappeared persistently, despite being struck down as unconstitutional in courts or being turned back by voters. Thus, it was in an atmosphere of intolerance and discrimination against individuals based on their sexual orientation that a proposed resolution on gender, sexual orientation, and the *Library Bill of Rights* came before the ALA's Council. Specifically, the resolution directed that Article V of the *Library Bill of Rights* be amended to add the words "gender" and "sexual orientation" after the word "age," with the amended section to read thus: "A person's right to use the library should not be denied or abridged because of origin, age, gender, sexual orientation, background, or views." The proposed resolution was referred to the Intellectual Freedom Committee for review and recommendation.

The IFC became concerned with the impulse and momentum for amending the *Library Bill of Rights,* pointing out the long-standing "laundry list" problem in Article V, where it sometimes has been assumed that any characteristic not specifically listed is thereby excluded. The 1980 revisions to the *Library Bill of Rights* deliberately broadened the language of Article V to cover all possibilities; and, in response to a request of the Minority Concerns Committee in 1989 to review the *Library Bill of Rights* to ensure that it addressed language and economic status, the Intellectual Freedom Committee declined to amend the document; it opted instead to incorporate those concerns into revisions of Interpretations. In addition, amending the *Library Bill of Rights* would mean that thousands of libraries across the country that had adopted the document as part of their operating principles and practices would need to readopt a revised version. Ordinarily, this would be a matter of routine. The repressive national atmosphere at the time, however, aroused concern that the process of adopting a revised version of the *Library Bill of Rights* would invite vigorous assault by conservative pressure groups that had identified the document as a target and had worked in various localities to secure its removal from local library policy.

Faced with these concerns, the Intellectual Freedom Committee elected to present a substitute resolution reaffirming that the *Library Bill of Rights* did include gender and sexual orientation. In her Report to Council, Intellectual Freedom Committee chair Candace Morgan explained:

> We took this action for several reasons: first, our Association's commitment to nondiscrimination with regard to gender and sexual orientation has always been part of the meaning of all Articles of the *Library Bill of Rights,* not just Article V; second, terminology in the *Library Bill of Rights,* particularly in Article V, is deliberately broad to prohibit discrimination targeted at any class of individuals on the basis of arbitrary distinctions; third, we have frequently been asked to add language to Article V, and we have refused to do so in the belief that the addition of specific classifications implies that other classes not explicitly included are therefore excluded; and fourth, this organization has never, in our memory, amended the *Library Bill of Rights* without broad distribution for comment from all divisions and other interested bodies.

The Council accepted the Intellectual Freedom Committee's substitute resolution. At that same Midwinter Meeting, the IFC also recommended, and the Council adopted, a more generic "Resolution on Gay Rights and Materials," designed to be useful and immediately available in localities where antigay initiatives were springing up with regularity.

In addition to adopting these two resolutions, however, the Council directed the Intellectual Freedom Committee to bring to the 1993 Annual Conference in New Orleans specific language to revise the *Library Bill of Rights* so as to address the issue of sexual orientation.

In New Orleans, the Committee's concerns about revising the *Library Bill of Rights* were as strong as they had been at the Midwinter Meeting. Battles over maintaining the current version of the *Library Bill of Rights* had just been fought in both North Carolina and Nevada. Given the atmosphere of attack on the *Library Bill of Rights* already evident in many communities, the Committee believed the wiser course would be to present a very strongly worded Interpretation of the *Library Bill of Rights* to the Council for its adoption. Such an Interpretation would state specifically that the document already covers gays, lesbians, and anyone else, with regard to both their access to materials and the necessity of maintaining collections that contain materials by and about homosexuals. The Council had directed that language to amend the *Library Bill of Rights* be prepared, however. The Intellectual Freedom Committee was faced with the dilemma of responding to the Council's directive despite strong reservations about the approach to the problem that the Council apparently wanted to take. In addition to proposed language to revise the *Library Bill of Rights*, a draft Interpretation on gender and sexuality was prepared and circulated to all ALA units prior to the Annual Conference soliciting response on this approach to the issue. The draft, and the approach of adopting an Interpretation rather than amending the *Library Bill of Rights* itself, was enthusiastically received and endorsed by a number of the ALA's divisions and committees, including the Association for Library Service to Children, Public Library Association, American Library Trustee Association, Young Adult Library Services Association, the Committee on Professional Ethics, and the Intellectual Freedom Round Table. Given that response, Intellectual Freedom Committee chair Candace Morgan explained in her 1993 Annual Conference Report to Council that the Committee had decided—with the support of the above-named divisions, committees, and round table—to recommend the option of adopting an Interpretation only and leaving the *Library Bill of Rights* as is. Morgan acknowledged in her report:

> There is no question that materials by and about gays, lesbians,
> and bisexuals, and on the subject of homosexuality in general, are

at the top of the agenda of organized pressure groups that are attacking libraries all over the country for including such materials in their collections. There is also no question that gays, lesbians, and bisexuals themselves are the victims and the targets of unprecedented attacks aimed at codifying discrimination against homosexuals into law. Finally, there is no question that the library profession's commitment to intellectual freedom and the responsibility of libraries and librarians to protect and defend access to information from all points of view, requires including materials in libraries on homosexuality to serve the needs of all library users, including gays, lesbians, and bisexuals. This commitment to free expression also mandates that we take positive action to protect the rights of access for all persons regardless of sexuality, gender, or age.

Morgan went on to explain that, ironically, the *Library Bill of Rights* had recently come under attack in Nevada and North Carolina by opponents of intellectual freedom because those opponents assumed that the document, unamended, already protected materials by, about, or of interest to gays, lesbians, and bisexuals. The battles to protect the *Library Bill of Rights* in state and local policy had been hard fought and narrowly won. Many of the fighters, including public and school librarians in many other states, reported that in the current climate of attacks on the freedom to read, adopting a newly amended *Library Bill of Rights* would be politically impossible. Believing that the document would be useless to the profession if not incorporated into local library policy, Morgan explained the Committee's strong belief that it would be unwise to initiate an opportunity to exclude the document from local policy by forcing local libraries to consider readopting an amended version. Issuing an Interpretation for governing bodies and librarians would guide their understanding of the *Library Bill of Rights* as it was already incorporated in policy. Finally, Morgan explained the "laundry list" problem, in which revision of Article V of the *Library Bill of Rights* to include specific characteristics renders it vulnerable to requests that a long list of characteristics be added and creates the implication that any characteristic not explicitly included is, therefore, excluded. One of the first comments the Intellectual Freedom Committee received when the possibility of revision to include gender and sexual orientation was announced was that if disability was not currently covered, as a move to amend implied, the word "ability" should be included to cover mental, emotional, or physical conditions. Health, race, national origin, and language were also suggested as additions to the list. The Committee itself added "financial status" to the language for the proposed amendment because, at the time, it was still considering a request of the Minority Concerns Committee to address economic status and language in the *Library Bill of Rights* while simultaneously working on a proposed Interpretation to do just that.

The Intellectual Freedom Committee's reasoning was persuasive, and the Council rejected amendments to the *Library Bill of Rights*. Instead, it adopted a new Interpretation of the *Library Bill of Rights*, "Access to Library Resources and Services regardless of Gender or Sexual Orientation," which makes absolutely clear that censorship of material based on sexuality, or discrimination against library users based on gender or sexual orientation, is and always has been totally inappropriate and violative of the *Library Bill of Rights*.

As part of its overall review of all of the Interpretations in 1999–2000, the IFC proposed removal of references to terms of sexual orientation in the belief that terms can become dated or offensive, or both. The committee also affirmed that all materials— regardless of format or services—are protected by the *Library Bill of Rights*; and referenced ALA policy 52.5.2, "Sex Education Materials in Libraries," in the Interpretation. On July 12, 2000, the ALA Council adopted the Interpretation as amended.

2.4

Access to Resources and Services in the School Library Media Program

An Interpretation of the *Library Bill of Rights*

The school library media program plays a unique role in promoting intellectual freedom. It serves as a point of voluntary access to information and ideas and as a learning laboratory for students as they acquire critical thinking and problem solving skills needed in a pluralistic society. Although the educational level and program of the school necessarily shapes the resources and services of a school library media program, the principles of the *Library Bill of Rights* apply equally to all libraries, including school library media programs.

School library media professionals assume a leadership role in promoting the principles of intellectual freedom within the school by providing resources and services that create and sustain an atmosphere of free inquiry. School library media professionals work closely with teachers to integrate instructional activities in classroom units designed to equip students to locate, evaluate, and use a broad range of ideas effectively. Through resources, programming, and educational processes, students and teachers experience the free and robust debate characteristic of a democratic society.

School library media professionals cooperate with other individuals in building collections of resources appropriate to the developmental and maturity levels of students. These collections provide resources which support the curriculum and are consistent with the philosophy, goals, and objectives of the school district. Resources in school library media collections represent diverse points of view on current as well as historical issues.

While English is, by history and tradition, the customary language of the United States, the languages in use in any given community may vary. Schools serving communities in which other languages are used make efforts to accommodate the needs of students for whom English is a second language. To support these efforts, and to ensure equal access to resources and services, the school library media program provides resources which reflect the linguistic pluralism of the community.

Members of the school community involved in the collection development process employ educational criteria to select resources unfettered by their personal, political, social, or religious views. Students and educators served by the school library media program have access to resources and services free of constraints resulting from personal, partisan, or doctrinal disapproval. School library media professionals resist efforts by individuals or groups to define what is appropriate for all students or teachers to read, view, hear, or access via electronic means.

Major barriers between students and resources include but are not limited to: imposing age or grade level restrictions on the use of resources, limiting the use of interlibrary loan and access to electronic information, charging fees for information in specific formats, requiring permission from parents or teachers, establishing restricted shelves or closed collections, and labeling. Policies, procedures, and rules related to the use of resources and services support free and open access to information.

The school board adopts policies that guarantee students access to a broad range of ideas. These include policies on collection development and procedures for the review of resources about which concerns have been raised. Such policies, developed by persons in the school community, provide for a timely and fair hearing and assure that procedures are applied equitably to all expressions of concern. School library media professionals implement district policies and procedures in the school.

Adopted July 2, 1986; amended January 10, 1990; July 12, 2000, by the ALA Council.

HISTORY

Access to Resources and Services in the School Library Media Program

During the early 1950s, as the anticommunist reaction of McCarthyism swept across the United States, school librarians and school curriculum planners were affected no less than people in journalism, entertainment, and government. Schools were coerced to ban works that were alleged to contain "un-American" thinking. The issue of selecting school library materials was raised during the meeting of the Board of Directors of the American Association of School Librarians (AASL) during the 1953 ALA Annual Conference in Los Angeles. Sue Hefley, chair of the school libraries discussion group at the second Conference on Intellectual Freedom (held at Whittier College, June 20–21), reported on her group's consensus concerning the need for a policy statement on the matter of selection. In response to Hefley's report, the board voted

> that a committee be appointed to consider the advisability of preparing a statement on book selection in defense of liberty in schools of a democracy, and in considering this problem to make use of the excellent statement prepared at the Conference on Intellectual Freedom. Furthermore, that this committee make recommendations as to what further action AASL should take in this matter.[1]

In preparation for the AASL meeting at the 1954 Annual Conference in Minneapolis, the Committee on Book Selection in Defense of Liberty in Schools of a Democracy submitted a draft for a *School Library Bill of Rights.* At the 1955 Midwinter Meeting, the AASL officially accepted the *School Library Bill of Rights,* and on July 8, 1955, it was adopted by the ALA Council.

In the years following the adoption of the *School Library Bill of Rights,* the ALA's *Library Bill of Rights* underwent several basic changes. (For full discussion, see part I, section 1, *Library Bill of Rights.*) Because of changes in the *Library Bill of Rights,* affirmed by the *School Library Bill of Rights* of 1955, as well as changes in the conception of the range of materials to be provided by libraries, the AASL Board of Directors appointed a committee in 1968 to consider revising the 1955 *School Library Bill of Rights.*

At the 1969 ALA Annual Conference in Atlantic City, the revised *School Library Bill of Rights* was brought before the AASL Board of Directors. Making only minor corrections, the board voted to accept the revised version:

> The American Association of School Librarians reaffirms its belief in the *Library Bill of Rights* of the American Library Association. Media personnel are concerned with generating understanding of American freedoms through the development of informed and responsible citizens. To this end the American Association of School Librarians asserts that the responsibility of the school library media center is:
>
> To provide a comprehensive collection of instructional materials selected in compliance with basic written selection principles, and to provide maximum accessibility to these materials;
>
> To provide materials that will support the curriculum, taking into consideration the individual's needs, and the varied interests, abilities, socioeconomic backgrounds, and maturity levels of the students served;
>
> To provide materials for teachers and students that will encourage growth in knowledge, and that will develop literary, cultural, and aesthetic appreciation, and ethical standards;
>
> To provide materials which reflect the ideas and beliefs of religious, social, political, historical, and ethnic groups and their contribution to the American and world heritage and culture, thereby enabling students to develop an intellectual integrity in forming judgments;

To provide a written statement, approved by the local boards of education, of the procedures for meeting the challenge of censorship of materials in school library media centers; and

To provide qualified professional personnel to serve teachers and students.

It soon became clear, however, that the existence of two documents with very similar titles could be a source of confusion. Moreover, with the 1967 amendment of the *Library Bill of Rights* to oppose discrimination against library users by age, the *School Library Bill of Rights* became largely redundant. As increasing numbers of librarians pointed out, the school document simply repeated in different language the principles enunciated more forcefully in the *Library Bill of Rights*. This served only to detract attention from and, hence, to weaken the impact of the Association's most basic document on intellectual freedom.

The problem was discussed extensively in both the Intellectual Freedom Committee and the AASL. At the 1976 Annual Conference in Chicago, the Board of Directors of the American Association of School Librarians withdrew the *School Library Bill of Rights* and endorsed the *Library Bill of Rights.*

Since 1976 and particularly in the 1980s, the challenge to materials in school libraries and media centers has increased in volume and intensity. The need became apparent for an Interpretation of the *Library Bill of Rights* that spoke directly to the unique role of school libraries and media centers in the educational process. A clear statement of the responsibility of school library media professionals for the selection process and of the centrality of intellectual freedom principles in this process was perceived as the central focus for this Interpretation.

In 1985–86, an Interpretation was drafted by the AASL with the cooperation of the IFC. At the 1986 Annual Conference in New York, "Access to Resources and Services in the School Library Media Program" was adopted by the ALA Council. It read as follows:

The school library media program plays a unique role in promoting intellectual freedom. It serves as a point of voluntary access to information and ideas and as a learning laboratory for students as they acquire critical thinking and problem solving skills needed in a pluralistic society. Although the educational level and program of the school necessarily shape the resources and services of a school library media program, the principles of the *Library Bill of Rights* apply equally to all libraries, including school library media programs.

School library media professionals assume a leadership role in promoting the principles of intellectual freedom within the school by providing resources and services that create and sustain an atmosphere of free inquiry. School library media professionals work closely with teachers to integrate instructional activities in classroom units designed to equip students to locate, evaluate, and use a broad range of ideas effectively. Through resources, programming, and educational processes, students and teachers experience the free and robust debate characteristic of a democratic society.

School library media professionals cooperate with other individuals in building collections of resources appropriate to the developmental and maturity levels of students. These collections provide resources which support the curriculum and are consistent with the philosophy, goals, and objectives of the school district. Resources in school library media collections represent diverse points of view and current as well as historic issues.

Members of the school community involved in the collection development process employ educational criteria to select resources unfettered by their personal, political, social, or religious views. Students and educators served by the school library media program have access to resources and services free of constraints resulting from personal, partisan, or doctrinal disapproval. School library media professionals resist efforts by individuals to define what is appropriate for all students or teachers to read, view, or hear.

Major barriers between students and resources include imposing age or grade level restrictions on the use of resources, limiting the use of interlibrary loan and access to electronic information, charging fees for information in specific formats, requiring permissions from parents or teachers, establishing restricted shelves or closed collections, and labeling. Policies, procedures, and rules related to the use of resources and services support free and open access to information.

The school board adopts policies that guarantee student access to a broad range of ideas. These include policies on collection development and procedures for the review of resources about which concerns have been raised. Such policies, developed by persons in the school community, provide for a timely and fair hearing and ensure that procedures are applied equitably to all expressions of concern. School library media professionals implement district policies and procedures in the school.

A revised Interpretation was circulated for comment in the fall of 1989. The sole substantive change was the addition of a paragraph stating that the school library media program should attempt to accommodate the needs of students for whom English is a second language. To ensure equality of access, librarians must provide resources reflecting the linguistic pluralism of the community that they serve.

At the 1990 Midwinter Meeting, comments received from the American Association of School Librarians, Office for Library Personnel Resources (now known as Human Resources Development and Recruitment), Standing Committee on Library Education, and the Professional Ethics Committee resulted in minor editorial changes. The revised policy was recommended to the Council and adopted on January 10, 1990.

As part of its review of all of the Interpretations in 1999–2000, the IFC proposed editorial changes in the Interpretation (the addition of "should" in some instances, and the substitution of "that cross" for "across"). On July 12, 2000, the amended Interpretation was adopted by the ALA Council.

NOTE

1. *School Libraries* 3, no. 1:8 (October 1953).

2.5
Challenged Materials

An Interpretation of the
Library Bill of Rights

The American Library Association declares as a matter of firm principle that it is the responsibility of every library to have a clearly defined materials selection policy in written form which reflects the *Library Bill of Rights,* and which is approved by the appropriate governing authority.

Challenged materials which meet the criteria for selection in the materials selection policy of the library should not be removed under any legal or extra-legal pressure. The *Library Bill of Rights* states in Article I that "Materials should not be excluded because of the origin, background, or views of those contributing to their creation," and in Article II, that "Materials should not be proscribed or removed because of partisan or doctrinal disapproval." Freedom of expression is protected by the Constitution of the United States, but constitutionally protected expression is often separated from unprotected expression only by a dim and uncertain line. The Constitution requires a procedure designed to focus searchingly on challenged expression before it can be suppressed. An adversary hearing is a part of this procedure.

Therefore, any attempt, be it legal or extra-legal, to regulate or suppress materials in libraries must be closely scrutinized to the end that protected expression is not abridged.

Adopted June 25, 1971; amended July 1, 1981; amended January 10, 1990, by the ALA Council.

HISTORY

Challenged Materials

The *Library Bill of Rights* states that library materials should not be "excluded because of the origin, background, or views" of their creators. The document states further that "Materials should not be proscribed or removed because of partisan or doctrinal disapproval." Nevertheless, libraries are still pressured by many groups and individuals to remove certain materials because they find their sexual, political, or religious content objectionable.

Particularly when sexually explicit materials are the object of censorship efforts, librarians and boards of trustees are often unaware of the legal procedures required to effect the removal of such items. Many attorneys, even when employed by state or local governing bodies, are not aware of the procedures to determine whether or not a work is obscene under the law. According to U.S. Supreme Court decisions, a work is not obscene until found to be so by a court of law and only after an adversary hearing to determine the question of obscenity. Until a work is specifically found to be unprotected by the First Amendment, the title remains a legal library acquisition and need not be removed.

In 1971, several attempts to ban publications from libraries involved charges that the works were obscene and therefore not legal or proper acquisitions for the library. In Groton, Connecticut, in a case involving *Evergreen Review,* the librarian and the board of trustees were threatened with prosecution under a state obscenity statute if they refused to remove the magazine from the library. The board, after several months of resisting efforts to remove the magazine, capitulated in the face of this threat to prosecute them as individuals.

The Groton, Connecticut, case prompted the Intellectual Freedom Committee, with the aid of legal counsel, to study U.S. Supreme Court and federal circuit court decisions concerning procedures whereby materials are determined to be obscene. Three cases in particular were reviewed: *Bantam Books, Inc.* v. *Sullivan* (372 U.S. 58, 83 S. Ct. 631 [1963]); *Marcus* v. *Search Warrants* (367 U.S. 717, 732; 81 S. Ct. 1708, 1716 [1961]); and *A Quantity of Copies of Books* v. *Kansas* (378 U.S. 205, 211; 84 S. Ct. 1723 [1964]).

Using the language of these three decisions as a basis, the Intellectual Freedom Committee developed "Resolution on Challenged Materials." The statement was submitted to the ALA Council during the 1971 Annual Conference in Dallas and was adopted as an ALA policy on June 25, 1971. It read as follows:

WHEREAS, The *Library Bill of Rights* states that no library materials should be proscribed or removed because of partisan or doctrinal disapproval; and

WHEREAS, Constitutionally protected expression is often separated from unprotected expression only by a dim and uncertain line; and

WHEREAS, Any attempt, be it legal or extra-legal, to regulate or suppress material must be closely scrutinized to the end that protected expression is not abridged in the process; and

WHEREAS, The Constitution requires a procedure designed to focus searchingly on the question before speech can be suppressed; and

WHEREAS, The dissemination of a particular work which is alleged to be unprotected should be completely undisturbed until an independent determination has been made by a judicial officer, including an adversary hearing;

THEREFORE, THE PREMISES CONSIDERED, BE IT RESOLVED, That the American Library Association declares as a matter of firm principle that no challenged library material should be removed from any library under any legal or extra-legal pressure, save after an independent determination by a judicial officer in a court of competent jurisdiction and only after an adversary hearing, in accordance with well-established principles of law.

A decade later, legal standards for determining obscenity had changed significantly. Nevertheless, the basic principle—that expression is protected by the First Amendment until it has been determined through an adversary procedure that such expression is obscene, libelous, or otherwise unprotected—remained firmly established in U.S. constitutional law. In reviewing the 1971 resolution in 1981, however, the IFC found that a major revision still was necessary. The principal difficulties were twofold. The first problem was the rather simple matter of format. Written as a formal resolution, with an implementary paragraph preceded by a series of "whereas clauses," "Resolution on Challenged Materials" was inconsistent in form with other Interpretations of the *Library Bill of Rights,* and lacked clarity and force as a document directed toward the general public as well as library professionals.

The second problem was more substantive. The materials selection policies of most libraries correctly provide opportunities for patron comments and citizen requests for reconsideration of library materials. Yet the policy seemed to make a mockery of such procedures by declaring in advance that "no challenged library material should be removed" unless the library were ordered to do so by a court of law. Moreover, many librarians complained that such an inflexible declaration served to tie the library's own hands in its efforts to correct the inevitable mistakes that occur in any selection process.

With these considerations in mind, the IFC presented the Council with a new version of the document, written in a format similar to the other Interpretations of the *Library Bill of Rights* and more appropriate for a broader audience. The new version linked the decision to remove or retain challenged materials to the maintenance of clear guidelines consistent with the *Library Bill of Rights* and established by the library's materials selection policy. The revision designated the maintenance of a "clearly defined" selection policy a "responsibility" of all libraries. The new version offered libraries and patrons alike greater flexibility in the consideration of challenges while at the same time reaffirming the principles of the *Library Bill of Rights,* calling for the closest scrutiny of all efforts to remove materials, and maintaining due process in the reconsideration procedure. On July 1, 1981, the Council adopted the revised statement "Challenged Materials" as a policy of the American Library Association:

The American Library Association declares as a matter of firm principle that it is the responsibility of every library to have a clearly defined materials selection policy in written form which reflects the *Library Bill of Rights,* and which is approved by the appropriate governing authority.

Challenged materials which meet the materials selection policy of the library should not be removed under any legal or extralegal pressure. The *Library Bill of Rights* states in Article I that "Materials should not be excluded because of the origin, background, or views of those contributing to their creation," and in Article II, that "Materials should not be proscribed or removed because of partisan or doctrinal disapproval." Freedom of expression is protected by the Constitution of the United States, but constitutionally protected expression is often separated from unprotected expression only by a dim and uncertain line. The Constitution requires a procedure designed to focus searchingly on challenged expression before it can be suppressed. An adversary hearing is a part of this procedure.

Therefore, any attempt, be it legal or extra-legal, to regulate or suppress materials in libraries must be closely scrutinized to the end that protected expression is not abridged.

In 1986, in response to inquiries from librarians facing book or material challenges for the first time, the Intellectual Freedom Committee developed the following list of definitions to clarify terminology associated with challenges:

Expression of Concern. An inquiry that has judgmental overtones.

Oral Complaint. An oral challenge to the presence and/or appropriateness of the material in question.

Written Complaint. A formal, written complaint filed with the institution (library, school, etc.), challenging the presence and/or appropriateness of specific material.

Public Attack. A publicly disseminated statement challenging the value of the material, presented to the media and/or others outside the institutional organization in order to gain public support for further action.

Censorship. A change in the access status of material, based on the content of the work and made by a governing authority or its representatives. Such changes include exclusion, restriction, removal, or age/grade level changes.

As part of the Interpretation review process initiated in 1989, one minor change was made in this policy to state explicitly that materials must meet criteria stated in materials selection policies rather than simply meeting the policy, per se. No substantive changes were recommended.

On January 10, at the 1990 Midwinter Meeting, the Council adopted the "Challenged Materials" Interpretation, as amended.

In line with the ongoing practice of periodic review, the IFC reviewed "Challenged Materials" during 1999–2000, and did not recommend any changes.

2.6
Diversity in Collection Development

An Interpretation of the
Library Bill of Rights

Throughout history, the focus of censorship has fluctuated from generation to generation. Books and other materials have not been selected or have been removed from library collections for many reasons, among which are prejudicial language and ideas, political content, economic theory, social philosophies, religious beliefs, sexual forms of expression, and other topics of a potentially controversial nature.

Some examples of censorship may include removing or not selecting materials because they are considered by some as racist or sexist; not purchasing conservative religious materials; not selecting materials about or by minorities because it is thought these groups or interests are not represented in a community; or not providing information on or materials from non-mainstream political entities.

Librarians may seek to increase user awareness of materials on various social concerns by many means, including, but not limited to, issuing bibliographies and presenting exhibits and programs. Librarians have a professional responsibility to be inclusive, not exclusive, in collection development and in the provision of interlibrary loan. Access to all materials legally obtainable should be assured to the user, and policies should not unjustly exclude materials even if they are offensive to the librarian or the user. Collection development should reflect the philosophy inherent in Article II of the *Library Bill of Rights:* "Libraries should provide materials and information presenting all points of view on current and historical issues. Materials should not be proscribed or removed because of partisan or doctrinal disapproval." A balanced collection reflects a diversity of materials, not an equality of numbers. Collection development responsibilities include selecting materials in the languages in common use in the community which the library serves. Collection development and the selection of materials should be done according to professional standards and established selection and review procedures.

There are many complex facets to any issue, and variations of context in which issues may be expressed, discussed, or interpreted. Librarians have a professional responsibility to be fair, just, and equitable and to give all library users equal protection in guarding against violation of the library patron's right to read, view, or listen to materials and resources protected by the First Amendment, no matter what the viewpoint of the author, creator, or selector. Librarians have an obligation to protect library collections from removal of materials based on personal bias or prejudice, and to select and support the access to materials on all subjects that meet, as closely as possible, the needs and interests of all persons in the community which the library serves. This includes materials that reflect political, economic, religious, social, minority, and sexual issues.

Intellectual freedom, the essence of equitable library services, provides for free access to all expressions of ideas through which any and all sides of a question, cause, or movement may be explored. Toleration is meaningless without tolerance for what some may consider detestable. Librarians cannot justly permit their own preferences to limit their degree of tolerance in collection development, because freedom is indivisible.

Adopted July 14, 1982; amended January 10, 1990, by the ALA Council.

HISTORY

Diversity in Collection Development

During the 1971 Midwinter Meeting in Los Angeles, the ALA Intellectual Freedom Committee met with representatives of the Executive Board of the International Conference of Police Associations. The meeting was to provide a forum for discussing police efforts to remove William Steig's *Sylvester and the Magic Pebble* from public and school libraries. During the meeting, the officers raised a provocative and embarrassing question for librarians. They asked why some librarians were quick to comply with requests to remove another children's book, *Little Black Sambo*, from their collections when blacks complained that its illustrations were degrading; yet now, when police officers found William Steig's pigs dressed as law enforcement officers to be degrading, librarians objected vociferously to taking the book out of their collections.

The evasive response from the IFC was generally to the effect that the Committee had difficulty impressing upon members of the library profession the importance of the principles of intellectual freedom. The inability to answer the officers' charge adequately acknowledged the accusation implicit in the question: some librarians do employ a double standard when it comes to their practice of intellectual freedom and their commitment to it. Many librarians express a strong commitment to the principles of intellectual freedom but fail to grasp that the concept of intellectual freedom, in its pure sense, promotes no causes, furthers no movements, and favors no viewpoints. *Little Black Sambo* and *Sylvester and the Magic Pebble* did not bring new issues before the library profession. These books only inherited the cloak of controversy that had already surrounded such diverse works as *The Adventures of Huckleberry Finn, Mother Goose Nursery Rhymes and Fairy Tales, Doctor Doolittle,* and *The Merchant of Venice.*

Until 1980, Article II of the *Library Bill of Rights* stated that "no library materials should be proscribed or removed from libraries because of partisan or doctrinal disapproval." The phrase "no library materials" did not appear by accident. Before June 1967, the sentence concluded, "books or other reading matter of sound factual authority should not be proscribed or removed from library shelves because of partisan or doctrinal disapproval." Article II was revised in 1967 because some librarians used an alleged lack of "sound factual authority" as a basis for removing library materials. To determine which materials lacked sound factual authority, many deferred to their personal conceptions of fact and authority. One of the most extreme examples, cited at the time of the revision, was of a Catholic librarian who excluded Protestant publications because they were not of "sound factual authority." Today, the even broader phrase "Materials should not be proscribed or removed" in the *Library Bill of Rights* leaves no room for interpretation. The revised statement reflects the philosophy that freedom is indivisible and that tolerance, if it is to be meaningful, must hold for all points of view.

At the 1972 Midwinter Meeting in Chicago, the Intellectual Freedom Committee reported its intention to prepare a statement making clear the meaning of the *Library Bill of Rights* as it pertains to attempts to censor library materials because of alleged racism, sexism, or any other "isms." The statement was approved by the IFC on June 25, 1972. It was subsequently submitted to the ALA Council at the 1973 Midwinter Meeting in Washington, D.C., and approved as an ALA policy on February 2, 1973. Entitled "Sexism, Racism, and Other -Isms in Library Materials," it read as follows:

> Traditional aims of censorship efforts have been to suppress political, sexual, or religious expressions. The same three subjects have also been the source of most complaints about materials in library collections. Another basis for complaints, however, has become more and more frequent. Due, perhaps, to increased awareness of the rights of minorities and increased efforts to secure those rights, libraries are being asked to remove, restrict or

reconsider some materials which are allegedly derogatory to specific minorities or which supposedly perpetuate stereotypes and false images of minorities. Among the several recurring "isms" used to describe the contents of the materials objected to are "racism" and "sexism."

Complaints that library materials convey a derogatory or false image of a minority strike the personal social consciousness and sense of responsibility of some librarians who—accordingly—comply with the requests to remove such materials. While such efforts to counteract injustices are understandable, and perhaps even commendable as reflections of deep personal commitments to the ideal of equality for all people, they are—nonetheless—in conflict with the professional responsibility of librarians to guard against encroachments upon intellectual freedom.

This responsibility has been espoused and reaffirmed by the American Library Association in many of its basic documents on intellectual freedom over the past thirty years. The most concise statement of the Association's position appears in Article II of the *Library Bill of Rights,* which states that "Libraries should provide books and materials presenting all points of view concerning the problems and issues of our times; no library materials should be proscribed or removed because of partisan or doctrinal disapproval."

While the application of this philosophy may seem simple when dealing with political, religious, or even sexual expressions, its full implications become somewhat difficult when dealing with ideas, such as racism or sexism, which many find abhorrent, repugnant, and inhumane. But, as stated in "The Freedom to Read":

> It is inevitable in the give and take of the democratic process that the political, the moral, or the aesthetic concepts of an individual or group will occasionally collide with those of another individual or group. In a free society each individual is free to determine for himself what he wishes to read, and each group is free to determine what it will recommend to its freely associated members. But no group has the right to take the law into its own hands, and to impose its own concept of politics or morality upon other members of a democratic society. Freedom is no freedom if it is accorded only to the accepted and the inoffensive. . . . We realize that the application of these propositions may mean the dissemination of ideas and manners of expression that are repugnant to

many persons. We do not state these propositions in the comfortable belief that what people read is unimportant. We believe rather that what people read is deeply important; that ideas can be dangerous; but that the suppression of ideas is fatal to a democratic society. Freedom itself is a dangerous way of life, but it is ours.

Some find this creed acceptable when dealing with materials for adults but cannot extend its application to materials for children. Such reluctance is generally based on the belief that children are more susceptible to being permanently influenced—even damaged—by objectionable materials than are adults. The *Library Bill of Rights*, however, makes no distinction between materials and services for children and adults. Its principles of free access to all materials available apply to every person; as stated in Article V, "The rights of an individual to the use of a library should not be denied or abridged because of his age, race, religion, national origins or social or political views."

Some librarians deal with the problem of objectionable materials by labeling them or listing them as "racist" or "sexist." This kind of action, too, has long been opposed by the American Library Association through its Statement on Labeling, which says,

> If materials are labeled to pacify one group, there is no excuse for refusing to label any item in the library's collection. Because authoritarians tend to suppress ideas and attempt to coerce individuals to conform to a specific ideology, the American Library Association opposes such efforts which aim at closing any path to knowledge.

Others deal with the problem of objectionable materials by instituting restrictive circulation or relegating materials to closed or restricted collections. This practice, too, is in violation of the *Library Bill of Rights* as explained in Restricted Access to Library Materials, which says

> Too often only "controversial" materials are the subject of such segregation, leading to the conclusion that factors other than theft and mutilation were the true considerations. The distinction is extremely difficult to make, both for the librarian and the patron. Selection policies, carefully developed on the basis of principles of intellectual freedom and the *Library Bill of Rights*, should not be vitiated by administrative practices such as restricted access.

The American Library Association has made clear its position concerning the removal of library materials because of partisan or doctrinal disapproval, or because of pressures from interest groups, in another policy statement, the Resolution on Challenged Materials:

> The American Library Association declares as a matter of firm principle that no challenged material should be removed from any library under any legal or extra-legal pressure, save after an independent determination by a judicial officer in a court of competent jurisdiction and only after an adversary hearing, in accordance with well-established principles of law.

Intellectual freedom, in its purest sense, promotes no causes, furthers no movements, and favors no viewpoints. It only provides for free access to all ideas through which any and all sides of causes and movements may be expressed, discussed, and argued. The librarian cannot let his own preferences limit his degree of tolerance, for freedom is indivisible. Toleration is meaningless without toleration for the detestable.

It soon became apparent that this lengthy and somewhat unwieldy document had been formulated to address a specific situation arising in the late 1960s and early 1970s. During this time many people of a liberal or leftist political orientation, who in the past had stood in the forefront of the anticensorship battle, were falling, intentionally or not, into the very practice they had previously opposed when espoused by others. By the end of the 1970s, however, although the problem addressed by the policy continued, new instances of censorship had arisen in which other would-be censors also sought to justify their actions by support for broadly accepted social values. In reviewing the policy in the early 1980s, the IFC concluded that a broader statement covering the influence of conflicting values, philosophies, and points of view on library collections, and reaffirming the library's commitment to the inclusion of all, would be more appropriate.

At first the Committee tried to expand the number of "isms" covered by the policy to include such phenomena as anti-Semitism, communism and anticommunism, homosexuality, and the like. It quickly became obvious, however, that this approach would not only be extremely awkward but, like the original policy, would tie the document to the temporal particularities of the period in which it was written. The Committee therefore decided to formulate and present to the Council a new Interpretation, expanding more broadly on the call in the *Library Bill of Rights* for libraries "to provide materials and information presenting all points of view on current and historical issues."

The new policy was titled "Diversity in Collection Development." These words were not lightly chosen. Indeed, the IFC initially had preferred the title "Balanced Collections." In the early 1980s, however, several groups and individuals actively involved in increasing censorship pressures, largely from the right of center, also had raised the demand for "balance" in library holdings. Insofar as this was a call for libraries to be more inclusive in collection development, it was welcomed by the ALA. Many, however, also saw in the demand for "balance" a dangerous, if hidden, threat of censorship.

The concept of balanced collections may be misunderstood to presuppose a bias toward moderation and to place limitations on the acquisition of materials thought to be "extreme," because these might skew the "balance" of the collection. The requirement that a library collection be "balanced" could be construed to imply, for instance, that leftist materials cannot be acquired if there is no equivalent material from the right, or vice versa. If balance is sought in this formal sense, librarians are placed in a position that requires them to act as validators of opinion by assigning values, or "weights," to differing points of view across the spectrum of opinion. In other words, a misconceived if well-intentioned requirement for balance may also make of the librarian a kind of censor.

Recognizing this possible misapplication of the notion of balance, the Committee opted to emphasize instead the concept of diversity. Not only is the library obliged to include many differing views in its collection, but materials representing the broadest diversity of human thought and creativity should, in general, be actively sought, irrespective of the opinions, prejudices, values, and tastes of the librarian, and whether or not a given numerical or other balance of views can be achieved at a given moment. The Committee completed work on the document at the 1982 Annual Conference in Philadelphia and on July 14, 1982, the Council approved the new Interpretation of the *Library Bill of Rights*, noting that it replaced the former policy on "Sexism, Racism, and Other -Isms in Library Materials," which was then rescinded. The new policy read as follows:

Throughout history, the focus of censorship has vacillated from generation to generation. Books and other materials have not been selected or have been removed from library collections for many reasons, among which are prejudicial language and ideas, political content, economic theory, social philosophies, religious beliefs, and/or sexual forms of expression.

Some examples of this may include removing or not selecting materials because they are considered by some as racist or sexist; not purchasing conservative religious materials; not selecting materials about or by minorities because it is thought these groups or interests are not represented in a community; or not providing information on or materials from nonmainstream political entities.

Librarians may seek to increase user awareness of materials on various social concerns by many means, including, but not limited to, issuing bibliographies and presenting exhibits and programs.

Librarians have a professional responsibility to be inclusive, not exclusive, in collection development and in the provision of interlibrary loan. Access to all materials legally obtainable should be assured to the user, and policies should not unjustly exclude materials even if offensive to the librarian or the user. Collection development should reflect the philosophy inherent in Article II of the *Library Bill of Rights:* "Libraries should provide materials and information presenting all points of view on current and historical issues. Materials should not be proscribed or removed because of partisan or doctrinal disapproval." A balanced collection reflects a diversity of materials, not an equality of numbers. Collection development and the selection of materials should be done according to professional standards and established selection and review procedures.

There are many complex facets to any issue, and variations of context in which issues may be expressed, discussed, or interpreted. Librarians have a professional responsibility to be fair, just, and equitable and to give all library users equal protection in guarding against violation of the library patrons' liberty to read, view, or listen to materials and resources protected by the First

Amendment, no matter what the viewpoint of the author, creator, or selector. Librarians have an obligation to protect library collections from removal of materials based on personal bias or prejudice, and to select and support the access to materials on all subjects that meet, as closely as possible, the needs and interests of all persons in the community which the library serves. This includes materials that reflect political, economic, religious, social, minority, and sexual issues.

Intellectual freedom, the essence of equitable library services, promotes no causes, furthers no movements, and favors no viewpoints. It only provides for free access to all expressions of ideas through which any and all sides of a question, cause, or movement may be explored. Toleration is meaningless without tolerance for what some may consider detestable. Librarians cannot justly permit their own preferences to limit their degree of tolerance in collection development, because freedom is indivisible.

Note: This policy replaces the policy "Sexism, Racism, and Other -Isms in Library Materials."

The Interpretation "Diversity in Collection Development" was revised in 1989 to acknowledge the responsibility of all librarians to be sensitive to the language(s) in common use in the community the library serves. Finally, the phrase claiming that intellectual freedom "promotes no causes, furthers no movements, and favors no viewpoints" was deleted from the text.

The newly revised Interpretation was adopted by the Council on January 10, 1990.

No changes in "Diversity in Collection Development" were recommended as part of the 1999–2000 periodic review of all Interpretations by the IFC.

2.7

Economic Barriers to Information Access

An Interpretation of the *Library Bill of Rights*

A democracy presupposes an informed citizenry. The First Amendment mandates the right of all persons to free expression, and the corollary right to receive the constitutionally protected expression of others. The publicly supported library provides free and equal access to information for all people of the community the library serves. While the roles, goals and objectives of publicly supported libraries may differ, they share this common mission.

The library's essential mission must remain the first consideration for librarians and governing bodies faced with economic pressures and competition for funding.

In support of this mission, the American Library Association has enumerated certain principles of library services in the *Library Bill of Rights*.

Principles Governing Fines, Fees, and User Charges

Article I of the *Library Bill of Rights* states:

> Books and other library resources should be provided for the interest, information, and enlightenment of all people of the community the library serves.

Article V of the *Library Bill of Rights* states:

> A person's right to use a library should not be denied or abridged because of origin, age, background, or views.

The American Library Association opposes the charging of user fees for the provision of information by all libraries and information services that receive their major support from public funds. All information resources that are provided directly or indirectly by the library, regardless of technology, format, or methods of delivery, should be readily, equally, and equitably accessible to all library users.

Libraries that adhere to these principles systematically monitor their programs of service for potential barriers to access and strive to eliminate such barriers when they occur. All library policies and procedures, particularly those involving fines, fees, or other user charges, should be scrutinized for potential barriers to access. All services should be designed and implemented with care, so as not to infringe on or interfere with the provision or delivery of information and resources for all users. Services should be re-evaluated on a regular basis to ensure that the library's basic mission remains uncompromised.

Librarians and governing bodies should look for alternative models and methods of library administration that minimize distinctions among users based on their economic status or financial condition. They should resist the temptation to impose user fees to alleviate financial pressures, at long-term cost to institutional integrity and public confidence in libraries.

Library services that involve the provision of information, regardless of format, technology, or method of delivery, should be made available to all library users on an equal and equitable basis. Charging fees for the use of library collections, services, programs, or facilities that were purchased with public funds raises barriers to access. Such fees effectively abridge or deny access for some members of the community because they reinforce distinctions among users based on their ability and willingness to pay.

Principles Governing
Conditions of Funding

Article II of the *Library Bill of Rights* states:

> Materials should not be proscribed or removed because of partisan or doctrinal disapproval.

Article III of the *Library Bill of Rights* states:

> Libraries should challenge censorship in the fulfillment of their responsibility to provide information and enlightenment.

Article IV of the *Library Bill of Rights* states:

> Libraries should cooperate with all persons and groups concerned with resisting abridgment of free expression and free access to ideas.

The American Library Association opposes any legislative or regulatory attempt to impose content restrictions on library resources, or to limit user access to information, as a condition of funding for publicly supported libraries and information services.

The First Amendment guarantee of freedom of expression is violated when the right to receive that expression is subject to arbitrary restrictions based on content.

Librarians and governing bodies should examine carefully any terms or conditions attached to library funding and should oppose attempts to limit through such conditions full and equal access to information because of content. This principle applies equally to private gifts or bequests and to public funds. In particular, librarians and governing bodies have an obligation to reject such restrictions when the effect of the restriction is to limit equal and equitable access to information.

Librarians and governing bodies should cooperate with all efforts to create a community consensus that publicly supported libraries require funding unfettered by restrictions. Such a consensus supports the library mission to provide the free and unrestricted exchange of information and ideas necessary to a functioning democracy.

The Association's historic position in this regard is stated clearly in a number of Association policies: 50.3, "Free Access to Information"; 50.8, "Financing of Libraries"; 51.2, "Equal Access to Library Service" (superseded); 53, "Intellectual Freedom"; 59.1, "Policy Objectives"; and 61, "Library Services for the Poor."

Adopted by the ALA Council, June 30, 1993.

HISTORY

Economic Barriers
to Information Access

In 1989, the American Library Association's Minority Concerns Committee requested that the Council direct the Intellectual Freedom Committee to review the *Library Bill of Rights* to ensure that it included protection for intellectual freedom without regard to language or economic status. The ALA Council issued that directive, thereby launching a three-year process of review of all of the Interpretations of the *Library Bill of Rights,* of which all save one were amended to address the question of language. Throughout its discussions, the IFC discussed whether a separate or new Interpretation, specifically dealing with questions relating to economic status, was needed; it concluded that the prevalence of questions about fees for library services necessitated a new Interpretation.

The process of gathering information for what became "Economic Barriers to Information Access" began at the 1991 Annual Conference in Atlanta, where the IFC sponsored an open hearing on fees for library service to receive comments from librarians working in all areas of library service and types of libraries. A first draft of an Interpretation was developed at the 1992 Midwinter Meeting in San Antonio, and widely circulated for comment prior to and during the 1992 Annual Conference in San Francisco. Continuing its process of receiving comments and suggestions on the draft, the Committee met, at the 1993 Midwinter Meeting in Denver, with representatives of the Library of Congress (LC), who themselves were contemplating charging fees for library services.

Since 1977, the American Library Association has had on the books a policy (50.4) opposing fees for library services, specifically information services. But libraries have always felt pressure both from funding agencies and internally to recover the cost of providing certain types of services, particularly in times of economic hardship. In 1993, the atmosphere of fiscal restraint was being felt by all types of libraries all over the country, and had reached to the Library of Congress itself.

Judith Farley, Daniel Molhollan, and Winston Tabb, representatives of the Library of Congress, met with the IFC at the 1993 Midwinter Meeting to discuss a bill then pending before Congress dealing with the LC's funding and fees. While expressing concerns about user charges, they were troubled by statements in the then-current draft Interpretation flatly opposing the charging of user fees. At that time, the LC was the subject of a funding bill in Congress defining three different types of library service: core, national, and specialized. Core services would be free, national services would have fees related to distribution costs only, and specialized services would be provided on a full cost-recovery basis. The proposal generated intensive discussion at the Intellectual Freedom Committee meeting during that 1993 Midwinter Meeting. The net result of the discussion was to solidify the Committee's belief that an Interpretation of the *Library Bill of Rights* addressing economic barriers to information access must be unequivocal with regard to the provision of information in libraries—an information "have and have-not" society, based upon the ability to pay for information services in libraries, must be avoided. As IFC chair Candace Morgan explained in her Report to Council for that Midwinter Meeting, the draft was revised to "address the Committee's growing concern over the creeping acceptance, by governing bodies and funding sources, of the idea that libraries should be required to recover some costs through user charges, which have the potential to create barriers to access based on economic status."

Another issue that was raised during the discussion was potential restrictions and conditions imposed upon information access by donors. Libraries sometimes receive donations of money or materials which carry with them conditions imposing restrictions upon access which discriminate against some library users.

Finally, the pervasive atmosphere of fiscal restraint had generated pressures from local government upon libraries to charge fees for services. The Committee noted that much of that pressure reflected a lack of understanding of the unique mission of publicly supported libraries—no other agency serves as a public forum through which the ideals of the First Amendment may be realized. The Committee added introductory language to the draft Interpretation to place libraries "firmly within the realm of essential public services, and to address how libraries, which must compete for funding, can examine their policies to ensure that the essential mission of providing free access to information is protected." The Committee wanted to encourage libraries to educate their funding agencies about their unique role and to urge them to insist on being treated as unique by local governments. The new introductory language in the revised draft Interpretation squarely placed libraries within the arena of First Amendment law—as public forums for access to information subject to First Amendment principles and responsible to their users to provide information access without charge.

Following consideration of testimony presented at the 1991 hearing, comments made on the draft, and the concerns of the representatives of the Library of Congress, a substantially revised version was circulated for comment to the ALA Executive Board, the ALA Council, ALA committees, divisions, round tables, chairs of state intellectual freedom committees, and interested librarians, prior to the 1993 Annual Conference. Additional written and oral comments continued to be received until and during the Conference, where the Committee again met with representatives of the Library of Congress. A final draft was offered to the Council for its adoption at that 1993 Annual Conference in New Orleans.

The final version takes a strong position against the charging of fees and urges libraries to examine their policies and practices to ensure that information access is not restricted by being based upon the ability to pay. Although the Interpretation was adopted by the Council at the 1993 Annual Conference, the discussion of the principles it states continues. Many libraries, still suffering severe budgetary constraints, have contended that the document is too idealistic and sets a standard that libraries cannot realistically meet. Others acknowledge that the document states central matters of principle in deliberately strong terms, that libraries must stake their ground and refuse to accede to demands to charge fees and become "entre-preneurial." Instead, they should demand that the essential services they provide be adequately funded and new services not be mandated unless appropriate budgets to pay for them are supplied by funding agencies.

The debate over charges for information services is sure to continue as more sophisticated, and more expensive, modes of information access find their way into libraries. Providing patrons with access to the Internet, as well as other electronic networks and database services, some of which are themselves fee-based, will continue to be a budgetary issue for libraries, and the temptation to charge fees for the use of newer technologies is ever present. In the process of developing "Economic Barriers to Information Access," a history of charging fees for new technologies in many libraries emerged. The Intellectual Freedom Committee determined that the best way to describe the resources provided by publicly supported libraries that the Committee believed should be free of all user charges was through the use of the expression "information resources and services." The document does not preclude the possibility of charging fees for noninformation services, such as photocopying. The language of the Interpretation is intentionally broad, however, in order to preclude the possibility of extended bickering over what constitutes, for example, "core" service or the provision of information for which user charges should not be imposed. The final document sets forth an ideal toward which libraries are encouraged to aspire, and it encourages the continuous scrutiny of library policy, procedure, and operation for potential economic barriers in order to ensure that access to information is not proscribed according to the ability to pay.

No changes in "Economic Barriers to Information Access" were recommended as part of the 1999–2000 periodic review of all Interpretations by the IFC.

2.8

Evaluating Library Collections

An Interpretation of the
Library Bill of Rights

The continuous review of library materials is necessary as a means of maintaining an active library collection of current interest to users. In the process, materials may be added and physically deteriorated or obsolete materials may be replaced or removed in accordance with the collection maintenance policy of a given library and the needs of the community it serves. Continued evaluation is closely related to the goals and responsibilities of libraries and is a valuable tool of collection development. This procedure is not to be used as a convenient means to remove materials presumed to be controversial or disapproved of by segments of the community. Such abuse of the evaluation function violates the principles of intellectual freedom and is in opposition to the Preamble and Articles I and II of the *Library Bill of Rights*, which state:

> The American Library Association affirms that all libraries are forums for information and ideas, and that the following basic policies should guide their services.
>
> I. Books and other library resources should be provided for the interest, information, and enlightenment of all people of the community the library serves. Materials should not be excluded because of the origin, background, or views of those contributing to their creation.

II. Libraries should provide materials and information presenting all points of view on current and historical issues. Materials should not be proscribed or removed because of partisan or doctrinal disapproval.

The American Library Association opposes such "silent censorship" and strongly urges that libraries adopt guidelines setting forth the positive purposes and principles of evaluation of materials in library collections.

Adopted February 2, 1973; amended July 1, 1981, by the ALA Council.

HISTORY

Evaluating
Library Collections

In both theory and practice, library collections undergo continual reevaluation to ensure that they fulfill and remain responsive to the goals of the institution and the needs of library patrons. The reevaluation process, however, can also be used to achieve the purposes of the censor, purposes manifestly inconsistent with Articles I and II of the *Library Bill of Rights*.

At the 1972 Midwinter Meeting in Chicago, the Intellectual Freedom Committee realized the necessity of an Interpretation of the *Library Bill of Rights* with regard to the more general issues involved in reevaluating library collections. Accordingly, the Committee announced its intent to prepare a statement on reevaluation. The document was approved by the Intellectual Freedom Committee at the 1972 Annual Conference in Chicago. It was submitted to the ALA Council at the 1973 Midwinter Meeting in Washington, D.C., and was adopted on February 2, 1973, under the title "Reevaluating Library Collections."

> The continuous review of library collections to remove physically deteriorated or obsolete materials is one means to maintain active library collections of current interest to users.* Continued reevaluation is closely related to the goals and responsibilities of libraries,

---

*The traditional term "weeding," implying "the removal of a noxious growth," is purposely avoided because of the imprecise nature of the term.

and is a valuable tool of collection building. This procedure, however, is sometimes used as a convenient means to remove materials thought to be too controversial or disapproved of by segments
of the community. Such abuse of the reevaluation function violates
the principles of intellectual freedom and is in opposition to
Articles I and II of the *Library Bill of Rights,* which state that:

> As a responsibility of library service, books and other library
> materials selected should be chosen for values of interest, informa-
> tion, and enlightenment of all the people of the community. In no
> case should library materials be excluded because of the race or
> nationality or the social, political, or religious views of the authors.
>
> Libraries should provide books and other materials presenting
> all points of view concerning the problems and issues of our times;
> no library materials should be proscribed or removed from
> libraries because of partisan or doctrinal disapproval.

The American Library Association opposes such "silent censorship," and recommends that libraries adopt guidelines setting
forth the positive purposes and principles for reevaluation of
materials in library collections.

In 1981, the policy was rewritten by the IFC to reflect the
changes that had been made in the 1980 version of the *Library Bill of
Rights.* In the process, a number of editorial changes were made in
the text with the aim of increasing its forcefulness. The most significant amendment recommended by the IFC was a change in the title
of the document from "Reevaluating Library Collections" to
"Evaluating Library Collections." The change was suggested
because the process of evaluating library materials for acquisition or
retention is a single ongoing process and, in principle, is never completed and then redone. Moreover, the Intellectual Freedom
Committee thought that it could be falsely inferred from the word
"reevaluating" that initial evaluations of works had been incorrect.
The revision was approved by the Council on July 1, 1981.

In line with the ongoing practice of periodic review, the IFC
reviewed "Evaluating Library Collections" during 1999–2000, and
did not recommend any changes.

2.9
Exhibit Spaces and Bulletin Boards

An Interpretation of the
Library Bill of Rights

Libraries often provide exhibit spaces and bulletin boards. The uses made of these spaces should conform to the *Library Bill of Rights:* Article I states, "Materials should not be excluded because of the origin, background, or views of those contributing to their creation." Article II states, "Materials should not be proscribed or removed because of partisan or doctrinal disapproval." Article VI maintains that exhibit space should be made available "on an equitable basis, regardless of the beliefs or affiliations of individuals or groups requesting their use."

In developing library exhibits, staff members should endeavor to present a broad spectrum of opinion and a variety of viewpoints. Libraries should not shrink from developing exhibits because of controversial content or because of the beliefs or affiliations of those whose work is represented. Just as libraries do not endorse the viewpoints of those whose works are represented in their collections, libraries also do not endorse the beliefs or viewpoints of topics which may be the subject of library exhibits.

Exhibit areas often are made available for use by community groups. Libraries should formulate a written policy for the use of these exhibit areas to assure that space is provided on an equitable basis to all groups which request it.

Written policies for exhibit space use should be stated in inclusive rather than exclusive terms. For example, a policy that the library's exhibit space is open "to organizations engaged in educational, cultural, intellectual, or charitable activities" is an inclusive statement of the limited uses of the exhibit space. This defined limitation would permit religious groups to use the exhibit space because they engage in intellectual activities, but would exclude most commercial uses of the exhibit space.

A publicly supported library may limit use of its exhibit space to strictly "library-related" activities, provided that the limitation is clearly circumscribed and is viewpoint neutral.

Libraries may include in this policy rules regarding the time, place, and manner of use of the exhibit space, so long as the rules are content-neutral and are applied in the same manner to all groups wishing to use the space. A library may wish to limit access to exhibit space to groups within the community served by the library. This practice is acceptable provided that the same rules and regulations apply to everyone, and that exclusion is not made on the basis of the doctrinal, religious, or political beliefs of the potential users.

The library should not censor or remove an exhibit because some members of the community may disagree with its content. Those who object to the content of any exhibit held at the library should be able to submit their complaint and/or their own exhibit proposal to be judged according to the policies established by the library.

Libraries may wish to post a permanent notice near the exhibit area stating that the library does not advocate or endorse the viewpoints of exhibits or exhibitors.

Libraries which make bulletin boards available to public groups for posting notices of public interest should develop criteria for the use of these spaces based on the same considerations as those outlined above. Libraries may wish to develop criteria regarding the size of material to be displayed, the length of time materials may remain on the bulletin board, the frequency with which material may be posted for the same group, and the geographic area from which notices will be accepted.

Adopted July 2, 1991, by the ALA Council.

HISTORY

Exhibit Spaces
and Bulletin Boards

U se of library exhibit spaces and meeting rooms became a subject of developing controversy in the 1970s. These years saw several publicized efforts to deny access to such facilities to controversial groups or exhibitors. In North Carolina, for example, an exhibit sponsored by the Ku Klux Klan at a public library sparked a violent confrontation with protesters. At the University of California library at Berkeley, Turkish students protested the "one-sidedness" of an exhibit on the early 20th-century massacre of Armenians by Turks, which had been placed in the library by students of Armenian ancestry. In several places, attempts were made to deny use of such facilities to certain groups on the grounds either that the groups themselves were advocates of violence or that the threat of violence associated with their meetings—including threats made against these meetings by the groups' opponents—posed a danger to library employees and patrons or to library property. At the same time, exhibits mounted by libraries themselves sometimes came under fire. In Virginia, for instance, an exhibit of books about homosexuality in a public library collection was accused of promoting this practice and of obscenity. All these efforts to censor library exhibits were in violation of Article VI of the *Library Bill of Rights*.

Yet the 1970s were also marked by some confusion within the ALA about the applicability of Article VI, as it was formulated in the 1967 version of the *Library Bill of Rights*. In particular, academic and school libraries pointed out that the provision was written to apply in reality only to public libraries, and public librarians noted that not enough flexibility existed even to accommodate the varying situations of public libraries.

The 1980 revision of the *Library Bill of Rights* took account of these objections, and the revision of Article VI in that year successfully remedied its major defects. (See part II, section 1, *"Library Bill of Rights:* History.") At the 1980 Annual Conference in New York, however, the IFC, with Frances C. Dean as chair, decided that, given both the increasing number of incidents and the admitted complexity of applying even the revised Article in practice, a written policy interpreting the Article would be desirable.

The Intellectual Freedom Committee agreed that the key to applying the Article was the need to maintain flexibility, while upholding a standard of fairness. On this basis a policy was prepared and, at the 1981 Midwinter Meeting in Washington, D.C., presented to the Council, which adopted it as an ALA policy on February 4, 1981. It read as follows:

> As part of their program of service, many libraries provide meeting rooms and exhibit spaces for individuals and groups. Article VI of the *Library Bill of Rights* states that such facilities should be made available to the public served by the given library "on an equitable basis, regardless of the beliefs or affiliations of individuals or groups requesting their use."
>
> In formulating this position, the American Library Association sought to accommodate the broad range of practices among public, academic, school and other libraries, while upholding a standard of fairness. Libraries maintaining exhibit and meeting room facilities for outside groups and individuals should develop and publish policy statements governing their use. These statements can properly define and restrict eligibility for use as long as the qualifications do not pertain to the content of a meeting or exhibit or to the beliefs or affiliations of the sponsors.
>
> It is appropriate for a library to limit access to meeting rooms or exhibit space to members of the specific community served by the library or to groups of a specific category. It is not proper to apply such limitations in ways which favor points of view or organizations advocating certain viewpoints. For example, some libraries permit religious groups to use meeting facilities, while others do not. According to Article VI, both policies are acceptable

as long as all religious groups are treated in the same way, irrespective of their doctrines.

Exhibits and meetings sponsored by the library itself should be organized in a manner consistent with the *Library Bill of Rights,* especially Article II which states that "libraries should provide materials and information presenting all points of view." However, in granting meeting or exhibit space to outside individuals and groups, the library should make no effort to censor or amend the content of the exhibit or meeting. Those who object to or disagree with the content of any exhibit or meeting held at the library should be entitled to submit their own exhibit or meeting proposals which should be judged according to the policies established by the library.

The library may properly limit the use of its meeting rooms to meetings which are open to the public, or it may make space available for both public and private sessions. Again, however, the same standard should be applicable to all.

In 1989, revisions were undertaken to reflect nondiscrimination on the basis of language or economic status. Discussion on appropriate changes in the Interpretation continued through June 26, 1990, at which time the Committee voted to rescind two sentences of the Interpretation as an interim measure.

For example, some libraries permit religious groups to use meeting facilities, while others do not. According to Article VI, both policies are acceptable as long as all religious groups are treated in the same way, irrespective of their doctrines.

The sentences were rescinded in light of a recent court decision in favor of a religious organization that had been denied use of a library meeting room. (See part V, section 5, "Public Libraries as Limited Public Fora for Access to Information.") The policy then read as follows:

As part of their program of service, many libraries provide meeting rooms and exhibit spaces for individuals and groups. Article VI of the *Library Bill of Rights* states that such facilities should be made available to the public served by the given library "on an equitable basis, regardless of the beliefs or affiliations of individuals or groups requesting their use."

In formulating this position, the American Library Association sought to accommodate the broad range of practices among public, academic, school and other libraries, while upholding a standard of fairness. Libraries maintaining exhibit and meeting room facilities for outside groups and individuals should develop and publish policy statements governing their use. These statements can properly define and restrict eligibility for use as long as the qualifications do not pertain to the content of a meeting or exhibit or to the beliefs or affiliations of the sponsors.

It is appropriate for a library to limit access to meeting rooms or exhibit space to members of the specific community served by the library or to groups of a specific category. The library may properly limit the use of its meeting rooms to meetings which are open to the public, or it may make space available for both public and private sessions. It is not proper to apply such limitations in ways which favor points of view or organizations advocating certain viewpoints.

Exhibits and meetings sponsored by the library itself should be organized in a manner consistent with the *Library Bill of Rights,* especially Article II which states that "libraries should provide materials and information presenting all points of view." However, in granting meeting or exhibit space to outside individuals and groups, the library should make no effort to censor or amend the content of the exhibit or meeting. Those who object to or disagree with the content of any exhibit or meeting held at the library should be entitled to submit their own exhibit or meeting proposals which should be judged according to the policies established by the library.

Following adoption of the interim language, continuing concerns about the meaning of "viewpoint neutral restrictions," the rules governing designated public forums, and commercial uses of library meeting rooms led to a consensus decision to rewrite the policy totally.

In January 1991, two separate Interpretations—"Meeting Rooms" and "Exhibit Spaces and Bulletin Boards"—were introduced. Recent court decisions supporting the right of religious groups to have access to public forums for their meetings raised questions that were best dealt with in a discrete meeting-room policy, rather than under the same policy rubric that included meeting rooms, exhibit spaces, and bulletin boards. After additional discussion about fees, commercial uses, and disclaimers to clarify the library's position as a neutral host and not an advocate of particular meetings or exhibits, the Committee voted to adopt the two Interpretations for circulation to all ALA units, the Council, and the Executive Board for comment.

The two policies were adopted as revised on July 2, 1991, at the Annual Conference. (For the policy "Meeting Rooms," see part II, section 2.14.)

No changes in "Exhibit Spaces and Bulletin Boards" were recommended as part of the 1999–2000 periodic review of all Interpretations by the IFC.

2.10

Expurgation
of Library Materials

An Interpretation of the
Library Bill of Rights

Expurgating library materials is a violation of the *Library Bill of Rights*. Expurgation as defined by this Interpretation includes any deletion, excision, alteration, editing, or obliteration of any part(s) of books or other library resources by the library, its agent, or its parent institution (if any). By such expurgation, the library is in effect denying access to the complete work and the entire spectrum of ideas that the work intended to express. Such action stands in violation of Articles I, II, and III of the *Library Bill of Rights*, which state that "Materials should not be excluded because of the origin, background, or views of those contributing to their creation," that "Materials should not be proscribed or removed because of partisan or doctrinal disapproval," and that "Libraries should challenge censorship in the fulfillment of their responsibility to provide information and enlightenment."

The act of expurgation has serious implications. It involves a determination that it is necessary to restrict access to the complete work. This is censorship. When a work is expurgated, under the assumption that certain portions of that work would be harmful to minors, the situation is no less serious.

Expurgation of any books or other library resources imposes a restriction, without regard to the rights and desires of all library users, by limiting access to ideas and information.

Further, expurgation without written permission from the holder of the copyright on the material may violate the copyright provisions of the United States Code.

Adopted February 2, 1973; amended July 1, 1981; amended January 10, 1990, by the ALA Council.

HISTORY

Expurgation
of Library Materials

The December 1971 issue of *School Library Journal* (page 7) carried the following report submitted by one of its readers:

> Maurice Sendak might faint but a staff member of Caldwell Parish Library [Louisiana], knowing that the patrons of the community might object to the illustrations in *In the Night Kitchen,* solved the problem by diapering the little boys with white tempera paint. Other libraries might wish to do the same.

In response, Ursula Nordstrom, publisher of Harper Junior Books, sent a statement to more than 380 librarians, professors, publishers, authors, and artists throughout the United States:

> [The news item sent to *School Library Journal*] is representative of several such reports about Maurice Sendak's *In the Night Kitchen,* a book for children, that have come out of public and school libraries throughout the country.
>
> At first, the thought of librarians painting diapers or pants on the naked hero of Sendak's book might seem amusing, merely a harmless eccentricity on the part of some prim few. On reconsideration, however, this behavior should be recognized for what it is: an act of censorship by mutilation rather than by obvious suppression.

More than 425 persons signed the statement of protest circulated by Miss Nordstrom.

The expurgation of *In the Night Kitchen* was brought to the attention of the Intellectual Freedom Committee by the Children's Book Council in June 1972. During its meeting at the 1972 ALA Annual Conference in Chicago, the Committee decided, after considering whether expurgation was already covered by the *Library Bill of Rights*, that a statement should be issued specifically on expurgation. During the 1973 Midwinter Meeting in Washington, D.C., the Committee approved a statement on expurgation of library materials and sent it to the ALA Council for approval. The statement which was adopted by the Council as an ALA policy on February 2, 1973, read as follows:

> Library materials are chosen for their value and interest to the community the library serves. If library materials were acquired for these reasons and in accordance with a written statement on materials selection, then to expurgate must be interpreted as a violation of the *Library Bill of Rights*. For purposes of this statement, expurgation includes deletion, excision, alteration or obliteration. By such expurgation, the library is in effect denying access to the complete work and the full ideas that the work was intended to express; such action stands in violation of Article II of the *Library Bill of Rights*, which states that "no library materials should be proscribed or removed from libraries because of partisan or doctrinal disapproval."
>
> The act of expurgation has serious implications. It involves a determination by an individual that it is necessary to restrict the availability of that material. It is, in fact, censorship.
>
> When a work is expurgated, under the assumption that certain sections of that work would be harmful to minors, the situation is no less serious. Expurgation of any library materials imposes a restriction, without regard to the rights and desires of all library users.

In 1981, during the review of all the Interpretations of the *Library Bill of Rights*, the IFC reviewed the policy on expurgation and made several changes designed to add clarity to and strengthen the document. Most important, the IFC recommended basing the argument of the Interpretation not only on Article II of the *Library Bill of Rights* but on Articles I and III as well. The revision was adopted by the Council on July 1, 1981, and read as follows:

Books and other library resources are selected for their value, interest, and importance to the people of the community the library serves. Since books and other library resources are acquired for these reasons and in accordance with a written statement on materials selection, then expurgating them must be interpreted as a violation of the *Library Bill of Rights*. Expurgation as defined by this Interpretation includes any deletion, excision, alteration, or obliteration of any part(s) of books or other library resources by the library. By such expurgation, the library is in effect denying access to the complete work and the entire spectrum of ideas that the work intended to express; such action stands in violation of Articles I, II, and III of the *Library Bill of Rights,* which state that "Materials should not be excluded because of the origin, background, or views of those contributing to their creation"; that "Materials should not be proscribed or removed because of partisan or doctrinal disapproval"; and that "Libraries should challenge censorship in the fulfillment of their responsibility to provide information and enlightenment."

The act of expurgation has serious implications. It involves a determination that it is necessary to restrict complete access to that material. This is censorship. When a work is expurgated, under the assumption that certain portions of that work would be harmful to minors, the situation is no less serious.

Expurgation of any books or other library resources imposes a restriction, without regard to the rights and desires of all library users, by limiting access to ideas and information.

At the 1989 ALA Annual Conference in Dallas, the Interpretation "Expurgation of Library Materials" was revised in accordance with the request of the Minority Concerns Committee for review of the *Library Bill of Rights* to ensure that discrimination on the basis of language and economic status would be addressed. The IFC adopted a revised version, which was subsequently circulated for comments. At the 1990 Midwinter Meeting, minor editorial changes were made, and the new draft was adopted and recommended to the Council. On January 10, 1990, the Interpretation became ALA policy.

In 1999–2000, "Expurgation of Library Materials" was carefully reviewed by the IFC and no changes were recommended.

2.11

Free Access to Libraries
for Minors

An Interpretation of the
Library Bill of Rights

Library policies and procedures which effectively deny minors equal access to all library resources available to other users violate the *Library Bill of Rights.* The American Library Association opposes all attempts to restrict access to library services, materials, and facilities based on the age of library users.

Article V of the *Library Bill of Rights* states, "A person's right to use a library should not be denied or abridged because of origin, age, background, or views." The "right to use a library" includes free access to, and unrestricted use of, all the services, materials, and facilities the library has to offer. Every restriction on access to, and use of, library resources, based solely on the chronological age, educational level, or legal emancipation of users violates Article V.

Libraries are charged with the mission of developing resources to meet the diverse information needs and interests of the communities they serve. Services, materials, and facilities which fulfill the needs and interests of library users at different stages in their personal development are a necessary part of library resources. The needs and interests of each library user, and resources appropriate to meet those needs and interests, must be determined on an individual basis. Librarians cannot predict what resources will best fulfill the needs and interests of any individual user based on a single criterion such as chronological age, level of education, or legal emancipation.

The selection and development of library resources should not be diluted because of minors having the same access to library resources as adult users. Institutional self-censorship diminishes the credibility of the library in the community, and restricts access for all library users.

Librarians and governing bodies should not resort to age restrictions on access to library resources in an effort to avoid actual or anticipated objections from parents or anyone else. The mission, goals, and objectives of libraries do not authorize librarians or governing bodies to assume, abrogate, or overrule the rights and responsibilities of parents or legal guardians. Librarians and governing bodies should maintain that parents—and only parents—have the right and the responsibility to restrict the access of their children—and only their children—to library resources. Parents or legal guardians who do not want their children to have access to certain library services, materials or facilities, should so advise their children. Librarians and governing bodies cannot assume the role of parents or the functions of parental authority in the private relationship between parent and child. Librarians and governing bodies have a public and professional obligation to provide equal access to all library resources for all library users.

Librarians have a professional commitment to ensure that all members of the community they serve have free and equal access to the entire range of library resources regardless of content, approach, format, or amount of detail. This principle of library service applies equally to all users, minors as well as adults. Librarians and governing bodies must uphold this principle in order to provide adequate and effective service to minors.

Adopted June 30, 1972; amended July 1, 1981; July 3, 1991, by the ALA Council.

HISTORY

Free Access
to Libraries for Minors

The question of whether or not intellectual freedom in libraries applies to children and young adults has been debated by librarians since the early years of the profession's involvement with intellectual freedom. The question was considered many times by the Intellectual Freedom Committee and led to the preconference institute titled Intellectual Freedom and the Teenager, held in San Francisco on June 23–25, 1967.

Sponsored jointly by the Intellectual Freedom Committee, the Young Adult Services Division, and the American Association of School Librarians, and attended by approximately 400 librarians, the preconference featured a variety of speakers of national reputation, including author Kenneth Rexroth, attorneys Stanley Fleishman and Alex P. Allain, book review editor Robert Kirsh, and library young-adult consultant Esther Helfand. The most outspoken panelist was Edgar L. Freidenberg, author of *Coming of Age in America*, who told participants:

> The library is just one more place where the kids are taught they are second-class citizens. They learn this not only from the books pressed upon them by the helpful librarian but even more so from the very atmosphere of the place.[1]

In his summary of the three-day meeting, Ervin Gaines, chair of the IFC, dwelt at length on Freidenberg's comments:

He made the assumption that intellectual freedom was an inalienable right and that age is not a morally relevant factor and that adults have themselves no right to determine for youth access to ideas. This assumption which came at the very beginning of this talk echoed and re-echoed throughout the conference. There was surprising unanimity of opinion on this particular point.[2]

As the preconference progressed, there was also surprising unanimity on the position that not only teenagers, but all young people, were the focus of the discussions. This was reflected in one of the major recommendations of the institute, "that free access to all books in a library collection be granted to young people."[3]

Later, during the 1967 ALA Annual Conference, Gaines moved that the Council adopt a revised version of the *Library Bill of Rights*. He introduced his motion with the following remarks:

At a meeting of the Intellectual Freedom Committee yesterday two minor amendments were suggested to this text [the revised *Library Bill of Rights*]. In section 5 we suggest that the word "age" be inserted. . . . This suggestion comes as a result of recommendations from the preconference on Intellectual Freedom and the Teenager, which was held last week.

The change was approved by the Council, and the Association, well in advance of society in general, took a significant stand, approving free access for minors to all the materials in a library collection.

After 1967, the word "age" in the *Library Bill of Rights* was a constant source of confusion. Did it mean children should be able to take home any materials in a library collection, or were some restrictions permissible? What about double card systems or multiple card systems, restricting minors to the use of only part of the collection? These and other questions accrued until the IFC's 1972 Midwinter Meeting. Twenty hours of meetings were dominated by discussions of minors and library access problems, all related to the word "age" in the *Library Bill of Rights*.

After the meeting, the Committee announced plans to develop a position statement concerning access to libraries for minors. A draft was subsequently sent, in the spring of 1972, to the boards of the Public Library Association, the American Association of School Librarians, the Children's Services Division, the Young Adult Services

Division, and the American Library Trustee Association. At its annual meeting in June 1972, the IFC approved the statement and recommended it to the ALA Council, which adopted it on June 30, 1972, as an ALA policy titled "Free Access to Libraries for Minors." The statement read as follows:

Some library procedures and practices effectively deny minors access to certain services and materials available to adults. Such procedures and practices are not in accord with the *Library Bill of Rights* and are opposed by the American Library Association.

Restrictions take a variety of forms, including, among others, restricted reading rooms for adult use only, library cards limiting circulation of some materials to adults only, closed collections for adult use only, and interlibrary loan service for adult use only.

All limitations in minors' access to library materials and services violate Article V of the *Library Bill of Rights,* which states, "The rights of an individual to the use of a library should not be denied or abridged because of age. . . ." Limiting access to some services and materials to only adults abridges the use of libraries for minors. "Use of the library" includes use of, and access to, all library materials and services.

Restrictions are often initiated under the assumption that certain materials are "harmful" to minors, or in an effort to avoid controversy with parents who might think so. The librarian who would restrict the access of minors to materials and services because of actual or suspected parental objection should bear in mind that he is not in loco parentis in his position as librarian. Individual intellectual levels and family backgrounds are significant factors not accommodated by a uniform policy based upon age.

In today's world, children are exposed to adult life much earlier than in the past. They read materials and view a variety of media on the adult level at home and elsewhere. Current emphasis upon early childhood education has also increased opportunities for young people to learn and to have access to materials, and has decreased the validity of using chronological age as an index to the use of libraries. The period of time during which children are interested in reading materials specifically designed for them grows steadily shorter, and librarians must recognize and adjust to this change if they wish to maintain the patronage of young people.

The American Library Association holds that it is the parent—and only the parent—who may restrict his children—and only his children—from access to library materials and services. The parent who would rather his child did not have access to certain materials should so advise the child.

The word "age" was incorporated into Article V of the *Library Bill of Rights* as a direct result of a preconference titled Intellectual Freedom and the Teenager, held in San Francisco in June 1967. One recommendation of the preconference participants was "that free access to all books in a library collection be granted to young people." The preconference generally concluded that young people are entitled to the same access to libraries and to the materials in libraries as are adults and that materials selection should not be diluted on that account.

This does not mean, for instance, that issuing different types of borrowers' cards to minors and adults is, per se, contrary to the *Library Bill of Rights.* If such practices are used for purposes of gathering statistics, the various kinds of cards carry no implicit or explicit limitations on access to materials and services. Neither does it mean that maintaining separate children's collections is a violation of the *Library Bill of Rights,* provided that no patron is restricted to the use of only certain collections.

The Association's position does not preclude isolating certain materials for legitimate protection of irreplaceable or very costly works from careless use. Such "restricted-use" areas as rare book rooms are appropriate if the materials so classified are genuinely rare, and not merely controversial.

Unrestrictive selection policies, developed with care for principles of intellectual freedom and the *Library Bill of Rights,* should not be vitiated by administrative practices which restrict minors to the use of only part of a library's collections and services.

Following adoption of the 1980 revision of the *Library Bill of Rights,* the IFC reviewed the document anew. Working closely with the intellectual freedom committees of the Young Adult Services Division and the Association for Library Service to Children (previously the Children's Services Division), at the 1981 Midwinter Meeting and Annual Conference, the Committee made several changes aimed not only at eliminating sex-linked language but also at strengthening the impact of the Interpretation. Reference to the 1967 preconference was deleted as a historical detail irrelevant to a broad public statement of policy, and several key paragraphs were rewritten to communicate the Association's stand with greater force and clarity.

The Intellectual Freedom Committee also decided to delete from the document all references to specific administrative practices such as dual-card systems and restricted-use areas—which, although not always in violation of the principles of the *Library Bill of Rights*, have been employed at times in ways that unfairly limit minors' access to library resources. Limiting discussion of the intellectual freedom implications of such administrative practices to their effects on minors' access in itself tended to legitimize their misuse; and, the Committee concluded, the treatment in the document weakened its overall thrust by appearing to qualify the policy and limit its application. The Committee therefore decided to discuss such practices separately and in a more all-sided way by developing a new Interpretation, to be titled "Administrative Policies and Procedures Affecting Access to Library Resources and Services." That Interpretation was adopted in 1982 but rescinded in 1992, when the Committee adopted "Guidelines for the Development and Implementation of Policies, Regulations and Procedures Affecting Access to Library Materials, Services and Facilities." (See part III, section 8.)

On July 1, 1981, the revision of "Free Access to Libraries for Minors" was adopted by the Council. It read as follows:

> Some library procedures effectively deny minors access to certain services and materials available to adults. Such procedures and practices are not in accord with the *Library Bill of Rights* and are opposed by the American Library Association.
>
> Restrictions take a variety of forms, including, among others, restricted reading rooms for adult use only, library cards limiting circulation of some materials to adults only, closed collections for adult use only, collections limited to teacher use, or restricted according to a student's grade level, and interlibrary loan service for adult use only.
>
> Article V of the *Library Bill of Rights* states that, "A person's right to use a library should not be denied or abridged because of origin, age, background, or views." All limitations on minors'

access to library materials and services violate that Article. The "right to use a library" includes use of, and access to, all library materials and services. Thus, practices which allow adults to use some services and materials which are denied to minors abridge the use of libraries based on age.

Material selection decisions are often made and restrictions are often initiated under the assumption that certain materials may be "harmful" to minors, or in an effort to avoid controversy with parents. Libraries or library boards which would restrict the access of minors to materials and services because of actual or suspected parental objections should bear in mind that they do not serve in loco parentis. Varied levels of intellectual development among young people and differing family background and child-rearing philosophies are significant factors not accommodated by a uniform policy based upon age.

In today's world, children are exposed to adult life much earlier than in the past. They read materials and view a variety of media on the adult level at home and elsewhere. Current emphasis upon early childhood education has also increased opportunities for young people to learn and to have access to materials, and has decreased the validity of using chronological age as an index to the use of libraries. The period of time during which children are interested in reading materials specifically designed for them grows steadily shorter, and librarians must recognize and adjust to this change if they wish to serve young people effectively. Librarians have a responsibility to ensure that young people have access to a wide range of informational and recreational materials and services that reflects sufficient diversity to meet the young person's needs.

The American Library Association opposes libraries restricting access to library materials and services for minors and holds that it is the parents—and only parents—who may restrict their children—and only their children—from access to library materials and services. Parents who would rather their children did not have access to certain materials should so advise their children. The library and its staff are responsible for providing equal access to library materials and services for all library users.

The word "age" was incorporated into Article V of the *Library Bill of Rights* because young people are entitled to the same access to libraries and to the materials in libraries as are adults. Materials selection should not be diluted on that account.

Ten years later, at the 1991 Midwinter Meeting, a further revised "Free Access to Libraries for Minors" was adopted by the IFC. The Committee had extensively reworked the document to make the protections for minors' access more explicit and to outline with greater precision librarians' responsibilities toward minors and all library users. The new policy emphasized the role of librarians as information providers and placed the burden of guiding minors squarely on the shoulders of parents.

The definition of library usage was expanded to include use of facilities as well as materials and services. Library trustees were implicated in the new policy as being co-responsible with librarians for providing equal access to all library resources for all library users.

The Midwinter version also included a list of practices that librarians have used to restrict indirectly minors' access to expensive, controversial, or otherwise objectionable materials, including issuing limited-access cards; barring entry to stacks, reserve areas, or reading rooms; charging fees; and simply refusing to perform a service based solely on the age or educational level of the user. This list was intended to alert librarians to specific practices that inhibited minors' access to library materials, services, and facilities, and to discourage these all-too-common practices.

At the 1991 Annual Conference, the Council deleted the list of examples from the final Interpretation before approving it as ALA policy. Many councilors believed that the ALA's official position would be more effective and adaptable to changing societal circumstances if the Interpretation were written in broad terms, without a list of potential violations of the principle.

The list of examples that follows is not comprehensive, but suggestive of some of the most commonly used practices that violate the *Library Bill of Rights*. Copies are available upon request from the Office for Intellectual Freedom.

Examples of Age-Based Access Limitations

Some specific examples of denial of equal access include, but are not limited to, the following:

restricting access to reading or reference rooms, or to otherwise open stack areas, on the basis of the age or school grade level of the user;

issuing limited access library cards, or otherwise restricting the circulation of materials, on the basis of the age or school grade level of the user;

assigning materials to special collections, such as parenting, teacher-professional, historical-genealogical collections, and restricting access to these collections, on the basis of the age or school grade level of the user;

using manual or computerized registration or circulation systems that restrict access to materials, on the basis of the age or school grade level of the user;

sequestering or otherwise restricting access to material because of its content, on the basis of the age or school grade level of the user;

requiring or soliciting written permission from a parent or guardian to gain or restrict access to materials because of their content, on the basis of the age or school grade level of the user;

restricting access to interlibrary loan, fax, and electronic reference services, on the basis of the age or school grade level of the user;

restricting access to materials because of their format or their cost—such as computer software, compact discs, periodicals, microfilm-fiche, and videocassettes, on the basis of the age or school grade level of the user;

charging fees or requiring deposits to gain access to services, materials, or facilities, on the basis of the age or school grade level of the user;

refusing to process interlibrary loans, reserves, or reference requests for materials classified as juvenile;

assigning professional-nonprofessional staff to reference searches, on the basis of the age or school grade level of the user;

restricting access to library-sponsored programs or events otherwise designed for general audiences, on the basis of the age or school grade level of the user;

restricting access to public facilities, such as meeting rooms, display cases, and notice boards, on the basis of the age or school grade level of the user.

During 1999–2000, in line with their ongoing practice of periodic review of all Interpretations, the IFC carefully reviewed "Free Access to Libraries for Minors," especially in regard to its applicability to the Internet. The committee did not recommend any changes.

NOTES

1. *San Francisco Examiner and Chronicle,* June 25, 1967.
2. *Newsletter on Intellectual Freedom* 16:54 (September 1967).
3. Ibid., p. 55.

2.12

Intellectual Freedom Principles for Academic Libraries

An Interpretation of the
Library Bill of Rights

A strong intellectual freedom perspective is critical to the development of academic library collections and services that dispassionately meet the education and research needs of a college or university community. The purpose of this statement is to outline how and where intellectual freedom principles fit into an academic library setting, thereby raising consciousness of the intellectual freedom context within which academic librarians work. The following principles should be reflected in all relevant library policy documents.

1. The general principles set forth in the *Library Bill of Rights* form an indispensable framework for building collections, services, and policies that serve the entire academic community.

2. The privacy of library users is and must be inviolable. Policies should be in place that maintain confidentiality of library borrowing records and of other information relating to personal use of library information and services.

3. The development of library collections in support of an institution's instruction and research programs should transcend the personal values of the selector. In the interests of research and learning, it is essential that collections contain materials representing a variety of perspectives on subjects that may be considered controversial.

4. Preservation and replacement efforts should ensure that balance in library materials is maintained and that controversial materials are not removed from the collections through theft, loss, mutilation, or normal wear and tear. There should be alertness to efforts by special interest groups to bias a collection through systematic theft or mutilation.

5. Licensing agreements should be consistent with the *Library Bill of Rights,* and should maximize access.

6. Open and unfiltered access to the Internet should be conveniently available to the academic community in a college or university library. Content filtering devices and content-based restrictions are a contradiction of the academic library mission to further research and learning through exposure to the broadest possible range of ideas and information. Such restrictions are a fundamental violation of intellectual freedom in academic libraries.

7. Freedom of information and of creative expression should be reflected in library exhibits and in all relevant library policy documents.

8. Library meeting rooms, research carrels, exhibit spaces, and other facilities should be available to the academic community regardless of research being pursued or subject being discussed. Any restrictions made necessary because of limited availability of space should be based on need, as reflected in library policy, rather than on content of research or discussion.

9. Whenever possible, library services should be available without charge in order to encourage inquiry. Where charges are necessary, a free or low-cost alternative (e.g., downloading to disc rather than printing) should be available when possible.

10. A service philosophy should be promoted that affords equal access to information for all in the academic community with no discrimination on the basis of race, values, gender, sexual orientation, cultural or ethnic background, physical or learning disability, economic status, religious beliefs, or views.

11. A procedure ensuring due process should be in place to deal with requests by those within and outside the academic

community for removal or addition of library resources, exhibits, or services.

12. It is recommended that this statement of principle be endorsed by appropriate institutional governing bodies, including the faculty senate or similar instrument of faculty governance.

Approved by the ACRL Board of Directors, June 29, 1999.

Adopted July 12, 2000, by the ALA Council.

Endorsed by the American Association of University Professors, November 11, 2000.

HISTORY

Intellectual Freedom Principles
for Academic Libraries

The Association of College and Research Libraries' Intellectual Freedom Committee began work on "Intellectual Freedom Principles for Academic Libraries" during the fall of 1998. By the 1999 ALA Midwinter Meeting in Philadelphia, the document had gone through two drafts. At the Midwinter Meeting, the Committee endorsed a third draft which was published in the June issue of *C&RL News*. Accompanying the draft was notice of an open hearing scheduled for June 28 at the 1999 ALA Annual Conference in New Orleans. At the same time, response was solicited from readers of the third draft. IFC deliberations before and after the 1999 Annual Conference hearing provided the basis for the fourth draft, which was submitted to the ACRL Board of Directors for approval. The ACRL Board unanimously approved the document on June 29, 1999. Subsequently, on January 16, 2000, the statement was endorsed by the ALA's Intellectual Freedom Committee. The ALA Council adopted the document as an Interpretation on July 12, 2000.

On November 11, 2000, the American Association of University Professors endorsed the document, stating their concern that college and university librarians are designated the same rights afforded to other faculty in regard to intellectual freedom, and requesting that their endorsement be prefaced with the following language from the "Joint Statement on Faculty Status of College and University Librarians," as contained in *AAUP: Policy Documents and Reports*, 1995 edition:

College and university librarians share the professional concerns of faculty members. Academic freedom, for example, is indispensable to librarians, because they are trustees of knowledge with responsibility of ensuring the availability of information and ideas, no matter how controversial, so that teachers may freely teach and students may freely learn. Moreover, as members of the academic community, librarians should have latitude in the exercise of their professional judgement within the library, a share in shaping policy within the institution, and adequate opportunities for professional development and appropriate reward.

2.13

Library-Initiated Programs as a Resource

An Interpretation of the *Library Bill of Rights*

Library-initiated programs support the mission of the library by providing users with additional opportunities for information, education, and recreation. Article I of the *Library Bill of Rights* states: "Books and other library resources should be provided for the interest, information, and enlightenment of all people of the community the library serves."

Library-initiated programs take advantage of library staff expertise, collections, services and facilities to increase access to information and information resources. Library-initiated programs introduce users and potential users to the resources of the library and to the library's primary function as a facilitator of information access. The library may participate in cooperative or joint programs with other agencies, organizations, institutions, or individuals as part of its own effort to address information needs and to facilitate information access in the community the library serves.

Library-initiated programs on site and in other locations include, but are not limited to, speeches, community forums, discussion groups, demonstrations, displays, and live or media presentations.

Libraries serving multilingual or multicultural communities should make efforts to accommodate the information needs of those for whom English is a second language. Library-initiated programs that cross language and cultural barriers introduce otherwise unserved populations to the resources of the library and provide access to information.

Library-initiated programs "should not be proscribed or removed (or canceled) because of partisan or doctrinal disapproval" of the contents of the program or the views expressed by the participants, as stated in Article II of the *Library Bill of Rights*. Library sponsorship of a program does not constitute an endorsement of the content of the program or the views expressed by the participants, any more than the purchase of material for the library collection constitutes an endorsement of the contents of the material or the views of its creator.

Library-initiated programs are a library resource, and, as such, are developed in accordance with written guidelines, as approved and adopted by the library's policy-making body. These guidelines should include an endorsement of the *Library Bill of Rights* and set forth the library's commitment to free and open access to information and ideas for all users.

Library staff select topics, speakers and resource materials for library-initiated programs based on the interests and information needs of the community. Topics, speakers and resource materials are not excluded from library-initiated programs because of possible controversy. Concerns, questions or complaints about library-initiated programs are handled according to the same written policy and procedures which govern reconsiderations of other library resources.

Library-initiated programs are offered free of charge and are open to all. Article V of the *Library Bill of Rights* states: "A person's right to use a library should not be denied or abridged because of origin, age, background, or views."

The "right to use a library" encompasses all of the resources the library offers, including the right to attend library-initiated programs. Libraries do not deny or abridge access to library resources, including library-initiated programs, based on an individual's economic background and ability to pay.

Adopted January 27, 1982; amended June 26, 1990; July 12, 2000, by the ALA Council.

HISTORY

Library-Initiated Programs
as a Resource

A s libraries have sought in recent years to broaden their appeal and to strengthen their ties with the communities they serve, library-initiated programs such as invited public speeches, film showings, reading clubs, and children's game groups have become an increasingly important and visible part of library service. Such programming, however, also has increasingly become a target for would-be censors. In the 1970s, many communities witnessed efforts to ban controversial speakers from appearing in libraries. Elsewhere, showings of R-rated or allegedly "explicit" films were attacked. In New Rochelle, New York, an Italian-American group objected to a library showing of *The Godfather*, and in North Carolina, a French comedy about a homosexual couple, *La Cage aux Folles*, was successfully banned from a public library.

In the early 1980s, some parents' groups objected to several library-sponsored "theme" programs for children, especially those emphasizing magic or the occult. In a few communities, citizens concerned about the alleged spread of occultism and witchcraft sought to terminate the use of library facilities for organized playing of the popular game "Dungeons and Dragons."

In response to incidents of this sort and a growing number of inquiries from librarians and library users about the applicability of the *Library Bill of Rights* to such programs, in 1981, at the urging of the intellectual freedom committees of the Young Adult Services Division and the Association for Library Service to Children, the IFC, with J. Dennis Day as chair, decided to develop a policy statement. At the 1982 ALA Midwinter Meeting in Denver, the Committee approved the statement and recommended it to the Council, which adopted it on January 27, 1982, as an Interpretation of the *Library Bill of Rights,* entitled "Library-Initiated Programs as a Resource." It read as follows:

> Library-initiated programming is a library resource that provides information, education, and recreation to library users. Library-initiated programming utilizes library staff, books, library and community resources, resource people, displays, and media presentations. The library often incorporates cooperative programming with other agencies, organizations, and educational institutions, as well as other resources, to communicate with library users. Library-initiated programs should provide "for the interest, information, and enlightenment of all the people of the community the library serves," as stated in Article I of the *Library Bill of Rights.*
>
> The American Library Association believes that library-sponsored programs, as well as library resources, "should not be proscribed or removed (or canceled) because of partisan or doctrinal disapproval" (Article II of the *Library Bill of Rights*).
>
> A person's right to attend a library-initiated program should not be denied or abridged because of origin, age, background, or views (Article V of the *Library Bill of Rights*).
>
> A written policy on library-initiated programming, approved by the library's policy-making body, should reflect the library's philosophy regarding free access to information and ideas. Similarly, concerns expressed regarding library-initiated programs should be handled as they are for library resources.
>
> Selection of library program topics, speakers, courses, classes, and resource materials should be made by library staff on the basis of the interests and needs of library users and the community. Library programming should not exclude topics, books, speakers, media, and other resources because they might be controversial.

Review of the Interpretation "Library-Initiated Programs as a Resource" began in January 1989. A draft of a revised document was circulated in the spring of 1990. Comments received on the proposed draft raised questions of fees, access for handicapped and deaf patrons, and the practical problems of abolishing age-based restrictions on program attendance.

As a result of these comments, the Interpretation was expanded to include library programs held on- and off-site, and those produced in cooperation with other groups. Provisions were included to encourage librarians to formulate written policies on programming that conform to the intellectual freedom standards set by the *Library Bill of Rights*.

In addition, librarians were exhorted to consider the multicultural or multilingual composition of their communities in planning library events and not to shrink from addressing controversial topics. A special provision was added to emphasize the librarian's duty to assure equal access to all patrons, explicitly stating that economic background and ability to pay cannot be used to restrict access to library-sponsored events. The new Interpretation was adopted by the Council on June 26, 1990.

As part of the ongoing review of the Interpretations in 1999–2000, the IFC proposed some grammatical corrections. On July 12, 2000, the Council adopted the Interpretation as amended.

2.14
Meeting Rooms

An Interpretation of the
Library Bill of Rights

Many libraries provide meeting rooms for individuals and groups as part of a program of service. Article VI of the *Library Bill of Rights* states that such facilities should be made available to the public served by the given library "on an equitable basis, regardless of the beliefs or affiliations of individuals or groups requesting their use."

Libraries maintaining meeting room facilities should develop and publish policy statements governing use. These statements can properly define time, place, or manner of use; such qualifications should not pertain to the content of a meeting or to the beliefs or affiliations of the sponsors. These statements should be made available in any commonly used language within the community served.

If meeting rooms in libraries supported by public funds are made available to the general public for non-library sponsored events, the library may not exclude any group based on the subject matter to be discussed or based on the ideas that the group advocates. For example, if a library allows charities and sports clubs to discuss their activities in library meeting rooms, then the library should not exclude partisan political or religious groups from discussing their activities in the same facilities. If a library opens its meeting rooms to a wide variety of civic organizations, then the library may not deny access to a religious organization. Libraries may wish to post a permanent notice near the meeting room stating that the library does not advocate or endorse the viewpoints of meetings or meeting room users.

Written policies for meeting room use should be stated in inclusive rather than exclusive terms. For example, a policy that the library's facilities are open "to organizations engaged in educational, cultural, intellectual, or charitable activities" is an inclusive statement of the limited uses to which the facilities may be put. This defined limitation would permit religious groups to use the facilities because they engage in intellectual activities, but would exclude most commercial uses of the facility.

A publicly supported library may limit use of its meeting rooms to strictly "library-related" activities, provided that the limitation is clearly circumscribed and is viewpoint neutral.

Written policies may include limitations on frequency of use, and whether or not meetings held in library meeting rooms must be open to the public. If state and local laws permit private as well as public sessions of meetings in libraries, libraries may choose to offer both options. The same standard should be applicable to all.

If meetings are open to the public, libraries should include in their meeting room policy statement a section which addresses admission fees. If admission fees are permitted, libraries shall seek to make it possible that these fees do not limit access to individuals who may be unable to pay, but who wish to attend the meeting. Article V of the *Library Bill of Rights* states that "a person's right to use a library should not be denied or abridged because of origin, age, background, or views." It is inconsistent with Article V to restrict indirectly access to library meeting rooms based on an individual's or group's ability to pay for that access.

Adopted July 2, 1991, by the ALA Council.

HISTORY

Meeting Rooms

The Interpretation "Meeting Rooms" was developed concurrently with the Interpretation "Exhibit Spaces and Bulletin Boards." See part II, section 2.9, for that history.

"Meeting Rooms" was reviewed as part of the 1999–2000 review of all Interpretations by the IFC. No changes were recommended.

2.15
Restricted Access
to Library Materials

An Interpretation of the
Library Bill of Rights

Libraries are a traditional forum for the open exchange of information. Attempts to restrict access to library materials violate the basic tenets of the *Library Bill of Rights.*

Historically, attempts have been made to limit access by relegating materials into segregated collections. These attempts are in violation of established policy. Such collections are often referred to by a variety of names, including "closed shelf," "locked case," "adults only," "restricted shelf," or "high demand." Access to some materials also may require a monetary fee or financial deposit. More recently, some libraries have applied filtering software to their Internet stations that prevent users from finding targeted categories of information, much of which is constitutionally protected. In any situation which restricts access to certain materials, a barrier is placed between the patron and those materials. That barrier may be age related, linguistic, economic, or psychological in nature.

Because restricted materials often deal with controversial, unusual, or "sensitive" subjects, having to ask a librarian or circulation clerk for access to them may be embarrassing or inhibiting for patrons desiring the materials. Needing to ask for materials may pose a language barrier or a staff service barrier. Because restricted materials often feature information that some library patrons consider "objectionable," the potential user may be predisposed to think of the materials as "objectionable" and, therefore, are reluctant to ask for access to them.

Barriers between the materials and the patron which are psychological, or are affected by language skills, are nonetheless limitations on access to information. Even when a title is listed in the catalog with a reference to its restricted status, a barrier is placed between the patron and the publication. (See also "Statement on Labeling.")

There may be, however, countervailing factors to establish policies to protect library materials—specifically, for reasons of physical preservation including protection from theft or mutilation. Any such policies must be carefully formulated and administered with extreme attention to the principles of intellectual freedom. This caution is also in keeping with ALA policies, such as "Evaluating Library Collections," "Free Access to Libraries for Minors," and the "Preservation Policy."

Finally, in keeping with the "Joint Statement on Access" of the American Library Association and Society of American Archivists, restrictions that result from donor agreements or contracts for special collections materials must be similarly circumscribed. Permanent exclusions are not acceptable. The overriding impetus must be to work for free and unfettered access to all documentary heritage.

Adopted February 2, 1973; amended July 1, 1981; July 3, 1991; July 12, 2000, by the ALA Council.

HISTORY

Restricted Access to Library Materials

O n January 11, 1971, the City Council of San Jose, California, received a formal request from T. J. Owens, president of the San Jose branch of the National Association for the Advancement of Colored People (NAACP), that the book *Epaminondas and His Auntie* be removed from general circulation in the San Jose libraries. Owens charged that the book depicts a black child in a manner that makes him look "completely idiotic and stupid."[1]

Subsequent to a discussion of the book with Owens, Homer L. Fletcher, city librarian, recommended to the city council that *Epaminondas and His Auntie* be retained on open shelf in all the city's libraries and that the option remain for children's librarians to reorder the book should they choose to do so. Fletcher's recommendation was based on his view that any other action would be inconsistent with the *Library Bill of Rights*, which stated that "no library materials should be proscribed or removed from libraries because of partisan or doctrinal disapproval." Despite the recommendation of the city librarian, the San Jose City Council voted to remove the book from general circulation in city libraries, and to put the book on reserve, thereby necessitating that each individual who wished to use it make a special request to the librarian. On March 29, 1971, however, the City Council reconsidered its action and, upon recommendation of the Library Commission, adopted the *Library Bill of Rights* as city policy and removed the restrictions on the book.

An advisory statement concerning restricted circulation of library materials, drafted in response to the problem in San Jose, was approved by the Intellectual Freedom Committee during the 1971 ALA Annual Conference in Dallas. This statement, in slightly amended form, was submitted to the Council at the 1973 Midwinter Meeting in Washington, D.C., and approved as an ALA policy on February 2, 1973:

> Restricting access of certain titles and certain classes of library materials is a practice common to many libraries in the United States. Collections of these materials are referred to by a variety of names such as "closed shelf," "locked case," "adults only," or "restricted shelf" collections.
>
> Three reasons generally advanced to justify restricted access are:
>
> 1. It provides a refuge for materials that belong in the collection but which may be considered "objectionable" by some library patrons.
> 2. It provides a means for controlling distribution of materials which allegedly should not be read by those who are not "prepared" for such materials by experience, education, or age.
> 3. It provides a means to protect certain materials from theft and mutilation.
>
> Though widely used—and often practical—restricted access to library materials is frequently in opposition to the principles of intellectual freedom. While the limitation differs from direct censorship activities, such as removal of library materials or refusal to purchase certain publications, it nonetheless constitutes censorship, albeit in a subtle form. As a form of censorship, restricted access violates the spirit of the *Library Bill of Rights* in the following ways:
>
> 1. It violates that portion of Article II which states that "no library materials should be proscribed . . . because of partisan or doctrinal disapproval."
>
> The word "proscribed," as used in Article II, means "suppressed." Restricted access achieves de facto suppression of certain materials.
>
> Even when a title is listed in the card catalog with a reference to its restricted shelf status, a barrier is placed between the patron and

the publication. Because a majority of materials placed in restricted collections deal with controversial, unusual, or "sensitive" subjects, asking a librarian or circulation clerk for them is an embarrassment for patrons desiring the materials. Because restricted collections are often composed of materials which some library patrons consider "objectionable," the potential user is predisposed to thinking of the materials as "objectionable," and is accordingly inhibited from asking for them. Although the barrier between the materials and the patron is psychological, it is nonetheless a tangible limitation on his access to information.

2. It violates Article V, which states that "the rights of an individual to the use of a library should not be denied or abridged because of his age. . ."

Limiting access of certain materials to adults only abridges the use of the library for minors. "Use of the library" includes use of, and access to, library materials. Such restrictions are generally instituted under the assumption that certain materials are "harmful" to minors, or in an effort to avoid controversy with parents who might think so.

The librarian who would restrict the availability of materials to minors because of actual or suspected parental objection should bear in mind that he is not in loco parentis in his position as librarian. The American Library Association holds that it is the parent—and only the parent—who may restrict his children—and only his children—in reading matter. The parent who would rather his child did not read certain materials or certain kinds of materials should so advise the child.*

When restricted access is implemented to protect materials from theft or mutilation, the use of the practice may be legitimate. However, segregation of materials to protect them must be administered with extreme attention to the rationale for restricting access. Too often only "controversial" materials are the subject of such segregation, leading to the conclusion that factors other than theft and mutilation were the true considerations. The distinction is extremely difficult to make, for both the librarian and the patron.

Selection policies, carefully developed on the basis of principles of intellectual freedom and the *Library Bill of Rights*, should

---

See also "'Free Access to Libraries for Minors," adopted June 30, 1972, by the ALA Council.

not be vitiated by administrative practices such as restricted access.

As part of the overall review of all Interpretations of the *Library Bill of Rights* following that document's revision in 1980, the IFC recommended several relatively minor changes in the policy on restricted access, mainly aimed at removing sex-linked pronoun usage and strengthening the arguments against restricting access for minors. The recommendations were presented to the Council, which adopted the revised policy on July 1, 1981. It read as follows:

Restricting access of certain titles and classes of library materials is a practice common to many libraries in the United States. Collections of these materials are referred to by a variety of names such as "closed shelf," "locked case," "adults only," or "restricted shelf."

Three reasons generally advanced to justify restricted access are:

1. It provides a refuge for materials that belong in the collection but which may be considered "objectionable" by some library patrons;
2. It provides a means for controlling distribution of materials, to those who are allegedly not "prepared" for such materials or who have been labeled less responsible, because of experience, education, or age;
3. It provides a means to protect certain materials from theft and mutilation.

Restricted access to library materials is frequently in opposition to the principles of intellectual freedom. While the limitation differs from direct censorship activities, such as removal of library materials or refusal to purchase certain publications, it nonetheless constitutes censorship, albeit in a subtle form. Restricted access often violates the spirit of the *Library Bill of Rights* in the following ways:

1. It violates that portion of Article II which states that "No library materials should be proscribed . . . because of partisan or doctrinal disapproval."

    "Materials . . . proscribed" as used in Article II includes "suppressed" materials. Restricted access achieves de facto suppression of certain materials.

Even when a title is listed in the catalog with a reference to its restricted status, a barrier is placed between the patron and the publication. Because a majority of materials placed in restricted collections deal with controversial, unusual, or "sensitive" subjects, asking a librarian or circulation clerk for them may be embarrassing for patrons desiring the materials. Because restricted collections are often composed of materials which some library patrons consider "objectionable" the potential user is predisposed to thinking of the materials as "objectionable" and may be reluctant to ask for them. Although the barrier between the materials and the patron is psychological, it is nonetheless a limitation on access to information.

2. It violates Article V, which states that, "A person's right to use a library should not be denied or abridged because of . . . age."

Limiting access of certain materials only to adults abridges the use of the library for minors. Access to library materials is an integral part of the right to use a library. Such restrictions are generally instituted under the assumption that certain materials are "harmful" to minors, or in an effort to avoid controversy with adults who might think so.

Libraries and library boards who would restrict the availability of materials to minors because of actual or anticipated parental objection should bear in mind that they do not serve in loco parentis. The American Library Association holds that it is parents—and only parents—who may restrict their children—and only their children—from access to library materials and services. Parents who would rather their children not have access to certain materials should so advise their children.

When restricted access is implemented solely to protect materials from theft or mutilation, the practice may be legitimate. However, segregation of materials to protect them must be administered with extreme attention to the reason for restricting access. Too often only "controversial" materials are the subject of such segregation, indicating that factors other than theft and mutilation—including content—were the true considerations. When loss rates of items popular with young people are high, this cannot justify the labeling of all minors as irresponsible and the adoption of prejudiced restrictions on the right of minors to use library services and materials.

Selection policies, carefully developed to include principles of intellectual freedom and the *Library Bill of Rights*, should not be vitiated by administrative practices such as restricted access.

Note: See also "Free Access to Libraries for Minors," adopted June 30, 1972; amended July 1, 1981, by ALA Council.

In 1990, "Restricted Access to Library Materials" was substantially revised. Barriers between materials and patrons which were deemed psychological, linguistic, or related to other patron characteristics were addressed. New language relating to preservation of library materials was added that also referenced related Interpretations of the *Library Bill of Rights*, including "Evaluating Library Collections" and "Free Access to Libraries for Minors," as well as the ALA's "Preservation Policy." Also added was an explanation of how the *Library Bill of Rights* applies to restrictions resulting from agreements made with donors of materials or contracts for special collections materials. The new version of "Restricted Access to Library Materials" was adopted by the Council on July 3, 1991.

As part of the ongoing review of the Interpretations in 1999–2000, the IFC proposed some grammatical corrections and the addition of the following sentence: "More recently, some libraries have applied filtering software to their Internet stations that prevent users from finding targeted categories of information, much of which is constitutionally protected." On July 12, 2000, the Council adopted the amended Interpretation.

NOTE

1. *San Jose News*, March 2, 1971.

2.16
Statement on Labeling

An Interpretation of the
Library Bill of Rights

Labeling is the practice of describing or designating materials by affixing a prejudicial label and/or segregating them by a prejudicial system. The American Library Association opposes these means of predisposing people's attitudes toward library materials for the following reasons:

1. Labeling is an attempt to prejudice attitudes and as such, it is a censor's tool.
2. Some find it easy and even proper, according to their ethics, to establish criteria for judging publications as objectionable. However, injustice and ignorance rather than justice and enlightenment result from such practices, and the American Library Association opposes the establishment of such criteria.
3. Libraries do not advocate the ideas found in their collections. The presence of books and other resources in a library does not indicate endorsement of their contents by the library.

A variety of private organizations promulgate rating systems and/or review materials as a means of advising either their members or the general public concerning their opinions of the contents and suitability or appropriate age for use of certain books, films, recordings, or other materials. For the library to adopt or enforce any of these private systems, to attach such ratings to library materials, to include them in bibliographic records, library catalogs, or other finding aids, or otherwise to endorse them would violate the *Library Bill of Rights.*

While some attempts have been made to adopt these systems into law, the constitutionality of such measures is extremely questionable. If such legislation is passed which applies within a library's jurisdiction, the library should seek competent legal advice concerning its applicability to library operations.

Publishers, industry groups, and distributors sometimes add ratings to material or include them as part of their packaging. Librarians should not endorse such practices. However, removing or obliterating such ratings—if placed there by or with permission of the copyright holder—could constitute expurgation, which is also unacceptable.

The American Library Association opposes efforts which aim at closing any path to knowledge. This statement, however, does not exclude the adoption of organizational schemes designed as directional aids or to facilitate access to materials.

Adopted July 13, 1951. Amended June 25, 1971; July 1, 1981; June 26, 1990, by the ALA Council.

HISTORY

Statement on Labeling

In late 1950, the Intellectual Freedom Committee received a report that the Montclair, New Jersey, chapter of the Sons of the American Revolution (SAR) was exerting pressure on New Jersey libraries to put a prominent label or inscription on "publications which advocate or favor communism, or which are issued or distributed by any communist organization or any other organization formally designated by any authorized government official or agency as communistic or subversive." The SAR said further that such publications "should not be freely available in libraries to readers or in schools to pupils, but should be obtainable only by signing suitable applications."[1]

Rutherford D. Rogers, at the time chair of the IFC, reported the matter to the ALA Council on July 13, 1951, and said groups other than the SAR have tried to use such labeling as a means of limiting the freedom to read. He cited religious groups that sometimes asked libraries to label publications "objectionable," and he mentioned that other "patriotic" organizations were moving toward similar proposals. Rogers also reported that in April 1951 the Association received a letter from the Montclair chapter of the SAR requesting the ALA to adopt a policy advocating that communistic and subversive materials not only be labeled but also be segregated from other materials in the library collection and given out only upon written and signed application.

The Intellectual Freedom Committee believed that such practices violated the principles of intellectual freedom and that the labeling of books according to points of view should not be undertaken by any library. The Committee also noted that it was not clear who would do such labeling, who would decide what is communistic or subversive, or by what criteria such decisions would be made. In addition, the process was envisioned as expensive and time consuming, involving examination of all materials in a library collection. The impracticality and financial problems of such a project, however, were not deemed relevant to the Association's policy concerning the practice. As Rogers pointed out, policy was to be based on the principle involved.

The IFC's study of the SAR proposal resulted in a six-point statement. Before presenting the statement to the Council for adoption as an ALA policy, the Committee conducted an informal survey of 24 libraries around the country. Twenty responded, all agreeing that labeling violated basic principles of intellectual freedom and should not be practiced by libraries. The IFC's six-point "Statement on Labeling" was approved by the Council as an ALA policy on July 13, 1951:

> 1. Although totalitarian states find it easy and even proper, according to their ethics, to establish criteria for judging publications as "subversive," injustice and ignorance rather than justice and enlightenment result from such practices, and the American Library Association has a responsibility to take a stand against the establishment of such criteria in a democratic state.
>
> 2. Libraries do not advocate the ideas found in their collections. The presence of a magazine or book in a library does not indicate an endorsement of its contents by the library.
>
> 3. No one person should take the responsibility of labeling publications. No sizeable group of persons would be likely to agree on the types of materials which should be labeled or the sources of information which should be regarded with suspicion. As a practical consideration, a librarian who labeled a book or magazine procommunist might be sued for libel.
>
> 4. Labeling is an attempt to prejudice the reader, and as such, it is a censor's tool.
>
> 5. Labeling violates the spirit of the *Library Bill of Rights.*
>
> 6. Although we are all agreed that communism is a threat to the free world, if materials are labeled to pacify one group, there

is no excuse for refusing to label any item in the library's collection. Because communism, fascism, or other authoritarianisms tend to suppress ideas and attempt to coerce individuals to conform to a specific ideology, American librarians must be opposed to such "isms." We are, then, anticommunist, but we are also opposed to any other group which aims at closing any path to knowledge.

The 1951 "Statement on Labeling" was adopted as policy by many libraries and, over the years, was a useful tool in combating this brand of censorship. One incident involving an attempt to label library materials occurred at the St. Charles County Library, St. Charles, Missouri, in 1968 and concluded with a unique twist. The case began when Nina S. Ladof, the librarian, was presented with a petition requesting the removal of *Ramparts* magazine. The library dismissed the petition, explaining that *Ramparts* was purchased in accordance with the library's book selection policy, which included the *Library Bill of Rights* and "The Freedom to Read."

After the initial attempt to remove *Ramparts*, several months passed. Eventually, though, the original complainant presented the librarian with a sheaf of petitions from the Veterans of Foreign Wars, the American Legion, the Lions Club, and a church. With variations, the petitions read as follows:

> We, the undersigned, do hereby petition the Library Board of the County of St. Charles, requesting that any book or publication on file in the St. Charles County Library System authored, published, or edited by any individual or group of individuals having been cited by any official Federal or State UnAmerican Activities Committee or Fact-Finding Committee as subversive or unAmerican in nature or belonging to any organization having been cited as subversive or unAmerican, be so explicitly labeled in a conspicuous manner for the information of the patrons of the St. Charles County Libraries.

Ladof pointed out that Dr. Benjamin Spock, author of *The Common Sense of Baby Care,* was sentenced on charges of aiding young men to avoid military service. Would this book require a label? Pursuing this example further, Ladof wrote to Spock's publishers to ask what action they would take if she did, in fact, affix a label to his works. Two replied that they would consider it possible grounds for legal action against the library. Dr. Spock's own attorney concurred.

Both the American Civil Liberties Union and the Freedom of Information Center at the University of Missouri provided Nina Ladof with the legal opinion that labeling a work, as requested in the petition, would be grounds for a libel action by the author whose works were involved because of the injury to the sale of his works that might result. Even if the label were factual, such as "so-and-so was a member of the Communist Party in 1941," he would have grounds to prove such injury. In fact, injury need not actually occur; it need only be a possibility for a court to award substantial damages to a plaintiff in such a case. And, since library boards of trustees cannot be sued as a body, each member would be liable for the damages awarded.

Armed with this information, and with the board's unanimous belief that labels are forms of censorship—and, as such, are completely opposed to basic library policies—the library issued a firm statement rejecting the proposed labeling. The statement included information from legal sources and paraphrased and expanded the six points of the ALA "Statement on Labeling." All persons interested in the matter were sent copies with an explanatory letter. *Ramparts* and other literature written by so-called subversives continued to circulate unlabeled.

The 1951 "Statement on Labeling" stood without revision until 1971. At that time, study of the policy confirmed that some sections were framed in language that reflected the Association's response to a specific threat—the labeling as "subversive" or "communist" of specific materials. The Intellectual Freedom Committee concluded that, although these sections once met a particular need, they limited the document's usefulness.

To make the "Statement on Labeling" applicable to a broader range of labeling problems, even encompassing "harmful matter," the Intellectual Freedom Committee recommended a revised version to the Council. The 1971 revision was designated an Interpretation of the *Library Bill of Rights* to emphasize the relationship between Articles I, II, and III of that document and the "Statement on Labeling." The revision was adopted by the Council on June 25, 1971:

Because labeling violates the spirit of the *Library Bill of Rights*, the American Library Association opposes the technique of labeling as a means of predisposing readers against library materials for the following reasons:

1. Labeling* is an attempt to prejudice the reader, and as such it is a censor's tool.

2. Although some find it easy and even proper, according to their ethics, to establish criteria for judging publications as objectionable, injustice and ignorance rather than justice and enlightenment result from such practices, and the American Library Association must oppose the establishment of such criteria.

3. Libraries do not advocate the ideas found in their collections. The presence of a magazine or book in a library does not indicate an endorsement of its contents by the library.

4. No one person should take the responsibility of labeling publications. No sizeable group of persons would be likely to agree either on the types of material which should be labeled or the sources of information which should be regarded with suspicion. As a practical consideration, a librarian who labels a book or magazine might be sued for libel.

5. If materials are labeled to pacify one group, there is no excuse for refusing to label any item in the library's collection. Because authoritarians tend to suppress ideas and attempt to coerce individuals to conform to a specific ideology, the American Library Association opposes such efforts which aim at closing any path to knowledge.

Following the 1980 revision of the *Library Bill of Rights,* the IFC again reviewed the statement, recommending three major changes. First, the Committee noted that relegating definition of the labeling practice to a footnote detracted from the policy's unity and effectiveness and suggested incorporating the definition in the opening paragraph. Second, the Committee recommended that points 4 and 5

---

*"Labeling," as it is referred to in the "Statement on Labeling," is the practice of describing or designating certain library materials, by affixing a prejudicial label to them or segregating them by a prejudicial system, so as to predispose readers against the materials.

be dropped, because these were not considerations of principle but, rather, "practical" objections to labeling.

Although librarians should certainly be aware that the labeling of library materials could provoke legal action, and although it is certainly true that adoption of labels at the instigation of one group might open a veritable Pandora's box of labeling demands by others, neither of these considerations lies at the basis of the Association's opposition to labeling. The American Library Association opposes labeling of library materials not because this is impractical or legally dangerous but because this practice flagrantly violates both the spirit and the letter of the *Library Bill of Rights* and stands in fundamental opposition to the most basic principles of intellectual freedom.

In addition, the Committee recommended adding a sentence to the statement indicating that the Association's objections to labeling should not be construed as opposition to legitimate organizational schemes designed to facilitate access. The second revision of the "Statement on Labeling" was adopted by the Council on July 1, 1981. It read as follows:

> Labeling is the practice of describing or designating certain library materials by affixing a prejudicial label to them or segregating them by a prejudicial system. The American Library Association opposes this as a means of predisposing people's attitudes towards library materials for the following reasons:
>
> 1. Labeling is an attempt to prejudice attitudes and as such, it is a censor's tool.
>
> 2. Some find it easy and even proper, according to their ethics, to establish criteria for judging publications as objectionable. However, injustice and ignorance rather than justice and enlightenment result from such practices, and the American Library Association opposes the establishment of such criteria.
>
> 3. Libraries do not advocate the ideas found in their collections. The presence of books and other resources in a library does not indicate endorsement of their contents by the library.
>
> The American Library Association opposes efforts which aim at closing any path to knowledge. This statement does not, however, exclude the adoption of organizational schemes designed as directional aids or to facilitate access to materials.

In keeping with the review of *Library Bill of Rights* Interpretations, undertaken in response to the 1988 Minority Concerns Committee resolution, the "Statement on Labeling" was the first to be revised by the Intellectual Freedom Committee at the 1989 ALA Annual Conference. The importance of this policy increased significantly in light of attempts, in 1990, to pass legislation in Congress requiring warning labels for musical recordings with allegedly obscene lyrics or lyrics deemed offensive or unsuitable for minors.

Policy revisions made clear the ALA's opposition to labeling, and emphasized librarians' responsibility to prevent the imposition of private or voluntary labeling schemes on library materials, while leaving permanently affixed labels intact to avoid expurgation of copyrighted material. The new Interpretation also encourages librarians to become familiar with local laws and regulations on the issue.

Following adoption by the IFC in June 1989, the revised "Statement on Labeling" was circulated to other ALA units. At the 1990 Midwinter Meeting, the revision was reconsidered in light of comments received from the other units. The final version of this Interpretation was accepted by the Committee and then adopted by the Council on June 26, 1990.

In 1999–2000, as part of its ongoing practice of periodic review of all Interpretations, the IFC reviewed the "Statement on Labeling." No changes were recommended.

NOTE

1. *ALA Bulletin* 45:241 (July–August 1951).

2.17

The Universal Right
to Free Expression

An Interpretation of the
Library Bill of Rights

Freedom of expression is an inalienable human right and the foundation for self-government. Freedom of expression encompasses the freedoms of speech, press, religion, assembly, and association, and the corollary right to receive information.

The American Library Association endorses this principle, which is also set forth in the Universal Declaration of Human Rights, adopted by the United Nations General Assembly. The Preamble of this document states that ". . . recognition of the inherent dignity and of the equal and inalienable rights of all members of the human family is the foundation of freedom, justice, and peace in the world. . ." and ". . . the advent of a world in which human beings shall enjoy freedom of speech and belief and freedom from fear and want has been proclaimed as the highest aspiration of the common people. . . ."

Article 18 of this document states:

> Everyone has the right to freedom of thought, conscience, and religion; this right includes freedom to change his religion or belief, and freedom, either alone or in community with others and in public or private, to manifest his religion or belief in teaching, practice, worship, and observance.

Article 19 states:

> Everyone has the right to freedom of opinion and expression; this right includes freedom to hold opinions without interference and to seek, receive and impart information and ideas through any media regardless of frontiers.

Article 20 states:

> 1. Everyone has the right to freedom of peaceful assembly and association.
> 2. No one may be compelled to belong to an association.

We affirm our belief that these are inalienable rights of every person, regardless of origin, age, background, or views. We embody our professional commitment to these principles in the *Library Bill of Rights* and "Code of Ethics," as adopted by the American Library Association.

We maintain that these are universal principles and should be applied by libraries and librarians throughout the world. The American Library Association's policy on International Relations reflects these objectives: ". . . to encourage the exchange, dissemination, and access to information and the unrestricted flow of library materials in all formats throughout the world."

We know that censorship, ignorance, and limitations on the free flow of information are the tools of tyranny and oppression. We believe that ideas and information topple the walls of hate and fear and build bridges of cooperation and understanding far more effectively than weapons and armies.

The American Library Association is unswerving in its commitment to human rights and intellectual freedom; the two are inseparably linked and inextricably entwined. Freedom of opinion and expression is not derived from or dependent on any form of government or political power. This right is inherent in every individual. It cannot be surrendered, nor can it be denied. True justice comes from the exercise of this right.

We recognize the power of information and ideas to inspire justice, to restore freedom and dignity to the oppressed, and to change the hearts and minds of the oppressors.

Courageous men and women, in difficult and dangerous circumstances throughout human history, have demonstrated that freedom lives in the human heart and cries out for justice even in the face of threats, enslavement, imprisonment, torture, exile, and death. We draw inspiration from their example. They challenge us to remain steadfast in our most basic professional responsibility to promote and defend the right of free expression.

There is no good censorship. Any effort to restrict free expression and the free flow of information aids the oppressor. Fighting oppression with censorship is self-defeating.

Threats to the freedom of expression of any person anywhere are threats to the freedom of all people everywhere. Violations of human rights and the right of free expression have been recorded in virtually every country and society across the globe.

In response to these violations, we affirm these principles:

> The American Library Association opposes any use of governmental prerogative that leads to the intimidation of individuals which prevents them from exercising their rights to hold opinions without interference, and to seek, receive, and impart information and ideas. We urge libraries and librarians everywhere to resist such abuse of governmental power, and to support those against whom such governmental power has been employed.

> The American Library Association condemns any governmental effort to involve libraries and librarians in restrictions on the right of any individual to hold opinions without interference, and to seek, receive, and impart information and ideas. Such restrictions pervert the function of the library and violate the professional responsibilities of librarians.

> The American Library Association rejects censorship in any form. Any action which denies the inalienable human rights of individuals only damages the will to resist oppression, strengthens the hand of the oppressor, and undermines the cause of justice.

> The American Library Association will not abrogate these principles. We believe that censorship corrupts the cause of justice, and contributes to the demise of freedom.

Adopted by the ALA Council, January 16, 1991.

HISTORY

The Universal Right to Free Expression

Out of a long and emotional debate about support for sanctions—including books and informational materials—against South Africa, a new Interpretation of the *Library Bill of Rights* was created. Modeled after Article 19 of the United Nations Universal Declaration of Human Rights, the "Universal Right to Free Expression" advocates the free flow of information within all countries across national boundaries.

In 1989, the ALA was asked to support the Association of American Publishers (AAP) in its efforts to end the book boycott against South Africa. The ALA Council asked the Intellectual Freedom Committee for its recommendation. Concurrently, the Social Responsibilities Round Table had proposed a set of guidelines for librarians interacting with South Africa that were opposed by the IFC. The debate within the ALA over South African policy was emotional, vigorous, and sometimes vituperative. It became clear that no extant ALA policy provided an adequate framework from which to respond fully to the complicated questions about international intellectual freedom and human rights raised during the course of the debate.

In 1990, the IFC began work on an international free flow of information policy to address this glaring need. The new policy was to provide a secure foundation from which to respond to the AAP's request and from which to address other international intellectual freedom issues. The drafters used Articles 18, 19, and 20 of the Universal Declaration of Human Rights as models for the new policy.

In January 1991, the IFC considered comments on the "Free Flow of Information" draft. The title of the Interpretation was changed to "The Universal Right to Free Expression," and the IFC voted to seek endorsements of other units of the ALA and to present the Interpretation to the Council.

On January 16, 1991, the Council voted to adopt the policy as the most recent addition to the *Library Bill of Rights* and its Interpretations.

"The Universal Right to Free Expression" was reviewed in 1999–2000 by the IFC as part of its ongoing periodic review of all Interpretations. No changes were recommended.

PART III

Protecting the Freedom to Read

1

The Freedom to Read
Policy Statement

The freedom to read is essential to our democracy. It is continuously under attack. Private groups and public authorities in various parts of the country are working to remove or limit access to reading materials, to censor content in schools, to label "controversial" views, to distribute lists of "objectionable" books or authors, and to purge libraries. These actions apparently rise from a view that our national tradition of free expression is no longer valid; that censorship and suppression are needed to avoid the subversion of politics and the corruption of morals. We, as citizens devoted to reading and as librarians and publishers responsible for disseminating ideas, wish to assert the public interest in the preservation of the freedom to read.

Most attempts at suppression rest on a denial of the fundamental premise of democracy: that the ordinary citizen, by exercising critical judgment, will accept the good and reject the bad. The censors, public and private, assume that they should determine what is good and what is bad for their fellow citizens.

We trust Americans to recognize propaganda and misinformation, and to make their own decisions about what they read and believe. We do not believe they need the help of censors to assist them in this task. We do not believe they are prepared to sacrifice their heritage of a free press in order to be "protected" against what others think may be bad for them. We believe they still favor free enterprise in ideas and expression.

These efforts at suppression are related to a larger pattern of pressures being brought against education, the press, art and images, films, broadcast media, and the Internet. The problem is not only one of actual censorship. The shadow of fear cast by these pressures leads, we suspect, to an even larger voluntary curtailment of expression by those who seek to avoid controversy.

Such pressure toward conformity is perhaps natural to a time of accelerated change. And yet suppression is never more dangerous than in such a time of social tension. Freedom has given the United States the elasticity to endure strain. Freedom keeps open the path of novel and creative solutions, and enables change to come by choice. Every silencing of a heresy, every enforcement of an orthodoxy, diminishes the toughness and resilience of our society and leaves it the less able to deal with controversy and difference.

Now as always in our history, reading is among our greatest freedoms. The freedom to read and write is almost the only means for making generally available ideas or manners of expression that can initially command only a small audience. The written word is the natural medium for the new idea and the untried voice from which come the original contributions to social growth. It is essential to the extended discussion that serious thought requires, and to the accumulation of knowledge and ideas into organized collections.

We believe that free communication is essential to the preservation of a free society and a creative culture. We believe that these pressures toward conformity present the danger of limiting the range and variety of inquiry and expression on which our democracy and our culture depend. We believe that every American community must jealously guard the freedom to publish and to circulate, in order to preserve its own freedom to read. We believe that publishers and librarians have a profound responsibility to give validity to that freedom to read by making it possible for the readers to choose freely from a variety of offerings. The freedom to read is guaranteed by the Constitution. Those with faith in free people will stand firm on these constitutional guarantees of essential rights and will exercise the responsibilities that accompany these rights.

We therefore affirm these propositions:

1. *It is in the public interest for publishers and librarians to make available the widest diversity of views and expressions, including those that are unorthodox or unpopular with the majority.*

   Creative thought is by definition new, and what is new is different. The bearer of every new thought is a rebel until that idea is refined and tested. Totalitarian systems attempt to maintain themselves in power by the ruthless suppression of any concept that challenges the established orthodoxy. The power of a democratic system to adapt to change is vastly strengthened by the freedom of its citizens to choose widely from among conflicting opinions offered freely to them. To stifle every nonconformist idea at birth would mark the end of the democratic process. Furthermore, only through the constant activity of weighing and selecting can the democratic mind attain the strength demanded by times like these. We need to know not only what we believe but why we believe it.

2. *Publishers, librarians, and booksellers do not need to endorse every idea or presentation they make available. It would conflict with the public interest for them to establish their own political, moral, or aesthetic views as a standard for determining what should be published or circulated.*

   Publishers and librarians serve the educational process by helping to make available knowledge and ideas required for the growth of the mind and the increase of learning. They do not foster education by imposing as mentors the patterns of their own thought. The people should have the freedom to read and consider a broader range of ideas than those that may be held by any single librarian or publisher or government or church. It is wrong that what one can read should be confined to what another thinks proper.

3. *It is contrary to the public interest for publishers or librarians to bar access to writings on the basis of the personal history or political affiliations of the author.*

   No art or literature can flourish if it is to be measured by the political views or private lives of its creators. No society of free people can flourish that draws up lists of writers to whom it will not listen, whatever they may have to say.

4. *There is no place in our society for efforts to coerce the taste of others, to confine adults to the reading matter deemed suitable for adolescents, or to inhibit the efforts of writers to achieve artistic expres*sion.

To some, much of modern expression is shocking. But is not much of life itself shocking? We cut off literature at the source if we prevent writers from dealing with the stuff of life. Parents and teachers have a responsibility to prepare the young to meet the diversity of experiences in life to which they will be exposed, as they have a responsibility to help them learn to think critically for themselves. These are affirmative responsibilities, not to be discharged simply by preventing them from reading works for which they are not yet prepared. In these matters values differ, and values cannot be legislated; nor can machinery be devised that will suit the demands of one group without limiting the freedom of others.

5. *It is not in the public interest to force a reader to accept with any expression the prejudgment of a label characterizing it or its author as subversive or dangerous.*

The ideal of labeling presupposes the existence of individuals or groups with wisdom to determine by authority what is good or bad for the citizen. It presupposes that individuals must be directed in making up their minds about the ideas they examine. But Americans do not need others to do their thinking for them.

6. *It is the responsibility of publishers and librarians, as guardians of the people's freedom to read, to contest encroachments upon that freedom by individuals or groups seeking to impose their own standards or tastes upon the community at large.*

It is inevitable in the give and take of the democratic process that the political, the moral, or the aesthetic concepts of an individual or group will occasionally collide with those of another individual or group. In a free society individuals are free to determine for themselves what they wish to read, and each group is free to determine what it will recommend to its freely associated members. But no group has the right to take the law into its own hands, and to impose its own concept of politics or morality upon other members of a democratic society. Freedom is no freedom if it is accorded only to the accepted and the inoffensive.

7. *It is the responsibility of publishers and librarians to give full meaning to the freedom to read by providing books that enrich the quality and diversity of thought and expression. By the exercise of this affirmative responsibility, they can demonstrate that the answer to a "bad" book is a good one, the answer to a "bad" idea is a good one.*

The freedom to read is of little consequence when the reader cannot obtain matter fit for that reader's purpose. What is needed is not only the absence of restraint, but the positive provision of opportunity for the people to read the best that has been thought and said. Books are the major channel by which the intellectual inheritance is handed down, and the principal means of its testing and growth. The defense of the freedom to read requires of all publishers and librarians the utmost of their faculties, and deserves of all citizens the fullest of their support.

We state these propositions neither lightly nor as easy generalizations. We here stake out a lofty claim for the value of the written word. We do so because we believe that it is possessed of enormous variety and usefulness, worthy of cherishing and keeping free. We realize that the application of these propositions may mean the dissemination of ideas and manners of expression that are repugnant to many persons. We do not state these propositions in the comfortable belief that what people read is unimportant. We believe rather that what people read is deeply important; that ideas can be dangerous; but that the suppression of ideas is fatal to a democratic society. Freedom itself is a dangerous way of life, but it is ours.

This statement was originally issued in May of 1953 by the Westchester Conference of the American Library Association and the American Book Publishers Council, which in 1970 consolidated with the American

Educational Publishers Institute to become the Association of American Publishers.

Adopted June 25, 1953; revised January 28, 1972; January 16, 1991; July 12, 2000, by the ALA Council and the AAP Freedom to Read Committee.

A Joint Statement by:

American Library Association
Association of American Publishers

Subsequently Endorsed by:

American Association of University Professors
American Booksellers Foundation for Free Expression
American Society of Journalists and Authors
American Society of Newspaper Editors
Anti-Defamation League of B'nai B'rith
Association of American University Presses
Center for Democracy & Technology
The Children's Book Council
The Electronic Frontier Foundation
Feminists for Free Expression
Freedom to Read Foundation
International Reading Association
The Media Institute
National Coalition Against Censorship
National PTA
Parents, Families and Friends of Lesbians and Gays
People for the American Way
Student Press Law Center
The Thomas Jefferson Center for the Protection of Free Expression

HISTORY

The Freedom to Read

" **T**he Freedom to Read," best known of the American Library Association's documents supporting the principles of intellectual freedom as embodied in the *Library Bill of Rights,* had its beginnings during the Intellectual Freedom Committee's 1953 Midwinter Meeting in Chicago.[1] At that meeting, Chair William S. Dix suggested the committee "discuss the current wave of censorship and attacks on books and libraries" and "help clarify the stand which libraries might take and point to ways in which our own position might be strengthened in the minds of the public." The Committee directed Dix to consider a small, off-the-record conference with in-depth discussion of the matter.

Dix's efforts resulted in a conference on the freedom to read, sponsored jointly by the American Library Association and the American Book Publishers Council, held at the Westchester Country Club, in Rye, New York, on May 2–3, 1953. The object of the meeting was to bring together nationally known figures representing librarians, publishers, and the public interest. Spokesmen for the public interest, viewed as vitally important to the success of the conference, included representatives of business, foundations, law, and education. Luther Evans, former Librarian of Congress—and head of the United Nations Educational, Scientific and Cultural Organization—served as chair of the conference.

In their invitation to potential participants, the joint sponsors said:

Recent months have seen the emergence in our country of a pattern of pressures whose effect must be to limit the range and variety of expression. This pattern has affected in one way or another all the media of communications and indeed the entire area of free inquiry. Books are the last of the communications media to be affected by these pressures toward conformity. They remain preeminently the medium for the free expression of facts, ideas, and human experience in all its varieties. Librarians and publishers feel a deep responsibility for doing their part to see that this continues to be so, and they share with thoughtful men in every profession a conviction that freedom of communication is indispensable to a creative culture and a free society.

The objectives of the conference were the following:

1. To define the rights and responsibilities of publishers and librarians in maintaining the freedom of Americans to read what they choose;
2. To assay recent developments tending to restrict this freedom;
3. To consider where lines should be drawn between permissible expression and impermissible expression, and who is to draw the lines; and
4. To ascertain the public interest in this area and, if the group agrees, consider ways of asserting it.

Debate at the conference focused on the specific problem areas of obscenity and pornography and disloyalty and subversive materials. The participants considered a number of questions: What is the function of publishers and librarians in circulating ideas? Should they be responsible guides or simply caterers to public taste? Do they have a special responsibility to make available nonconforming expression and unpopular views? Do citizens have a right to read everything not expressly prohibited by law? Should a book be judged only by its content, and the political and personal background of the author ignored? Is the role of the public library entirely neutral? Can books be subversive?

The conference resulted in substantial agreement on principles. A Continuations Committee was appointed to draft a statement based on the proceedings and to consider action and research projects designed to publicize and explore further the matters discussed. The Continuations Committee consisted of Arthur A. Houghton Jr., president of Steuben Glass; Harold D. Lasswell, professor of law and political science at Yale Law School; Bernard Berelson, director of the Behavioral Sciences Division at the Ford Foundation; William S. Dix, librarian at Princeton University; and Dan Lacy, managing director of the American Book Publishers Council.

By the end of May, the Continuations Committee, with the assistance of other individuals, produced a final version of "The Freedom to Read" for the approval of the Westchester Conference participants. On June 18, 1953, the following statement was endorsed by the Board of Directors of the American Book Publishers Council and on June 25, 1953, by the Council of the American Library Association:

> The freedom to read is essential to our democracy. It is under attack. Private groups and public authorities in various parts of the country are working to remove books from sale, to censor textbooks, to label "controversial" books, to distribute lists of "objectionable" books or authors, and to purge libraries. These actions apparently rise from a view that our national tradition of free expression is no longer valid; that censorship and suppression are needed to avoid the subversion of politics and the corruption of morals. We, as citizens devoted to the use of books and as librarians and publishers responsible for disseminating them, wish to assert the public interest in the preservation of the freedom to read.
>
> We are deeply concerned about these attempts at suppression. Most such attempts rest on a denial of the fundamental premise of democracy: that the ordinary citizen, by exercising his critical judgment, will accept the good and reject the bad. The censors, public and private, assume that they should determine what is good and what is bad for their fellow-citizens.
>
> We trust Americans to recognize propaganda, and to reject obscenity. We do not believe they need the help of censors to assist them in this task. We do not believe they are prepared to sacrifice their heritage of a free press in order to be "protected" against what others think may be bad for them. We believe they still favor free enterprise in ideas and expression.

We are aware, of course, that books are not alone in being subjected to efforts at suppression. We are aware that these efforts are related to a larger pattern of pressures being brought against education, the press, films, radio, and television. The problem is not only one of actual censorship. The shadow of fear cast by these pressures leads, we suspect, to an even larger voluntary curtailment of expression by those who seek to avoid controversy.

Such pressure toward conformity is perhaps natural to a time of uneasy change and pervading fear. Especially when so many of our apprehensions are directed against an ideology, the expression of a dissident idea becomes a thing feared in itself, and we tend to move against it as against a hostile deed, with suppression.

And yet suppression is never more dangerous than in such a time of social tension. Freedom has given the United States the elasticity to endure strain. Freedom keeps open the path of novel and creative solutions, and enables change to come by choice. Every silencing of a heresy, every enforcement of an orthodoxy, diminishes the toughness and resilience of our society and leaves it the less able to deal with stress.

Now as always in our history, books are among our greatest instruments of freedom. They are almost the only means for making generally available ideas or manners of expression that can initially command only a small audience. They are the natural medium for the new idea and the untried voice from which come the original contributions to social growth. They are essential to the extended discussion which serious thought requires and to the accumulation of knowledge and ideas into organized collections.

We believe that free communication is essential to the preservation of a free society and a creative culture. We believe that these pressures towards conformity present the danger of limiting the range and variety of inquiry and expression on which our democracy and our culture depend. We believe that every American community must jealously guard the freedom to publish and to circulate, in order to preserve its own freedom to read. We believe that publishers and librarians have a profound responsibility to give validity to that freedom to read by making it possible for the reader to choose freely from a variety of offerings.

The freedom to read is guaranteed by the Constitution. Those with faith in free men will stand firm on these constitutional guarantees of essential rights and will exercise the responsibilities that accompany these rights.

We therefore affirm these propositions:

1. *It is in the public interest for publishers and librarians to make available the widest diversity of views and expressions, including those which are unorthodox or unpopular with the majority.*

   Creative thought is by definition new, and what is new is different. The bearer of every new thought is a rebel until that idea is refined and tested. Totalitarian systems attempt to maintain themselves in power by the ruthless suppression of any concept which challenges the established orthodoxy. The power of a democratic system to adapt to change is vastly strengthened by the freedom of its citizens to choose widely from among conflicting opinions offered freely to them. To stifle every nonconformist idea at birth would mark the end of the democratic process. Furthermore, only through the constant activity of weighing and selecting can the democratic mind attain the strength demanded by times like these. We need to know not only what we believe but why we believe it.

2. *Publishers and librarians do not need to endorse every idea or presentation contained in the books they make available. It would conflict with the public interest for them to establish their own political, moral, or aesthetic views as the sole standard for determining what books should be published or circulated.*

   Publishers and librarians serve the educational process by helping to make available knowledge and ideas required for the growth of the mind and the increase of learning. They do not foster education by imposing as mentors the patterns of their own thought. The people should have the freedom to read and consider a broader range of ideas than those that may be held by any single librarian or publisher or government or church. It is wrong that what one man can read should be confined to what another thinks proper.

3. *It is contrary to the public interest for publishers or librarians to determine the acceptability of a book solely on the basis of the personal history or political affiliations of the author.*

A book should be judged as a book. No art or literature can flourish if it is to be measured by the political views or private lives of its creators. No society of free men can flourish which draws up lists of writers to whom it will not listen, whatever they may have to say.

4. *The present laws dealing with obscenity should be vigorously enforced. Beyond that, there is no place in our society for extralegal efforts to coerce the taste of others, to confine adults to the reading matter deemed suitable for adolescents, or to inhibit the efforts of writers to achieve artistic expression.*

To some, much of modern literature is shocking. But is not much of life itself shocking? We cut off literature at the source if we prevent serious artists from dealing with the stuff of life. Parents and teachers have a responsibility to prepare the young to meet the diversity of experiences in life to which they will be exposed, as they have a responsibility to help them learn to think critically for themselves. These are affirmative responsibilities, not to be discharged simply by preventing them from reading works for which they are not yet prepared. In these matters taste differs, and taste cannot be legislated; nor can machinery be devised which will suit the demands of one group without limiting the freedom of others. We deplore the catering to the immature, the retarded, or the maladjusted taste. But those concerned with freedom have the responsibility of seeing to it that each individual book or publication, whatever its contents, price or method of distribution, is dealt with in accordance with due process of law.

5. *It is not in the public interest to force a reader to accept with any book the prejudgment of a label characterizing the book or author as subversive or dangerous.*

The idea of labeling presupposes the existence of individuals or groups with wisdom to determine by authority what is good or bad for the citizen. It presupposes that each individual must be directed in making up his mind about the ideas he examines. But Americans do not need others to do their thinking for them.

6. *It is the responsibility of publishers and librarians, as guardians of the people's freedom to read, to contest encroachments upon that freedom by individuals or groups seeking to impose their own standards or tastes upon the community at large.*

It is inevitable in the give and take of the democratic process that the political, the moral, or the aesthetic concepts of an individual or group will occasionally collide with those of another individual or group. In a free society each individual is free to determine for himself what he wishes to read, and each group is free to determine what it will recommend to its freely associated members. But no group has the right to take the law into its own hands, and to impose its own concept of politics or morality upon other members of a democratic society. Freedom is no freedom if it is accorded only to the accepted and the inoffensive.

7. *It is the responsibility of publishers and librarians to give full meaning to the freedom to read by providing books that enrich the quality of thought and expression. By the exercise of this affirmative responsibility, bookmen can demonstrate that the answer to a bad book is a good one, the answer to a bad idea is a good one.*

The freedom to read is of little consequence when expended on the trivial; it is frustrated when the reader cannot obtain matter fit for his purpose. What is needed is not only the absence of restraint, but the positive provision of opportunity for the people to read the best that has been thought and said. Books are the major channel by which the intellectual inheritance is handed down, and the principal means of its testing and growth. The defense of their freedom and integrity, and the enlargement of their service to society, requires of all bookmen the utmost of their faculties, and deserves of all citizens the fullest of their support.

From a deceptively comfortable position in the middle of the 1960s, most librarians looked forward to the 1970s with optimism, hoping for a favorable climate for intellectual freedom. The U.S. Supreme Court extended constitutional support and protection in many areas of human and civil rights. Very encouraging to librarians was the expansion of freedom of expression and other First

Amendment rights to allow publications that could not have been found 15 years earlier. An unfettered climate in which all ideas could be freely exchanged seemed imminent.

But the sense of optimism was soon undercut as increased American involvement in the Vietnam War prompted rancorous divisions among citizens and members of the government. And then came 1968: on April 4, Dr. Martin Luther King Jr. was assassinated in Memphis, and the riots provoked in Washington, D.C., and elsewhere led President Lyndon B. Johnson to call out troops to restore order. By April 14, violence had erupted in 29 states. On June 6, Robert F. Kennedy died in Los Angeles, also a victim of an assassin's bullet. From August 25 to 29, the Democratic National Convention in Chicago became the scene of violent clashes between the police and National Guard troops on one side and more than 10,000 antiwar demonstrators on the other. This period of violent dissent, countered by equally violent reactions, continued into 1970 with the Kent State and Jackson, Mississippi, incidents and battles between the Black Panther Party and police, and between the radical Weathermen group and police.

It became increasingly clear that such incidents of violent dissent and violent reactions were gradually eroding prospects for the open society many had envisioned. The "permissive" atmosphere collided with demands for law and order. One effect of the collision was that, little by little, the supports for intellectual freedom in the society at large were weakened.

In the form of subpoenas, pressure was brought against news reporters, photographers, and television broadcasting corporations to divulge sources of information and to produce unpublished materials deleted from final reports. Vice President Spiro Agnew gave a series of speeches condemning the news media for biased reporting and calling on citizens to protest such reporting. President Richard M. Nixon promised to appoint conservatives to the Supreme Court.

Recognizing the increasing conservatism of the nation, and mindful that "The Freedom to Read" might be tied too closely to the McCarthy era, the IFC began, in the fall of 1968, to consider the need for and desirability of a new statement to serve the 1970s. A careful review of the document resulted in the following points:

1. Article 4, urging the vigorous enforcement of "the present laws dealing with obscenity," should be revised or deleted entirely.
2. The basic sentiments expressed in "The Freedom to Read" remain valid and should not be distorted.
3. The document has historical significance.
4. A new statement is needed dealing specifically with the pressures on today's society and those foreseen arising during the next decade.

Believing a new statement should at least be attempted, the IFC asked the National Book Committee (NBC) and the American Book Publishers Council (ABPC), co-sponsor of "The Freedom to Read," whether they were interested in joining the undertaking. Both replied affirmatively. Theodore Waller and Peter Jennison met with the IFC during the 1969 Midwinter Meeting in Washington, D.C., and formed a subcommittee composed of representatives from the ABPC, ALA, and NBC, charged with determining content and preparing a draft document.

Meeting during the 1969 ALA Annual Conference in Atlantic City, the subcommittee—composed of Edwin Castagna, Peter Jennison, Judith F. Krug, Dan Lacy, and Theodore Waller—discussed the two major items: (1) Should "The Freedom to Read" be revised, or should a new document be produced? (As the IFC did, they decided to design a new statement meeting the challenge of the 1970s); and (2) What kind of ammunition is needed to meet the challenge of the 1970s? The subcommittee also considered such questions as: Can freedom to read be separated from intellectual freedom? Is a broader concept of intellectual freedom, embracing the First Amendment together with other aspects of the Bill of Rights, such as the invasion of privacy, needed? Should all media, not just books, be considered? Should complete intellectual freedom be called for, or must one retreat in the end to the principle of the freedom to read?

The subcommittee next met in August of that year, with a membership augmented by the presence of William DeJohn, Freeman Lewis, Harriet Pilpel, and Richard Sullivan. They drafted several statements and asked Jennison to assemble them into one cohesive document. Five drafts were subsequently produced, and the IFC, in

a ten-to-one mail vote, approved the fifth draft. At the time of the
1970 Midwinter Meeting, however, a sixth draft had been prepared.

The ABPC Board of Directors received the draft and approved
it by acclamation on January 28. The sixth draft was resubmitted to
the IFC, which approved it in a ten-to-one vote.

Following the 1970 Midwinter Meeting, the staff of the Office
for Intellectual Freedom carefully reviewed the sixth draft of the
document, tentatively entitled *The Promise of the First Freedom: A
Statement of Free Men*. The staff could not join with the IFC in
endorsing this document and recommended to the IFC that "The
Freedom to Read" be revised, as opposed to rewritten, to meet contemporary needs. This decision was based on several factors:

1. The major part of "The Freedom to Read" remained valid.
2. Among those parts that needed change were the specific references to books, for libraries were concerned with all types of
   materials.
3. Although "The Freedom to Read" had historical significance,
   subsequent policy statements, as well as actions, of the Association were in opposition to a few parts, primarily Article 4.
4. The few parts in opposition were believed to be serious matters
   and should not be permitted to stand.

The revision was undertaken by the Office for Intellectual
Freedom and W. Lester Smith of the Association of American
Publishers (AAP), successor to the combined ABPC and the
American Educational Publishers Institute. The new document differed from the 1953 version on only a few significant points: the earlier call for "vigorous enforcement of present obscenity laws" was
omitted, as was the reference to "the immature, the retarded, and
the maladjusted taste."

The revised "Freedom to Read" statement was approved by
the ALA Council at the 1972 Midwinter Meeting and by the AAP
as follows:

> The freedom to read is essential to our democracy. It is contin-
> uously under attack. Private groups and public authorities in var-
> ious parts of the country are working to remove books from sale,
> to censor textbooks, to label "controversial" books, to distribute

lists of "objectionable" books or authors, and to purge libraries. These actions apparently rise from a view that our national tradition of free expression is no longer valid; that censorship and suppression are needed to avoid the subversion of politics and the corruption of morals. We, as citizens devoted to the use of books and as librarians and publishers responsible for disseminating them, wish to assert the public interest in the preservation of the freedom to read.

We are deeply concerned about these attempts at suppression. Most such attempts rest on a denial of the fundamental premise of democracy: that the ordinary citizen, by exercising his critical judgment, will accept the good and reject the bad. The censors, public and private, assume that they should determine what is good and what is bad for their fellow-citizens.

We trust Americans to recognize propaganda and to reject it. We do not believe they need the help of censors to assist them in this task. We do not believe they are prepared to sacrifice their heritage of a free press in order to be "protected" against what others think may be bad for them. We believe they still favor free enterprise in ideas and expression.

We are aware, of course, that books are not alone in being subjected to efforts at suppression. We are aware that these efforts are related to a larger pattern of pressures being brought against education, the press, films, radio, and television. The problem is not only one of actual censorship. The shadow of fear cast by these pressures leads, we suspect, to an even larger voluntary curtailment of expression by those who seek to avoid controversy.

Such pressure toward conformity is perhaps natural to a time of uneasy change and pervading fear. Especially when so many of our apprehensions are directed against an ideology, the expression of a dissident idea becomes a thing feared in itself, and we tend to move against it as against a hostile deed, with suppression.

And yet suppression is never more dangerous than in such a time of social tension. Freedom has given the United States the elasticity to endure strain. Freedom keeps open the path of novel and creative solutions, and enables change to come by choice. Every silencing of a heresy, every enforcement of an orthodoxy, diminishes the toughness and resilience of our society and leaves it the less able to deal with stress.

Now as always in our history, books are among our greatest instruments of freedom. They are almost the only means for making generally available ideas or manners of expression that can initially command only a small audience. They are the natural medium for the new idea and the untried voice from which come the original contributions to social growth. They are essential to the extended discussion which serious thought requires, and to the accumulation of knowledge and ideas into organized collections.

We believe that free communication is essential to the preservation of a free society and a creative culture. We believe that these pressures towards conformity present the danger of limiting the range and variety of inquiry and expression on which our democracy and our culture depend. We believe that every American community must jealously guard the freedom to publish and to circulate, in order to preserve its own freedom to read. We believe that publishers and librarians have a profound responsibility to give validity to that freedom to read by making it possible for the readers to choose freely from a variety of offerings.

The freedom to read is guaranteed by the Constitution. Those with faith in free people will stand firm on these constitutional guarantees of essential rights and will exercise the responsibilities that accompany these rights.

We therefore affirm these propositions:

1. *It is in the public interest for publishers and librarians to make available the widest diversity of views and expressions, including those which are unorthodox or unpopular with the majority.*

   Creative thought is by definition new, and what is new is different. The bearer of every new thought is a rebel until that idea is refined and tested. Totalitarian systems attempt to maintain themselves in power by the ruthless suppression of any concept which challenges the established orthodoxy. The power of a democratic system to adapt to change is vastly strengthened by the freedom of its citizens to choose widely from among conflicting opinions offered freely to them. To stifle every nonconformist idea at birth would mark the end of the democratic process. Furthermore, only through the constant activity of weighing and selecting can the democratic mind attain the strength demanded by times like these. We need to know not only what we believe but why we believe it.

2. *Publishers, librarians, and booksellers do not need to endorse every idea or presentation contained in the books they make available. It would conflict with the public interest for them to establish their own political, moral, or aesthetic views as a standard for determining what books should be published or circulated.*

Publishers and librarians serve the educational process by helping to make available knowledge and ideas required for the growth of the mind and the increase of learning. They do not foster education by imposing as mentors the patterns of their own thought. The people should have the freedom to read and consider a broader range of ideas than those that may be held by any single librarian or publisher or government or church. It is wrong that what one can read should be confined to what another thinks proper.

3. *It is contrary to the public interest for publishers or librarians to determine the acceptability of a book on the basis of the personal history or political affiliations of the author.*

A book should be judged as a book. No art or literature can flourish if it is to be measured by the political views or private lives of its creators. No society of free men can flourish which draws up lists of writers to whom it will not listen, whatever they may have to say.

4. *There is no place in our society for efforts to coerce the taste of others, to confine adults to the reading matter deemed suitable for adolescents, or to inhibit the efforts of writers to achieve artistic expression.*

To some, much of modern literature is shocking. But is not much of life itself shocking? We cut off literature at the source if we prevent writers from dealing with the stuff of life. Parents and teachers have a responsibility to prepare the young to meet the diversity of experiences in life to which they will be exposed, as they have a responsibility to help them learn to think critically for themselves. These are affirmative responsibilities, not to be discharged simply by preventing them from reading works for which they are not yet prepared. In these matters taste differs, and taste cannot be legislated; nor can machinery be devised which will suit the demands of one group without limiting the freedom of others.

5. *It is not in the public interest to force a reader to accept with any book the prejudgment of a label characterizing the book or author as subversive or dangerous.*

The idea of labeling presupposes the existence of individuals or groups with wisdom to determine by authority what is good or bad for the citizen. It presupposes that each individual must be directed in making up his mind about the ideas he examines. But Americans do not need others to do their thinking for them.

6. *It is the responsibility of publishers and librarians, as guardians of the people's freedom to read, to contest encroachments upon that freedom by individuals or groups seeking to impose their own standards or tastes upon the community at large.*

It is inevitable in the give and take of the democratic process that the political, the moral, or the aesthetic concepts of an individual or group will occasionally collide with those of another individual or group. In a free society each individual is free to determine for himself what he wishes to read, and each group is free to determine what it will recommend to its freely associated members. But no group has the right to take the law into its own hands, and to impose its own concept of politics or morality upon other members of a democratic society. Freedom is no freedom if it is accorded only to the accepted and the inoffensive.

7. *It is the responsibility of publishers and librarians to give full meaning to the freedom to read by providing books that enrich the quality and diversity of thought and expression. By the exercise of this affirmative responsibility, bookmen can demonstrate that the answer to a bad book is a good one, the answer to a bad idea is a good one.*

The freedom to read is of little consequence when expended on the trivial; it is frustrated when the reader cannot obtain matter fit for his purpose. What is needed is not only the absence of restraint, but the positive provision of opportunity for the people to read the best that has been thought and said. Books are the major channel by which the intellectual inheritance is handed down, and the principal means of its testing and growth. The defense of their freedom and integrity; and the enlargement of their service to society, requires of all bookmen the utmost of their faculties, and deserves of all citizens the fullest of their support.

We state these propositions neither lightly nor as easy generalizations. We here stake out a lofty claim for the value of books. We do so because we believe that they are good, possessed of enormous variety and usefulness, worthy of cherishing and keeping free. We realize that the application of these propositions may mean the dissemination of ideas and manners of expression that are repugnant to many persons. We do not state these propositions in the comfortable belief that what people read is unimportant. We believe rather that what people read is deeply important; that ideas can be dangerous; but that the suppression of ideas is fatal to a democratic society. Freedom itself is a dangerous way of life, but it is ours.

The document was subsequently endorsed by many other organizations: American Booksellers Association; American Civil Liberties Union; American Federation of Teachers, AFL-CIO; Anti-Defamation League of B'nai B'rith; Association of American University Presses; Bureau of Independent Publishers and Distributors; Children's Book Council; Freedom of Information Center; Freedom to Read Foundation; Magazine Publishers Association; Motion Picture Association of America; National Association of College Stores; National Board of the Young Women's Christian Association of the U.S.A.; National Book Committee; National Council of Negro Women; National Council of Teachers of English; National Library Week Program; P.E.N.–American Center; Periodical and Book Association of America; Sex Information and Education Council of the U.S.; and Women's National Book Association.

By 1990, both the IFC and the AAP Freedom to Read Committee were in agreement that "The Freedom to Read" needed minor revisions. In addition, it recently had gone out of print. At the Annual Conference in June, Richard Kleeman of the Association of American Publishers recommended minor changes, including removal of gender-specific language. It also was suggested that the new draft incorporate international concerns about the freedom to read.

A major question in regard to a revised statement was whether it should be more explicitly inclusive of the arts and music—targets of many then-recent censorship battles. Again the view was strongly expressed that the statement had stood the test of time and would only be diminished by major revisions. The IFC agreed to proceed with a review and report back at the 1991 Midwinter Meeting. Richard Kleeman said the AAP Freedom to Read Committee would follow the same timetable.

In January 1991, the IFC considered two new drafts: one without gender-specific language and the other with a new international focus. Ultimately, the Committee decided to adopt only the first version and to address international and other concerns in separate documents. On January 16, 1991, the Committee adopted "The Freedom to Read" as revised and so informed the Council. Given the editorial nature of the changes, no action by the Council was required. On the same date, at its regular monthly meeting, the AAP Freedom to Read Committee adopted the same revision.

In line with the ongoing practice of periodic review, the IFC carefully reviewed all statements, including "The Freedom to Read," during 1999–2000, especially in regard to their applicability to the Internet. At the 2000 Midwinter Meeting, IFC member Carolyn Caywood, who had been assigned the task of reviewing "The Freedom to Read," presented a revision which she said did not tamper with the spirit of the statement but only updated certain phrases and terminologies. After discussion by the IFC, Caywood, along with IFC members Vivian Wynn and Paul Vermouth, drafted further refinements which they felt broadened the statement beyond print material. The revised document was adopted by the ALA Council and the AAP Freedom to Read Committee on July 12, 2000, and reads as follows.

> The freedom to read is essential to our democracy. It is continuously under attack. Private groups and public authorities in various parts of the country are working to remove or limit access to reading materials, to censor content in schools, to label "contro-

versial" views, to distribute lists of "objectionable" books or authors, and to purge libraries. These actions apparently rise from a view that our national tradition of free expression is no longer valid; that censorship and suppression are needed to avoid the subversion of politics and the corruption of morals. We, as citizens devoted to reading and as librarians and publishers responsible for disseminating ideas, wish to assert the public interest in the preservation of the freedom to read.

Most attempts at suppression rest on a denial of the fundamental premise of democracy: that the ordinary citizen, by exercising critical judgment, will accept the good and reject the bad. The censors, public and private, assume that they should determine what is good and what is bad for their fellow citizens.

We trust Americans to recognize propaganda and misinformation, and to make their own decisions about what they read and believe. We do not believe they need the help of censors to assist them in this task. We do not believe they are prepared to sacrifice their heritage of a free press in order to be "protected" against what others think may be bad for them. We believe they still favor free enterprise in ideas and expression.

These efforts at suppression are related to a larger pattern of pressures being brought against education, the press, art and images, films, broadcast media, and the Internet. The problem is not only one of actual censorship. The shadow of fear cast by these pressures leads, we suspect, to an even larger voluntary curtailment of expression by those who seek to avoid controversy.

Such pressure toward conformity is perhaps natural to a time of accelerated change. And yet suppression is never more dangerous than in such a time of social tension. Freedom has given the United States the elasticity to endure strain. Freedom keeps open the path of novel and creative solutions, and enables change to come by choice. Every silencing of a heresy, every enforcement of an orthodoxy, diminishes the toughness and resilience of our society and leaves it the less able to deal with controversy and difference.

Now as always in our history, reading is among our greatest freedoms. The freedom to read and write is almost the only means for making generally available ideas or manners of expression that can initially command only a small audience. The written word is the natural medium for the new idea and the untried voice from which come the original contributions to social growth. It is essential to the extended discussion that serious thought requires, and to the accumulation of knowledge and ideas into organized collections.

We believe that free communication is essential to the preservation of a free society and a creative culture. We believe that these pressures toward conformity present the danger of limiting the range and variety of inquiry and expression on which our democracy and our culture depend. We believe that every American community must jealously guard the freedom to publish and to circulate, in order to preserve its own freedom to read. We believe that publishers and librarians have a profound responsibility to give validity to that freedom to read by making it possible for the readers to choose freely from a variety of offerings. The freedom to read is guaranteed by the Constitution. Those with faith in free people will stand firm on these constitutional guarantees of essential rights and will exercise the responsibilities that accompany these rights.

We therefore affirm these propositions:

1. *It is in the public interest for publishers and librarians to make available the widest diversity of views and expressions, including those that are unorthodox or unpopular with the majority.*

   Creative thought is by definition new, and what is new is different. The bearer of every new thought is a rebel until that idea is refined and tested. Totalitarian systems attempt to maintain themselves in power by the ruthless suppression of any concept that challenges the established orthodoxy. The power of a democratic system to adapt to change is vastly strengthened by the freedom of its citizens to choose widely from among conflicting opinions offered freely to them. To stifle every nonconformist idea at birth would mark the end of the democratic process. Furthermore, only through the constant activity of weighing and selecting can the democratic mind attain the strength demanded by times like these. We need to know not only what we believe but why we believe it.

2. *Publishers, librarians, and booksellers do not need to endorse every idea or presentation they make available. It would conflict with the public interest for them to establish their own political,*

moral, or aesthetic views as a standard for determining what should be published or circulated.

Publishers and librarians serve the educational process by helping to make available knowledge and ideas required for the growth of the mind and the increase of learning. They do not foster education by imposing as mentors the patterns of their own thought. The people should have the freedom to read and consider a broader range of ideas than those that may be held by any single librarian or publisher or government or church. It is wrong that what one can read should be confined to what another thinks proper.

3. *It is contrary to the public interest for publishers or librarians to bar access to writings on the basis of the personal history or political affiliations of the author.*

No art or literature can flourish if it is to be measured by the political views or private lives of its creators. No society of free people can flourish that draws up lists of writers to whom it will not listen, whatever they may have to say.

4. *There is no place in our society for efforts to coerce the taste of others, to confine adults to the reading matter deemed suitable for adolescents, or to inhibit the efforts of writers to achieve artistic expression.*

To some, much of modern expression is shocking. But is not much of life itself shocking? We cut off literature at the source if we prevent writers from dealing with the stuff of life. Parents and teachers have a responsibility to prepare the young to meet the diversity of experiences in life to which they will be exposed, as they have a responsibility to help them learn to think critically for themselves. These are affirmative responsibilities, not to be discharged simply by preventing them from reading works for which they are not yet prepared. In these matters values differ, and values cannot be legislated; nor can machinery be devised that will suit the demands of one group without limiting the freedom of others.

5. *It is not in the public interest to force a reader to accept with any expression the prejudgment of a label characterizing it or its author as subversive or dangerous.*

The ideal of labeling presupposes the existence of individuals or groups with wisdom to determine by authority what is good or bad for the citizen. It presupposes that individuals must be directed in making up their minds about the ideas they examine. But Americans do not need others to do their thinking for them.

6. *It is the responsibility of publishers and librarians, as guardians of the people's freedom to read, to contest encroachments upon that freedom by individuals or groups seeking to impose their own standards or tastes upon the community at large.*

It is inevitable in the give and take of the democratic process that the political, the moral, or the aesthetic concepts of an individual or group will occasionally collide with those of another individual or group. In a free society individuals are free to determine for themselves what they wish to read, and each group is free to determine what it will recommend to its freely associated members. But no group has the right to take the law into its own hands, and to impose its own concept of politics or morality upon other members of a democratic society. Freedom is no freedom if it is accorded only to the accepted and the inoffensive.

7. *It is the responsibility of publishers and librarians to give full meaning to the freedom to read by providing books that enrich the quality and diversity of thought and expression. By the exercise of this affirmative responsibility, they can demonstrate that the answer to a "bad" book is a good one, the answer to a "bad" idea is a good one.*

The freedom to read is of little consequence when the reader cannot obtain matter fit for that reader's purpose. What is needed is not only the absence of restraint, but the positive provision of opportunity for the people to read the best that has been thought and said. Books are the major channel by which the intellectual inheritance is handed down, and the principal means of its testing and growth. The defense of the freedom to read requires of all publishers and librarians the utmost of their faculties, and deserves of all citizens the fullest of their support.

We state these propositions neither lightly nor as easy generalizations. We here stake out a lofty claim for the value of the written word. We do so because we believe that it is possessed of enormous variety and usefulness, worthy of cherishing and keeping free. We realize that the application of these propositions may mean the dissemination of ideas and manners of expression that are repugnant to many persons. We do not state these propositions in the comfortable belief that what people read is unimportant. We believe rather that what people read is deeply important; that ideas can be dangerous; but that the suppression of ideas is fatal to a democratic society. Freedom itself is a dangerous way of life, but it is ours.

NOTE

1. For full details of national and international events surrounding the development of "The Freedom to Read," see Everett T. Moore, "Intellectual Freedom," in *Research Librarianship: Essays in Honor of Robert B. Downs,* ed. Jerrold Orne (New York: Bowker, 1971).

2
Libraries:
An American Value
Policy Statement

Libraries in America are cornerstones of the communities they serve. Free access to the books, ideas, resources, and information in America's libraries is imperative for education, employment, enjoyment, and self-government.

Libraries are a legacy to each generation, offering the heritage of the past and the promise of the future. To ensure that libraries flourish and have the freedom to promote and protect the public good in the twenty-first century, we believe certain principles must be guaranteed.

To that end, we affirm this contract with the people we serve:

- We defend the constitutional rights of all individuals, including children and teenagers, to use the library's resources and services;
- We value our nation's diversity and strive to reflect that diversity by providing a full spectrum of resources and services to the communities we serve;
- We affirm the responsibility and the right of all parents and guardians to guide their own children's use of the library and its resources and services;
- We connect people and ideas by helping each person select from and effectively use the library's resources;
- We protect each individual's privacy and confidentiality in the use of library resources and services;

- We protect the rights of individuals to express their opinions about library resources and services;
- We celebrate and preserve our democratic society by making available the widest possible range of viewpoints, opinions and ideas, so that all individuals have the opportunity to become lifelong learners—informed, literate, educated, and culturally enriched.

Change is constant, but these principles transcend change and endure in a dynamic technological, social, and political environment.

By embracing these principles, libraries in the United States can contribute to a future that values and protects freedom of speech in a world that celebrates both our similarities and our differences, respects individuals and their beliefs, and holds all persons truly equal and free.

Adopted by the ALA Council, February 3, 1999.

HISTORY

Libraries:
An American Value

" ibraries: An American Value" is intended to inform the public about a library's role in the community, particularly in the face of accelerating change and uncertainty. It was the first major intellectual freedom policy adopted by the American Library Association in nearly twenty years, and it was the first one available for distribution and discussion via the Internet and e-mail.

In 1997, ALA president-elect Ann K. Symons asked her organizing committee to explore writing a new basic policy for the ALA. The first step was to determine the purpose of the policy and its relation to existing policies, such as the *Library Bill of Rights*, the "Freedom to Read" statement, and the "Code of Ethics." The committee, chaired by June Pinnell-Stephens, met with ALA members at the 1998 Midwinter Meeting, where discussion centered around the need to reaffirm intellectual freedom principles and the democratic mandates on which they are based in the face of the changing legal, technological, and political environment. The participants agreed that a new document should contain the library's implicit contract with the community and that the primary difference between "Libraries: An American Value" and the *Library Bill of Rights* should be the targeted audience: the first, directed to the public, explaining the role of the library in a democracy and the second, directed to both libraries and the public, addressing the library's obligations to the individual. The other documents clearly differed from the proposed new policy, with the "Freedom to Read" statement describing the underlying value of reading to the individual and society, and the "Code of Ethics" addressing appropriate professional behavior.

A drafting committee met in Chicago in February 1998 to write the first draft of the policy. This was circulated to ALA members for comment and was the subject of a hearing at the 1998 Annual Conference in Washington, D.C. In September 1998, a final draft was released. Between e-mail messages and speakers at the hearing, the committee received more than 200 comments and suggestions, ranging from complete agreement to total rewrites. By the time the document came to the ALA Council for adoption, every ALA division and fifty-six state chapters and school media associations had endorsed it. It was adopted by the Council on February 3, 1999.

3

Policy on Confidentiality
of Library Records
Policy Statement

The Council of the American Library Association strongly recommends that the responsible officers of each library, cooperative system, and consortium in the United States:

1. Formally adopt a policy which specifically recognizes its circulation records and other records identifying the name of library users to be confidential in nature.*

2. Advise all librarians and library employees that such records shall not be made available to any agency of state, federal, or local government except pursuant to such process, order, or subpoena as may be authorized under the authority of, and pursuant to, federal, state, or local law relating to civil, criminal, or administrative discovery procedures or legislative investigative power.

3. Resist the issuance or enforcement of any such process, order, or subpoena until such time as a proper showing of good cause has been made in a court of competent jurisdiction.**

Note: See also ALA "Code of Ethics," point III: "We protect each library user's right to privacy and confidentiality with respect to information sought or received, and materials consulted, borrowed, acquired or transmitted."

**Note:* Point 3, above, means that upon receipt of such process, order, or subpoena, the library's officers will consult with their legal counsel to determine if such process, order, or subpoena is in proper form and if there is a showing of good cause for its issuance; if the process, order, or subpoena is not in proper form or if good cause has not been shown, they will insist that such defects be cured.

Adopted January 20, 1971; revised July 4, 1975; July 2, 1986, by the ALA Council.

Suggested Procedures
for Implementing
"Policy on Confidentiality
of Library Records"

When drafting local policies, libraries should consult with their legal counsel to insure these policies are based upon and consistent with applicable federal, state, and local law concerning the confidentiality of library records, the disclosure of public records, and the protection of individual privacy.

Suggested procedures include the following:

1. The library staff member receiving the request to examine or obtain information relating to circulation or other records identifying the names of library users, will immediately refer the person making the request to the responsible officer of the institution, who shall explain the confidentiality policy.

2. The director, upon receipt of such process, order, or subpoena, shall consult with the appropriate legal officer assigned to the institution to determine if such process, order, or subpoena is in good form and if there is a showing of good cause for its issuance.

3. If the process, order, or subpoena is not in proper form or if good cause has not been shown, insistence shall be made that such defects be cured before any records are released. (The legal process requiring the production of circulation or other library records shall ordinarily be in the form of subpoena duces tecum [bring your records] requiring the responsible officer to attend court or the taking of his/her deposition and may require

him/her to bring along certain designated circulation or other specified records.)

4. Any threats or unauthorized demands (i.e., those not supported by a process, order, or subpoena) concerning circulation and other records identifying the names of library users shall be reported to the appropriate legal officer of the institution.

5. Any problems relating to the privacy of circulation and other records identifying the names of library users which are not provided for above shall be referred to the responsible officer.

Adopted by the ALA Intellectual Freedom Committee, January 9, 1983; revised January 11, 1988.

HISTORY

Policy on Confidentiality
of Library Records

During the spring of 1970, the Milwaukee Public Library was visited by agents of the U.S. Treasury Department, who were requesting permission to examine the circulation records of books and materials on explosives. Initially rebuffed by the assistant librarian, the agents later returned with an opinion from the city attorney's office that circulation records were public records and that the agents should be allowed access to the files. The library complied. At about the same time, the ALA Office for Intellectual Freedom received reports of similar visits from Treasury agents at public libraries in Cleveland, Ohio, and Richmond, California. On July 1 of that year, a report was received from Atlanta, Georgia, stating that in the Atlanta area, twenty-seven libraries and branches were visited.

On July 21, the ALA Executive Board issued an emergency advisory statement urging all libraries to make circulation records confidential as a matter of policy. The advisory statement read:

> The American Library Association has been advised that the Internal Revenue Service of the Treasury Department has requested access to the circulation records of public libraries in Atlanta, Georgia, and Milwaukee, Wisconsin, for the purpose of determining the identity of persons reading matter pertaining to the construction of explosive devices. The Association is further advised that such requests were not based on any process, order, or subpoena authorized by federal, civil, criminal, or administrative discovery procedures.

The Executive Board of the ALA believes that the efforts of the federal government to convert library circulation records into "suspect lists" constitute an unconscionable and unconstitutional invasion of the right of privacy of library patrons and, if permitted to continue, will do irreparable damage to the educational and social value of the libraries of this country.

Accordingly, the Executive Board of the American Library Association strongly recommends that the responsible officers in each U.S. library:

1. Formally adopt a policy which specifically recognizes its circulation records to be confidential in nature.
2. Advise all librarians and library employees that such records shall not be made available to any agency of state, federal, or local government except pursuant to such process, order, or subpoena as may be authorized under the authority of, and pursuant to, federal, state, or local law relating to civil, criminal, or administrative discovery procedures or legislative investigatory power.
3. Resist the issuance or enforcement of any such process, order, or subpoena until such time as a proper showing of good cause has been made in a court of competent jurisdiction.

David H. Clift, ALA executive director, and staff members met with Randolph W. Thrower, commissioner of the Internal Revenue Service (IRS), on August 5, 1970, to discuss their mutual concern over the inquiries. Little was agreed upon at the meeting except that "efforts would begin, in a spirit of cooperation, to develop guidelines acceptable to the American Library Association and the Internal Revenue Service." That afternoon, Clift received a copy of a letter sent to Senator Sam J. Ervin Jr., chair of the Senate Subcommittee on Constitutional Rights, by Secretary of the Treasury David M. Kennedy in response to Senator Ervin's earlier expressed concern about the IRS inquiries. Secretary Kennedy's letter stated that the visits had been conducted to "determine the advisability of the use of library records as an investigative technique to assist in quelling bombings. That survey . . . has terminated and will not be repeated." But the door was not being closed on future surveys. The secretary added that "it is our judgment that checking such records in certain limited circumstances is an appropriate investigative technique" and that the Alcohol, Tobacco, and Firearms Division of the Treasury Department has the authority, under federal statute, to conduct limited investigations in specific cases.[1]

The ALA indicated its awareness of the Internal Revenue Service's responsibility to enforce the statutes, but noted that the Association's primary concern was not the enforcement itself but, rather, the means by which this enforcement was undertaken regarding libraries. While not intending to hinder effective enforcement of federal statutes, the Association made it clear that circulation records were "not to be made available to any agency of state, federal, or local government except pursuant to such process, order, or subpoena as may be authorized under the authority of, and pursuant to, federal, state, or local law relating to civil, criminal, or administrative discovery procedures or legislative investigatory power."

In anticipation of presenting the matter to the ALA Council at the 1971 Midwinter Meeting in Los Angeles, Intellectual Freedom Committee members were polled by telegram in October 1970, concerning a proposed draft of a policy statement. Suggestions for modification of the July statement were made by the IFC and the Executive Board at the latter's 1970 fall meeting. The Board suggested that the original introductory paragraph be shortened, that the phrase "and other records identifying the names of library users with specific materials" be added to Article 1, and that Article 3 be clarified.

The "Policy on Confidentiality of Library Records" was formally adopted by the IFC at a special meeting in December 1970. It was submitted to the ALA Council at the 1971 Midwinter Meeting in Los Angeles, and was approved on January 20, 1971. On that date, in his progress report to the Council, IFC chair David K. Berninghausen stated the following:

> When the time comes in any society that government officials seek information as to what people are reading, it must be presumed that they expect to use these records as evidence of dangerous thinking. And when a government takes action to control what its citizens are thinking, it is a tell-tale sign that all is not well in that society.
>
> We recognize that the U.S. Treasury agents probably did not realize that their investigations would be viewed as an invasion of

privacy of readers or as an infringement on the freedom of thought guaranteed by the U.S. Constitution and Bill of Rights. But it is such small, beginning steps that lead a nation down the road to tyranny. We are pleased to note that these programs of inquiry have been stopped. We are proud of ALA's prompt action which helped to bring the investigations to an end.[2]

At the 1975 Annual Conference in San Francisco, a new problem of confidentiality was considered by the IFC. Earlier, the Intellectual Freedom Committee of the Washington Library Association had called the ALA's attention to the fact that the policy on the confidentiality of library records "identifying the names of library users with specific materials" had been used to justify the release of other kinds of library records on patrons to police officers.

After reviewing this issue, the IFC voted to recommend to the Council that the phrase "with specific materials" be deleted from the policy, thus making it applicable to all patron records. The IFC's recommendation was accepted by the Council at its meeting on July 4, 1975.

During the 1980–82 revision of the ALA's intellectual freedom policies, the IFC considered several suggested revisions of the "Policy on Confidentiality of Library Records." After considerable discussion and consultation with ALA counsel, however, the Committee decided not to recommend any changes in the policy. At the 1983 Midwinter Meeting in San Antonio, however, it was voted to append to the document a note referring to point III of the ALA "Code of Ethics" protecting the library user's right to privacy. At San Antonio, the IFC also adopted a series of "suggested procedures" for implementing the confidentiality policy.

At the 1988 Midwinter Meeting in San Antonio, the IFC amended the suggested procedures. The emendations were made to bring the language in this document into conformance with the language in the policy, to stress the need for a court order before any records are released, and to emphasize the need for libraries to consult applicable federal, state, and local law when drafting such a policy for local use. Later in 1988, responding to concerns about whether the language in the "Policy on Confidentiality of Library Records" was sufficient to cover all records, rather than just registration or circulation records, the IFC reviewed both the policy and the procedures for implementing it. The Committee decided that the language of the policy was sufficient but that the language in the procedures was not uniformly inclusive and should be revised. The Committee chair noted that the procedures should include a direction to librarians to ascertain the status of their state law on confidentiality of library records. In addition, the chair suggested that all state IFCs be encouraged to review their state statutes to determine the inclusivity of the records covered.

A new draft of the procedure incorporating the above-mentioned concerns was adopted by the Intellectual Freedom Committee on January 11, 1988. The suggested procedures for implementing the policy are institutional in nature and not official ALA policy; action by the Council, therefore, was not needed.

In line with the ongoing practice of periodic review, in 1999–2000 the IFC reviewed the "Policy on Confidentiality of Library Records" and recommended no changes.

NOTES

1. David M. Kennedy, letter to Sen. Sam J. Ervin Jr., July 29, 1970 (copy in ALA files).

2. American Library Association, "Minutes of Council Meetings," vol. 14, 1971–72, p. 76.

4

Policy concerning Confidentiality of Personally Identifiable Information about Library Users
Policy Statement

The ethical responsibilities of librarians, as well as statutes in most states and the District of Columbia, protect the privacy of library users. Confidentiality extends to "information sought or received, and materials consulted, borrowed or acquired," and includes database search records, reference interviews, circulation records, interlibrary loan records, and other personally identifiable uses of library materials, facilities, or services.

The First Amendment's guarantee of freedom of speech and of the press requires that the corresponding rights to hear what is spoken and read what is written be preserved, free from fear of government intrusion, intimidation, or reprisal. The American Library Association reaffirms its opposition to "any use of government prerogatives which lead to the intimidation of the individual or the citizenry from the exercise of free expression . . . [and] encourages resistance to such abuse of government power. . . .": (ALA policy 53.4). In seeking access or in the pursuit of information, confidentiality is the primary means of providing the privacy that will free the individual from fear of intimidation or retaliation.

Libraries are one of the great bulwarks of democracy. They are living embodiments of the First Amendment because their collections include voices of dissent as well as assent. Libraries are impartial resources providing information on all points of view, available to all persons regardless of age, race, religion, national origin, social or political views, economic status, or any other characteristic. The role of libraries as such a resource must not be compromised by an erosion of the privacy rights of library users.

The American Library Association regularly receives reports of visits by agents of federal, state, and local law enforcement agencies to libraries, where it is alleged they have asked for personally identifiable information about library users. These visits, whether under the rubric of simply informing libraries of agency concerns or for some other reason, reflect an insensitivity to the legal and ethical bases for confidentiality, and the role it plays in the preservation of First Amendment rights, rights also extended to foreign nationals while in the United States. The government's interest in library use reflects a dangerous and fallacious equation of what a person reads with what that person believes or how that person is likely to behave. Such a presumption can and does threaten the freedom of access to information. It also is a threat to a crucial aspect of First Amendment rights: that freedom of speech and of the press include the freedom to hold, disseminate, and receive unpopular, minority, "extreme," or even "dangerous" ideas.

The American Library Association recognizes that, under limited circumstances, access to certain information might be restricted due to a legitimate "national security" concern. However, there has been no showing of a plausible probability that national security will be compromised by any use made of unclassified information available in libraries. Thus, the right of access to this information by individuals, including foreign nationals, must be recognized as part of the librarian's legal and ethical responsibility to protect the confidentiality of the library user.

The American Library Association also recognizes that law enforcement agencies and officers may occasionally believe that library records contain information which would be helpful to the investigation of criminal activity. If there is a reasonable basis to believe such records are necessary to the progress of an investigation or prosecution, the American judicial system provides the mechanism for seeking release of such confidential records: the issuance of a court order, following a showing of good cause based on specific facts, by a court of competent jurisdiction.

Adopted July 2, 1991, by the ALA Council.

HISTORY

Policy concerning Confidentiality of Personally Identifiable Information about Library Users

In 1989, the Intellectual Freedom Committee prepared a statement sent to then-FBI director William Sessions, outlining the ALA's concerns about the FBI Library Awareness Program. (For more on the FBI Library Awareness Program, see part I, section 1, "ALA and Intellectual Freedom: A Historical Overview.") Although the FBI had indicated it would exchange a similar statement of its own about the program, none was ever received by the ALA. Inquiries to the Office for Intellectual Freedom from librarians seeking assistance in handling law enforcement requests for confidential information about library users continued.

In response to the increasing number of inquiries, the lack of cooperation from the FBI, and concern about law enforcement requests for personally identifiable information about patrons whether found in library records per se or not, the ALA Council requested that a policy addressing the FBI and law enforcement issues be drafted.

The IFC revised and reformatted the statement prepared for the FBI in 1989 to explain library concerns about confidentiality to produce the "Policy concerning Confidentiality of Personally Identifiable Information about Library Users."

In 1991, the first draft was further revised to broaden the language concerning what constitutes personally identifiable information about library users. This was done in response to a case in Oregon, where law enforcement officials took fingerprints from library materials as part of a criminal investigation. Members ques-

tioned whether fingerprints could be considered personally identifiable information according to the policy

The new draft also included a statement expressing the ALA's
contention that the use of unclassified materials in libraries cannot
reasonably be deemed a national security threat, as alleged by the
FBI in an attempt to justify the Library Awareness Program. The
final version of the new policy was adopted by the Council on July 2,
1991.

In line with the ongoing review of all policies in 1999–2000, the
IFC reviewed this policy and made no changes.

5

Resolution on the Use
of Filtering Software
in Libraries

WHEREAS, On June 26, 1997, the United States Supreme Court issued a sweeping re-affirmation of core First Amendment principles and held that communications over the Internet deserve the highest level of constitutional protection; and

WHEREAS, The Court's most fundamental holding is that communications on the Internet deserve the same level of constitutional protection as books, magazines, newspapers, and speakers on a street corner soapbox. The Court found that the Internet "constitutes a vast platform from which to address and hear from a world-wide audience of millions of readers, viewers, researchers, and buyers," and that "any person with a phone line can become a town crier with a voice that resonates farther than it could from any soapbox"; and

WHEREAS, For libraries, the most critical holding of the Supreme Court is that libraries that make content available on the Internet can continue to do so with the same constitutional protections that apply to the books on libraries' shelves; and

WHEREAS, The Court's conclusion that "the vast democratic fora of the Internet" merit full constitutional protection will also serve to protect libraries that provide their patrons with access to the Internet; and

WHEREAS, The Court recognized the importance of enabling individuals to receive speech from the entire world and to speak to the entire world. Libraries provide those opportunities to many who would not otherwise have them; and

WHEREAS, The Supreme Court's decision will protect that access; and

WHEREAS, The use in libraries of software filters which block constitutionally protected speech is inconsistent with the United States Constitution and federal law and may lead to legal exposure for the library and its governing authorities; now, therefore, be it

RESOLVED, That the American Library Association affirms that the use of filtering software by libraries to block access to constitutionally protected speech violates the *Library Bill of Rights*.

Adopted by the ALA Council, July 2, 1997.

Statement on Library Use of Filtering Software
Policy Statement

On June 26, 1997, the United States Supreme Court in *Reno, Attorney General of the United States, et al.* v. *American Civil Liberties Union, et al.*, issued a sweeping reaffirmation of core First Amendment principles and held that communications over the Internet deserve the highest level of constitutional protection.*

The Court's most fundamental holding was that communications on the Internet deserve the same level of constitutional protection as books, magazines, newspapers, and speakers on a street corner soapbox. The Court found that the Internet "constitutes a vast platform from which to address and hear from a world-wide audience of millions of readers, viewers, researchers, and buyers," and that "any person with a phone line can become a town crier with a voice that resonates farther than it could from any soapbox."

For libraries, the most critical holding of the Supreme Court is that libraries that make content available on the Internet can continue to do so with the same constitutional protections that apply to the books on libraries' shelves. The Court's conclusion that "the vast democratic fora of the Internet" merit full constitutional protection serves to protect libraries that provide their patrons with access to the Internet. The Court recognized the

*The full text of the Supreme Court's decision is available at www.ciec.org/SC_appeal/decision.shtml.

importance of enabling individuals to receive speech from the entire world and to speak to the entire world. Libraries provide those opportunities to many who would not otherwise have them. The Supreme Court's decision protects that access.

The use in libraries of software filters to block constitutionally protected speech is inconsistent with the United States Constitution and federal law and may lead to legal exposure for the library and its governing authorities. The American Library Association affirms that the use of filtering software by libraries to block access to constitutionally protected speech violates the *Library Bill of Rights.*

What Is Blocking/ Filtering Software?

Blocking/filtering software is a mechanism used to:

- restrict access to Internet content, based on an internal database of the product, or;
- restrict access to Internet content through a database maintained external to the product itself, or;
- restrict access to Internet content to certain ratings assigned to those sites by a third party, or;
- restrict access to Internet content by scanning text, based on a keyword or phrase or text string, or;
- restrict access to Internet content by scanning pixels, based on color or tone, or;
- restrict access to Internet content based on the source of the information.

Problems with the Use of Blocking/ Filtering Software in Libraries

- Publicly supported libraries are governmental institutions subject to the First Amendment, which forbids them from restricting information based on viewpoint or content discrimination.

- Libraries are places of inclusion rather than exclusion. Current blocking/filtering software not only prevents access to what some may consider "objectionable" material, but also blocks information protected by the First Amendment. The result is that legal and useful material will inevitably be blocked.
- Filters can impose the producer's viewpoint on the community.
- Producers do not generally reveal what is being blocked, or provide methods for users to reach sites that were inadvertently blocked.
- Criteria used to block content are vaguely defined and subjectively applied.
- The vast majority of Internet sites are informative and useful. Blocking/filtering software often blocks access to materials it is not designed to block.
- Most blocking/filtering software was designed for the home market and was intended to respond to the preferences of parents making decisions for their children. As these products have moved into the library market, they have created a dissonance with the basic mission of libraries. Libraries are responsible for serving a broad and diverse community with different preferences and views. Blocking Internet sites is antithetical to library missions because it requires the library to limit information access.
- Filtering all Internet access is a one-size-fits-all "solution," which cannot adapt to the varying ages and maturity levels of individual users.
- A role of librarians is to advise and assist users in selecting information resources. Parents and only parents have the right and responsibility to restrict their own children's access—and only their own children's access—to library resources, including the Internet. Librarians do not serve in loco parentis.
- Library use of blocking/filtering software creates an implied contract with parents that their children *will not* be able to access material on the Internet that they do not wish their children to read or view. Libraries will be unable to fulfill this

implied contract, due to the technological limitations of the software.

- Laws prohibiting the production or distribution of child pornography and obscenity apply to the Internet. These laws provide protection for libraries and their users.

What Can Your Library Do to Promote Access to the Internet?

- Educate yourself, your staff, library board, governing bodies, community leaders, parents, elected officials, etc., about the Internet and how best to take advantage of the wealth of information available. Information on libraries and the Internet is available on the OIF Web site at www.ala.org/alaorg/oif/filtersandfiltering.html.
- Uphold the First Amendment by establishing and implementing written guidelines and policies on Internet use in your library in keeping with your library's overall policies on access to library materials. Information on Internet use policies is available on the OIF Web site at www.ala.org/alaorg/oif/internetusepolicies.html. (See also "Internet Filtering Statements of State Library Associations" at www.ala.org/alaorg/oif/stateresolutions.html and "Access to Electronic Information, Services, and Networks: An Interpretation of the Library Bill of Rights" at www.ala.org/alaorg/oif/electacc.html.)
- Promote Internet use by facilitating user access to Web sites that satisfy user interest and needs.
- Create and promote library Web pages designed both for general use and for use by children. These pages should point to sites that have been reviewed by library staff.
- Consider using privacy screens or arranging terminals away from public view to protect a user's confidentiality.
- Provide Internet information and training for parents and children on Internet use which will include: the wide variety

of useful resources on the Internet, child safety on the Internet, limitations of filtering software, and library rules regarding time, place, and manner restriction.
- Establish and implement user behavior policies.

Adopted by the ALA Intellectual Freedom Committee, July 1, 1997; revised November 17, 2000.

HISTORY

Resolution on the Use of Filtering Software in Libraries and Statement on Library Use of Filtering Software

A s we entered the new century, the major intellectual freedom issue facing libraries in the United States revolved around the Internet. The issue, however, did not suddenly appear in the year 2000; it became every librarian's concern when the Communications Decency Act (CDA) was signed into law in February 1996.

Although a legal challenge to the CDA was immediately filed (see part IV, section 2, "Libraries and the Internet"), the IFC nevertheless began working on a "Statement on Library Use of Filtering Software" (July 1, 1997; www.ala.org/alaorg/oif/filt_stm.html) at the 1997 Midwinter Meeting. During the 1997 Annual Conference, the draft document was the subject of a lengthy discussion by the IFC during which many points were made:

- Parental empowerment is not a negative value, but a positive one. Parents must participate with their children on the Internet. (For more information on families and the Internet, see "GetNetWise" at www.getnetwise.org/.)
- An official statement is much more "rigid" than a discussion piece and the IFC may wish, instead, to develop a question-and-answer guide, describing why filtering does not fit well in libraries.
- Filtering keeps people from information; the traditional role of librarians and libraries is to bring people and information together.

- Since libraries stand for individual choice, libraries could provide blocking mechanisms, if they were available, to enable patrons to make individual choices. Parents who do not want their children in the library without limits being placed should come in with their children to set such limits.
- Children and young people are one of the major constituencies of all libraries. The ALA has never treated children as the "possessions" of parents.
- Filters do not block all objectionable sites, and if a library uses them, a warning should be issued stating that fact. It is impossible to guarantee that any filter prevents children from accessing what some may believe are objectionable sites, and this situation creates liability for the library. Moreover, filters also block constitutionally protected speech while blocking objectionable sites.

After the discussion, the IFC agreed that any statement the Committee issued would not please everyone, but that the conference should not end without clear guidelines for librarians regarding filters. The IFC had always considered the statement to be an explanation of the proposed "Resolution on the Use of Filtering Software in Libraries" (July 2, 1997; www.ala.org/alaorg/oif/filt_res.html), on which the Committee had been working since the 1997 Midwinter Meeting. During the course of the conference, the Committee refined the resolution, and after intensive, and sometimes heated, debate, voted to take the document to the Council.

On July 2, 1997, IFC chair Ann K. Symons presented the resolution to the ALA Council. An amendment to the Committee's wording of the "resolved paragraph" had already been received and accepted by the IFC. The amended "resolved clause," brought by Gordon Conable, IFC member and councilor-at-large, read:

> RESOLVED, That the American Library Association affirms that the use of filtering software by libraries to block access to *constitutionally* protected speech violates the *Library Bill of Rights*.

Considerable debate on the resolution followed its presentation to the Council. Of grave concern was the position in which libraries would be placed if they were directed to install filtering software. It was pointed out that the *Library Bill of Rights* is a statement of professional principles to which libraries are urged to strive to adhere. The resolution explained the significance of the *Library Bill of Rights* in regard to filtering Internet content. It is always unfortunate when libraries find some of their practices to be not in total conformance with the principles of the ALA. The resolution, however, was offered both as a confirmation of what the ALA stands for and what the ALA understands to be the constitutional obligations of publicly supported libraries. The "Statement on Library Use of Filtering Software" was attached to the IFC report to Council. It elaborated the policy articulated in the "Resolution on the Use of Filtering Software in Libraries" and, like other Committee guidelines and statements, did not require Council adoption.

After a motion to close debate passed, ALA president Mary Somerville asked all those in favor of the resolution to rise, and then all those opposing the resolution to rise. The ALA Council endorsed the "Resolution on the Use of Filtering Software in Libraries" on July 2, 1997. As soon as President Somerville announced that the resolution passed, applause arose in the Council.

6

Policy on Governmental Intimidation
Policy Statement

The American Library Association opposes any use of governmental prerogatives which leads to the intimidation of the individual or the citizenry from the exercise of free expression. ALA encourages resistance to such abuse of governmental power and supports those against whom such governmental power has been employed.

Adopted February 2, 1973; amended July 1, 1981, by the ALA Council.

HISTORY

Policy on Governmental Intimidation

The issue of the federal government's abuse of authority was brought before the ALA membership at the Association's 1971 Annual Conference in Dallas. At the general membership meeting on June 23, Zoia Horn and Patricia Rom (then librarians at Bucknell University in Lewisburg, Pennsylvania) introduced a resolution on governmental intimidation. Approved by the membership and two days later amended and approved by the ALA Council, the original ALA statement on governmental intimidation read as follows:

WHEREAS, ALA is concerned with the preservation of intellectual freedom; and

WHEREAS, The freedom to think, to communicate, and discuss alternatives are essential elements of intellectual freedom; and

WHEREAS, These freedoms have been threatened by actions of the federal government through the use of informers, electronic surveillance, grand juries, and indictments under the Conspiracy Act of 1968 as demonstrated in the case of the Harrisburg 6;

NOW THEREFORE BE IT RESOLVED,

1. That the ALA Membership Meeting at Dallas recognizes the danger to intellectual freedom presented by the use of spying in libraries by government agencies;
2. That ALA go on record against the use of the grand jury procedure to intimidate anti-Vietnam War activists and people seeking justice for minority communities;

3. That ALA deplore and go on record against the use of the Conspiracy Act of 1968 as a weapon against the citizens of this country who are being indicted for such overt acts as meeting, telephoning, discussing alternative methods of bringing about change, and writing letters;
4. That the ALA Membership at Dallas assert the confidentiality of the professional relationships of librarians to the people they serve, that these relationships be respected in the same manner as medical doctors to their patients, lawyers to their clients, priests to the people they serve; and
5. That ALA assert that no librarian would lend himself to a role as informant, whether of voluntarily revealing circulation records or identifying patrons and their reading habits.

In March 1972, the Social Responsibilities Round Table asked the Executive Board to give the Association's moral support and financial aid to a librarian who had been called to testify in a federal court and, after refusing, had been jailed for civil contempt. The Social Responsibilities Round Table held that the "Dallas Resolution on Governmental Intimidation" committed the ALA to supporting this librarian. The Executive Board directed the IFC to review the resolution and "develop a statement which would interpret the resolution in terms of guidance for possible action."

At the 1972 Annual Conference in Chicago, the IFC spent a great portion of its scheduled meetings trying to fulfill this charge. The Committee felt that it was unable to develop an interpretive statement because, in the Committee's words, the 1971 statement was "good in intent, but inoperable . . . due to its narrowness of focus." Because the 1971 statement was tied to a specific piece of legislation and a specific incident, the Intellectual Freedom Committee felt the document was difficult to apply. Rather than develop an interpretive statement, the Committee promised to develop a new resolution, expressing similar concerns, for presentation to the ALA Council at the Association's 1973 Midwinter Meeting. The IFC turned its full attention to preparing a new statement at the 1973 Midwinter Meeting. The new document was presented to the Council on February 2, 1973.

The Committee originally moved that the resolution be adopted and substituted in its entirety for the 1971 Dallas statement.

However, the Council felt that the new resolution omitted one important concern: an affirmation of the confidential nature of the librarian-patron relationship, covered by Articles 4 and 5 of the Dallas resolution. To ensure that this point would be retained as part of official ALA policy, the Council rescinded all of the Dallas resolution except for Articles 4 and 5. In addition, the Council amended the IFC's resolution, confirming the ALA's support of all those against whom governmental power has been employed. The "Resolution on Governmental Intimidation," approved by the ALA Council on February 2, 1973, read as follows:

WHEREAS, The principle of intellectual freedom protects the rights of free expression of ideas, even those which are in opposition to the policies and actions of government itself; and

WHEREAS, The support of that principle is guaranteed by the First Amendment, thus insuring constitutional protection of individual or collective dissent; and

WHEREAS, Government, at whatever level, national, state, or local, must remain ever vigilant to the protection of that principle; and

WHEREAS, Government, although properly empowered to promulgate, administer, or adjudicate law, has no right to use illicitly its legally constituted powers to coerce, intimidate, or harass the individual or the citizenry from enunciating dissent; and

WHEREAS, The illegitimate uses of legitimate governmental powers have become increasingly a matter of public record, among them being the misuse of the Grand Jury and other investigative procedures, the threat to deny licenses to telecommunications media, the indictment of citizens on charges not relevant to their presumed offenses, and the repressive classification, and hence denial, of documentary material to the very public taxed for its accumulation; and

WHEREAS, These illicit uses not only constitute an abrogation of the right to exercise the principle of freedom of expression but also, and perhaps more dangerously, prefigure a society no longer hospitable to dissent;

NOW THEREFORE BE IT RESOLVED, That the American Library Association, cognizant that in the scales of justice the strength of individual liberty may outweigh the force of power, express its unswerving opposition to any use of governmental prerogative which leads to the intimidation of the individual or the citizenry from the exercise of the constitutionally protected right of free expression; and

BE IT FURTHER RESOLVED, That the American Library Association encourage its members to resist such improper uses of governmental power; and

FURTHER, That the American Library Association support those against whom such governmental power has been employed.

During the review of the ALA intellectual freedom policies and statements which followed the Council's adoption in 1980 of the revision of the *Library Bill of Rights,* the Intellectual Freedom Committee determined that two problems existed with the "Resolution on Governmental Intimidation." The first was the matter of format. It was a resolution and included a series of "whereas clauses," which were helpful in explaining the policy section (i.e., the "resolved clauses") but were not theoretically a part of the policy. The second problem related to the policy section itself, which the Committee believed should stand alone without the necessity of explanatory phrases. As in all cases when examples are used, these tend to date the policy to the period of time in which it was originally created. They also tend to dilute the clarity and force of the policy statement.

The Committee agreed that any policy on governmental intimidation should strongly oppose this activity and that, in addition, the policy should indicate ALA support of those who resist governmental intimidation. In presenting the amended policy to the ALA Council, the Intellectual Freedom Committee decided that the 1973 version would be maintained in full in the historical file and that it would be made available as necessary. The amended policy on governmental intimidation was adopted by the ALA Council on July 1, 1981.

In 1999–2000, as part of the periodic review of all policies, the IFC reviewed "Policy on Governmental Intimidation" and did not recommend any changes.

7

Resolution on Access to the Use of Libraries and Information by Individuals with Physical or Mental Impairment

WHEREAS, The Intellectual Freedom Committee is concerned with freedom of access; and

WHEREAS, The *Library Bill of Rights* states that "books and other library resources should be provided for the interest, information, and enlightenment of all people of the community the library serves" and "a person's right to use a library should not be denied or abridged . . ."; and

WHEREAS, Federal and state constitutional and statutory laws forbid public institutions from discriminating against handicapped individuals, i.e., persons who have a physical or mental impairment; and

WHEREAS, Court opinions have clearly interpreted said laws as proscribing discrimination against persons who have acquired immune deficiency syndrome ("AIDS"), AIDS-related complex ("ARC"), or who test positive for the human immunodeficiency virus ("HIV"); and

WHEREAS, The American Medical Association and the United States Department of Health and Human Services have opined that while the human immunodeficiency virus that causes AIDS is a contagious disease, it cannot be transmitted by casual contact;

NOW THEREFORE BE IT RESOLVED, That the *Library Bill of Rights* of the American Library Association which insures access to library facilities, materials and services by all people of the community, includes individuals with physical or mental impairments; and

BE IT FURTHER RESOLVED, That the American Library Association deplores discrimination against and denial or abridgment of library and information access to persons of all ages who have acquired immune deficiency syndrome ("AIDS"), AIDS-related complex ("ARC"), or who test positive for the human immunodeficiency virus ("HIV").

Adopted January 13, 1988, by the ALA Council.

HISTORY

Resolution on Access to the Use of Libraries and Information by Individuals with Physical or Mental Impairment

Immediately before the 1988 Midwinter Meeting in San Antonio, the Intellectual Freedom Committee received a request for a statement of the ALA's position concerning access to libraries and information by those with physical and mental impairments, particularly persons with the AIDS virus.

The occasion for this request was the barring of a child in Lake City, Tennessee, from attendance at the public school because the child had AIDS. Public librarians in the area perceived a need for their boards to adopt a clear policy about the access rights of persons with AIDS. In the search for existing policy statements, the Intellectual Freedom Committee was contacted, but no such statements were found.

Recognizing the need for definitive language affirming the access rights of all physically and mentally impaired persons and in light of a rising hysteria over AIDS, the IFC took to the ALA Council the following: "Resolution on Access to the Use of Libraries and Information by Individuals with Physical or Mental Impairment." It was adopted by the Council on January 13, 1988.

In line with the practice of periodic review, the IFC reviewed "Resolution on Access to the Use of Libraries and Information by Individuals with Physical or Mental Impairment" in 1999–2000 and recommended no changes.

8

Guidelines for the Development and Implementation of Policies, Regulations and Procedures Affecting Access to Library Materials, Services and Facilities

Publicly supported libraries exist within the context of a body of law derived from the United States Constitution and appropriate state constitutions, defined by statute, and implemented by regulations, policies and procedures established by their governing bodies and administrations. These regulations, policies and procedures establish the mission of the library, define its functions, services and operations and ascertain the rights and responsibilities of the clientele served by the library.

Publicly supported library service is based upon the First Amendment right of free expression. The publicly supported library provides free and equal access to information for all people of the community it serves. Thus, publicly supported libraries are governmental agencies designated as limited public forums for access to information. Libraries that make meeting rooms, exhibit spaces and/or bulletin boards available for public use are also designated as limited public forums for the exchange of information.

Many libraries adopt administrative policies and procedures regulating the organization and use of library materials, services and facilities. These policies and procedures affect access and may have the effect of restricting, denying or creating barriers to access to the library as a public forum, including the library's resources, facilities and services. Library policies and procedures that impinge upon First Amendment rights are subject to a higher standard of review than may be required in the policies of other public services and facilities.

Policies, procedures or regulations that may result in denying, restricting or creating physical or economic barriers to access to the library's public forum must be based on a compelling government interest. However, library governing authorities may place reasonable and narrowly drawn restrictions on the time, place or manner of access to library resources, services or facilities, provided that such restrictions are not based upon arbitrary distinctions between individuals or classes of individuals.

The American Library Association has adopted the *Library Bill of Rights* and Interpretations of the *Library Bill of Rights* to provide library governing authorities, librarians and other library staff and library users with guidelines on how constitutional principles apply to libraries in the United States of America.

The American Library Association's Intellectual Freedom Committee recommends that publicly supported libraries use the following guidelines, based on constitutional principles, to develop policies, regulations and procedures.

Guidelines

All library policies, regulations and procedures should be carefully examined to determine if they may result in denying, restricting or creating barriers to access. If they may result in such restrictions, they:

1. should be developed and implemented within the legal framework that applies to the library. This includes: the United States Constitution, including the First and Fourteenth Amendments, due process and equal treatment under the law; the applicable state constitution; federal and state civil rights legislation; all other applicable federal, state and local legislation; and applicable case law;
2. should cite statutes or ordinances upon which the authority to make that policy is based, when appropriate;
3. should be developed and implemented within the framework of the *Library Bill of Rights* and its Interpretations;

4. should be based upon the library's mission and objectives;
5. should only impose restrictions on the access to, or use of library resources, services or facilities when those restrictions are necessary to achieve the library's mission and objectives;
6. should narrowly tailor prohibitions or restrictions, in the rare instances when they are required, so they are not more restrictive than needed to serve their objectives;
7. should attempt to balance competing interests and avoid favoring the majority at the expense of individual rights, or allowing individual users' rights to interfere materially with the majority's rights to free and equal access to library resources, services and facilities;
8. should avoid arbitrary distinctions between individuals or classes of users, and should not have the effect of denying or abridging a person's right to use library resources, services or facilities based upon arbitrary distinctions such as origin, age, background or views;

In the *Library Bill of Rights* and all of its Interpretations, it is intended that: "origin" encompasses all the characteristics of individuals that are inherent in the circumstances of their birth; "age" encompasses all the characteristics of individuals that are inherent in their levels of development and maturity; "background" encompasses all the characteristics of individuals that are a result of their life experiences; and "views" encompasses all the opinions and beliefs held and expressed by individuals;

9. should not target specific users or groups of users based upon an assumption or expectation that such users might engage in behavior that will materially interfere with the achievement of substantial library objectives;
10. must be clearly stated so that a reasonably intelligent person will have fair warning of what is expected;
11. must provide a means of appeal;
12. must be reviewed regularly by the library's governing authority and by its legal counsel;
13. must be communicated clearly and made available in an effective manner to all library users;

14. must be enforced evenhandedly, and not in a manner intended to benefit or disfavor any person or group in an arbitrary or capricious manner;

Libraries should develop an ongoing staff training program designed to foster the understanding of the legal framework and principles underlying library policies and to assist staff in gaining the skill and ability to respond to potentially difficult circumstances in a timely, direct and open manner. This program should include training to develop empathy and understanding of the social and economic problems of some library users;

15. should, if reasonably possible, provide adequate alternative means of access to information for those whose behavior results in the denial or restriction of access to any library resource, service or facility.

Adopted June 28, 1994, by the ALA Intellectual Freedom Committee.

HISTORY

Guidelines for the Development and Implementation of Policies, Regulations and Procedures Affecting Access to Library Materials, Services and Facilities

As part of the review of all of the Interpretations of the *Library Bill of Rights*, begun in 1989 in response to a request by the Minority Concerns Committee that the policy reflect equity of access without regard to language or economic status, the Intellectual Freedom Committee took up the Interpretation entitled "Administrative Policies and Procedures Affecting Access to Library Resources and Services." In 1991, that Interpretation was revised substantially and retitled "Regulations, Policies and Procedures Affecting Access to Library Resources and Services." The newly revised Interpretation responded to issues raised in two 1991 court cases which had important implications for libraries. The policy also addressed intellectual freedom concerns raised by challenges to materials that were inappropriately handled where the challenges had originated within libraries by librarians, library administration, or library staff.

The two court cases referenced in the Interpretation were *Rust v. Sullivan*[1] and *Kreimer v. Morristown*.[2] In *Rust v. Sullivan*, the United States Supreme Court upheld Department of Health and Human Services regulations prohibiting the recipients of Title X funds (primarily, family planning clinics) from providing information about abortion or any abortion counseling whatsoever to their clients. In a close 5-4 decision, the Court held that the prohibition was a permissible government choice, favoring some activities over others. In a stinging dissent, Justice Harry A. Blackmun pointed out that, for the first time, the Court had sanctioned outright viewpoint-based discrimination in a federally funded program. In other words, the

Supreme Court had said that it was permissible for the federal government to selectively fund speech promoting one point of view while prohibiting the mention of the opposing position.

The decision was significant for libraries because, although libraries take no position on the underlying issue, they do provide materials and information from all points of view on topics of current and historical interest, including abortion. Librarians realized that, if medical professionals working in facilities supported by federal funds could be "gagged," so could libraries that received public money. The *Rust* decision was issued in an atmosphere of severe fiscal conservancy, when many public libraries already had experienced massive funding cuts. The potential of those cuts to be linked to ideological, viewpoint-based restrictions on library collections was clear.

The other significant court decision addressed in the 1991 revision of the Interpretation was *Kreimer* v. *Morristown*, a case that came from the United States District Court in New Jersey. Richard Kreimer, a homeless man, challenged rules and regulations of the Morristown, New Jersey, Public Library, on the grounds that they, on their face, discriminated against homeless and economically disadvantaged patrons.[3] Library officials, in turn, contended that Kreimer had annoyed other patrons, exuded a body odor so offensive as to interfere with other patrons' use of the library, stared at people, and followed children around the stacks. According to the court's decision, the library admitted that some of the regulations had specifically been designed to bar Kreimer from the institution.

The district court found that the library's regulations prohibiting patrons from staring or annoying other patrons were overbroad and vague and, therefore, unconstitutional. The court recognized and firmly supported the right and the responsibility of public libraries to make rules governing their use and governing patron behavior, but the court also firmly upheld the First Amendment right to receive information in publicly funded libraries. The court held that, in the interest of all patrons, library rules should be specific, necessary, and neutral, and not susceptible of discriminatory application. In addition, they must not be so vague that their application is subject to the whims of individual library staff members.

The *Morristown* decision firmly upheld First Amendment rights to receive information in libraries and provided a powerful argument supporting libraries' resistance to censorship. At the same time, the judge recognized the necessity of specific, necessary, and neutral rules governing patron behavior to ensure equal access for all.

The Morristown Library appealed the district court's decision to the United States Court of Appeals for the Third Circuit. That court reversed the lower court's decision, finding that the Morristown Library's rules were constitutional on their face. However, the court also found that rules that could result in the expulsion of a person from a public library do implicate First Amendment rights and must be analyzed under First Amendment principles. In addition, the court held that public libraries are limited public fora for access to information. This is a highly significant holding, placing public libraries squarely within the First Amendment realm and recognizing, for the first time by any court, that libraries have a unique position in the fulfillment of the First Amendment right to receive information.

The Intellectual Freedom Committee believed it would be beneficial to produce a policy statement of the American Library Association that placed the ALA's intellectual freedom policy squarely within the realm of First Amendment law. Such placement would counter accusations by opposition pressure groups that the American Library Association's policies were simply the ALA's opinion and not in any way binding in effect. Whereas it is true that no library is compelled to adopt the ALA's policies, publicly supported libraries are subject to First Amendment legal principles. The newly revised Interpretation made this explicit by quoting language from both the *Rust* and *Morristown* decisions.

The document adopted by the Council at the 1991 Annual Conference included quotes from the district court's opinion in the *Morristown* case, which was subsequently reversed by the Third Circuit, necessitating a review for possible revision. The process of revising the Interpretation began at the Annual Conference in 1993. At the 1994 Midwinter Meeting in Los Angeles, it became apparent that the Interpretation attempted to address very broad areas of library operation, which could conceivably be addressed in many different library policies; revision was proving difficult. Given the difficulty the IFC had had in attempting revision, the Committee concluded that it might be more appropriate and successful to revise the Interpretation into a set of guidelines. A draft of "Guidelines for the Development of Policies, Regulations and Procedures Affecting Access to Library Materials, Services and Facilities" was produced at the Midwinter Meeting and circulated to ALA units for comment following that meeting. At the 1994 Annual Conference in Miami Beach, the Committee revised and renamed the document, and formally adopted it. "Guidelines for the Development and Implementation of Policies, Regulations and Procedures Affecting Access to Library Materials, Services and Facilities" was presented to the Council for its information, together with a recommendation that the Interpretation of the *Library Bill of Rights* entitled "Regulations, Policies and Procedures Affecting Access to Library Resources and Services" be rescinded. The Council acted on the IFC's recommendation, rescinding the Interpretation. The "Guidelines" were made available to libraries contemplating new or revised policies.

The "Guidelines" were intended to provide signposts for libraries as they develop policies, procedures, and regulations governing many areas of library operation, encouraging libraries to consider at the outset the First Amendment implications of their policies, as well as the potential applicability of state constitutional principles and federal, state, and local law. In addition, the "Guidelines" suggest that policies address considerations such as due process and equity of access, and that they ensure nondiscrimination between classes of library patrons.

In line with the ongoing practice of periodic review, the IFC carefully reviewed all statements during 1999–2000, especially in regard to their applicability to the Internet. No changes were recommended in these guidelines.

NOTES

1. *Rust* v. *Sullivan,* 59 U.S.L.W 4451, 111 S.Ct. 1759 (1991).
2. *Richard R. Kreimer* v. *Bureau of Police for the Town of Morristown, et al.,* 765 F.Supp 181 (D.N.J. 1991), rev'd and remanded, 958 F.2d 1242 (3rd Cir. 1992).
3. For more on the *Morristown case,* see part IV, section 5, "Public Libraries as Limited Public Fora for Access to Information."

9

Guidelines for the Development of Policies and Procedures regarding User Behavior and Library Usage

Libraries are faced with problems of user behavior that must be addressed to insure the effective delivery of service and full access to facilities. Library governing bodies must approach the regulation of user behavior within the framework of the ALA "Code of Ethics," the *Library Bill of Rights,* and the law, including local and state statutes, constitutional standards under the First and Fourteenth Amendments, due process and equal treatment under the law.

Publicly supported library service is based upon the First Amendment right of free expression. Publicly supported libraries are recognized as limited public forums for access to information. At least one federal court of appeals has recognized a First Amendment right to receive information in a public library. Library policies and procedures that could impinge upon such rights are subject to a higher standard of review than may be required in the policies of other public services and facilities.

There is a significant government interest in maintaining a library environment that is conducive to all users' exercise of their constitutionally protected right to receive information. This significant interest authorizes publicly supported libraries to maintain a safe and healthy environment in which library users and staff can be free from harassment, intimidation, and threats to their safety and well-being. Libraries should provide appropriate safeguards against such behavior and enforce policies and procedures addressing that behavior when it occurs.

In order to protect all library users' right of access to library facilities, to ensure the safety of users and staff, and to protect library resources and facilities from damage, the library's governing authority may impose reasonable restrictions on the time, place, or manner of library access.

Guidelines

The American Library Association's Intellectual Freedom Committee recommends that publicly supported libraries use the following guidelines, based upon constitutional principles, to develop policies and procedures governing the use of library facilities:

1. Libraries are advised to rely upon existing legislation and law enforcement mechanisms as the primary means of controlling behavior that involves public safety, criminal behavior, or other issues covered by existing local, state, or federal statutes. In many instances, this legal framework may be sufficient to provide the library with the necessary tools to maintain order.
2. If the library's governing body chooses to write its own policies and procedures regarding user behavior or access to library facilities, services, and resources, the policies should cite statutes or ordinances upon which the authority to make those policies is based.
3. Library policies and procedures governing the use of library facilities should be carefully examined to insure that they are not in violation of the *Library Bill of Rights.*
4. Reasonable and narrowly drawn policies and procedures designed to prohibit interference with use of the facilities and services by others, or to prohibit activities inconsistent with achievement of the library's mission statement and objectives, are acceptable.
5. Such policies and the attendant implementing procedures should be reviewed frequently and updated as needed by the library's legal counsel for compliance with federal and state

constitutional requirements, federal and state civil rights legislation, all other applicable federal and state legislation, and applicable case law.

6. Every effort should be made to respond to potentially difficult circumstances of user behavior in a timely, direct, and open manner. Common sense, reason and sensitivity should be used to resolve issues in a constructive and positive manner without escalation.

7. Libraries should develop an ongoing staff training program based upon their user behavior policy. This program should include training to develop empathy and understanding of the social and economic problems of some library users.

8. Policies and regulations that impose restrictions on library access:

   a. should apply only to those activities that materially interfere with the public's right of access to library facilities, the safety of users and staff, and the protection of library resources and facilities;

   b. should narrowly tailor prohibitions or restrictions so that they are not more restrictive than needed to serve their objectives;

   c. should attempt to balance competing interests and avoid favoring the majority at the expense of individual rights, or allowing individual users' rights to supersede those of the majority of library users;

   d. should be based solely upon actual behavior and not upon arbitrary distinctions between individuals or classes of individuals. Policies should not target specific users or groups of users based upon an assumption or expectation that such users might engage in behaviors that could disrupt library service;

   e. should not restrict access to the library by persons who merely inspire the anger or annoyance of others. Policies based upon appearance or behavior that is merely annoying or which merely generates negative subjective reactions from others, do not meet the necessary standard. Such policies should employ a reasonable, objective standard based on the behavior itself;

f. must provide a clear description of the behavior that is prohibited and the various enforcement measures in place, so that a reasonably intelligent person will have both due process and fair warning; this description must be continuously and clearly communicated in an effective manner to all library users;

g. to the extent possible, should not leave those affected without adequate alternative means of access to information in the library;

h. must be enforced evenhandedly, and not in a manner intended to benefit or disfavor any person or group in an arbitrary or capricious manner.

The user behaviors addressed in these Guidelines are the result of a wide variety of individual and societal conditions. Libraries should take advantage of the expertise of local social service agencies, advocacy groups, mental health professionals, law enforcement officials, and other community resources to develop community strategies for addressing the needs of a diverse population.

Adopted January 24, 1993, by the ALA Intellectual Freedom Committee; revised November 17, 2000.

HISTORY

Guidelines for the Development of Policies and Procedures regarding User Behavior and Library Usage

In the wake of the 1991 district court decision in *Kreimer* v. *Morristown*,[1] a case involving a challenge to regulations implemented by the Morristown, New Jersey, Public Library, the Intellectual Freedom Committee recognized a need for guidance in the development of library policies governing patron behavior. At the 1991 ALA Annual Conference in Atlanta, the Committee established a task force to draft guidelines. The task force was charged with seeking expert legal advice in developing suggestions to assist local libraries in reviewing or drafting policies to deal with problem patrons that would meet constitutional standards. From the very beginning, the Intellectual Freedom Committee recognized that it would be impossible to present a set of model regulations, because the legal considerations governing actual behavior in differing jurisdictions vary. Instead, the Committee took the approach of providing a constitutional framework and encouraging libraries to consider carefully local statutory law, which might apply to particular patron-behavior situations.

The task force, chaired by then Public Library Association IFC chair Candace Morgan, presented a draft at the 1992 Midwinter Meeting in San Antonio. In presenting the draft to the Committee, Morgan explained that it was based almost entirely on advice obtained from the ALA and Freedom to Read Foundation legal counsel firm Jenner & Block. The Committee also sponsored an open hearing at that Midwinter Meeting to receive additional comment on the draft from librarians. Despite explanations of why it would be unwise and probably impossible to provide a model set of rules, many librarians who testified and offered comments requested more specificity. Following the hearing, the task force met and agreed that, although it would be difficult to promulgate specific regulations within the context of widely varying local and state law, the task force could address the need for specificity by highlighting the necessity to refer to that local law. The task force also decided to address, in a similar, general way, health and safety regulations, equal access concerns, civil rights and due process, and so forth. Reference to staff training was also added. Another open forum was held at the 1992 Annual Conference in San Francisco to receive additional comment on a revised draft addressing these issues.

Throughout the development of the guidelines, the library community continued to discuss the *Kreimer* v. *Morristown* case. The Intellectual Freedom Committee and the task force to develop the guidelines took great pains to inform the library community that the guidelines were not meant as a specific response to the *Morristown* case. The subject of the task force's hearings was not the *Morristown* case but the draft guidelines, which went far beyond the specifics of that dispute. The task force stressed that it was attempting to provide a constitutional framework in which libraries could proceed in the development of their own regulations regarding user behavior of all types, not just the conduct addressed by the rules of the Morristown library that were challenged in the litigation.

However, because questions and misunderstandings persisted about the legal issues involved, Judge H. Lee Sarokin, the federal district court judge who rendered the original opinion in the *Kreimer* v. *Morristown* case, appeared at the 1992 Annual Conference in San Francisco to speak generally about those legal issues. The reception he received from some librarians in the audience, many of whom had not read his opinion and did not understand the legal status of the case, could only be described as openly hostile. Librarians from New Jersey continued to focus on the alleged behavior of one library patron, Richard Kreimer, and were patently uninterested in the broader legal issues the judge addressed.

Following Judge Sarokin's appearance, the task force once again revised the draft guidelines. The intent was to make the guidelines as broad and general as possible so that local libraries would have a framework in which to formulate their own rules with reference to both local law and constitutional principles. The task force stressed that the guidelines did not, and were not intended to, constitute an ALA response to the *Morristown* decision. The IFC voted to approve the revised draft and to circulate it once again for additional comment.

After final editorial revisions in light of additional comments, the IFC adopted the final version of the "Guidelines for the Development of Policies and Procedures regarding User Behavior and Library Usage" and presented it for information to the ALA Council at the 1993 Midwinter Meeting in Denver.

In line with the ongoing practice of periodic review, the IFC carefully reviewed all statements during 1999–2000, especially in regard to their applicability to the Internet. The IFC recommended only slight editorial changes to this policy, with one exception. Under point 8, paragraph f, the IFC included the phrase "and the various enforcement measures in place," so that it is clearer that not only should a fair warning measure be in place, but also a means for due process.

NOTE

1. *Richard R. Kreimer* v. *Bureau of Police for the Town of Morristown, et al.,* 765 F.Supp. 181 (D.N.J. 1991); rev'd in part and remanded, 958 F.2d 1242 (3rd Cir. 1992). For more on the *Morristown* case, see part IV, section 5, "Public Libraries as Limited Public Fora for Access to Information."

10

Dealing with Concerns
about Library Resources
Procedural Statement

As with any public service, libraries receive complaints and expressions of concern. One of the librarian's responsibilities is to handle these complaints in a respectful and fair manner. The complaints that librarians often worry about most are those dealing with library resources or free access policies. The key to successfully handling these complaints is to be sure the library staff and the governing authorities are all knowledgeable about the complaint procedures and their implementation. As normal operating procedure each library should:

1. *Maintain a materials selection policy.* It should be in written form and approved by the appropriate governing authority. It should apply to all library materials equally.
2. *Maintain a library service policy.* This should cover registration policies, programming and services in the library that involve access issues.
3. *Maintain a clearly defined method for handling complaints.* The complaint must be filed in writing and the complainant must be properly identified before action is taken. A decision should be deferred until fully considered by appropriate administrative authority. [See figure 1 for a sample complaint form.] The process should be followed, whether the complaint originates internally or externally.
4. *Maintain in-service training.* Conduct periodic in-service training to acquaint staff, administration, and the governing

FIGURE I
Request for Reconsideration of Library Resources

[This is where you identify who in your own structure
has authorized use of this form—director, Board of Trustees,
Board of Education, etc.—and to whom to return the form.]

EXAMPLE: The school board of Mainstream County, U.S.A., has delegated the responsibility for selection and evaluation of library/educational resources to the school library media specialist/curriculum committee, and has established reconsideration procedures to address concerns about those resources. Completion of this form is the first step in those procedures. If you wish to request reconsideration of school or library resources, please return the completed form to the Coordinator of Library Media Resources, Mainstream School Dist., 1 Mainstream Plaza, Anytown, U.S.A.

Name _____ Date _____

Address _____

City _____ State _____ Zip Code_____

Phone _____

Do you represent yourself? _____ Your organization? _____

1. Resource on which you are commenting: ____ Book ____ Textbook

   ____ Video ____ Display ____ Magazine ____ Library Program

   ____ Audio Recording ____ Newspaper

   ____ Electronic information/network (please specify):

   _____

   ____ Other: _____

   Title: _____

   Author/Producer: _____

2. What brought this resource to your attention?

   _____

3. Have you examined the entire resource?

   _____

4. What concerns you about the resource? (Use other side or additional pages if necessary.)

   _____

5. Are there resource(s) you suggest to provide additional information and/or other viewpoints on this topic?

_____

Revised by the ALA Intellectual Freedom Committee, June 27, 1995.

authority with the materials selection policy and library service policy and procedures for handling complaints.

5. *Maintain lines of communication with civic, religious, educational, and political bodies of the community.* Library board and staff participation in local civic organizations and presentations to these organizations should emphasize the library's selection process and intellectual freedom principles.

6. *Maintain a vigorous public information program on behalf of intellectual freedom.* Newspapers, radio, and television should be informed of policies governing resource selection and use, and of any special activities pertaining to intellectual freedom.

7. *Maintain familiarity with any local municipal and state legislation pertaining to intellectual freedom and First Amendment rights.*

Following these practices will not preclude receiving complaints from pressure groups or individuals but should provide a base from which to operate when these concerns are expressed. When a complaint is made, follow one or more of the steps listed below:

a. Listen calmly and courteously to the complaint. Remember the person has a right to express a concern. Use of good communication skills helps many people understand the need for diversity in library collections and the use of library resources. In the event the person is not satisfied, advise the complainant of the library policy and procedures for handling library resource statements of concern. If a person does fill out a form about their concern, make sure a prompt written reply related to the concern is sent.

b. It is essential to notify the administration and/or the governing authority (library board, etc.) of the complaint and assure them that the library's procedures are being followed. Present full, written information giving the nature of the complaint and identifying the source.

c. When appropriate, seek the support of the local media. Freedom to read and freedom of the press go hand in hand.

d. When appropriate, inform local civic organizations of the facts and enlist their support. Meet negative pressure with positive pressure.

e. Assert the principles of the *Library Bill of Rights* as a professional responsibility. Laws governing obscenity, subversive material and other questionable matter are subject to interpretation by courts. Library resources found to meet the standards set in the materials selection or collection development policy should not be removed or restricted from public access until after an adversary hearing resulting in a final judicial determination.

f. Contact the ALA Office for Intellectual Freedom and your state intellectual freedom committee to inform them of the complaint and to enlist their support and the assistance of other agencies.

The principles and procedures discussed above apply to all kinds of resource related complaints or attempts to censor and are supported by groups such as the National Education Association, the American Civil Liberties Union and the National Council of Teachers of English, as well as the American Library Association. While the practices provide positive means for preparing for and meeting pressure group complaints, they serve the more general purpose of supporting the *Library Bill of Rights*, particularly Article III, which states that "Libraries should challenge censorship in the fulfillment of their responsibility to provide information and enlightenment."

Revised by the ALA Intellectual Freedom Committee, January 12, 1983; November 17, 2000.

HISTORY

Dealing with Concerns
about Library Resources

The *Library Bill of Rights* and its Interpretations are all broad statements of policy. Their purpose is to clarify application of the basic principles of intellectual freedom to libraries. As statements of policy, they offer general guidance for the resolution of practical problems, but they are not in and of themselves practical or procedural documents. Yet in the course of applying the principles of the *Library Bill of Rights,* librarians frequently encounter pressures and concerns from those who, consciously or not, may seek to distort the library into an instrument of their own beliefs. "Dealing with Concerns about Library Resources" outlines basic procedural and practical measures for responding to such pressure.

"Dealing with Concerns about Library Resources" is a procedural document. Its goal is to assist librarians in implementing the ALA's intellectual freedom policies; it is not itself a policy statement. Its roots, however, lie in a previous document, titled "How Libraries and Schools Can Resist Censorship," first adopted in 1962 but rescinded by the ALA Council at the request of the IFC in 1981.

The early 1960s saw increased censorship attacks on libraries and strenuous assaults on the freedom to read; "witch hunts" in Georgia, censorship of some best-sellers, and heated controversy over Henry Miller's Tropic of Cancer were prominent during the period. In response to this situation, a group of librarians and publishers met in Washington, D.C., on January 5, 1962, to draft a statement on censorship. The committee was composed of David H. Clift, executive director of the American Library Association; Dan

Lacy, managing director of the American Book Publishers Council; Margaret Dudley, executive secretary of the National Book Committee; Emerson Greenaway, chair of the ALA Legislative Committee; and Archie McNeal, chair of the ALA Intellectual Freedom Committee. The statement this group wrote, titled "How Libraries and Schools Can Resist Censorship," gave support and step-by-step guidelines whereby a library can thwart the censor.

In introducing the statement to the ALA Council, McNeal urged its support, especially in light of the nationwide attempts at censorship. "How Libraries and Schools Can Resist Censorship" was approved unanimously by the ALA Council on February 1, 1962. The statement was endorsed by the Adult Education Association's Executive Committee, the American Book Publishers Council, the American Civil Liberties Union, the National Book Committee, the National Council of Teachers of English, the National Education Association's Commission on Professional Rights and Responsibilities, and the National Education Association's Department of Class Room Teachers.

At the 1972 Midwinter Meeting of the Intellectual Freedom Committee, the original statement on resisting censorship was altered to include all types of libraries, not just school and public libraries; and "library materials" was substituted for "books." The new document, "How Libraries Can Resist Censorship," was adopted by the ALA Council on January 28, 1972:

> Libraries of all sizes and types continue to be targets of pressure from groups and individuals who wish to use the library as an instrument of their own tastes and views. The problem differs somewhat between the public library, with a responsibility to present as wide a spectrum of materials as its budget can afford, and the school or academic library, whose collection is designed to support the educational objectives of the institution. Both, however, involve the freedom of the library to meet its professional responsibilities to the whole community.
>
> To combat censorship efforts from groups and individuals, every library should take certain measures to clarify policies and establish community relations. While these steps should be taken regardless of any attack or prospect of attack, they will provide a firm and clearly defined position if selection policies are challenged. As normal operating procedure, each library should:

1. Maintain a definite materials selection policy. It should be in written form and approved by the appropriate regents or other governing authority. It should apply to all library materials equally.
2. Maintain a clearly defined method for handling complaints. Basic requirements should be that the complaint be filed in writing and the complainant be properly identified before his request is considered. Action should be deferred until full consideration by appropriate administrative authority.
3. Maintain lines of communication with civic, religious, educational, and political bodies of the community. Participation in local civic organizations and in community affairs is desirable. Because the library and the school are key centers of the community, the librarian should be known publicly as a community leader.
4. Maintain a vigorous public relations program on behalf of intellectual freedom. Newspapers, radio, and television should be informed of policies governing materials selection and use, and of any special activities pertaining to intellectual freedom.

Adherence to the practices listed above will not preclude confrontations with pressure groups or individuals but may provide a base from which to counter efforts to place restraints on the library. If a confrontation does occur, librarians should remember the following:

1. Remain calm. Don't confuse noise with substance. Require the deliberate handling of the complaint under previously established rules. Treat the group or individual who complains with dignity, courtesy, and good humor. Given the facts, most citizens will support the responsible exercise of professional freedom by teachers and librarians, and will insist on protecting their own freedom to read.
2. Take immediate steps to assure that the full facts surrounding a complaint are known to the administration and the governing authority. The school librarian-media specialist should go through the principal to the superintendent and the school board; the public librarian, to the board of trustees or to the appropriate governing authority of the

community; the college or university librarian, to the president and through him to the board of trustees. Present full, written information giving the nature of the complaint and identifying the source.

3. Seek the support of the local press when appropriate. The freedom to read and freedom of the press go hand in hand.

4. Inform local civic organizations of the facts and enlist their support when appropriate. Meet negative pressure with positive pressure.

5. In most cases, defend the principle of the freedom to read and the professional responsibility of teachers and librarians. Only rarely is it necessary to defend the individual item. Laws governing obscenity, subversive material, and other questionable matter are subject to interpretation by courts. Responsibility for removal of any library materials from public access rests with this established process.

6. Inform the ALA Office for Intellectual Freedom and other appropriate national and state organizations concerned with intellectual freedom of the nature of the problem. Even though censorship must be fought at the local level, there is value in the support and assistance of agencies outside the area which have no personal involvement. They can often cite parallel cases and suggest methods of meeting an attack.

The foregoing principles and procedures apply to all kinds of censorship attacks and are supported by groups such as the National Education Association, the American Civil Liberties Union, and the National Council of Teachers of English, as well as the American Library Association. Whereas the practices provide positive means for preparing for and meeting pressure group complaints, they serve the more general purpose of supporting the *Library Bill of Rights*, particularly Article III, which states that "censorship should be challenged by libraries in the maintenance of their responsibility to provide public information and enlightenment." Adherence to this principle is especially necessary when the library is under pressure.

During 1980–81, following the 1980 revision of the *Library Bill of Rights*, the Intellectual Freedom Committee reviewed "How Libraries Can Resist Censorship" and found that the bulk of the document was simply a procedural elaboration and repetitive of other policies. Stripped to its essentials, its main use was as a concise statement of practical measures libraries can and should take in preparing for and responding to potentially censorious complaints and pressures. At the 1981 Annual Conference, the IFC voted to request the ALA Council to rescind the document, which the Council did. Later that year, "Dealing with Complaints about Resources," based in part on the former document and on discussions by the IFC, was published as a procedural statement. At the 1983 Midwinter Meeting in San Antonio, the statement was again revised by the Committee and retitled "Dealing with Concerns about Library Resources." This document is the basis for part V of this manual, Before the Censor Comes: Essential Preparations.

In line with the ongoing practice of periodic review, the IFC carefully reviewed all statements during 1999–2000, especially in regard to their applicability to the Internet. The IFC recommended only slight editorial changes to this policy. Under point 7, paragraph e, the IFC substituted the word "resources" for "materials," included both materials selection "or collection development," and emphasized that library resources must be neither removed nor "restricted."

II

Guidelines and Considerations for Developing a Public Library Internet Use Policy

Intellectual Freedom's Meaning and Scope

Libraries are a major information source in our society for access to the larger world of human expression. For some, they are the only available access point. Libraries connect individuals with the ideas, information, and images they seek. Libraries that raise the barrier to access damage their credibility with their users.

By providing information across the spectrum of human interests, and making it available and accessible to anyone who wants it, libraries allow individuals to exercise their First Amendment right to seek and receive all types of expression, from all points of view. Materials in any given library cover the spectrum of human experience and thought, even those that some people may consider false, offensive, or dangerous.

In the millions of Web sites available on the Internet, there are some—often loosely called "pornography"—that parents, or adults generally, do not want children to see. A very small fraction of those sexually explicit materials is actually obscenity or child pornography, which are not constitutionally protected. The rest, like the overwhelming majority of materials on the Internet, is protected by the First Amendment.

Obscenity and child pornography are illegal. Federal and state statutes, the latter varying slightly depending on the jurisdiction, proscribe such materials. The U.S. Supreme Court has settled most questions about what obscenity and child pornography statutes are constitutionally sound.

According to the Court:

Obscenity must be determined using a three-part test. To be obscene, (1) the average person, applying contemporary community standards, must find that the work, taken as a whole, appeals to prurient interests; (2) the work must depict or describe, in a patently offensive way, sexual conduct as specified in the applicable statutes; and (3) the work, taken as a whole, must lack serious literary, artistic, political, or scientific value.

Child pornography may be determined using a slightly less rigorous test. To be child pornography, the work must involve depictions of sexual conduct specified in the applicable statutes and use images of children below a specified age.

Many states and some localities have "harmful to minors" laws. These laws regulate free speech with respect to minors, typically forbidding the display or dissemination of certain sexually explicit materials to children, as further specified in the laws.

According to the U.S. Supreme Court:

Materials *harmful to minors* include descriptions or representations of nudity, sexual conduct, or sexual excitement that appeal to the prurient, shameful, or morbid interest of minors; are patently offensive to prevailing standards in the adult community as a whole with respect to what is suitable material for minors; and lack serious literary, artistic, political, or scientific value for minors.

Knowing what materials are actually obscenity or child pornography is difficult, as is knowing when minors are involved, and what materials are actually "harmful to minors." The applicable statutes and laws, together with the written decisions of courts that have applied them in actual cases, are the only official guides. Libraries and librarians are not in a position to make those decisions for library users or for citizens generally. Only courts have constitutional authority to determine, in accordance with due process, what materials are obscenity, child pornography, or "harmful to minors."

Obscenity and child pornography statutes apply to materials on the Internet; such materials are currently being regulated there. The applicability of particular "harmful to minors" laws to materials on the Internet is unsettled, however. Because of the uncertainty, various federal and state legislative proposals are pending specifically to "protect" children from sexually explicit materials on the Internet.

Intellectual Freedom's First Amendment Foundations

Courts have held that the public library is a "limited public forum." "Limited" means it is a place for access to free and open communication, subject to reasonable restrictions as to the time, place, and manner for doing so. As with any public forum the government has opened for people to use for communication, the First Amendment protects people's right to use the forum without the government interfering with what is communicated there. This is the very essence of the Constitution's guarantee of freedom of speech.

In a public forum, the government is prohibited from exercising discrimination with respect to the content of communication, unless the government demonstrates that the restriction is necessary to achieve a "compelling" government interest and there is no less restrictive alternative for achieving that interest. This means public libraries cannot exclude books about abortion just because they discuss the subject of abortion. That would be discrimination with respect to content. Books can be selected on the basis of content-neutral criteria such as the quality of the writing, their position on best-seller lists, the presence or absence of other materials in the collection related to certain time periods or historical figures, and the like; they can be deselected on the basis of wear and tear, the availability of more current materials, and similar criteria. Libraries, however, cannot deliberately suppress the record of human thought on a particular subject or topic.

Internet filters are mechanisms designed to discriminate with respect to the content of communication. Filters are incapable of doing what computer software engineers have designed them to do—typically, block "hard-core pornography" and other "offensive" sites on the Internet. But even at their hypothetical best, mechanisms to screen and block content on the Internet exclude far more than just obscenity and child pornography. They exclude a wide range of sexually explicit materials protected under the Constitution. For instance, materials that depict homosexual relations, variations on conventional heterosexuality, and even nudity and heterosexual relations channeled toward reproduction and family life represent distinct subjects or topics. Their suppression is discrimination with respect to the content of communication.

The rapid expansion of Web sites on the Internet and the sheer impossibility of keeping up with this growth are factors that limit the reliability of filtering devices. Neither humans nor machines are capable of processing and reviewing everything available, with the result that filters will block some materials while other equivalent materials will remain unblocked.

Moreover, there is legal precedent that suggests that government agencies like libraries cannot adopt and enforce private rating schemes. When libraries restrict access based on content ratings developed and applied by a filtering vendor, sometimes with no knowledge of how these ratings are applied or what sites have been restricted, they are delegating their public responsibility to a private agency.

Filtering and other means to block content on the Internet only can be utilized if the government—in this case, the public library—can demonstrate both that the need is compelling and that the method chosen to achieve the purpose is the least restrictive method possible. The lawsuit brought by the American Library Association—*American Library Association* v. *United States Department of Justice,* consolidated with and decided by the U.S. Supreme Court under the name of *Reno* v. *American Civil Liberties Union*—invalidated the provisions of the Communications Decency Act of 1996 that criminalized "indecent" and "patently offensive" electronic communication. The Court did so on the ground that those provisions, suppressing speech addressed to adults, reduced the entire population only to what is fit for children. It recognized "the governmental interest in protecting children from harmful materials," but found that less restrictive means were available to achieve that interest.

It is well documented that filtering software is over-inclusive, blocking not only sites that may have sexual content, strong language, or unconventional ideas considered harmful or offensive—but also sites having no controversial content whatsoever. This over-inclusive blocking violates the First Amendment rights of youth and children, as well as adults, to access constitutionally protected materials. In the context of limiting or avoiding children's exposure to possibly "harmful" materials on library computers with Internet access, less restrictive means than the use of filters are available.

Adults' reading cannot be reduced to the level of what is fit for children, and the public library, therefore, cannot restrict them to Internet-access computers with filtering software. Young adults and children also have First Amendment rights, although such rights are variable, depending on the age of the minor and other factors, including maturity, not yet settled in the law. Even though minors' First Amendment rights are not as extensive as those of adults, the public library cannot restrict them solely to computers with filtering software. This is why libraries advocate that parents guide their children's use of the Internet. Only unfiltered Internet access accommodates both parental guidance and sensitive recognition of the First Amendment rights of young people.

Librarians and the strength of their commitment to professional standards and values assure that, at least through the public library, the least restrictive means available to achieve the government's interest in protecting children will be implemented.

Specific Internet Use Policy Provisions

The position of the American Library Association is set forth in several documents adopted by the Council, its governing body. The Interpretation of the *Library Bill of Rights* entitled "Access to Electronic Information, Services, and Networks" calls for free and unfettered access to the Internet for any library user, regardless of age. The "Resolution on the Use of Filtering Software in Libraries" and the "Statement on Library Use of Filtering Software" reiterate the U.S. Supreme Court's declaration in *Reno* v. *American Civil Liberties Union* that the Internet is a forum of free expression deserving full constitutional protection. The "Resolution" and "Statement" condemn as a violation of the *Library Bill of Rights* any use of filtering software by libraries that blocks access to constitutionally protected speech.

Consistent with these policies, which collectively embody the library profession's understanding of First Amendment constraints on library Internet use, the Intellectual Freedom Committee offers guidelines to public libraries, as follows:

- Adopt a comprehensive, written Internet use policy that, among other things, should:

    - set forth reasonable time, place, and manner restrictions;

    - expressly prohibit any use of library equipment to access material that is obscene, child pornography, or "harmful to minors" (consistent with any applicable state or local law);

    - provide for the privacy of users with respect to public terminals; and

    - protect the confidentiality of records, electronic or otherwise, that identify individual users and link them to search strategies, sites accessed, or other specific data about the information they retrieved or sought to retrieve.

- Communicate the relevant policies for use of Internet-access computers to all library users, and include the parents of children who may use the library without direct parental supervision. Do so in a clear and conspicuous manner sufficient to alert library users that filtering software is not utilized.

- Post notices at all Internet-access computers that use of library equipment to access the illegal materials specified in the Internet use policy is prohibited.

- Offer a variety of programs, at convenient times, to educate library users, including parents and children, on the use of the Internet. Publicize them widely.

- Offer library users recommended Internet sites. For youth and children, especially, offer them, according to age group, direct links to sites with educational and other types of material best suited to their typical needs and interests (e.g., the American Library Association's "700+ Great Sites for Kids and the Adults Who Care about Them" and its Internet guide for young adults, "TEENHoopla").

Samples of Internet use policies are located on the Office for Intellectual Freedom's Web page, "Internet Use Policies," at www.ala.org/alaorg/oif/internetusepolicies.html.

Answers to Objections

Various metaphors have been offered, both by opponents of free and open access in libraries, as well as proponents, to explain the use of the Internet in libraries and the impact of filtering software. Two metaphors offered by opponents and the arguments built around them deserve close examination:

The "selection" metaphor. Filtering Internet resources is tantamount to selecting materials in a library. Since libraries, opponents of unfettered Internet access say, are not constrained to select any particular materials for their collections, filtering is constitutionally unobjectionable.

This metaphor is faulty. Filtering the Internet is not selecting materials. The only selection decisions involved in use of the Internet in libraries are those as to whether, for instance, the World Wide Web will be offered with other tools based on special Internet protocols, e.g., *ftp* (file transfer protocol) or *telnet*. Selecting the World Wide Web for the library means selecting the entire resource, just as selecting *Time* means selecting the entire magazine. A library cannot select *Time* and then decide to redact or rip out the pages constituting the "American Scene" feature or the "Washington Diary." That would be censorship. It is the same with the World Wide Web. It is not an accident of terminology that the Web consists of a vast number of Web *pages* and that browser software permits the user to *bookmark* those that are interesting or useful.

The "interlibrary loan" metaphor. Internet access is tantamount to interlibrary loan service. Typing a Web site URL into a browser's location entry box and pressing the <Enter> key amounts to an interlibrary loan request that the library, opponents of unfettered access say, is free to deny.

This metaphor is faulty, too. Far more frequently than typing and entering URLs, surfers of the World Wide Web click on hot links for automatic access to the Web pages they wish to see. More significantly, absent financial constraints, any public library true to its function as a public forum makes available to users any constitutionally protected material, whether that means locating the material within the library itself or obtaining it elsewhere through interlibrary loan.

As articulated by the U.S. Supreme Court in the American Library Association case culminating in *Reno* v. *American Civil Liberties Union*, the Internet represents a vast library. It is a virtual library already present within any public library that selects Internet access. The fundamental First Amendment question is: given the free availability of a near-infinite range of content on the Internet, can the library ever deliberately deprive a library user of the constitutionally protected materials he or she seeks? The emphatic answer of the librarian informed by principles of intellectual freedom is: *absolutely not.*

But what about obscenity and child pornography, as well as, when minors are involved, materials "harmful to minors"?

- As for obscenity and child pornography, prosecutors and police have adequate tools to enforce criminal laws. Libraries are not a component of law enforcement efforts naturally directed toward the source, i.e., the publishers, of such material.
- As for materials "harmful to minors," it is true that, in some jurisdictions, libraries that choose not to utilize filtering or other means to block content on the Internet may find themselves in a "bind"; under some circumstances, they may be subject to liability under "harmful to minors" laws.

Libraries should be cautioned that laws differ from state to state, and they should seek advice on laws applicable in their jurisdiction from counsel versed in First Amendment principles. In particular, they should determine whether any "harmful to minors" law applies to materials available at the library, either through Internet access or otherwise. They should specifically inquire whether they are expressly exempt from the particular "harmful to minors" laws in their jurisdiction, as libraries frequently are.

Moreover, libraries should be aware that the legal framework and context of regulation is rapidly changing; federal, state, and local governments have begun to legislate specifically in the area of library Internet use. Libraries should actively oppose proposed legislation that exposes them to new liabilities and negatively impacts intellectual freedom. As always, they should be vigilant about new regulations of free speech.

For information on filtering and other legal issues affecting libraries, see the Freedom to Read Foundation's Web page, "Memoranda to Freedom to Read Foundation from Jenner & Block" (its legal counsel), at www.ftrf.org/memos_jb.html, and the Office for Intellectual Freedom's Web page, "Filters and Filtering," at www.ala.org/alaorg/oif/filtersandfiltering.html.

Adopted by the ALA Intellectual Freedom Committee, June 1998; revised November 2000.

HISTORY

Guidelines and Considerations for Developing a Public Library Internet Use Policy

To guide librarians in developing Internet use policies, the American Library Trustee Association, the Association for Library Service to Children, and the Public Library Association published "Children and the Internet: Guidelines for Developing Public Library Policy." To complement this and other materials intended to help librarians develop such policies, the Intellectual Freedom Committee requested that the Office for Intellectual Freedom write "Guidelines and Considerations for Developing a Public Library Internet Use Policy," which was designed to answer specific policy questions from an intellectual freedom perspective. The guidelines are not legal advice, but were written to reinforce the principle that libraries, because they link individuals with knowledge, information, literature, and other resources people seek, are the information source in our society and that it is never libraries' role to keep individuals from what other people have to say. The guidelines were to provide a useful resource for those writing Internet use policies. Written in 1998, the guidelines were discussed by the IFC at their June 1998 meeting and then presented to the ALA Council as part of the Intellectual Freedom Committee's report on July 1, 1998.

In line with the ongoing practice of periodic review, the IFC carefully reviewed these guidelines during 1999–2000, especially in regard to their applicability to the Internet. The IFC revised the "Guidelines and Considerations for Developing a Public Library Internet Use Policy" for clarity, removed outdated filtering examples, but emphasized that filters either are under-inclusive or over-inclusive. The concepts of privacy and confidentiality were included as important points in any Internet use policy. In addition, the committee included URLs to related OIF and Freedom to Read Foundation Web sites.

PART IV

Intellectual Freedom
and the Law

I

ALA Intellectual Freedom Policies and the First Amendment

BRUCE J. ENNIS

[From time to time, the Freedom to Read Foundation receives questions regarding the relationship of the ALA intellectual freedom policies to the First Amendment. People often want to know whether or not the ALA's policies go beyond the First Amendment. Since the question is key to Foundation activities, we asked our counsel to comment. His response follows:]

You requested our input on the following two questions: (1) whether the American Library Association (ALA) goes beyond judicially mandated First Amendment protections in its policies; and (2) if it is not a violation of First Amendment rights to control access to some materials because of a theft or vandalism problem, whether it would be a constitutional violation to control access to material because it may be inappropriate for children below a certain age. We address each issue separately.

First, the policies of the ALA are based on, and consistent with, federal and state constitutional protections as interpreted by the judiciary. Thus, ALA policies safeguard the rights of free speech of all patrons to the extent protected by either the federal or state constitution. It is manifest that the ALA policies safeguard all speech protected by the First Amendment of the United States Constitution. Additionally, ALA policies protect all speech secured by a state

This article was first published in vol. 19 (1994), no. 1 of *Freedom to Read Foundation News*.

constitution even if those protections are broader than those encompassed in the federal Constitution. For example, the First Amendment of the federal Constitution has been interpreted as providing more limited protection for commercial as opposed to political speech. If a state constitution were interpreted as providing greater protection for commercial speech in a particular jurisdiction, that speech would be encompassed in the ALA policies. A state might choose not to place any restrictions on speech. (Libraries in each state, however, should check with their state statutes to see whether or what kind of obscenity or "harmful to minors" laws exist, and they should ask their attorneys whether such laws apply to the library.) ALA policies would, therefore, direct that all expressive materials in that particular state were constitutionally protected and encompassed within the ALA policies. In the spirit of providing the greatest access to information and ideas, ALA policies were intended to encompass the broadest interpretation of protection for free speech.

Second, courts have held that children are entitled to the protections afforded by the First Amendment. Thus, courts have held that governments (including school boards) may not restrict minors' access to materials based on the viewpoint expressed therein. Although it may not violate the First Amendment to restrict access to a special or rare collection because of concerns of theft or vandalism, it would violate the First Amendment to restrict access to expressive materials, or ban them entirely, on the basis of viewpoint—even if the restrictions were directed to minors. The Supreme Court has held that the critical inquiry centers on motivation.

In *Board of Education, Island Trees Union Free School District No. 26* v. *Pico,* 457 U.S. 853 (1982), the Supreme Court considered whether a school board's removal of books from a school library violated the First Amendment rights of the students. A plurality held:

> [W]hether petitioners' removal of books from their school library denied respondents their First Amendment rights depends upon the motivation behind petitioners' actions. If petitioners *intended* by their removal decision to deny respondents access to ideas with which petitioners disagreed, and if this intent was the decisive factor in petitioners' decision, then petitioners have exercised their discretion in violation of the Constitution.

Id. At 871 (emphasis in text). The plurality opinion emphasized that "local school boards may not remove books from school library shelves simply because they dislike the ideas contained in those books and seek by their removal to 'prescribe what shall be orthodox in politics, nationalism, religion, or other matters of opinion.'" Id. At 872 (citation omitted).

Other courts have followed *Pico's* guidance that *motivation* is the key question in book removal cases. Thus, lower courts have suggested that although school boards have broader discretion in questions of school curriculum—provided the decisions are reasonably related to legitimate pedagogical concerns—removal of books from the *school library* implicates protected First Amendment rights. It follows that government would have even less justification to remove books or restrict access to books in the *public library* on the ground that such books are not suitable for children.

Public libraries wisely leave the decision of reading material to the patrons—or their parents. . . Unless there is an applicable Harmful to Minors Act, a policy of free access (limited only by parental decisions of appropriateness for very young children) provides the greatest insulation for the library from constitutional attack for restricting access to materials protected by the First Amendment. Restrictions on access that are not based on valid administrative reasons (such as reasonable concerns about theft and vandalism) could be interpreted as restrictions based on disagreement by the government with the views expressed in the material. Thus, if government officials sought to remove or restrict access to a book on the ground that government officials opposed an idea in that book, the removal of the book clearly would violate the First Amendment.

Third, it is possible that enabling statutes governing libraries could be useful. Checking those statutes will help determine whether they define the role of the library in removing materials. For example, in *Wexner v. Anderson,* 209 Cal. App. 3d 1438, 258 Cal. Rptr. 26 (Cal. App. 3d Dist. 1989), a California appellate court held that a school district could not forbid high school students from reading books in a school library collection on the ground that materials were not "socially acceptable." The California appellate court did not reach the constitutional issue. Instead, the appellate court held that the statutory authority provided to libraries did not permit removal of books from the school library (or presumably any public library in California) based on their content or "social acceptability." 258 Cal. Rptr. at 36. The court held that books could only be removed if they were "not fit for service" (interpreted by the court as "worn out") or "no longer needed by the course of study" (interpreted by the court to apply only to textbooks). 258 Cal. Rptr. at 36. The courts thus concluded that "*a county librarian* or superintendent of schools running a library has no authority, even with the approval of the board, to remove a book because of objectionable conduct." Id. (emphasis added).

2

Libraries and the Internet

JUDITH F. KRUG

A s Internet issues and problems consume more and more librarians' professional lives, the question arises, often in a humorous way, "What did we do before the Internet?" The truth is that we did the same thing before the advent of the Internet as we have been doing since, namely, bringing people together with the information they need and want.

The Internet hasn't changed that traditional role; it hasn't changed what librarians do. It has only changed, to some extent, how they do it.

What has not changed at all, however, is American librarians' commitment to intellectual freedom, or the place it holds in librarianship in the United States. In short, intellectual freedom is the heart and soul of the profession.

Intellectual freedom is based on the First Amendment to the United States Constitution, particularly the freedom of the press and freedom of speech clauses. Librarians have interpreted these clauses to mean that every person has the right to hold any belief or idea on any subject and to express those beliefs or ideas in whatever form they consider appropriate. The ability to express an idea or a belief is meaningless, however, unless there is an equal commitment to the right of unrestricted access to information and ideas regardless of the communication medium. Intellectual freedom, then, is

---

This article was originally published in vol. 26 (2000), no. 4 of *IFLA Journal*.

the right to express one's ideas and the right of others to be able to read, hear, or view them.

With intellectual freedom as their core value, American librarians have assumed the responsibility to provide, within their collections, ideas and information across the spectrum of social and political thought. Library patrons can then choose what they want to read, or listen to, or look at.

In today's world, information is available in a variety of formats— books, magazines, films, videos, CD-ROMs, sound recordings, paintings, sculptures, etc. To this mix, electronic communication, specifically the Internet, has been added. In some key ways, the Internet has changed how librarians bring information together with people.

Previously, librarians, limited by money and shelf space, selected the items that went into their collections. To a large extent, this still holds true. But it is no longer totally true. The Internet is allowing libraries, for the first time, to make the vast array of ideas and information available to everyone— and to permit each library user to act as his or her own selector. This has caused great anguish in certain quarters because some people are convinced that if young people have unfettered access to the Internet, they will be drawn to Web sites featuring explicit sex. There does not appear to be evidence to support such beliefs, but this lack of evidence has not changed the minds of those who so believe.

These same people also find the ALA's policies about children and young people to be misguided. The ALA's policies urge librarians to provide all users, regardless of age, with the information they need and want. The ALA's position has been willfully misinterpreted to mean that children not only do have— but also should have— access to what is termed "inappropriate" library materials. In this debate, the material that is allegedly "inappropriate" is not clearly defined. Indeed, it sometimes appears as if the definition is: "I don't like it— therefore, it is inappropriate." Such a label has been applied to material as widely varied as the lingerie ads in *Victoria's Secret*, the images of starlets in bikinis found in *People* magazine and movie star magazines, and information about medical matters (for instance, penile implants) and alternative lifestyles of which many people do not approve. There is no distinction made between "pornography," an umbrella term for material with sexual themes that people would like to have censored– but, in fact, is legal and protected by the First Amendment—and materials believed to be "obscene," "child pornography," or "harmful to minors," which are illegal. However, "obscene," "child pornography," or "harmful to minors" are terms of law, and only legal proceedings can determine if, indeed, a piece of material is illegal.

In many instances, these myths have been translated into legislative proposals. The first such proposal to become law was the Communications Decency Act (CDA), signed into law by President William Clinton on February 8, 1996, as part of the Telecommunications Reform Act of 1996. The CDA was about keeping "indecent" material from anyone under the age of eighteen. It said that if "merely" access was provided to the Internet, there was no liability. But, if anyone under eighteen was allowed to view "indecent" material, the provider was subject to fines of up to $250,000 and/or up to two years in prison. The CDA put libraries and librarians at risk because the term "indecent," was not defined in the legislation, and without a definition, librarians had no guidepost.

In February 1996, two separate lawsuits were filed challenging the constitutionality of the Communications Decency Act. *American Library Association* v. *U.S. Department of Justice* was filed after *American Civil Liberties Union* v. *Janet Reno;* the cases subsequently were consolidated and decided under the title *Reno* v. *ACLU.* Both legal actions argued three main points:

1. The prohibition of material on the Internet that was "indecent" or "patently offensive" was unconstitutional because these terms were undefined, vague, and overbroad. The legislation made no distinction between material on the Internet appropriate for a five-year old and that appropriate for a seventeen-year-old college student. In short, it was argued that government cannot limit adults (or nearly adults) solely to reading material that is appropriate for children.

2. There are alternate ways for parents to protect their minor children at home from materials on the Internet they consider inappropriate. Such ways, filters, for instance, would not violate the First Amendment rights of adults and would be more effective than this law. These alternative measures, however, were not considered by Congress, which held no hearings, nor invited any testimony on this issue before passing sweeping legislation.

3. The Internet is *not* a broadcast medium, like television and radio, on which courts have imposed content restrictions on what may be broadcast. Rather, the Internet is more like print– a newspaper, a bookstore, a library– because each member of the audience has control over what he or she can access, each has a choice. Accordingly, the Internet deserves the same First Amendment protection as books and newspapers, not the lesser protection granted to the broadcast media.

In June 1996, a lower court declared the CDA unconstitutional. The government appealed, and on June 26, 1997, by a 9-0 vote, the United States Supreme Court declared the Communications Decency Act unconstitutional.

The Supreme Court said:

1. Adults cannot be limited in their reading material to only that which is suitable for children;
2. There are alternate means, such as filters for parents to use at home, to protect their children;
3. The Internet is more like the print medium than like the broadcast medium, and deserves the same First Amendment protection enjoyed by print. The Court, in fact, went a step further and said electronic communications may be entitled to even more First Amendment protection than print!

The ALA's lawyer called the decision "the birth certificate of the Internet." It set the standard by which all future regulation of cyberspace communications would be judged by all other U.S. courts. By a unanimous Supreme Court decision, the freedom of expression on the Internet and access to that expression is protected in the United States. Nevertheless, that has not stopped the U.S. Congress, various state legislatures, and many local governments from spending vast amounts of time trying to figure out how to get around it and implement what some consider to be the solution to "bad stuff" on the Internet– namely, filters.

Contrary to popular belief, the American Library Association is not against filters. The ALA believes filters are appropriate devices for parents to use at home with their children. When they are used at home, parents can program them according to their value system and the principles they wish to instill in their children. But while the American Library Association believes that filters can be used by parents at home, the ALA does not believe filters are appropriate for public institutions. There are several reasons for this.

- Libraries are publicly supported governmental institutions and, as such, are subject to the First Amendment. The First Amendment forbids libraries from restricting information based on viewpoint or content.
- Libraries are places of inclusion rather than exclusion. Current blocking/filtering software prevents access not only to what some may consider to be "objectionable" material, but also to information protected by the First Amendment. The result is that legal, valuable, and useful information inevitably is blocked. For instance, sites that have been blocked by popular commercial blocking/filtering products include those on breast cancer, AIDS, women's rights, animal rights, the American Association of University Women, all groups known as "associations," the FBI, eBay, golfer Fred Couples, and the Mars exploration, which has the URL of "MARSEXPL."
- The filter manufacturers consider their blockages to be proprietary information and, therefore, will not reveal what is being blocked or how it is being blocked.
- Software developers are making selection decisions based on their biases or beliefs, not on the norms and values of the community employing the filter.
- Filters cannot—and do not—block all of the material that many prefer not to be accessible to children. Even the filtering manufacturers admit it is impossible to block all undesirable material. The Web is too vast and changes too quickly for filters to be effective. While research figures have varied widely, there is little debate that filters are not as effective as originally hoped. More importantly for librarians, filters eliminate up to 40 percent of sites that contain legal, valuable, and useful information. In truth, filters are merely mechanical devices—and mechanical devices have no judgmental capabilities or decision-making abilities. They are "things!"

For all of these reasons, then, filters are not appropriate for libraries.

When all is said and done, how a library handles the Internet is a local decision. Strategies to help libraries manage the Internet in accordance with the First Amendment have been developed. They include:

- Internet use policies that define the level of Web access based on age. Most libraries require young children to be accompanied by a parent or guardian.
- Codes of conduct that define appropriate use of library computers and the Internet (e.g., no participation in illegal activities such as child pornography or gambling).
- Internet training classes for children and parents to teach them how to do an online search and other techniques that can ensure a positive online experience.
- Links to pre-selected sites such as the American Library Association's "700+ Great Sites for Kids," and search engines specially designed for children such as "KidsClick!" or AOL's "NetFind for Kids."
- Privacy screens on workstations.
- Time limits and other rules for computer use in keeping with the library's mission statement and customer service practices.

Librarians' main responsibility is to bring people together with the information they need or want. The format in which that information appears has little bearing on that responsibility, as does the age of the user of the information. In fact, Article V of the *Library Bill of Rights* states: "A person's right to use a library should not be denied or abridged because of origin, age, background, or views." The librarian's role never has been, is not currently, and will not be in the future to keep people from the information they need and want.

Right now, fulfilling our responsibilities presents to librarians a challenge and an opportunity. The challenge, of course, comes from the many people and organizations who have decided they, rather than parents, are better able to determine what information on the Internet is appropriate for all children. The opportunity lies in helping all of our users understand the Internet, its pitfalls, and the growing role it will play in our lives as we move forward in the twenty-first century. It allows all people to access vastly more and more varied information than ever before in history. With librarians to help them, the public can harness this incredible resource and make it work for all of us.

3

School Libraries and the Courts

THERESA CHMARA

School Library Censorship and the Courts

Do minors have First Amendment rights? What role is played in the reading life of the minor by parents, teachers, school librarians, school administrators, school board members, and members of the community? Parents certainly have the right to guide and direct their own children to the reading materials to which they have access. Teachers plainly are entrusted with the mandate to develop the curriculum to guide and direct the pursuit of knowledge of their own students. School librarians have the task of providing all students with additional or alternative resources to enable them to independently study and pursue their interests. To what extent, then, can school administrators, school boards, or members of the community censor the reading materials available to minors in the school curriculum or the school library?

General First Amendment Principles in the School Context

It is well established that students do not shed their constitutional rights to freedom of speech or expression at the schoolhouse gate. In *Tinker* v. *Des Moines Independent Community School District*, 393

U.S. 503, 506 (1969), the United States Supreme Court ordered a public school to allow students to wear black armbands in protest against the Vietnam War, explaining that "[i]n our system, students may not be regarded as closed-circuit recipients of only that which the State chooses to communicate." Id. at 511. Since *Tinker,* the Court has made it clear that students' First Amendment rights include both the right to speak and the right to receive information. See, for example, *Board of Education, Island Trees Union Free School District No. 26 v. Pico,* 457 U.S. 853, 867 (1982).

Students' speech rights are different, however, than those of adults. The Supreme Court has held, in *Bethel School District No. 403 v. Fraser,* 478 U.S. 675, 682 (1986), that students' speech rights are not automatically coextensive with the rights of adults in other settings, and has generally applied those rights in light of the special characteristics of the school environment. See *Pico,* 457 U.S. at 868 (quoting *Tinker,* 393 U.S. at 506). In *Pico,* for example, although the Court's plurality opinion prohibited school officials from removing school library books based on the official's disagreement with the ideas expressed in the books, it noted that removal decisions motivated by concerns that a book was educationally unsuitable or pervasively vulgar would be constitutional. Id. at 871.

Likewise, the Court in *Hazelwood School District v. Kuhlmeier,* 484 U.S. 267 (1988), permitted a high school principal to order the removal of certain articles from a school newspaper. The newspaper, which was written and edited by a student journalism class, had planned to run several controversial stories about student pregnancy and the impact of divorce on the school's students. The principal justified the removal decision on the grounds that the articles were inappropriate for the maturity level of the intended readers; the privacy interests of the articles' subjects were not adequately protected; and the danger that the controversial views would be attributed to the school. Id. at 274. The Supreme Court rejected the students' First Amendment claims, finding that a lower standard of review should apply when there is a danger that student expression will be perceived as bearing the imprimatur of the school. Id. at 271 (holding that curriculum decisions are permissible if they are reasonably related to legitimate pedagogical concerns).

Similarly, in *Bethel School District,* the Court held that a student could be disciplined for having delivered a speech that was sexually explicit (but not legally obscene) at an official school assembly. 478 U.S. at 685-86. In upholding the school's disciplinary action, the Court held that "it was perfectly appropriate for the school to dissociate itself to make the point to the pupils that vulgar speech and lewd conduct are wholly inconsistent with the 'fundamental values' of public school education." Id. at 685-86.

What impact do the decisions in *Hazelwood* and *Bethel School District* have on the school library and attempts to censor materials in that venue? *Hazelwood* and *Bethel School District* are significant decisions but are of limited application to disputes involving student speech rights in public school libraries. School officials certainly cannot rely on those decisions to restrict students' speech at will, especially when that speech cannot reasonably be perceived as bearing the imprimatur of the school. Moreover, while courts plainly have given school officials a greater degree of control over decisions related to the school curriculum (see, for example, *Pico*, 457 U.S. at 864), these decisions do not directly implicate school libraries, which provide students with both curricular and extracurricular materials. See id. at 860.

Numerous lower court decisions have recognized the distinction in *Hazelwood* between curricular and non-curricular speech restrictions. In applying the *Hazelwood* case to other situations, lower courts have applied greater deference to school officials attempting to control curricular speech restrictions, holding that "[i]n matters pertaining to the curriculum, educators have been accorded greater control over expression than they may enjoy in other spheres of activity."[1] See *Virgil* v. *School Board of Columbia County, Florida*, 862 F.2d 1517, 1520 (11th Cir. 1989). In *Virgil*, for example, the court of appeals affirmed a school board's decision to remove selected portions of Geoffrey Chaucer's *The Miller's Tale* and Aristophanes' *Lysistrata* from a humanities course curriculum. In upholding the removal, the court emphasized that the disputed materials remained in the school library, id. at 1525, which, unlike a course curriculum, was a repository for voluntary inquiry. Id. at 1525 (quoting *Pico*, 457 U.S. at 869). But in *Pratt* v. *Independent School District No. 831*, 670 F.2d 771, 779 (8th Cir. 1982), a court refused to allow a school board to strike a film version of Shirley Jackson's short story, "The Lottery," from the school curriculum merely because the story remained available in the school library.

Students' First Amendment rights in the school library context, therefore, are broader than those in a class, a school-sponsored assembly, or other curriculum-based activities. In the context of book removals from libraries, courts must make the determination whether the removal is based on educational suitability or is an attempt to impose viewpoint or content discrimination.

The School Library

In *Board of Education* v. *Pico*, 457 U.S. 853 (1982), a school board had attempted to remove from a school library controversial titles such as Kurt Vonnegut's *Slaughterhouse Five* and Eldridge Cleaver's *Soul on Ice*. The school board's action did not restrict minors' own expression, as the bar on armbands in *Tinker* had, but the Supreme Court rejected the action because the board was restricting what minors could read. In a plurality opinion, the Court stated that the right to receive ideas is a necessary predicate to the recipient's meaningful exercise of his own rights of speech, press, and political freedom, id. at 867, and made clear that students too are beneficiaries of this principle. Id. at 868. Recent decisions of lower federal courts have echoed this reasoning and the result of *Pico*. See *Campbell* v. *St. Tammany Parish School Board*, 64 F.3d 184 (5th Cir. 1995); and *Case* v. *Unified School District No. 233*, 908 F. Supp. 864 (D. Kan. 1995).[2]

In *Campbell* v. *St. Tammany Parish School Board*, the court of appeals confirmed that the key inquiry in a book removal case is the school official's substantial motivation in arriving at the removal decision. Id. at 190. Considering the plaintiffs' constitutional challenge to a school board's decision to remove a book on voodoo from the town's school libraries, the court held that a determination of the board's motivation could not be made without a trial. The court observed that in light of the special role of the school library as a place where students may freely and voluntarily explore diverse topics, the school board's non-curricular decision to remove a book well after it had been placed in the public school libraries evokes the question whether that action might not be an unconstitutional attempt to strangle the free mind at its source. Id.

Similarly, the district court in *Case* v. *Unified School District No. 233* found a school board's removal of Nancy Garden's *Annie on My*

Mind unconstitutional where a substantial motivation behind the library removal was the officials' disagreement with the views expressed in the book. The defendants had claimed that the book was educationally unsuitable, a removal criterion deemed permissible by the Supreme Court's plurality decision in *Pico. Pico*, 457 U.S. at 871. Nonetheless, the court refused to credit the defendants' assertions, explaining that "[t]here is no basis in the record to believe that these Board members meant by 'educational suitability' anything other than their own disagreement with the ideas expressed in the book." *Case*, 908 F. Supp. at 875.

In a case that predates *Pico*, the court in *Minarcini v. Strongsville City School District*, 541 F.2d 577 (6th Cir. 1976), held that the First Amendment prohibited school officials from removing Joseph Heller's *Catch-22* and Vonnegut's *Cat's Cradle* from the school library solely because the books conflicted with the social or political tastes of the school board members. Id. at 582. Noting that "[a] library is a mighty resource in the free marketplace of ideas . . . specially dedicated to broad dissemination of ideas," id. at 582-83, the court distinguished the removal action from a decision not to approve or purchase certain texts, which the court found to be within the sound discretion of the school board.

Overall, courts carefully scrutinize any decision to remove a book from a school library, imposing stricter constitutional standards than those applicable to curricular decisions. Certainly, the case law forbids any removal action motivated by the school officials' disagreement with the views or ideas expressed in the book. Even purportedly viewpoint-neutral justifications—such as educational suitability—likely will be subjected to skeptical, exacting judicial review.

The Internet

How do these cases and principles apply in the Internet context? There are no cases that directly address the use of the Internet in public school libraries. The growing body of general Internet case law, however, is instructive in regard to the issues that are likely to arise in the context of school libraries.

On the federal level, Congress has attempted several times to impose broad restrictions on Internet use. The Supreme Court rejected the first such attempt—the Communications Decency Act (CDA)—in *Reno* v. *ACLU (Reno I)*,117 S. Ct. 2329 (1997), unanimously holding that the government could not criminalize Internet displays of material that would be indecent or patently offensive for minors. The Court reasoned that such a ban violated the First Amendment because it restricted adult access to constitutionally protected material. Congress subsequently passed the Child Online Protection Act (COPA), which, despite its differences from the CDA,[3] was promptly enjoined by a federal district court on First Amendment grounds. See *Reno* v. *ACLU (Reno II)*, 31 F.Supp.2d 473 (E.D. Pa. 1999). It seems clear from these decisions that an absolute ban on controversial material on the Internet will not pass constitutional muster.

Beyond complete bans, local officials have been moving toward more limited Internet restrictions. *Mainstream Loudoun* v. *Board of Trustees of Loudoun County Library*, 24 F.Supp.2d 552 (E.D. Va. 1998), for example, concerned a First Amendment challenge to a public library's restrictions on access to sexually explicit Internet sites. After concluding that the library was a limited public forum for the receipt and communication of online information,[4] the district court invalidated the library's filtering policy. The court held that even if the library board could demonstrate that the policy was reasonably necessary to further their compelling interests, the library could achieve that interest with less restrictive means.

The decision in *Loudoun* will not directly apply to a challenge to Internet filtering policies in public *school* libraries. School libraries typically do not serve adult patrons, so there is less danger of restricting adults' access to constitutionally protected material as was the case in *Loudoun*. Additionally, if a filtering program purported to exclude materials that are harmful to minors, it might be deemed to fall within the "educational suitability" or "pervasively vulgar" justifications identified as permissible in *Pico*, provided that the government entity imposing the restrictions could demonstrate that the filter served to exclude only those materials adjudged by a court of law to be harmful to minors. Importantly, however, no filter can make that legal determination, and given the general imperfections inherent in most filtering programs, the voluntary nature of school library facilities, and the general First Amendment rights enjoyed by students, a school Internet filtering program might not survive constitutional scrutiny.

In December 2000, Congress again attempted to impose restrictions on Internet use by requiring both public and school libraries that receive e-rate funding to utilize filters. At the time of this writing, the restrictions had not become effective, and this new attempt by Congress to restrict speech will be challenged in the courts.

Some schools may fear potential liability for *failure* to install any blocking technology on library Internet terminals. Such a claim against a public school library, however, would likely fail.[5] In *Kathleen R. v. City of Livermore*, No. V-015266-4, Superior Ct. of Cal., County of Alameda, Eastern Division, a woman sued a public library, claiming that her twelve-year-old son was able to view and download pornography at a public library in Livermore, California. The plaintiff's claims were summarily rejected, based in part on a provision in the federal Communications Decency Act, 47 U.S.C. 230, that immunizes service providers against state law liability for third parties' postings. See also *Zeran v. AOL*, 129 F.3d 327 (4th Cir. 1997), holding that Section 230 immunizes AOL against state law claims alleging (1) unreasonable delay in failing to remove defamatory messages posted by an unidentified third party, (2) refusing to post retractions, and (3) failing to screen for similar postings in future.

Conclusion

In sum, the school library serves as a special resource of information for students for both traditional print materials and Internet access. In its role outside the curriculum as an additional source of knowledge for intellectually curious students, the school library serves a different role for students. The courts have held repeatedly that minors have First Amendment rights at school in the classroom and beyond. School officials cannot restrict those rights at will. Plainly, minors have even greater First Amendment rights in the school library.

NOTES

1. See also, for example, *Virgil*, 862 F.2d at 1520-21 and n.3, citing cases rejecting First Amendment claims that challenged various curricular decisions.

2. Other cases in which the Supreme Court emphasized minors' right to receive information include *Erznoznik* v. *City of Jacksonville*, 422 U.S. 205, 213-14 (1975), holding that a "[s]peech . . . cannot be suppressed solely to protect the young from ideas or images that a legislative body thinks unsuitable for them"; and *Bolger* v. *Youngs Drug Products Corp.*, 463 U.S. 60, 75 n.30 (1983), criticizing a federal ban on mailing unsolicited contraceptive advertisements because it ignored adolescents' pressing need for information about contraception.

3. COPA differed from CDA in several ways. First, COPA restricted speech that is "harmful to minors," rather than "indecent or patently offensive" speech. Second, COPA restricted only speech provided on the Web for commercial purposes. Finally, COPA contained a variety of affirmative defenses to avoid prosecution (e.g., if a site requires the use of a credit card, adult access code, or personal identification number).

4. The "forum" designation for a given public space—whether it is deemed to be a public forum, limited public forum, or nonpublic forum—determines the level of scrutiny applied to speech restrictions in that space. See, for example, *Perry Education Assn.* v. *Perry Local Educators' Assn.*, 460 U.S. 37 (1983). In a limited public forum, content-based regulations of speech are subject to strict scrutiny.

5. As a general rule, courts are not inclined to hold a school liable simply because the school allows its students to read or view controversial material. See, for example, *Monteiro* v. *Temple Union High School District*, 158 F.3d 1022, 1029 (9th Cir. 1998), rejecting students' claims seeking to enjoin or attach civil liability to a school district's assignment of a book.

4

The Buckley Amendment
Student Privacy versus Parents' Right to Know

ANNE LEVINSON PENWAY

The Family Educational Rights and Privacy Act of 1974, 20 U.S.C. Section 1232(g)—commonly referred to as the Buckley Amendment after its sponsor, Senator James Buckley of New York—provides students over eighteen with access to their own school records, and provides the parents or guardians of minor students with access to the school records maintained on their minor children. It also protects the privacy of those records by prohibiting access to them by other persons without the knowledge or consent of students or their parents. Schools are required to provide parents, legal guardians, and students eighteen years or older a hearing for the purposes of challenging inaccurate, misleading, or false information contained in their school file. Should a school fail to comply, there is no private right to sue to enforce its terms. Instead, complaints about failure to abide by the terms of the law must be submitted to the Family Policy Compliance Office of the U.S. Department of Education.

It should be understood that the law does not *prohibit* disclosure of records—it simply imposes the penalty of loss of federal funds on schools that release records in violation of its terms: "Under the Family Educational Rights and Privacy Act (FERPA) and the Regulations thereunder, a school's release of a student's records or personally identifiable information to unauthorized persons will result in withholding of federal funds" (*Webster Groves School District* v. *Pulitzer Publishing Company*, 898 F.2d 1371, 1375 [8th Cir. 1990]).

The important question for school librarians is, does the Buckley Amendment apply to school library records? The precise definition of "education records," which are required to be disclosed to parents under the Buckley Amendment, has been the subject of much debate, very little case law, and little elaboration via the Code of Federal Regulations, where some additional explanation of the statute's terms may be found (see 32 C.F.R Section 99).

Nevertheless, school librarians may one day find themselves in the position of having to determine whether or not they are bound by law to release otherwise-confidential information about students to their parents or guardians. The language of the law, and the Department of Education's interpretation of it, are broad and inclusive, suggesting that all records containing personally identifiable information about a student are covered. But there are several exceptions in the definition section of the statute applicable to elementary and secondary school students. One of these exceptions covers records of instructional, supervisory, and administrative personnel, which are in the sole possession of the person who made them and which are not accessible or revealed to anyone else except a substitute.

Before even considering arguments about whether or not the Buckley Amendment should apply to school library records, librarians and school administrators should make sure they have a thorough understanding of the philosophy behind the professional, ethical, and often legal requirement that library records be kept confidential. Library circulation and registration records are maintained solely for administrative purposes—the only reason they are kept is for the library to keep track of its materials. They are not created as a means of spying on patrons' reading habits or of providing a government-sponsored intermediary between parent and child for the purpose of monitoring the child's reading habits. Ideally, parents should be guiding their own children's reading selections and should not rely on librarians to report on their children for them. Library patrons, including minors, will not feel free to exercise their constitutional right to receive information if they believe their selections are being monitored. Furthermore, it is inappropriate to call someone under suspicion, or to prejudge that person's character, because of his or her reading habits. A free society trusts its members to make their own individual decisions about what they choose to read and how they choose to act. Freedom of thought and conscience cannot be maintained in a society that does not allow its citizens to read and explore all points of view freely, without fear of social or governmental reprisal based upon the misguided assumption that what a person chooses to read is an absolute indicator of what that person believes or how that person is likely to behave.

Young people must be taught that they, too, have the right to read, and that they must learn to examine and distinguish between many different points of view and opinions in order to arrive at and defend their own in an intellectually sound and fully informed manner. In a democratic society, self-governing citizens must feel free to fully inform themselves, to become responsible participants in the democratic and social processes of a free nation.

For these sound philosophical reasons, free expression advocates, proponents of children's rights, and the ALA's Office for Intellectual Freedom oppose the application to school library records of the Buckley Amendment's requirement of disclosure to parents. First, one of the major purposes of the Buckley Amendment is to protect student privacy, something librarians are already committed to do. Librarians' professional ethics, and laws in forty-five states and the District of Columbia, protect the confidentiality of library records and either require or allow them to be withheld from anyone other than library personnel absent a court order.

Second, library records are not kept as a record of the scholastic development of a student. Circulation records are usually obliterated automatically when an item is returned, so one could argue that the records are not "maintained" in the manner contemplated by the statute. One of Senator Buckley's concerns in proposing the law, as explained in one of the few cases dealing with its terms, was that a single vindictive remark or inaccuracy could lurk undetected in a student's record, ruining future opportunities without the student's knowledge:

> An example of the type of abuse which FERPA was designed to prevent is the insertion of potentially prejudicial anecdotal comments and factual inaccuracies into a student's school records. When parents and students are not allowed to inspect such school records and make corrections, such material can have a devastatingly negative effect on the academic future and job prospects of an innocent, unaware student. A simple inaccuracy or a comment by a spiteful, neurotic teacher can potentially ruin a student's future. (*Bauer* v. *Kincaid*, 759 F.Supp. 575, 590 [W.D. Mo. 1991])

Library records do not contain personal observations and are therefore not the kind of records that could include such little "time bombs," which would need to be corrected, are not permanently maintained, and are not transmitted to anyone who could use them in any way against a student in the future. This, of course, is one of the reasons librarians keep such records confidential in the first place.

Maintaining the confidentiality of library records comports at least with the spirit of the Buckley Amendment with regard to privacy.

This interpretation of the status of school library records under the Buckley Amendment has never been tested directly in court. A 1991 federal court decision (in *Bauer* v. *Kincaid*, supra) defined school records narrowly to include only those "records relating to individual student academic performance, financial aid, or scholastic probation which are kept in individual student files." The court also explained the purpose of the act: "The underlying purpose of FERPA was not to grant individual students a right to privacy or access to educational records, but to stem the growing policy of many institutions to carelessly release educational information" (*Bauer* v. *Kincaid*, at 590). Again, library records contain no significant educational information and are already maintained as confidential. The decision in *Bauer* is not binding outside the district in which it was rendered, but since it is one of only a very few cases interpreting the statute, it sets a precedent upon which to base an argument for future cases.

The law governing the confidentiality of library records of minor patrons—and more broadly, the rights of children versus the rights of their parents—is indefinite and still developing. The ethical stance taken by librarians, however, is more clear: ALA policy and the Office for Intellectual Freedom advocate according the same confidentiality protection to minors as to adult patrons.

Children and young adults will not learn to exercise their own intellectual freedom if they are taught that the guarantees of the Constitution do not apply to them. Protecting their right to read freely and use library resources is critically important if we wish to raise new generations to be active First Amendment advocates and protectors of the Constitution, which provides the basis for government by and for all the people.

5

Public Libraries as Limited Public Fora for Access to Information

ANNE LEVINSON PENWAY

On March 23, 1992, the United States Court of Appeals for the Third Circuit handed down its decision in *Kreimer* v. *Morristown*.[1] The case, which involved a challenge to the patron behavior rules of the Morristown, New Jersey, Public Library, had been one of passionate debate in public library circles, much of which was, unfortunately, uninformed and misdirected. Indeed, the debate tended to focus on librarians' feelings about so-called problem patrons, including homeless patrons, and their alleged behavior, whereas the litigation focused only on whether the actual written rules adopted by the Morristown library were constitutionally acceptable.

The case arose out of a dispute between the Morristown library and one of its patrons, a homeless man named Richard Kreimer. Kreimer was accused of engaging in unacceptable behavior in the library, in violation of the library's rules for patron conduct. When Kreimer sued, contending that he had been barred from the library in violation of his constitutional right to have access to information, the library filed a motion for summary judgment, asking the court to rule, as a matter of law, that its rules were permissible under the Constitution. Rulings on motions for summary judgment are based on undisputed facts and make no factual rulings—instead, they address how the law applies to the facts at hand. In this case, the "undisputed facts" were the words of the rules themselves. Kreimer's specific behavior was not before the court and was not an element in its decision.

Initially, the federal district court, in a controversial opinion by Judge Lee Sarokin, found that the rules, which permitted ejecting a patron for "foul odor," "staring," and other infractions were over-broad. The library appealed to the United States Court of Appeals for the Third Circuit.

That court reversed the lower court's decision in part, but adopted the reasoning presented in separate amicus curiae briefs filed by the Freedom to Read Foundation and the New Jersey Library Association. The Third Circuit ruled, for the first time, that public libraries are designated limited public fora for access to information and that First Amendment rights are implicated when library rules and regulations threaten to restrict that access. The court also upheld the right of libraries to make reasonable rules to facilitate access for all library patrons. Finally, the court upheld the specific rules and regulations of the Morristown library, finding that they were either reasonable regulations on non-expressive activity or content-neutral restrictions on activity that might have an expres-sive element but interfered with the operation of the library

While press reports tended to focus on Kreimer's alleged con-duct, the court was careful to note that it did not make factual find-ings concerning that conduct. The ruling dealt only with the facial validity of Morristown's rules and regulations.

Following a careful review of Supreme Court precedents, the Third Circuit held that "our review of the Supreme Court's deci-sions confirms that the First Amendment does not merely prohibit the government from enacting laws that censor information, but additionally encompasses the positive right of public access to information and ideas. . . . [T]his right . . . includes the right to some level of access to a public library, the quintessential locus of the receipt of information."

Once it had recognized the constitutional right of public access to information and ideas in public libraries, the court took up the question of what kind of public forum analysis applies, "because the extent to which the government may limit access depends on whether the forum is public or non-public." The United States Supreme Court has, in several decisions, defined three types of such fora—public, limited or designated public, and nonpublic. The first type, *public fora,* encompasses places such as public streets, parks, and sidewalks, which have been traditional venues of freedom of expression and the dissemination of information by speakers to the public. *Limited or designated public fora* are places that have been set aside by the government for expressive activity In these two types of fora, the government may impose only "reasonable time, place and manner" restrictions on speech. *Nonpublic fora* are government buildings and other such areas, which do not have as their primary role acting as a venue for expression. More restrictive rules may be applied in such places.

The Third Circuit held that public libraries are designated or limited public fora:

> It is clear to us that a public library, albeit the quintessential locus for the exercise of the right to receive information and ideas, is sufficiently dissimilar to a public park, sidewalk or street that it cannot reasonably be determined to constitute a traditional public forum. Obviously, a library patron cannot be permitted to engage in most traditional First Amendment activities in any library, such as giving speeches or engaging in any other conduct that would disrupt the quiet and peaceful library environment. We thus rejected the District Court's conclusion that the library constitutes a "quintessential, traditional public forum whose accessibility affects the bedrock of our democratic system. . . ." In our view, . . . the library constitutes a limited public forum, a type of designated public fora.

A significant factor in the court's ruling was the Morristown library's mission statement and the stated purposes of the rules at issue in the case. These were to "allow all patrons of the Joint Free Public Library of Morristown and Morris Township to use its facilities to the maximum extent possible during its regularly scheduled hours." The Third Circuit was persuaded that this language established a governmental intent to open the library to the public for expressive activity, "namely, the communication of the written word." The court also noted that the record in the case indicated that the library exercised its authority to exclude a patron only after his or her violation of the library's rules. The rules themselves make clear that the library is open to the public only for specified purposes: reading, studying, or using library materials. The library has not opened its doors for the exercise of all First Amendment activities (such as demonstrations or soapbox speeches).

The court held that in a limited public forum, constitutional protection is afforded "only to expressive activity of a genre similar to those that government has admitted to the limited forum." Applying that standard, the court found "the library is obligated only to permit the public to exercise rights that are consistent with the nature of the library and consistent with the government's intent in designating the library as a public forum. Other activities need not be tolerated. "

Proceeding to an examination of the specific rules at issue, the court held that each of the challenged rules met the required standard of reasonableness and were not vague or overbroad. The court spent the most time analyzing the so-called smell rule, which prohibited patrons whose "bodily hygiene is so offensive as to constitute a nuisance" from remaining in the building. The court found that the "smell" rule was sufficiently narrow and that the library's purpose was served by the requirement that its patrons have non-offensive bodily hygiene. The rule left open alternative channels for communication, because all a patron had to do was comply with the rules in order to use the library's facilities. The court specifically stated that it did not read the rule as one that permanently barred a patron from reentering the library once the patron had complied with the requirements, in the absence of what the court termed "pervasive abuse." Interestingly, the Third Circuit noted,

> [W]hile the District Court was probably correct that the rule may disproportionately affect the homeless who have limited access to bathing facilities, this fact is irrelevant to a facial challenge and further would not justify permitting a would-be patron, with hygiene so offensive that it constitutes a nuisance, to force other patrons to leave the library or to inhibit library employees from performing their duties. Moreover, we do not face the more difficult scenario in which one individual possesses First Amendment rights and others do not. Here, if the First Amendment protects the right to reasonable access to a public library, as we hold it does, this is a right shared equally by all residents of Morristown and Morris Township. . . .Kreimer's right has no lesser, or greater, significance than that of other residents. Accordingly, his right to reasonable access to the library cannot be expanded to such an extent that it denies others the same guarantee.

Responding to the concern that enforcement of the "smell" rule depended on a third person's subjective reaction of being annoyed, the court observed that "the determination of whether a given patron's hygiene constitutes a nuisance involves an objective reasonableness test, not an annoyance test."

Thus, the court held that the Morristown library's rules were reasonable, that the library did not act in an arbitrary or discriminatory manner in enacting them, and that a violation of the rules would disrupt the smooth functioning of the library. It reversed the decision of the lower court and remanded the case for resolution of remaining issues and for entry of a partial summary judgment in favor of the library, upholding the facial constitutionality of its rules. Although the Third Circuit's decision is binding only in New Jersey, Pennsylvania, Delaware, and the Virgin Islands (the area of the Third Circuit's jurisdiction), it is the only federal appeals court decision that has directly ruled that libraries are designated public fora for access to information, and that infringements of that access must be analyzed under First Amendment principles. It therefore will be persuasive precedent for courts addressing similar issues in the future.

In response to the many requests that arose during the period this litigation was moving through the courts, the American Library Association's Intellectual Freedom Committee (IFC) developed "Guidelines for the Development of Policies and Procedures regarding User Behavior and Library Usage," which were designed to provide a framework of important considerations for libraries that were developing or revising patron behavior policies.[2]

The concept of libraries as limited public fora has also arisen in the context of library meeting-room use. The United States Court of Appeals for the Fifth Circuit ruled in 1989 that the Oxford, Mississippi, Public Library had established its meeting rooms as a limited public forum in that it allowed a wide variety of groups to meet there whether or not their meetings were library related or library sponsored. The local chapter of a conservative religious women's organization, Concerned Women for America, had requested the use of the room for a meeting that would include prayer. The library rejected the request, citing its policy of excluding religious uses of the meeting room, a policy that was probably developed in order to avoid the accusation that the library was violating the Establishment Clause of the First Amendment by sponsoring religious practices.

The group sued, claiming they had been unconstitutionally excluded because of the content of their speech—and the Fifth Circuit court agreed. Holding that the library had allowed groups such as the local swim club and military recruiters to use the room, groups that stretched the definition of those permitted in the library's own policy, the court found that the library had established a limited public forum in its meeting room and therefore could not discriminate against groups because of the content of the speech in which they wished to engage, including religious speech.[3]

Subsequently, the IFC revised an existing Interpretation of the *Library Bill of Rights* to reflect the court's reasoning, splitting it into two new Interpretations, one dealing specifically with meeting rooms and another dealing with exhibit spaces and bulletin boards. All three areas present issues that are appropriately considered using limited public forum analysis.[4]

Supporters of intellectual freedom viewed the decisions in *Kreimer* v. *Morristown* and in *Concerned Women for America* v. *Lafayette County* (the Oxford, Mississippi, case) as positive for libraries in general—they helped carve out First Amendment protection for libraries to make ideas and information from all points of view available and accessible. They place publicly supported libraries firmly within a well-established body of First Amendment law that will, in the future, provide more clarity and guidance in resolving issues of access, collection development, and the equitable provision of library services to all library patrons.

NOTES

1. *Kreimer* v. *Morristown*, 958 F.2d 1242 (3rd Cir. 1992).

2. See part II, section 9.

3. *Concerned Women for America* v. *Lafayette County*, 883 F.2d 32 (5th Cir. 1989).

4. See part II, sections 2.9 and 2.14.

PART V

Before the Censor Comes
Essential Preparations

1

Before the Censor Comes
Essential Preparation

BEVERLEY BECKER

Preparation is the key to preserving intellectual freedom in schools and libraries. Being prepared entails developing formal, written procedures, educating the library board and staff about those procedures—and intellectual freedom in general—and working to develop and maintain a strong foundation of support in the community you serve.

The first step is the development of written library policies and procedures. Once established and adopted, policies should be reviewed regularly and updated as needed.

Placing the policies in writing is key for several important reasons. Written policies encourage stability and continuity in the library's operations, while reducing ambiguity and confusion about procedures. They show everyone that the library is running a businesslike operation, giving credence to the library's actions, and informing the community about the library's intent, goals, and aspirations. People respect what is in writing, even though they may not agree with everything in the library's procedures manual. Written policies give the public a means to evaluate library performance and prove that the library is willing to be held accountable for its decisions. A well-written, board-approved policy will help disarm potential censors; unfounded accusations seldom prevail when the library's operations are based on clear-cut and timely written procedures that reflect thorough research, sound judgment, and careful planning.

Four procedures, at least, are vital for the good of the library and the defense of intellectual freedom: materials selection criteria, a complaints procedure, procedures that protect user confidentiality, and public relations procedures. Since most libraries now offer their users Internet access, an Internet use policy is a fifth, imperative procedure. In the following sections, these essential preparations are described in depth and practical guidelines are provided. These guidelines derive from and expand upon the basic outline of procedures offered in the document "Dealing with Concerns about Library Resources" (see part III, section 10, or http://www.ala.org/alaorg/oif/dealingwithconcerns.html), which should be reviewed in conjunction with the following sections. These policies also should have the endorsement of the library's governing body, thereby providing an even firmer foundation for supporting intellectual freedom if a censorship dispute arises.

Development of a Materials Selection Policy

The primary purpose of a materials selection or collection development policy is to promote the development of a collection based on institutional goals and user needs. A secondary purpose is to defend the principles of intellectual freedom.

The basis of a sound selection program is a materials selection statement, identifying specific criteria to be met for materials to be added to the collection.

A materials selection statement must relate to concrete practices. It should provide guidelines for strengthening and adding to the library's collection. Furthermore, if the statement is to fulfill its secondary purpose, that of defending intellectual freedom, it must be a viable, working document that relates to the specific, day-to-day operations of the library or library system of which it is a part. Large libraries may prefer to prepare both an overarching policy or mission statement describing the philosophy of collection development that will guide selection decisions, and a separate list of specific procedures that staff follows in carrying out the policy. Thus, the materials selection statement would reflect institutional policies, while a separate procedure manual would deal with the day-to-day applications of those policies.

A strong collection and intellectual freedom go hand in hand. It is more likely that problems will be resolved if the collection reflects the logical, coherent, and explicit statement from which it grows. In developing a materials selection statement, four basic factors must be considered: (1) service policy, (2) environmental characteristics, (3) collection specifications, and (4) current selection needs.

Service Policy

A service policy will provide practical operational guidelines to govern future collection development in accordance with the needs of the library's users and the goals of the library. In order to establish a service policy, it is necessary to determine what groups the library is striving to serve and what purposes it is attempting to achieve. To do so will entail a study of user-group characteristics and institutional objectives.

Environmental Characteristics

Librarians should determine which aspects of the environment surrounding the institution should influence the development of the library collection and the library's related activities. Environmental factors to consider include geographic location, economic structure, local industry, cultural makeup, and the presence or absence of colleges or universities.

Collection Specifications

Specifications should be established for each subject area or area of concern. For this section of the selection statement, each subject area should be carefully reviewed in order to determine the types of materials to be acquired in each and the depth in which materials are to be acquired.

Finally, a desired acquisition level should be specified for each area.

This section of the selection statement will specify the criteria to be used in selecting and reevaluating materials in terms of (1) types of materials (books, periodicals, newspapers, government publications, maps, records, films, etc.); (2) users' special needs because of occupation, cultural interest, language, etc.; and (3) users' age groups. This section will also specify policies to be used in handling such matters as gifts and special bequests.

Current Selection Needs

Current selection needs can be determined by the difference between the present collection and the collection specifications. In deciding what is currently needed, the desired state of affairs that may have been detailed under service policy should also be consulted. Once current needs are determined, other considerations come into play. Most prominent among these is the library's budget. Regardless of the amount of money available, the selection statement should indicate as clearly as possible which materials are to be added to the collection, and which are not.

Components of a Selection Policy Statement

After full consideration of the above four factors—service policy, environmental characteristics, collection specifications, and current selection needs—the next step is to prepare a final draft of the selection (or collection development) statement for submission to the library's governing body. Taking into account the factors discussed above, the statement should relate to and include all materials and services offered by the library.

A good policy statement will first discuss the library's objectives in acquiring materials and maintaining services. It will state in succinct terms what the library is trying to accomplish in its program of services, and the specific objectives in given areas of service.

The policy should be derived from the library's mission statement. It is helpful if the role of the library in society (or in the parent institution) is spelled out in the policy and related to the objectives of selection, collection development, and maintenance. The overarching goal may be expressed in the broadest terms. For example, a policy for a public library should include reference to the traditional function of the library in the marketplace of ideas. It could include language like the following: "The library serves a traditional role as a public forum for access to the full range of recorded information within the marketplace of ideas. Collection development shall be content neutral so that the library represents significant viewpoints on subjects of interest and does not favor any particular viewpoint."

A school library may declare that its main objective is "to make available to faculty and students a collection of materials that will enrich and support the curriculum and meet the educational needs of the students and faculty served." This may then be broken down into more specific objectives, such as to provide background materials to supplement classroom instruction, to provide access to classics of American and world literature, and to provide a broad range of materials on current issues of controversy to help students develop critical analytic skills.

The policy will precisely define the responsibility for selection of all types of library materials. It will name, by professional position, those persons responsible in each area of selection. While selection of materials will, of course, involve many people other than professionally trained librarians, ultimate responsibility should be delegated by the library's governing body to the professional staff. A public library's statement of responsibility might read: "The elected Library Board shall delegate to the Head Librarian the authority and responsibility for selection of all print and nonprint materials. Responsibilities for actual selection shall rest with appropriate professionally trained personnel who shall discharge this obligation consistent with the Board's adopted selection criteria and procedures." Depending upon the size and purpose of the library, the statement might continue by elaborating on any specialized selection responsibilities, the role of user input, and the like.

For subject matter covered, the policy will include criteria, and the application of criteria, relevant to the library's stated objectives. These will include artistic or literary excellence, appropriateness to level of user, authenticity, interest, cost, and circumstances of use. It is also appropriate to include technical criteria, such as clarity of sound in audio materials. To guide the professional staff with responsibility for selection, criteria should be spelled out as specifically as possible. Bibliographies, reviewing journals, and other selection aids to be consulted should be listed. Special criteria to be applied in exceptional cases should be clearly stated. For example, a public library that regularly purchases all books on the *New York*

Times best-seller list, even if these titles do not always meet other criteria, should state this clearly in the policy. A section should explain how the library will treat donated materials, and that such materials will be subject to the same selection criteria as materials the library purchases.

The policy should directly address problems associated with the acquisition of controversial materials. The document should include a statement on intellectual freedom and its importance to librarianship, as well as an affirmation of the *Library Bill of Rights*. Some libraries also include the text of the First Amendment to the U.S. Constitution. A statement on intellectual freedom might read: "The library subscribes in principle to the statements of policy on library philosophy as expressed in the American Library Association's *Library Bill of Rights*, a copy of which is appended to and made an integral part of this policy." The statement can also include the text of the "Freedom to Read" statement and the ALA's "Policy on Confidentiality of Library Records," which states that circulation records and other records identifying the names of library users are considered confidential.

The library's selection procedures should be described step by step from initial screening to final selection. The procedures should provide for coordination among departments and professional staff, for handling recommendations from library users, and for review of existing material. Any special procedures pertinent to collection development should be spelled out precisely in the materials selection statement. Some items to consider are sponsored materials, expensive or fragile materials, ephemeral materials, jobbers and salespersons, distribution of free materials, and handling of special collections. The document should review procedures for collection maintenance.

Finally, occasional objections to materials will be made despite the quality of the selection process. The procedure for review of challenged materials in response to expressed concerns of library users should be stated clearly. The procedure should establish a fair framework for registering complaints, while defending the principles of intellectual freedom, the library user's right of access, and professional responsibility and integrity. Each specific step to be taken when a request for reconsideration is made, and all possible avenues of appeal, should be listed.

The final format and organization of the materials selection statement will depend, of course, on the particularities of the library concerned. One possible table of contents, however, might look like this:

PART 1: Selection of Library Materials

I. Statement of Policy

II. Objectives of Selection

III. Responsibility for Selection

    A. Delegation of Responsibility to Professional Staff
    B. Particular Responsibilities of Staff Members

IV. Selection Criteria

    A. General Selection Criteria
    B. Specific Selection Criteria

V. Policy on Controversial Materials

    A. General Statement
    B. Library Bill of Rights
    C. "The Freedom to Read" statement
    D. ALA "Policy on Confidentiality of Library Records"

PART 2: Procedures for Selection of Library Materials

I. Procedures for Implementation

    A. Selection Aids
    B. Outside Recommendation Procedures
    C. Gifts
    D. Special Collections and Concerns

II. Collection Maintenance: Evaluation and Review of Existing Materials

III. Procedures for Dealing with Challenged Materials

    A. Request for Review
    B. The Review Committee
    C. Resolution and Appeal.

The preparation of a complete statement requires work—a great amount of it—which must be done before the censorship problem arises. Unfortunately, there are no shortcuts. The materials in this manual, including the texts of current ALA intellectual freedom policies, will be of some assistance. For school libraries, the American Association of School Librarians distributes a document entitled "Policies and Procedures for Selection of Instructional Materials." The ALA's Office for Intellectual Freedom (OIF) distributes a "Workbook for Selection Policy Writing" (http://www.ala.org/alaorg/oif/workbook_selection.html), with specific suggestions and examples of how to write a school library policy, the basic principles of which are also helpful in formulating policies for other types of libraries. The OIF and many state intellectual freedom committees have also collected sample selection statements which can serve as examples. It is, however, impossible to simply borrow a statement based on another institution's goals and needs; the statement must be a working document, a handbook for daily activities reflecting the specific needs of those who are to use it.

Procedures for Handling Complaints

All librarians must be aware that at some time there will be complaints about library service—and sometimes these complaints will center around a particular book, magazine, or other item that the library distributes. What should one do when a complaint of this kind is made? (See also "Dealing with Concerns about Library Resources" in part III, section 10, or http://www.ala.org/alaorg/oif/dealingwithconcerns.html.) Handling any type of complaint about library operations requires a courteous and calm approach. Above all, complainants must know that their objections will be given serious consideration and that interest in the library is welcome. Complainants should be listened to courteously and invited to file a complaint in writing, if the problem cannot be resolved through informal discussion. If the complaint comes by letter, it should be acknowledged promptly. In either case, the complainant should be offered a prepared questionnaire to be submitted formally. In addition, the rationale for having a formal complaint procedure should be explained.

Having a prepared form is not just an additional piece of record keeping. There are a number of advantages in having a complaint procedure available. First, knowing that a response is ready and a procedure is to be followed, the librarian will be relieved of much of the initial panic that inevitably strikes when confronted by an outspoken and perhaps irate library patron. Second, the complaint form asks complainants to state their objections in logical, unemotional terms, thereby allowing the librarian to evaluate the merits of the objections. In addition, the form benefits the complainant. When citizens with complaints are asked to follow an established procedure for lodging their objections, they feel assured they are being properly heard and that their objections will be considered.

The sample complaint form, entitled "Request for Reconsideration of Library Resources" (see figure 1 on p. 279), was adopted by the Intellectual Freedom Committee and most recently revised in 1995. Libraries and librarians should feel free to use it as a model, although alternative forms may be devised to reflect the specifics of a given library situation.

As soon as the complaint has been filed, the objections should be reviewed. The review should consist of specific steps, although the number will vary somewhat according to the individual library involved. Simultaneous with the review, the governing body (board of trustees, school board, etc.) should be routinely notified that a formal complaint has been made.

First, the person or committee that selected the item, or an ad hoc committee, should evaluate the original reasons for the purchase. The objections should be considered based on the library's materials selection statement, the principles of the *Library Bill of Rights,* and the opinions of the various reviewing sources used in materials selection. If the materials selection statement is sufficiently detailed to function as a guide for selection decisions, it should not be difficult to make a logical, strong response to the objections.

Second, the objections and the response should be forwarded to the acquisitions librarian who has final responsibility for selecting materials, and who, in turn, should review the response and if necessary either add relevant comments or return the response to the individual or committee for further clarification. At this point, then, either the acquisitions librarian or the selection committee can send a written response to the complainant.

It is critical that the review process be as objective as possible. If the challenged item does not meet the library's own criteria for selection (assuming, of course, that these criteria themselves are consistent with the principles of intellectual freedom), the library must be ready to acknowledge that the material is indeed unsuitable and withdraw it from the collection. If, on the other hand, as is most often the case, the material does meet the selection criteria and is deemed suitable for the collection, it is the responsibility of the library staff to respond to the complaint clearly and precisely. This response also should inform the complainant how to pursue the matter further. If the complainant is not satisfied, then the head administrator of the library (the person to whom the governing body has given authority) can serve as the person to whom an initial appeal is made. The complainant should be contacted promptly, given an explanation of the library's decision, and advised that further discussions are welcome.

If the complainant still feels that the problem has been dealt with inadequately, the complainant may make a final appeal (within the structure of the library) to the governing body of the institution. This body will take appropriate action—for example, conduct a public hearing—according to the established procedures for such appeals. It must be emphasized, however, that requests for action from the governing body should not be routine; such requests are best avoided by an adequate initial response to the complaint.

At each step of this process, the utmost courtesy toward and respect for the complainant should be maintained. There is no reason for a librarian to become defensive when a complaint is made. Not only is this counterproductive, but it runs counter to library efforts to encourage user involvement. Most complainants are sincere in their concerns and frequently can be prevailed upon to see the censorious implications of their actions. It should be recognized that many library users are intimidated by the librarian's authority and expertise, and for many patrons, the decision to complain may be an act of admirable personal courage and a reaffirmation of their democratic right to be involved.

The review procedure, including the written questionnaire, should be designed not only as a defense against potential censors, but also as a means to facilitate constructive dialogue. While these procedures do offer the library a defense against arbitrary attacks, they should never be permitted to degenerate into a bureaucratic smokescreen. In other words, the library should welcome constructive input even as it maintains firm barriers against censorship.

Conducting a Challenge Hearing

Challenges to materials only occasionally reach the stage of a full-blown administrative hearing; often they are resolved at an earlier step in the challenge resolution process. When a hearing is necessary, however, certain important do's and don'ts should be observed. A number of battles have been lost because of poorly organized challenge hearings. If procedures have been followed to the letter up to this point, the handling of the challenge hearing should not be the weak link in the process.

The challenge process begins when someone objects to materials in a library collection. At this point, providing (1) an explanation of selection procedures, (2) a copy of the selection policy, or (3) a copy of the reconsideration or complaint form, will often resolve the concern. A complainant sometimes may not return the reconsideration form, because he or she sees the logic of the selection process that emphasizes intellectual freedom and due process. The complainant tends to be satisfied in registering a concern and knowing the library is taking the concern seriously.

There are some, however, who will wish to follow through on the procedures established in the selection policy approved by the governing authority for handling complaints. To activate the reconsideration procedure, a complaint should be in writing. In fact, the written and approved selection policy should state that, to best serve the interests of all concerned, anonymous or unwritten complaints are not honored; action occurs only when the reconsideration or complaint form has been returned. When a written complaint is filed, the reconsideration committee, usually composed of representatives of all library users and the librarian (often, all are library staff—the actual composition of the committee is up to the individual institution), is formed. The committee should then undertake the following:

1. Read, view, or listen to the challenged material in its entirety;
2. Review the selection process and the criteria for selection;

3. Check reviews and recommended lists to determine recommendations by the experts and critics;
4. Meet to discuss the challenge; and
5. Make a recommendation to the administrator on removal, retention, or replacement.

Before the Hearing

After a formal, written request for reconsideration has been submitted and reviewed, and a recommendation for retention or removal has been made, the complainant should be notified of the committee's decision. At the same time, the procedure for appealing the decision should also be provided. The appeal may involve a hearing by a school board, a board of trustees, or a city or county board of commissioners or council. (The selection policy should clearly identify the chain of command.) The appeal must also be in writing in order for the chair of the governing authority to place it on the agenda for the next meeting. The librarian should follow up on this step to make certain the presiding officer is aware of the policies and procedures that should be followed, including open meetings laws and the agenda. Normally, the board conducts a challenge hearing that provides the forum for the complainant to air his or her objections to the title in the collection and for the recommendation of the reconsideration committee.

A hearing on challenged material is serious and often lengthy. Such a hearing may be the only item on the agenda; indeed, the best results are most often achieved this way.

Decide in advance on a length of time for the entire hearing. Have a definite beginning and ending time. Avoid overlong meetings when decisions may be made by small groups in the late hours. These have spelled disaster in some instances.

Never attempt to stage a hearing quietly. The entire community should be aware of the meeting and what has transpired up to this point. The hearing should be announced well in advance. Publicity is very important to assure good attendance at the meeting. Make the time and place very clear. Indicate in an announcement or news release that an open hearing is being held and that the public is invited. Try to obtain full coverage by the local press, radio, and television. Prepare a news release for each of these groups to ensure they have the facts correct. Deliver copies of the library's selection policies to them, along with a copy of the *Library Bill of Rights.* These policies, of course, should include procedures for handling complaints.

Seek help and advice from your state intellectual freedom committee, local and state colleges and universities, educational groups, teachers' professional organizations and coalitions, and the ALA Office for Intellectual Freedom. In addition, many nonlibrary groups have committees on intellectual freedom, freedom of speech, and academic freedom. Even when representatives from these groups cannot be present, written resolutions of support can be helpful.

Find people who will be willing to speak in support of the freedom to read, view, and listen. This pool of speakers should be contacted well in advance of the hearing. In fact, many librarians have lists of persons they have contacted previously and who are library supporters. The best spokespersons in hearings tend to be attorneys, ministers, people from the news media, educators, and, of course, librarians. Response to persons from the local community is usually more favorable than to people brought in from outside. Student speakers are also effective. They speak from the heart and have no vested interest other than maintaining their freedom of choice guaranteed by the Constitution.

Attempt to estimate in advance the size of the gathering for the hearing. Make certain the meeting place is large enough to prevent postponing the meeting or changing locations at the last minute. A late site change may result in losing part of the group attending.

Long before a hearing, members of the advisory board, the reconsideration committee, and governing board should have become well-schooled in intellectual freedom principles and procedures. It is the responsibility of the librarian to accomplish this, and it will ensure board support when a challenge hearing is necessary. All those selected to testify should be reminded they are defending a principle more than an individual title. The actual title in question should play a secondary role. It is very difficult to disagree with the freedom to read, view, and listen in a democratic society.

The Hearing

As people arrive for the hearing, they should be given a copy of the selection policy. If the *Library Bill of Rights* is not a formal part of the policy, it should be duplicated and distributed as well.

One or more persons should be stationed at the entrance to sign in people wishing to speak. Request that they identify the side on which they will be speaking. If at all possible, attempt to ensure that there will be a balanced number of speakers on both sides.

Begin the hearing on time. The chair of the governing board should preside, as at any other business meeting. After calling the meeting to order, he or she should review the procedures to be followed at the meeting, and the process followed up to this point for reconsideration of the material. The board should announce at the beginning of the hearing that it will issue its decision at the next regularly scheduled meeting, and that the meeting is simply to hear all sides of the issue. Speakers should be allowed to speak in the order they signed in. Limit each speaker to a specific amount of time, and appoint a timekeeper in advance. No participant should be allowed to speak a second time until everyone registered has been heard once. It is extremely important to adhere strictly both to the order of the speakers and to the time limits.

After the Hearing

The board should announce its decision publicly at its next regularly scheduled meeting. The agenda for that meeting should include an item showing that the board will announce its decision (but not the decision itself). The usual notices and publication of the agenda will alert the public; news releases also may be used to ensure coverage and attendance at the meeting if desired. Whatever the board's decision, the principles of the *Library Bill of Rights* should be reiterated, and the agreement of the decision with those principles should be explained. A very brief statement of the reason for the decision also should be made (e.g., "we have concluded that the material meets our selection criteria and will be retained without restriction").

By following this advice, the library board will be able to conduct a successful challenge hearing and improve the library's image in the process.

Developing an Internet Use Policy

Libraries should adopt and implement written Internet use policies in the same way they adopt other library use and access policies. A brief set of suggestions for developing an Internet policy follows. Librarians should also review "Guidelines and Considerations for Developing a Public Library Internet Use Policy" (see part III, section 11), prepared by the Intellectual Freedom Committee in June 1998.

The Internet use policy should be short, reflecting the library's mission statement, other access policies, and the community's needs. It may stand on its own or serve as an addition to existing library policy. Either way, it should incorporate the ideas in the *Library Bill of Rights*, and speak to access for all.

Policies will vary according to the individual library's mission. A typical policy will include a purpose statement, a code of conduct—including specific rules and consequences for violating those rules—and a statement of responsibility.

A purpose statement should clarify that the library provides Internet access in support of its mission to meet the information needs of its community. This statement should affirm the library's stand on intellectual freedom, and its support of the *Library Bill of Rights*.

The code of conduct should establish reasonable time, place, and manner restrictions. It should include specific do's and don'ts, and expressly prohibit any use of library equipment to access child pornography or material that is obscene or "harmful to minors."

State clearly the penalties for violating the policy, which may include loss of computer privileges, or even criminal prosecution. It is important to consider the need for due process in handling violations. Patrons should be notified of alleged violations and allowed to respond as they would to any other charge of misconduct.

A statement on privacy should be included in this section, or on its own. It should remind patrons to protect their own privacy while online, and to respect the privacy of other library patrons.

A statement of responsibility should communicate clearly that individuals are responsible for the information they access online, and that parents are responsible for their children. It should note that the library cannot guarantee the accuracy of information on the Internet.

Legal counsel should review the policy. A general discussion of the legal considerations surrounding Internet access in public libraries is available on the Freedom to Read Foundation Web site, http://www.ftrf.org/internetfilteringmemo.html.

Finally, the governing board should approve the Internet use policy. Make sure the board understands why the policy is needed and its implications. Keeping the board informed will encourage its support in case of future controversy. As always, review the policy regularly, and update it as needed.

It is important to keep the policy simple, avoid jargon, and make sure the language is easy to read and understand. It will be worthwhile to involve the library staff, board, and Friends group in the policy-writing process.

Communicate the relevant policies for use of Internet-access computers to all library users, and post notices on all Internet-access computers that use of library equipment to access the illegal materials specified in the Internet use policy is prohibited.

In addition to developing an Internet use policy, libraries may discourage controversy by implementing programs and policies that address community concerns about the Web. Libraries should teach children, young people, and adults how to use the Internet and to be critical users of information. Consider offering Internet training classes for all library users. Classes should cover the importance of intellectual freedom, how to search the Internet effectively, how to judge the validity of a Web site, and privacy and safety issues related to online searching. A good reference page to use in this training is "Especially for Children and Their Parents" (http://www.ala.org/alaorg/oif/children.html).

Whether the library faces challenges to print materials, videos, Internet access, or any other library resource, making these essential preparations—having written policies and procedures in place, making the library staff, board, and community aware of those policies and the underlying philosophy, and educating the entire community about the importance of intellectual freedom—will discourage censorship and ensure the best possible outcome to any challenge.

2
Developing a Confidentiality Policy

R ecent years have seen an increase in the number and frequency of challenges to the confidentiality of library records across the United States, and a new dimension has been added to confidentiality concerns. Throughout the 1980s, the Office for Intellectual Freedom (OIF) received queries from individual librarians who had been pressured by the FBI or local law enforcement agencies for information about library users, or who were afraid of being held liable for a patron's acts after providing information on such topics as bomb construction, weapons, or satanism. Some of these librarians were tempted to maintain special files on patrons who seemed "suspicious" or who made "unusual" requests. These queries revealed a lack of confidence in confidentiality procedures or a misunderstanding of the important links among confidentiality, intellectual freedom, and librarians' professional and legal obligations to uphold the privacy rights of patrons.

Why Is Confidentiality Crucial to Freedom of Inquiry?

Inquiries about patron reading habits raise serious questions for librarians and patrons. For example, are you what you read? Would you want others to base decisions affecting your life on their opinion of the books you read, the music you listen to, the information you access over the Internet or other electronic networks or database services, or the films you view? How would library use change if patrons thought their reading records and other information about their lives would be open for scrutiny? How widely would people read, knowing their choices might prejudice others against them? If libraries are to survive as centers for the free and uninhibited access to information so necessary to a democratic society, librarians must vigilantly guard their patrons' privacy and freedom of inquiry.

To support librarians in their role as defenders of the right to read, in 1971 the Intellectual Freedom Committee (IFC) proposed, and the ALA Council adopted, the "Policy on Confidentiality of Library Records" (revised in 1975). This important addition to the IFC's expanding inventory of tools for defending intellectual freedom was initiated in response to U.S. Treasury Department efforts to identify potentially "subversive" individuals based on their choice of reading material. Looking for the names of those who had borrowed or read books about the construction of explosives, Treasury agents conducted inquiries in libraries in Ohio, California, Georgia, and Wisconsin. Librarians sounded the alarm over these apparent "fishing expeditions," and the department ceased its inquiries— but not before some librarians had handed over their records.

The IFC, which is firmly committed to the freedom to read as a necessary corollary of freedom of expression, encouraged librarians to resist such open-ended government inquiries. One cannot exercise the right to read if the possible consequences include damage to one's reputation, ostracism from the community or workplace, or criminal penalties. Choice requires both a varied selection and the assurance that one's choice is not monitored. In the case of criminal investigations or other government inquiries, it is especially critical that a librarian preserve the patron's confidentiality because the consequences of releasing information about the individual(s) under investigation may be dire and the potential for abuse of information about a person's reading habits great.

A case in Decatur, Texas, dramatically illustrates this danger. Early in 1990, the Wise County district attorney's office, investigating a child-abandonment case, subpoenaed the records of the Decatur Public Library, requesting the names, addresses, and telephone numbers of all individuals who had checked out books on childbirth within the previous nine months, the titles they borrowed, and the dates the materials were checked out and returned. The police had no evidence indicating that the person who abandoned the child might have borrowed library books or otherwise used the library. Lacking any other leads, police were simply conducting a "fishing expedition."

The director of the Decatur Public Library refused to release the records. Instead, she chose to respond, with the help of the city attorney, by filing a motion to quash the subpoena on behalf of the library's patrons. On May 9, 1990, Texas District Court Judge John R. Lindsey ruled in favor of the library and quashed the subpoena.[1] The library director in this case was successful in defending her patrons, but imagine the consequences if she had failed: all patrons who had borrowed books on childbirth might have been subjected to police interrogation based solely upon their choice of reading materials. Thanks to this librarian's courageous implementation of the library confidentiality policy, patrons were not subject to such unjust and humiliating proceedings.

Threats to confidentiality arise within the library from loosely managed information or circulation systems, library staff or board members who are unaware of their responsibilities under existing confidentiality policy or state law, or from lack of any policy at all on the issue. Librarians or their staff may be asked for confidential information by patrons, journalists, students, or professors who wish to check on the reading habits of their students, or by parents of young children who must pay overdue fines or who wish to monitor their children's reading preferences. As more libraries become automated and computerize their patron information files, and as more libraries add access to the Internet, other electronic networks, database services, and e-mail services to the array of resources they offer their patrons, threats to privacy may arise from abusers of the system. Known as "hackers," these pranksters and vandals enter the system without authorization and attempt to spy on other users or sabotage the system as a whole, using software of their own design or by exploiting loopholes in the system, sometimes causing major system breakdowns.

Finally, many of the most difficult and complicated challenges come from local or federal law enforcement officials investigating criminal activities, or from feuding litigants in civil cases. Although these situations are relatively infrequent, they can be intimidating if a librarian, staff, and governing board are inadequately prepared to respond.

In 1989, responding to an increase in external threats and the clear need for further education on intellectual freedom and confidentiality for all librarians, the Intellectual Freedom Committee initiated *Confidentiality in Libraries: An Intellectual Freedom Modular Education Program*. Concurrently, the ALA Council requested a new and more specific policy to address the problem of confidentiality in the context of law enforcement inquiries, a trend sparked by the FBI Library Awareness Program and emulated by law enforcement agencies at all levels across the country—from county sheriffs to urban detectives. The IFC developed a new policy, and the Council adopted it at the June 1991 Annual Conference (see "Policy concerning Confidentiality of Personally Identifiable Information about Library Users," part III, section 4).

Confidentiality and the Law

Although librarians' main concern has been the potential chilling effect a violation of confidentiality could have on the exercise of First Amendment rights, a growing body of law exists that protects individual privacy rights and the confidentiality of library records, raising concerns of librarian liability when confidentiality is breached. The right to privacy is not among the rights enumerated in the Bill of Rights, but legal scholars and U.S. Supreme Court interpretations of the Constitution have found an implied right of privacy or zones of privacy surrounding the First Amendment freedom of expression.[2] Justice William O. Douglas stated that "the First Amendment has a penumbra where privacy is protected from governmental intrusion": the Fifth Amendment privilege against self-incrimination, the Fourteenth Amendment provision for due process and, above all, the Fourth Amendment protection against unreasonable search and seizure.

The Supreme Court, in two decisions, laid the foundation for recognizing a right to privacy in one's choice of reading materials and explained that freedom of expression includes the right to read. In *Lamont* v. *Postmaster General*,[3] the Court affirmed the right of an individual to receive controversial political materials through the U.S. mail. Later, in *Stanley* v. *Georgia*,[4] the Court made explicit the right of individual privacy in controversial reading material, holding that an individual may read as he or she chooses—even material alleged to be obscene, as was the case in *Stanley*—within the privacy of his or her home. In 1990, however, this right was limited in *Osborne* v. *Ohio*,[5] when the Supreme Court upheld an Ohio law banning the possession of child pornography, arguing for a narrow interpretation of *Stanley*, and stating that "the interests underlying child pornography prohibitions far exceed the interests justifying the Georgia law at issue in *Stanley*. Every court to address the issue has so concluded."[6]

Early Supreme Court interpretations of the Fourth Amendment sought to protect private property against government intrusion. This protection was expanded by later Court decisions, in cases such as *NAACP* v. *Alabama*[7] and *Griswold* v. *Connecticut*,[8] to protect a person and personal information, as opposed to a particular place or property. In the *NAACP* case, the Court recognized the "chilling effect on First Amendment rights of unauthorized disclosure of member lists." A 1967 ruling in *Katz* v. *United States*[9] took this recognition further, setting forth a standard for constitutionally protected zones of privacy. In this case, the individual's expectation of privacy was weighed against the government's interest in searching or invading that privacy. Based on *Katz* and preceding cases, the Court has interpreted the Fourth Amendment and the Bill of Rights as a whole to protect an individual's property, communications, personality, politics, and thoughts.

Although some Supreme Court decisions had favored the right to privacy, there remained a need for more explicit protections for individuals in an age of computer-based information systems. Seeking to address this need, Congress passed the Privacy Act of 1974,[10] prohibiting the maintenance of secret data files, ensuring the right of individuals to know what files are kept and what information they contain, and outlining a process by which individuals can correct false or misleading information found in records maintained about them.

The act was amended in 1988[11] to prevent (1) the establishment of a national data bank, merging information on individuals maintained in systems of records by other federal agencies; (2) the direct linking of computerized systems of records; (3) the computer matching of records not otherwise authorized by law; and (4) the disclosure of records for computer matching except to a federal, state, or local government agency. This attempt to legislate a right to privacy has had mixed success in the courts and has suffered some setbacks. To compensate for its inadequacies, nearly all states now recognize the right to privacy in their statutory law.

State Law Protection of Library Records

Forty-seven states and the District of Columbia also have laws that provide for the confidentiality of library records.[12] This protection usually takes one of two basic forms: affirmative protection of a patron's privacy rights; or exceptions to open public records or state freedom of information acts, exempting library records from public scrutiny. Direct protection is preferable, of course, because this format often provides for punitive action and redress if the law is broken; an exemption from an open public records act is not so easily enforced. Laws that do not specifically forbid revealing the information contained in library records are subject to varying interpretations and manipulation that might allow law enforcement agents easier access to privileged information.

It is imperative for librarians to know their legal rights and responsibilities and to create or revise confidentiality policies to conform with the law. Without taking these steps, the librarian may risk civil liability for harm suffered by a patron because the individual's library records were revealed to law enforcement agents, government officials, or others. Librarians may also be subjected to the penalties provided in state laws in the event that confidential records are revealed.

What Is a Librarian to Do?

Although questions of confidentiality can be complicated and have potentially serious consequences, they are exceedingly manageable and may be responded to in a way that protects both librarians and patrons. As all politics are local, so too are most attempts at censorship local in origin. Victories for the First Amendment are won (or lost) case by case and usually without fanfare through the conviction and dedication (or lack thereof) of individuals who stand up for freedom of expression, regardless of the alleged offensiveness of content or the good cause of the person requesting or demanding confidential information. This means that every librarian must understand the importance of maintaining confidentiality and be prepared to educate people with a wide range of interests and expertise about the role of confidentiality in protecting the intellectual freedom of all library users.

This critical responsibility is best managed by choosing to be proactive and take the initiative, rather than waiting for a crisis to develop. Protecting confidentiality requires a rapid and well-orchestrated defense, beginning with a library policy on confidentiality.

Writing a Policy

The basis in policy and law for the protection of confidentiality can be found in the following documents:

1. *Library Bill of Rights* and its Interpretations
2. American Library Association "Code of Ethics"
3. ALA "Policy on Confidentiality of Library Records"
4. ALA "Policy concerning Confidentiality of Personally Identifiable Information about Library Users"
5. First, Fourth, Fifth, and Fourteenth Amendments to the United States Constitution
6. Privacy Act of 1974, amended
7. State confidentiality of library records laws

An effective policy should include the following sections:

Objective: Who or what is to be protected? From whom or what? Why is the policy necessary?

Responsibility: Who is responsible for implementing the policy? Who will enforce it? Who has a right to know? A need to know?

Criteria: Which information will be protected? How will this be determined?

Procedures: What steps are to be taken by staff in identifying situations where the policy applies? How will the policy be implemented in response to such situations? How will the policy be adopted, amended, repealed? How will it be incorporated into the training of new staff, and what specific steps must staff follow under the policy? What provisions will there be for making the policy known to patrons and the public at large?

Circumstances, if any, under which records will be released.

Librarians will find it useful to append supporting documents (chosen from those in the foregoing list) to their policy. With these resources close at hand, librarians can prove formidable opponents for anyone who seeks access to confidential information.

Adopting a Policy

A policy stands a much better chance of being adopted if key board members have participated in the policy's development. This may involve consultation by phone or even a special meeting to explain the need for policy and seek board members' insights. This step, although perhaps cumbersome or inconvenient, will help smooth the way for board adoption of the final document.

Before the meeting at which the policy will be considered, copies of the draft, along with the agenda and other enclosures, should be sent to all board members. Enlisting supportive board members to "lobby" amongst their colleagues in advance is a valuable aid to the process.

Enlisting the most persuasive and supportive board member to present the policy to the entire board also may prove useful. In addition, library directors may want to invite the library's counsel to be present and support the policy from a legal perspective. If opposition to the policy is anticipated, the presenter should be ready to use data on other libraries in the state or region that already have confidentiality policies and on "real-life" examples of horrendous situations that can and do arise in the absence of such a policy.

Implementing a Policy

Once the policy has been successfully adopted by the governing board, the real work begins. Every member of the staff should be responsible for knowing the policy and his or her role in its implementation. This is important, even, and especially, for those who have no direct role to play. When initial attempts to obtain information through proper channels have been unsuccessful, determined and harried law enforcement officials, invasive journalists, and irate patrons have been known to try prying the information they seek from staff members who appear more easily intimidated than their supervisors.

The new policy should be incorporated into all training manuals and procedure books, especially those sections that involve the use of patron information: circulation, registration, and information services. The technology the library uses should be carefully assessed for weak points that could cause breaches of user confidentiality.

The governing board and legal counsel also must be familiar with the policy and the roles they will be expected to play when the library is faced with a challenge to the confidentiality of patron information. If board members and counsel have been involved in the policy process from the beginning, this aspect of the task will take care of itself.

NOTES

1. *Decatur Public Library* v. *District Attorney's Office of Wise County,* Case No. 90-05-192, letter opinion dated May 9, 1990.

2. *Griswold* v. *Connecticut,* 381 U.S. 479, 483 (1965).

3. *Lamont* v. *U.S. Postmaster General,* 381 U.S. 301 (1965).

4. *Stanley* v. *Georgia,* 394 U.S. 557 (1969).

5. *Clyde Osborne* v. *Ohio,* 109 L.Ed. 2d (1990).

6. Id., 108.

7. *NAACP* v. *Alabama,* 357 U.S. 449 (1958).

8. *Griswold* v. *Connecticut,* 381 U.S. 479 (1965).

9. *Katz* v. *United States,* 389 U.S. 347 (1967).

10. 5 U.S.C. #552(a).

11. "Computer Matching and Privacy Protection Act of 1988," P.L. 100-503. 5 U.S.C. #552(a).

12. As of this writing, only three states are without legislative protection for the confidentiality of library records: Hawaii, Kentucky, and, Ohio. Hawaii and Kentucky have Attorney General Advisory Opinions affirming the right of privacy in regard to library patron records.

3

Communicating the Intellectual Freedom Message

LINDA K. WALLACE

Libraries are democracy in action. For people of all ages and backgrounds, they provide free and open access to a spectrum of ideas and viewpoints that is often taken for granted—until it is challenged. Communicating the library's role in upholding intellectual freedom for all people should be of central concern to every library and librarian.

Highly publicized concerns about Internet access in libraries and challenges to books like *Harry Potter* have added urgency to the ongoing need to communicate about this aspect of the library's mission. A proactive public relations program designed to educate about the role of libraries and to advocate the importance of free access to information is the best way to address such concerns. This effort should be a key component of the library's overall communication program.

Developing an effective communications plan on intellectual freedom begins with an analysis of social and political attitudes and forces at the local level and how these relate to national trends. Other key elements also need to be identified.

The Audience

Who needs to hear the intellectual freedom message? Examples of key audiences are parents, teachers, government and religious leaders, members of the media, and business and labor groups. Be sure to include internal audiences—library users, staff, trustees, and

Friends of the library. Do not assume that anyone knows or understands what intellectual freedom is or the role of libraries and librarians in supporting it. It's also important to identify those who are potential supporters of censorship. What are their principal concerns? Knowing the philosophies and beliefs that threaten intellectual freedom will help in developing effective messages and engaging in meaningful dialogue. Also be sure to identify potential allies—individuals and groups who support civil liberties, the library, and its role in ensuring intellectual freedom. Identifying target audiences can save time and money. It can also increase effectiveness by providing a clear focus for your public relations efforts. Although some key audiences will remain the same, others may vary with time and circumstance.

The Message

The essence of a successful communications effort is a clear and consistent message. Sometimes known as a "sound bite," this key message should be no more than twenty-five words long. Try to use simple, clear language that is easily understood. The key message may be adapted for various audiences with slight modifications in wording or by changing the talking points and examples used. For example, the words "intellectual freedom" may resonate with some well-informed audiences, but talking about the "freedom to read, hear, or receive information" may be more appropriate for some.

Once you have defined the message, develop a message sheet that includes the key message, supporting points, facts and examples, and also sample questions and answers. The message sheet is an essential tool for designated spokespeople and should be shared with library staff, trustees, and advocates to support them in communicating the intellectual freedom message to library users, friends, neighbors, and others. It also provides a basis for speeches, fact sheets, brochures, and other communications and helps to ensure consistency in delivering the message.

In gathering and preparing information, it is important to avoid language that is negative or judgmental. The American Library Association opposes all practices that involve the prejudgment and labeling of groups or individuals as "censors." Libraries do not blacklist. It's important to acknowledge concerns as genuine and to address with respect those who express concerns or raise challenges.

Spokespeople

Effective communications depends on effective spokespeople. Because intellectual freedom is a complex and sometimes sensitive issue, it is particularly important to have knowledgeable, skilled spokespeople. And it is critical for speaking engagements and radio and television shows, where personal appearance and vocal technique are key to delivering the message successfully.

While the library director or board president is generally a library's official spokesperson, heads of departments, such as children's or collection development, may be called on in their area of expertise. The president of the Friends or library advocates network may also be asked for comment. All library staff, trustees, and Friends should know the procedures for dealing with questions from the media and public, whether it is referring questions directly to designated spokespeople or to the library's public relations staff.

While some people are gifted speakers, they may not be comfortable in high-pressure situations. Role-playing questions and answers should be part of the preparation process. In some cases, particularly those involving controversy, professional media training for designated spokespeople may be a wise investment.

You may also wish to organize a network of local advocates who are willing to speak out on intellectual freedom issues.[1] The American Library Association's Office for Intellectual Freedom maintains an Intellectual Freedom Action Network, an ad hoc group of volunteers who have identified themselves as willing to come forward in support of intellectual freedom in controversies in their localities. Members may be called on to attend board meetings, write letters to the editor, or simply lend moral support to librarians addressing censorship challenges. New volunteers are welcome.[2]

Delivering the Message

Once you have identified key audiences and defined your key message, the next step is to identify communications strategies. The mass media—newspapers, radio, and television—are generally considered the most powerful because of their effectiveness in reaching large numbers of people. But in every community and state, there are other opportunities which may, in fact, be equally or more effective. These include the Internet, speaking engagements, or community newsletters and other publications.

Speaking engagements and newsletters are particularly effective ways to reach key audiences who share particular interests and concerns. Many groups are looking for speakers to address timely topics and how they relate to their communities or campuses. Simply send a letter or make a phone call to program chairs of groups you wish to target. A draft script, which includes the library key message and talking points, should be provided for speakers. The script should be tailored to address the concerns of particular audiences such as business owners, clergy, or parents.

Be sure to include a section on the library's Web site about intellectual freedom and library policies. Ask partner groups to post articles or banners with links to the library's Web page. Create an electronic mailing list for those who wish to receive action alerts and updates on intellectual freedom issues. The library's newsletter, annual report, and other publications provide additional opportunities for educating about intellectual freedom, as do brochures created for specific audiences such as parents.

Recruiting other organizations that share an interest in First Amendment issues as allies is another effective strategy. Potential supporters might include law, journalism, education, and other professional or advocacy groups. Building a coalition of groups focused on a joint concern can be particularly effective in gaining credibility and influence with legislators and other elected officials.

Special events or promotions such as Banned Books Week: Celebrating the Freedom to Read, sponsored by the American Library Association and other concerned groups during the last week of September, provide opportunities to promote public understanding at the local level. Posters and a resource guide are available. See the Banned Books Week Web site at www.ala.org/bbooks/. National Library Week and Freedom of Information Day on March 16 provide other opportunities.[3] Planning local events in connection with these national observances can help attract media interest.

Programs and workshops directed at students, parents, educators, and other groups are excellent ways to communicate and educate about intellectual freedom issues. These can be on a wide range of topics such as guiding your child on the Internet, helping your child select good books, or the future of the First Amendment. Special workshops also may be held for trustees, staff, and Friends to familiarize them with the concept of intellectual freedom and the library's role.

When deciding which strategies to use, consider the following:

Who is the audience and what is the key message for that audience?

What is the best way to convey the information to the target audience—radio, television, direct mail, other? What kind of image do you want to project? Will it be an effective part of your total communications effort?

When is the deadline? Will your message be distributed in time to be effective?

Why is this the best strategy for this audience?

How much will it cost? Is this the most effective use of available funds?

Working with the Media

Because of its omnipresence in our lives, outreach to the media must be a key element in developing a public relations program. Journalists, in general, understand First Amendment issues and readily cover challenges to the public's right of access to library materials. Their support should never be assumed, however.

Preparation is key to dealing with the media successfully on intellectual freedom or any other issue. Make a list of media in your community or state. Be sure to include producers of radio and television talk shows, as well as news and feature editors of newspapers, and news assignment editors for radio and television. Note the names of contacts who are (or aren't) receptive to the intellectual freedom message.

Remember, regardless of their sympathies, reporters are paid to ask the tough questions their editors/readers/viewers/listeners want answered. Make sure you have a clear message and spokespeople prepared to deliver it. Also be prepared to provide supporting documents, copies of the library's intellectual freedom policies, fact sheets, and other documents that provide background and support for your message.

In dealing with members of the media, an effort should be made to build relationships based on trust and openness. Reporters are far more likely to give the library's message a fair treatment if they feel they are being treated honestly and respectfully. Return calls as quickly as possible, but make time to prepare an answer. Taking five minutes to review a message sheet can make a critical difference in how well the message is communicated. Tell the reporter you or a spokesperson will call back at a given time, and do so promptly. Avoid the infamous words "no comment." If you truly cannot comment, give a brief explanation: "I'm sorry I can't answer that question. I'll let you know as soon as I can." Or, "I'm sorry I can't answer that. Our board is still discussing this."

There are many ways of reaching out to the media. The most common is the press release highlighting an event or announcement of wide public interest. Begin with the most critical information in the first paragraph, with facts of lesser importance in descending order. Op-eds and letters to the editor provide opportunities for readers to express their views. Intellectual freedom advocates can use these forums to educate others about issues of concern in either national or local news. Op-eds are guest opinion columns that appear opposite the paper's own editorials.[4] Call the editor of the op-ed or editorial page and explain your idea briefly. Ask about length—most op-eds are about 750 words. Letters are generally much shorter and to the point.

The editorial board meeting is an opportunity to solicit the support of a newspaper. Call the editor of the editorial page to ask for an appointment and explain why. (Some radio and television stations offer these, too.) Prepare ahead of time to make a 15-minute presentation and to answer difficult questions. Editorial board meetings generally run around an hour and include key members of both the editorial and news staff.

The media frequently look for local people who can comment with authority on issues in the news, such as censorship. Where appropriate, members of state intellectual freedom committees may make themselves known as such a resource. To do this, send a brief letter to city and feature editors of key media. Such a letter could simply say: "Intellectual freedom issues are much in the news. If you are interested in a local point of view, I would be happy to help." Include a short biography highlighting relevant experience, or enclose a list of contact names, brief credentials, and contact information.

Talk show producers are frequently looking for guest speakers. Send a letter pitching your topic and its relevance to their audience, and also the qualifications of the guest you are proposing. Follow up with a phone call. Make sure the spokesperson understands and is comfortable with the needs of the broadcast media, that he or she is prepared to adapt the message for a particular audience and to answer any difficult questions.[5]

Keep in mind that hosts of talk shows may not be trained journalists. Rather, they may be advocates of a particular point of view. In today's highly competitive media market, their goal may also be to boost ratings by fanning the flames of controversy, sometimes at their guest's expense. Be sure to research the nature of a program (or publication) before seeking or accepting an interview.

Dealing with Controversy

All the elements of a good communications program become even more critical when dealing with controversy. These include a clear and consistent message, skilled spokespeople, targeted audiences, and effective communications strategies. Controversy, while generally not considered desirable, can provide a highly visible forum for educating the public about important intellectual freedom issues.

An ongoing public relations program and good media relations are the best way to avoid controversy. Every library should also have a crisis or controversy management plan, one that provides a clear road map for library staff, trustees, Friends, and advocates when dealing with high-pressure situations. Some of these—an organized move to limit Internet access in the library, objections to the library's *Playboy* subscription, or protests over an exhibit with sexually explicit art—can be anticipated and prepared for in advance.

It's important to prepare but not to overreact in dealing with such situations. If, for example, a local television station runs a "Sex at the Library" story about pornography on the Internet, a statement should be prepared but not necessarily released until you gauge reaction to the story. Many librarians have discovered that the public's good sense and confidence in libraries is able to withstand such sensationalized reporting. On the other hand, such a story may signal a need to intensify the library's Internet education efforts and prepare for any further media contacts the story may generate.[6]

Be strategic in your use of the media. A letter to the editor or op-ed clarifying the library's position can be helpful, especially if it is to correct a misrepresentation of fact. Engaging in a long, defensive battle of letters is probably not productive or a good use of advocates' energies.

Before accepting an appearance on a radio or television talk show, make sure you understand the nature and format of the program. Consider the size and nature of the audience and how receptive it is to your message. What is the format? Will there be someone from the opposition? Will there be call-ins? What is the host's position? If there is reason to believe the host will not provide a fair forum, it may be better to decline.

A crisis is not the time to build good media relations. Your library should have established relationships with key members of the media to call on at such times. If the library has a reputation for open and honest communication, journalists are more likely to be receptive and helpful in communicating the library's message.

The role of spokesperson becomes even more critical when dealing with controversy. Designating two or more spokespeople, one to deal with the media and one to handle concerns from staff and the public, is advisable if possible. In addition to message sheets and media coaching, spokespeople should receive prompt updates on new developments. All library staff and intellectual freedom advocates should be informed and involved in communicating the key message.

In dealing with hostile or negative situations, the following guidelines are suggested:

1. Anticipate difficult questions and develop answers ahead of time. Practice your answers with friends and colleagues. Also practice some easy ones so you won't be caught off guard.

2. Listen. Don't judge. Try to identify and address the real concern, fear, or issue being expressed.
3. Acknowledge. Pause to show you've given the question serious consideration. Frame your answer with a positive. For example, "You evidently have strong feelings about this," or "I respect your views, but let me give you another perspective." "We share your concern for children, but our approach is. . ."
4. Be factual. Make sure you have the information available. It is better to say "I don't know" than to give inaccurate information. If faced with a claim or information you are not familiar with, simply say "I hadn't heard that. I'll have to check," or "What I do know is . . ."
5. Don't repeat "hot" or negative words. If asked, "Why do librarians let children look at smut?", don't repeat the word "smut" in your answer.
6. Keep your answers to the point. Do not volunteer more information than is asked. Silence is a well-known technique used by reporters in the hope their subject will stray "off message."
7. Be truthful. Speak from your own experience. "In our library, our policy is. . . ," or "My experience is. . ."
8. Don't assume anything you say is "off the record." It can and may be used.
9. Maintain an open, calm, and friendly attitude. Avoid crossed arms, tapping feet, and other body language that conveys stress. Appearing defensive, angry, or out of control undermines credibility.
10. Above all, "stick to the high road." Do not criticize or get personal with an opponent. Stay focused on the key message.

Conclusion

The best way to promote intellectual freedom is to practice good public relations, which includes ongoing public education and being prepared for potential controversy. Evaluating the effectiveness of your communications efforts should be built into your communication program. Key indicators to consider include the number of challenges received by the library, the amount and extent of media coverage on intellectual freedom issues, the editorial support given the library, and expressions of both public concern and support. To improve on future efforts, make note of which strategies worked and didn't work.

Few institutions enjoy the credibility and goodwill that libraries have. Communicating openly, honestly, and with full understanding of the social, legal, and professional issues involved is the best way to promote intellectual freedom and uphold the image of the library and librarians. Those involved in the defense of intellectual freedom should work hard to avoid developing an adversary relationship with individuals or groups involved in censorship activity. It is much more productive to work toward developing relationships based on mutual respect. The more librarians and their supporters understand the feelings and beliefs of those who do not share their views, the easier it will be to relate to them as individuals with serious concerns.

Building a reputation for receptivity, openness, fairness, and friendliness toward the entire community can only enhance the standing of libraries and the concept of intellectual freedom.

NOTES

1. The *Library Advocate's Handbook*, which is available from the ALA Public Information Office, provides guidance on organizing an advocacy network. Call 800-545-2433, ext. 5041/5044, or see the ALA Web page at www.ala.org/advocacy/.

2. For more information on the Intellectual Freedom Action Network, call the Office for Intellectual Freedom, 800-545-2433, ext. 4221.

3. For calendars of library and literacy events sponsored by the American Library Association and others, see the ALA Web page at www.ala.org/pio/.

4. Copies of First Freedom op-ed pieces are available from the Office for Intellectual Freedom. Call 800-545-2433, ext. 4225, or see http://w3.trib.com/FACT/1st.oped.html.

5. For more ideas about programming to promote intellectual freedom, see the "Libraries: An American Value" tip sheet (*American Libraries*, June 1999).

6. Tips and guidance for communicating about the Internet can be found in "Libraries & the Internet Toolkit," available on the ALA Web site at http://www.ala.org/alaorg/oif/internettoolkit.html .

4

The Censor
Motives and Tactics

The term "censor" often evokes the mental picture of an irrational, belligerent individual. Such a picture, however, is misleading. In most cases, the one to bring a complaint to the library is a concerned parent or a citizen sincerely interested in the future well-being of the community. Although complainants may not have a broad knowledge of literature or of the principles of freedom of expression, their motives in questioning a book or other library material are seldom unusual. Any number of reasons are given for recommending that certain materials be removed from the library. Complainants may believe that the materials will corrupt children and adolescents, offend the sensitive or unwary reader, or undermine basic values and beliefs. Sometimes, for these reasons, they may argue that the materials are of no interest or value to the community.

Although an attempt to stereotype the censor would be unfair, one generalization can be made: regardless of specific motives, all would-be censors share one belief—that they can recognize "evil" and that other people must be protected from it. Censors do not necessarily believe their own morals should be protected, but they do feel compelled to save their fellows.

Why Censorship?

In general, there are four basic motivational factors that may lie behind a censor's actions. The four motivations are by no means mutually exclusive; indeed, they often merge, both in outward appearance and in the censor's mind.

Family values. In some cases, the censor may feel threatened by changes in the accepted, traditional way of life. Changes in attitudes toward the family and related customs are naturally reflected in library materials. Explicitly sexual works in particular are often viewed as obvious causes of repeated deviation from the norm. Because they challenge values, censors may want to protect children from exposure to works dealing frankly with sexual topics and themes.

Religion. The censor may also view explicitly sexual works and politically unorthodox ideas as attacks on religious faith. Antireligious works, or materials that the censor considers damaging to religious beliefs, cause concern about a society many see as becoming more and more hostile to religious training, and these works buttress beliefs about society's steady disintegration.

Political views. Changes in the political structure can be equally threatening. The censor may view a work that advocates radical change as subversive. (The fact that such works have been seen as attacking basic values is confirmed by the number of attempts to label library materials with such broad terms as "communistic," "un-American," or "ungodly.") If these works also contain less than polite language, it will not be difficult for the censor to formulate an attack on the grounds of obscenity in addition to—and sometimes to cover up—objections on political grounds.

Minority rights. Of course, not all censors are interested in preserving the traditional social order. The conservative censor has been joined by groups who want their own special group values recognized. For example, ethnic minorities and women struggling against long-established stereotypes are anxious to reject materials viewed as perpetuating those stereotypes. These groups too may use the devices of the censor.

Whatever the censor's motives, attempts to suppress certain library materials may also stem from a confused understanding of the role of the library and of the rights of other library users. The censor's concern about library materials is based upon a view of the library as an important social institution. But the censor may fail to see that the library fulfills its obligations to the community it serves by providing materials presenting all points of view, and that it is not the function of the library to screen materials according to arbitrary standards of acceptability. Would-be censors may think that it is the role of the library to support certain values or causes—which are, of course, their values and their causes.

In the United States, under the First Amendment, no citizen and no librarian can properly assume the duty or right to restrict or suppress legally protected expressions of ideas. The censor may not understand that a request that certain works be labeled or restricted, if fulfilled, would lead to an abridgment of the rights of other library users.

The Censor in Action

A censorship incident usually begins with a library user's complaint about specific library materials. In general, the immediate aim of the complainant is to inform the library that the materials in question are unacceptable. In some cases, the complainant may assume that the library will immediately agree that the materials are not appropriate and should not be in the library.

The censor may want to state publicly that he has found "objectionable" materials in the library, and may attend a meeting of the library board to announce his "discovery." Those sections of the work that are considered especially offensive may be read aloud or distributed in writing to the library board, the local press, and the public. The censor may also go one step further and organize an ad hoc censorship organization. Even if an ad hoc group is loosely organized, the censors could use it effectively to promote a statement of purposes among other community groups, to conduct a letter-to-the-editor campaign, and to circulate petitions. The organization could also influence public funding, the appointment of the library director, and the appointment or election of library board members.

Although most censorship incidents begin with an objection to a specific work, if the censors are unsuccessful in getting the item banned, they may turn their efforts to library policy. If they cannot bring about a change in the library's policy on materials selection and distribution, they may then ask that the library establish a closed shelf or adopt a policy of restricted access.

Opposing the Censor

Well in advance of the appearance of the censor, a materials selection program, a procedure for handling complaints, and a public relations program will, of course, have been established. After the censor comes, censorship of library materials can be resisted by informing a number of key support sources: (1) community leaders and community organizations who would support the position of the library, (2) local news media whose editorial support would be valuable, (3) other librarians in the community and state whose support could then be available if needed, (4) the publisher of the challenged work, who may have on file all its reviews and also may be interested in the legal questions raised by such practices as labeling and restricted access, (5) all library staff members and the governing board, (6) the library's legal counsel, (7) the state library association's intellectual freedom committee, and (8) the ALA's Office for Intellectual Freedom.

A censorship attempt presents the library with a good opportunity to explain the philosophy of intellectual freedom that underlies library service in the United States. For example, the library should prepare an article for local newspapers, explaining the role of the library and its commitment to the *Library Bill of Rights*. The article can emphasize the importance of the freedom to read as established by the First Amendment.

It is important to keep in mind that not every attempt to resist censorship will be successful; in many instances, developments will take a discouraging turn. However, it is certain that if the library is not prepared to offer any resistance, no battle will be won. And every battle won will contribute to establishing the library as an institution for free citizens in an open society.

5

Responding to Religious Right Censorship Attempts

ROB BOSTON

During the Christian Coalition's 1998 "Road to Victory" conference, a panel of right-wing activists addressed the issue of "Restoring Parental Rights." At a question-and-answer session that followed, a member of the audience asked what could be done about "immoral" materials in public libraries.

Patrick Fagan, identified as a "scholar" at the Heritage Foundation, a far-right group based in Washington, D.C., volunteered to field the question. His solution was simple: parents, he said, should check out books they find offensive and refuse to return them. If the library attempts to impose a fine, ignore it.

Other members of the panel seemed taken aback by Fagan's casual endorsement of theft, but several members of the audience nodded approvingly. Although ultraconservative groups frequently bemoan the alleged lack of morality in America and pine for moral absolutes, it seems at least a few believe that some laws can be broken in pursuit of larger goals, but without believing, as well, in accepting any consequences. In other words, they may look at their actions as a form of civil disobedience but would likely resist being fined or imprisoned for what they have done. This is not civil disobedience at all; it is merely an effort to keep books they don't like out of public libraries.

Perhaps more shocking than Fagan's proposal is the underlying assumption that America's libraries routinely stock "immoral" materials. While this might seem a curious assertion to many librarians, to members of the Religious Right it is an article of faith. To hear many Religious Right leaders and their followers talk, public libraries these days are little better than publicly funded X-rated bookstores.

Fortunately, most Americans reject the wild accusations and baseless charges that the Religious Right hurls against public libraries. Still, this is no time for complacency. There was a time in America when most people supported public education. Thanks to a relentless campaign of disinformation and attacks from far-right groups that advocate privatizing education, polls now show that growing numbers of Americans have a negative view of public schools at large (although many believe their local public school is just fine), and increasing numbers of people are backing privatization schemes, such as vouchers.[1] The people who work in public libraries should never assume that Religious Right-led smear campaigns are incapable of shifting public opinion.

What Is the Religious Right?

The Religious Right is a political movement that seeks to merge far-right politics with a literal, ultraconservative interpretation of the Bible. In its modern incarnation, the Religious Right has been active on the American scene since the late 1970s, which saw the rise of the Reverend Jerry Falwell's Moral Majority. Although he continues to lurk about on the fringes of the movement, Falwell has long since been eclipsed by other leaders, such as television preacher Pat Robertson, founder of the Christian Coalition, and radio counselor James C. Dobson, head of Focus on the Family.

Religious Right groups frequently advocate censorship of materials they dislike or consider to be immoral. Of course, most librarians know that censorship efforts can come from the right or the left. For example, some parents of a liberal bent have complained about racist language in Mark Twain's *The Adventures of Huckleberry Finn*. But these complaints tend to be sporadic, and usually spring from individuals at the local level—not from well-orchestrated campaigns sponsored by large, national organizations.

Many challenges to library materials from ultraconservative parents, on the other hand, result from information spread by national Religious Right groups. People who receive Religious Right magazines, watch television preachers, or listen to Religious

Right radio broadcasts may hear attacks on certain books, periodicals, and other media. They may be encouraged to find out if local libraries or bookstores make this material available and if so, to protest against it.

A handful of Religious Right organizations, well funded and national in scope, account for most of the right-wing attacks on libraries. In recent years, groups like the Christian Coalition, Focus on the Family, the Family Research Council, and others have stepped up their attacks on libraries. According to materials disseminated by these organizations, libraries are guilty of housing "pornography" or of failing to keep sexually explicit materials out of the hands of youngsters.

Most Religious Right organizations have a strong political bent. The Christian Coalition, founded by Robertson in the wake of his failed presidential bid in 1988, claims to be nonpartisan but is active in conservative politics nationwide. Many activists in these groups are not political neophytes; they know how to sway public opinion and are quite capable of running a sophisticated campaign against a library.

Thus, right-wing censorship advocates are likely to be backed by the resources of powerful national Religious Right groups. For example, Focus on the Family (FOF), headed by child psychologist and radio counselor Dobson in Colorado Springs, is a huge, ultraconservative evangelical ministry that reportedly reaches five million listeners a day. FOF publishes numerous magazines and makes other materials available to people involved in its ministry. Like Robertson, Dobson is very active in conservative politics. FOF has been attacking public libraries and the American Library Association with increasing regularity lately. In 1995, FOF's *Citizen* magazine ran a cover story highly critical of public libraries. It was illustrated by a drawing of innocent-looking children at a library reading *Playboy* magazine and books with bizarre titles like *Naked Tennis* and *Pipe Bombs Illustrated*. A sign on the wall reads, "ALA READING CORNER."[2]

The Family Research Council (FRC) is also active in this area. The FRC was originally an arm of Focus on the Family but is now legally separate. However, the two organizations remain closely connected, and Dobson sits on the FRC board. The FRC, based in Washington, D.C., was formerly run by Gary Bauer, who left the group in 1999 in an unsuccessful bid for the Republican presidential nomination. (The FRC also has chapters in most states.)

These organizations have staggering annual budgets. The Christian Coalition's budget is between $17 million and $25 million annually. The FRC's annual budget is $15 million. FOF's is an astounding $114 million.

Aside from these groups, literally dozens of smaller Religious Right groups dot the landscape. Some focus on a particular state or region of the country. These organizations include Concerned Women for America, the American Family Association, Coral Ridge Ministries, the Eagle Forum, the Christian Action Network, the Traditional Values Coalition, and Citizens for Excellence in Education.

Turning the Public against Libraries

An argument can be made that the Religious Right is trying to demonize libraries in the same way it has successfully demonized public schools. This strategy has two key components: convincing Americans that libraries are "antifamily" or that they maintain policies that harm children, and asserting that libraries are controlled by an outside force with a nefarious, ultraliberal, antifamily agenda—in this case the American Library Association.

Under this model, the ALA is analogous to the teachers' unions, which the Religious Right has successfully tarred as bloated bureaucracies obsessed with winning high pay for teachers (despite the fact that teaching remains a low-paying profession in many parts of the country) and blocking all innovative attempts at reform.

The analogy can be carried one step farther. The Religious Right has often portrayed public schools as agents for radical social change. Religious Right groups tell their followers that the people who work in public schools are working to undercut parental authority by turning children away from religion, telling students they don't have to listen to their parents, encouraging teenagers to experiment with sex, etc.

Similar claims are now being made about public libraries. Most Religious Right groups go immediately to the hot-button issue of sex, knowing that this concerns many parents, especially those with teenagers at home. According to the Religious Right, libraries fairly bristle with sex; in fact, they are so sexually charged they aren't even safe for children anymore.

Porno for All:
The "Sex-Crazed Library" Strategy

In 1995, Karen Jo Gounaud, head of Family Friendly Libraries, a group founded with support from Focus on the Family, told *Church & State* magazine that public libraries no longer offer a "safe browsing environment" for children.

"It used to be that the library was one of those places the kids could go and look around and the parents didn't have to worry about them running into pornography or wild and crazy sexual ideas. . . . Now that's no longer the case," Gounaud said. "The library is not even entirely safe to bring your child in with you."[3]

Gounaud was an enthusiastic supporter of the library board in Loudoun County, Virginia, which for several years in the late 1990s was dominated by Religious Right activists who scrapped the ALA's anticensorship statements and replaced them with their own, less strongly worded, policy. When members of the community attended a public meeting and complained, board chairman Dennis Pierce claimed that his opponents would favor allowing the library to rent the X-rated film *Deep Throat* to children. A local newspaper pointed out that the claim was somewhat hyperbolic, as the library does not rent X-rated videos. (In January 2000, a more moderate board voted 5-3 to reinstate the ALA policies.)

Religious Right activists are masters at a type of "bait-and-switch" maneuver that they have frequently used against libraries. In this case, the "bait" is a claim that libraries are stocked with "pornographic" materials. The "switch" comes when virtually any book, periodical, film, or other medium that deals with any aspect of human sexuality is deemed pornographic or obscene.

The Religious Right uses the terms "pornographic" and "obscene" very loosely. In fact, the law recognizes a legal definition of obscenity. While the precise definition is arguably difficult to determine—one is reminded of the Supreme Court justice who once remarked that while he could not define obscenity, "I know it when I see it"—it's likely that all of the material in public libraries that Religious Right groups call "obscene" or "pornographic" falls way short of the legal standard.

Gounaud, for example, has complained about books that deal with homosexuality. (In fact, her first campaign against a library was sparked because she was offended by the presence of a free gay newspaper distributed alongside other local periodicals in the library's lobby.) This topic is a frequent obsession of the Religious Right, which tends to be highly homophobic. But obviously every book that deals with homosexuality is not pornographic.

Other books that the Religious Right labels "pornography" may be merely erotic or include some scenes of a sexual nature. Parents have every right to steer their children away from this material in the library, but they do not have the right to take it out so no one can access it. After all, many modern (and not so modern) novels contain a sex scene or two, although sex may not be the subject of the book. The Religious Right may be quick to label such tomes "pornographic," but few others would agree, and in fact, none of these books would meet the legal definition of "obscenity." (Some Religious Right complaints really try to stretch that definition. In June 2000, a parent in Onalaska, Wisconsin, requested that the local elementary school library remove a 1993 adaptation of Hans Christian Andersen's "The Little Mermaid" because some of the illustrations in the book showed the Little Mermaid topless, though her hair was covering her chest. A school committee voted unanimously to keep the book.)

Given the chance, some Religious Right activists would stretch the definition of "pornography" to encompass anything they don't like in a library. In a celebrated incident from 1993, a member of Concerned Women for America in Cleveland, Tennessee, checked eighteen books out of the local public library and refused to return them. The woman had complained that the books were pornographic, yet some titles dealt with topics like AIDS and others had nothing to do with sex at all but concerned supernatural themes. (The woman eventually returned the books, but then asked local law enforcement officials to declare the books obscene; they refused.)

On this issue, it seems libraries can't win no matter what they do. In late July 2000, an FOF newsletter called *Citizen Issues Alert* attacked the ALA for daring to sponsor a workshop during its 2000 conference that focused on how material with sexual themes should be dealt with in collections. Thus, libraries can be criticized for even discussing the issue of how to handle controversial material.

Employing typical hyperbole, Phil Burress, a Gounaud ally at Family Friendly Libraries, interpreted the workshop as a sign that the ALA would soon advocate special pornography rooms in public libraries. "The pornography section is just the first step in many shocking plans they [the ALA] have for taxpayer-funded local libraries," he said.[4]

Aside from books dealing with sex, library materials that deal with occult or supernatural themes are frequent Religious Right targets. The phenomenal popularity of J. K. Rowling's *Harry Potter* books has sparked a raft of Religious Right-led challenges. (In Clarence, New York, a woman threatened to sue a local public school for using a *Harry Potter* book in class.) Here librarians stand on firmer ground. Some parents are wild about Harry and some are not, but the books are definitely not obscene; thus, there is no legal reason why any library would have to remove them. Many librarians have countered that the *Potter* books are merely the latest in a long line of children's books that feature fantastic themes, from the Brothers Grimm onward. If all of this material were purged from the libraries, there would be little left for children to read.

Tossing Out the Good Stuff: Libraries as Censors?

As they argue that public libraries are full of smut and witchcraft, Religious Right groups pursue a parallel line of attack that is more sophisticated: asserting that libraries are increasingly discarding "classics" in favor of sexually explicit materials.

In September 1995, Focus on the Family and the Family Research Council joined forces at a Washington, D.C., press conference to denounce libraries for allegedly weeding classics out of their collections. The groups claimed to have documentation for this startling claim. They had mailed surveys to 508 libraries across the country, deliberately excluding large, urban libraries. Librarians were asked to determine if they had copies of 100 titles deemed "classic" works by FOF and the FRC. Only 204 librarians responded. These replies became the basis for a report claiming that classics are rapidly disappearing from libraries. It was a clever strategy. The report, although pseudo-scientific in approach, had media appeal, and the groups captured some newspaper headlines.

Few reporters pointed out that FOF and the FRC had put libraries in a no-win situation. Not surprisingly, few libraries had all

100 titles on the FOF-FRC list. (Remember, large urban libraries—the ones most likely to have all of the titles—were deliberately excluded from the survey.) On the basis of a survey of 1.3 percent of the nation's libraries, FOF and the FRC concluded that "classics" are rapidly disappearing from library shelves.

However, the list of "classics" revealed a few curious features. FOF and the FRC asked libraries if they had copies of Mark Twain's *Following the Equator* but did not include any of his more familiar works. Similarly, libraries were scored for not having William Makepeace Thackeray's *The Irish Sketch Book* on hand, but his most famous work, *Vanity Fair*, which is probably found in every library in the country, is nowhere on the list. Libraries were expected to have Sir Walter Scott's *St. Ronan's Well*; *Ivanhoe* was not listed.

A good library, according to FOF and the FRC, should have a copy of Honoré de Balzac's *Old Goriot* on its shelves. Balzac wrote dozens of novels as part of his epic "Human Comedy" series; few libraries could have them all. The ones that don't have *Old Goriot* may instead have *Cousin Bette, Eugenie Grandet,* or *Lost Illusions.* (The same argument could be made for Émile Zola, who also wrote dozens of novels. The FRC and FOF hold it against libraries for not having *Nana* on hand. What if they have *Germinal* or *La Bête Humaine* instead?)

The list is also notable for the authors it omits: Herman Melville, Daniel Defoe, John Steinbeck, F. Scott Fitzgerald, John Bunyan, Voltaire, Theodore Dreiser, Leo Tolstoy, William Faulkner, Jane Austen, George Orwell, and all three Brontë sisters, among other well-known authors, are nowhere to be found.

The FOF-FRC press conference on the "vanishing classics" allegation was timed to coincide with the ALA's annual Banned Books Week. During the press conference, speakers ridiculed the ALA for daring to suggest that books are actually banned in the United States. They insisted that most censorship attempts fail and accused the ALA of engaging in scare-mongering, supposedly for the purpose of raising funds.

The real problem, FOF and the FRC insisted, is not censorship but allegedly rapidly vanishing classics. The groups went so far as to suggest that libraries might be plundering the classics for profit, suggesting that a lot of these volumes end up in used bookstores. Apparently, it did not occur to FOF or the FRC that classics, because they are much loved, get checked out frequently and are subjected to lots of handling; thus, they wear out faster and periodically must be replaced with new editions.

In reality, the "vanishing classics" allegation was yet another attempt by the Religious Right to shift public attention away from the problem of censorship and toward a bogus "problem" that doesn't really exist. Under fire for encouraging censorship, Religious Right groups tried to make public libraries the censor, a gambit they continue to pursue years later.

What Does the Religious Right Want?

The Religious Right hopes to successfully demonize libraries. Portraying them as distributors of pornography, places that gleefully pass out *Playboy* to children while tossing classic works in the trash can, is an integral part of this strategy.

What does the Religious Right hope to gain through all of this? Gounaud has been upfront that her goal is to have libraries remove all "pornography." (But again, her definition of what constitutes pornography is quite broad.) Originally, Gounaud called for libraries to divide their entire collection into different levels and restrict minors' access to certain areas. She now admits this is unrealistic and calls instead for an "opt-in" mechanism, which would allow parents to make it impossible for their children to check out adult fiction books.[5] Critics assert that the Religious Right's goal remains more ambitious: the expulsion of all material Religious Right groups do not like—for whatever reason.

Gounaud and many other Religious Right activists are also enthusiastic backers of Internet filters. These devices supposedly block access to pornographic sites on the World Wide Web, although some skeptics say filters can block non-pornographic sites as well.

Cyberspace appears to be the new frontier of censorship battles. The explosive growth of the Web and its popularity among young people have left many librarians unsure of what to do. While some library systems have installed filters, others have refused. Still others have installed them on computers in children's areas. Religious Right groups, as is their wont, seem to believe that a government-imposed fiat—in this case Internet filters—will magically solve a moral problem. For all of their talk about being "pro-family," they seem to have little faith in the ability of parents to accompany children to the library and guide them toward appropriate material.

Internet filters may be the next big battlefield. If libraries decline to install Internet filters, Religious Right activists may turn to pressure tactics. In 1999, members of the American Family Association in Holland, Michigan, put a measure on the ballot that would have required the local library to install filters or lose all municipal funding. In February 2000, voters in the conservative community voted down the proposal, 4,379 to 3,626.

Responding to Right-Wing Pressure Groups

Public libraries, like public schools, are under attack from the Religious Right. Some public schools have successfully fended off right-wing attacks. Libraries can learn from these experiences.

In 1993 educators in Gaston County, North Carolina, devised an ambitious education reform package they called "Educational Odyssey." The plan was based on the study of the humanities. A handful of local Religious Right activists apparently confused "humanities" with "humanism," a common far-right bogeyman. Led by a local minister, they went on the warpath.

In the end, the education plan stayed in effect. How did the school district win? Primarily by keeping the channels of communication open, answering inquiries promptly and honestly, and remaining courteous at all times.

Libraries can win censorship battles with the Religious Right. How? Here are key points to keep in mind:

> *Don't let Religious Right pressure groups portray your library as an institution that operates in secret, out of the public eye.* A certain degree of conspiratorial thinking is common in Religious Right groups. Religious Right activists may claim that decisions about the library are made without public input by an "elite" that thinks it knows best or that the local library is under the control of the ALA. Undercut this argument by stressing the role of the library board. Make certain that board meetings are open and encourage media and public attendance. Note the activities of other organizations, such as a local Friends of the Library, that are open to all community

members. Point out that volunteer opportunities exist, and that the library, as a taxpayer-funded institution, is responsible to the voters.

Maintain written copies of the library policies. All staff members should be familiar with library policies, especially policies that deal with access to material by children. Keep the policies in writing and share them with the public when asked.

Respond to reasonable requests for information promptly. A favorite tactic of the Religious Right is to demand information from a public institution and, if it does not arrive promptly, charge that the institution is unresponsive to the taxpayers. Undercut this tactic by responding to all requests for information—about the budget, library policies, acquisition of materials, etc.—as promptly as possible.

Stress the positive, pro-family activities at the library. Most libraries sponsor a wealth of truly pro-family activities—story hours for children, puppet shows, educational programs, and other special events. These programs can be an important line of defense against charges that the library is somehow "antifamily."

Respond to untrue charges and unfair criticism. Religious Right activists may use the local media to make baseless charges against the library. Someone should respond to these charges, if not a library official, then a member of the Friends of the Library or just an interested citizen.

Don't be intimidated by threatening letters. A favorite tactic of Religious Right groups is to have far-right legal groups mail letters to libraries and other government bodies containing thinly veiled threats of lawsuits unless certain actions are taken or policies adopted. In most cases, this is purely an intimidation tactic designed to scare the library into doing things the Religious Right's way. Librarians who are uncertain about what the law really says about issues such as obscenity, church-state separation, etc., should consult with national organizations that work in these areas.

Recognize that conservatives are not the library's enemy. The term "Religious Right" should not be used interchangeably with "conservative." Many conservatives oppose all forms of censorship. Many Republicans and conservatives support public libraries. Similarly, not every conservative Christian or evangelical buys into the Religious Right's anti-library line. Do not alienate potential supporters by lumping all conservatives or evangelical Christians together. Only those religious conservatives who are involved with the Religious Right and its brand of far-right politics are liable to criticize public libraries. These people account for a minority of conservative thought in the country.

Conclusion

Millions of Americans consider public libraries a great resource and will defend them in the face of Religious Right attacks. However, librarians, board members, and others who work in this field should never assume that public sentiment will automatically be on their side. The support of the public must be won, earned, and then earned again.

Religious Right organizations are working to undermine public support for libraries and are making various charges against them—mainly accusing them of housing "pornography." Librarians must work to counter such charges in a proactive manner to ensure that public sentiment remains on their side.

NOTES

1. For information about declining public support for public schools, see the annual survey conducted by *Phi Delta Kappa* magazine.

2. Scott DeNicola, "What Lurks in the Library?" in *Citizen*, September 18, 1995, pp. 1–4.

3. Rob Boston, "Censorship: Coming Soon to a Library Near You?" in *Church & State* (November 1995), pp. 8–12.

4. "An Erotica Section? ALA Ponders Idea at Convention," in *Citizen Issues Alert*, July 26, 2000.

5. John Reosti, "The Battle over Books," in *Montgomery Journal*, October 13, 1996.

PART VI

Working
for Intellectual
Freedom

I

Combating Censorship
Where to Go for Help

DON WOOD

The American Library Association, the Freedom to Read Foundation, the LeRoy C. Merritt Humanitarian Fund, state library associations' intellectual freedom committees, and intellectual freedom coalitions promote and defend intellectual freedom[1] in different ways. Collectively, they provide the means to protect the freedoms to read, speak, view, and access ideas and information for all Americans.

American Library Association

The American Library Association maintains a broad program for the promotion and defense of intellectual freedom. Its various components include the Intellectual Freedom Committee, which recommends policy to the ALA Council and sponsors educational programs; the Office for Intellectual Freedom, which implements ALA policy concerning the concept of intellectual freedom as embodied in the *Library Bill of Rights*[2]; the Intellectual Freedom Round Table, which provides the opportunity for ALA members to become involved in the promotion and defense of intellectual freedom; and the Intellectual Freedom Action Network, which is comprised of volunteers who have expressed a willingness to support the freedom to read in censorship controversies in their communities.

Intellectual Freedom Committee

According to its statement of responsibility, the purpose of the Intellectual Freedom Committee (IFC; www.ala.org/alaorg/oif/ifc_inf.html) is "to recommend such steps as may be necessary to safeguard the rights of library users, libraries, and librarians, in accordance with the First Amendment to the United States Constitution and the *Library Bill of Rights* as adopted by the ALA Council; to work closely with the Office for Intellectual Freedom and with other units and officers of the Association in matters touching intellectual freedom and censorship."[3]

To fulfill its charge, the IFC recommends policies concerning intellectual freedom to the ALA Council (www.ala.org/alaorg/oif/ifcreports.html). The Council-approved policy statements (e.g., Interpretations of the *Library Bill of Rights,* www.ala.org/work/freedom/interprt.html; "Libraries: An American Value," www.ala.org/alaorg/oif/lib_val.html; "Resolution on the Use of Filtering Software in Libraries," www.ala.org/alaorg/oif/filt_res.html) not only provide librarians with policies to adopt in their own libraries, but also establish a professional standard the ALA is committed to defend.

The IFC also writes and disseminates guidelines and other statements to assist librarians in promoting and defending intellectual freedom. Examples include "Dealing with Concerns about Library Resources" (www.ala.org/alaorg/oif/dealingwithconcerns.html), "Guidelines for the Development and Implementation of Policies, Regulations and Procedures Affecting Access to Library Materials, Services and Facilities" (www.ala.org/alaorg/oif/pol_reg.html), "Coping with Challenges: Strategies and Tips for Dealing with Challenges to Library Materials" (www.ala.org/alaorg/oif/coping_inf.html), and "Libraries & the Internet Toolkit" (www.ala.org/pio/internettoolkit/).

See also "ALA Intellectual Freedom Policies and the First Amendment" (www.ftrf.org/ennis.html), written by Bruce J. Ennis, and first published in vol. 19, no. 1 (1994) of *Freedom to Read Foundation News.*

In addition, the IFC works closely with the ALA Committee on Legislation to monitor current legislation activities and to develop strategies to defeat legislation aimed at restricting access to information.

Office for Intellectual Freedom

The Office for Intellectual Freedom (OIF; www.ala.org/alaorg/ oif/), the administrative arm of the IFC, implements ALA policies on intellectual freedom and educates librarians and the general public about the importance of intellectual freedom in libraries. Because the most effective safeguards for the rights of library users and librarians are an informed public and a library profession aware of repressive activities and how to combat them, the OIF maintains a wide-ranging program of projects, services, educational and informational publications, electronic discussion and business lists (www.ala.org/alaorg/oif/elists.html), and a Web site (www. ala.org/alaorg/oif/), on which is found all intellectual freedom policies and other related information.

One of the Intellectual Freedom Committee's most important publications is the bimonthly *Newsletter on Intellectual Freedom (NIF)*. The *NIF* was initiated in 1952 and has been edited and produced by the OIF staff since 1970. The *NIF* is addressed to both librarians and the general public concerned about intellectual freedom. It provides a comprehensive, national picture of censorship efforts, court cases, legislation, and current readings on the subject. Through original and reprinted articles, the *NIF* offers a forum for expressing varying views about intellectual freedom, while providing a means for reporting the activities of the IFC, the OIF, and the Freedom to Read Foundation. In 1982, the noted civil liberties authority Nat Hentoff named the *NIF* "the best small publication in America." Additional information about the *NIF* can be found at www.ala.org/alaorg/oif/nif_inf.html. It is available by subscription from the Office for Intellectual Freedom (1-800-545-2433, ext. 4223; oif@ala.org).

The OIF produces and distributes documents and articles concerning intellectual freedom to both librarians and the general public. Monographs, resource guides, training materials, and manuals (in addition to the *Intellectual Freedom Manual*) include the annually produced *Banned Books Week Resource Kit* (www.ala.org/bbooks/ resource.html); *Confidentiality in Libraries: An Intellectual Freedom Modular Education Program*; and *Censorship and Selection: Issues and Answers for Schools*, 3rd edition, by Henry Reichman (http://alas-tore.ala.org/). During nationwide controversies over individual titles, the OIF compiles press clippings, editorials, and public statements detailing the ways various libraries around the country handled requests to remove specific materials, and sends these out to others dealing with similar problems.

The OIF also seeks to make the library profession's support and concern for intellectual freedom known to the general public through the mass media and other forums. Both the IFC and the OIF cooperate with other national organizations (www.ala.org/alaorg/oif/first.html#advocates), such as the Association of American Publishers, the American Booksellers Association, the American Booksellers Foundation for Free Expression, The Media Coalition, People for the American Way, Americans United for Separation of Church and State, the National Coalition Against Censorship, and state and regional First Amendment organizations in activities that support free expression.

Challenge Support

One of the most often used and least heard-about functions of the OIF is its provision of advice and consultation (case support) to individuals in the throes of potential or actual censorship controversies. Rarely does a day go by without the OIF receiving a request for assistance with a challenge to library materials. The OIF provides reviews and information about the author of the challenged material, applicable ALA policies, advice about the implementation of reconsideration policies, and other counseling specific to the situation at hand. If needed, the OIF will provide a written position statement defending the principles of intellectual freedom in materials selection. As requested, the OIF provides the names of persons available to offer testimony or support before library boards, supplied from the ranks of the Intellectual Freedom Action Network and state library associations' intellectual freedom committees. The options chosen are always the prerogative of the individual requesting assistance.

When a censorship problem arises, librarians have at least three options. They can visit "Dealing with Challenges to Books and Other Library Materials" (www.ala.org/alaorg/oif/dealingwith-challenges.html), on which is found links to materials to help cope with challenges; they can visit "Reporting a Challenge" (www.ala. org/alaorg/oif/reporting.html), on which is found links and information on who to contact regarding a challenge; or they can contact directly the Office for Intellectual Freedom (50 East Huron Street, Chicago, Illinois 60611; phone: 1-800-545-2433, ext. 4223; oif@ala.org).

See also "What You Can Do" (www.ala.org/alaorg/oif/what youcando.html), a list of suggestions on how to combat censorship. This list is published as part of the ALAAction series brochure, No. 2, *Intellectual Freedom* (www.ala.org/alaorg/oif/ifbrochure.html), available from the ALA Public Information Office (1-800-545-2433, ext. 5041/5044; pio@ala.org; www.ala.org/pio). The online version of the list also includes links to information on intellectual freedom issues, intellectual freedom advocates, how to counter censorship in your community, how to celebrate your freedom to read, how to subscribe to various news and discussion e-lists, how to contact elected officials about issues and legislation related to intellectual freedom, and where to find news sources on intellectual freedom topics.

Censorship Database

In 1990 the Office for Intellectual Freedom established an electronic censorship database to record and report statistics on challenges to library materials across the country. The database is a useful tool for identifying trends in types of censorship cases and for documenting responses and solutions to these cases. Librarians are encouraged to document and report challenges and their outcome to the OIF. All identifying information is kept strictly confidential.

You may call in reports on attempted censorship of library and other materials, or you may send newspaper clippings, magazine articles, letters, or the OIF's reporting form—the Office for Intellectual Freedom Challenge Database Form (www.ala.org/alaorg/oif/chall.html).

In 2000 the OIF published its list of "The 100 Most Frequently Challenged Books of 1990–1999" (www.ala.org/alaorg/oif/top100 bannedbooks.html). The list was compiled from 5,718 challenges to library materials reported to or recorded by the Office for Intellectual Freedom from 1990 to 1999. Seventy-one percent of the challenges in that decade were to materials in schools or school libraries; another 26 percent were to materials in public libraries. Nearly 60 percent of challenges were brought by parents, 16 percent by library patrons, and 10 percent by administrators.

Electronic Discussion List

ALAOIF is an unmoderated electronic discussion list that the OIF maintains not only as an avenue of discussion, but also as a means to disseminate fast-breaking news items, updates on late-breaking censorship controversies or legislation that could affect intellectual freedom in libraries, and to alert subscribers to areas where they may find additional information or localities where their assistance is needed. It also provides information that may assist subscribers in the promotion and defense of intellectual freedom.

Information on subscribing to this or other lists (e.g., ACLU press releases) can be found at www.ala.org/alaorg/oif/elists.html.

Combating Repressive Legislation

Repressive legislation on such matters as obscenity and material deemed harmful to minors can severely restrict the activities of librarians striving to provide service in accordance with the principles of the *Library Bill of Rights.* When requested, therefore, the ALA, through the IFC and the OIF, as well as the Freedom to Read Foundation, supplies testimony, either singly or jointly, informing lawmakers of the potential effects of the legislation on the principles of intellectual freedom as applied to library service. Pending legislation in the United States Congress is frequently brought to the attention of these groups by the ALA Washington Office (www.ala.org/washoff/). With the assistance of legal counsel, the OIF will provide an analysis of proposed state or local statutes affecting intellectual freedom brought to its attention.

See also "Pending Internet Legislation" (www.ala.org/alaorg/oif/internetlegislation.html) and "News Sources for Information about Censorship, the Internet, Filters, Filtering, Intellectual Freedom, and the First Amendment" (www.ala.org/alaorg/oif/newssources.html), which link to news sources and other relevant links.

In addition, see "Intellectual Freedom in the News" (www.ala. org/alaorg/oif/news_inf.html), which includes links on how to contact elected officials about issues and legislation, information on pending legislation, where to find news sources, how to access online newspapers and journals, and various search engines to assist in locating information on intellectual freedom topics.

Freedom to Read Foundation:
Legal Support

The Freedom to Read Foundation (FTRF; www.ftrf.org/) was incorporated as a separate organization in 1969 by the ALA to act as its legal defense arm for intellectual freedom in libraries. Although it is a separate organization, the FTRF presents a report of its activities to the ALA Council at each ALA meeting (www.ftrf.org/ftrfreports.html). The purposes of the FTRF are:

1. Promoting and protecting the freedom of speech and of the press;
2. Protecting the public's right of access to information and materials stored in the nation's libraries;
3. Safeguarding libraries' right to include in their collections and to make available to the public any creative work they may legally acquire; and
4. Supporting libraries and librarians in their defense of First Amendment rights by supplying them with legal counsel or the means to secure it.

The FTRF's work has been divided into two primary activities:

1. The allocation and disbursement of grants to individuals and groups primarily for the purpose of aiding them in litigation; and
2. Direct participation in litigation dealing with freedom of speech and of the press.

The FTRF is devoted to the principle that the solution to offensive speech is more speech, and the suppression of speech on the grounds that it gives offense to some infringes on the rights of all to a free, open, and robust marketplace of ideas. The FTRF combats censorship through litigation of statutes or government actions that limit, or could have the effect of limiting, the availability and accessibility of constitutionally protected information in libraries. Librarians affected by repressive statutes or official actions should contact the FTRF. Librarians whose professional positions and personal well-being are endangered because of their defense of intellectual freedom, and library boards, librarians, and library employees threatened with legal action on such grounds, also should contact the FTRF.

For a select number of notable First Amendment cases, see www.ala.org/alaorg/oif/1stcases.html.

In addition, Jenner & Block, the general counsel of the FTRF, provides memoranda to assist librarians in combating censorship. Jenner & Block memoranda are posted on the FTRF Web site at www.ftrf.org/memos_jb.html. Although they are general discussions of issues and not opinion letters, they help librarians understand the legal implications of such issues as civil liability for an alleged hostile work environment related to patron or employee Internet use (www.ftrf.org/work_jb.html) and Internet filtering in public libraries (www.ftrf.org/internetfilteringmemo.html).

In 2000, a regular FTRF membership cost $35.00. By joining the FTRF, you

- Help defend the First Amendment in the courts, including the U.S. Supreme Court;
- Support librarians around the country besieged by attempts to restrict library materials and services;
- Expand the freedom to read by offering legal and financial help in cases involving libraries and librarians, authors, publishers, and booksellers;
- Receive the quarterly Freedom to Read Foundation News, which includes articles and timely reports on censorship trends, current court cases, and more. (The online version can be found at www.ftrf.org/ftrfnews.html); and
- Vote for and become eligible to run for trustee in the annual board elections.

For additional membership information, see www.ftrf.org/join ftrf.html.

LeRoy C. Merritt Humanitarian Fund: Financial Support

Librarians requiring immediate financial aid should contact the LeRoy C. Merritt Humanitarian Fund (www.ala.org/alaorg/oif/merritt.html). The Merritt Fund was established in recognition of the need for support at the moment an individual is in jeopardy or is fired in the cause of intellectual freedom or due to discrimination. Both the Freedom to Read Foundation and the Merritt Fund are administered through the OIF. For more information, contact the Merritt Fund at 1-800-545-2433, ext. 4226; merritt@ala.org.

Intellectual Freedom Round Table

The ALA encourages its members to become actively involved in the defense of intellectual freedom. The Intellectual Freedom Round Table (IFRT; www.ala.org/alaorg/oif/ifrt_inf.html), established in 1974, is a membership organization within the ALA. Participation in the IFRT allows ALA members to maintain close contact with the ALA's overall intellectual freedom program.

The IFRT sponsors the main intellectual freedom program at the ALA's Annual Conference, cosponsors other programs on various intellectual freedom-related subjects, and circulates its own newsletter. The IFRT, and individual IFRT members, are available to assist the IFC, the OIF, and the FTRF in various joint activities.

The IFRT administers the annual John Phillip Immroth Memorial Award for Intellectual Freedom and the State and Regional Achievement Award, and the biennial Eli M. Oboler Memorial Award (www.ala.org/alaorg/oif/ifrtawards.html). The Immroth Award recognizes extraordinary personal courage in the defense of intellectual freedom and may be presented to an individual or group of individuals. The State and Regional Achievement Award is an annual award to the state intellectual freedom committee that has implemented the most successful and creative state project during the preceding year. The Oboler Award, first presented in 1988, recognizes the best work in the area of intellectual freedom published in the two calendar years prior to the presentation of the award.

In response to IFRT members' requests for a more active voice in intellectual freedom issues, in the fall of 1994, the OIF established the Intellectual Freedom Action Network.

Intellectual Freedom Action Network

The Intellectual Freedom Action Network (IFAN; www.ala.org/ alaorg/oif/ifan_inf.html) is a grassroots, ad hoc group of volunteers who have identified themselves as willing to come forward in support of the freedom to read in censorship controversies in their communities.

The purpose of the IFAN is twofold. First, participants are asked to submit to the OIF information on groups that are attempting to censor materials in libraries. Although many of these groups are nationally based, they also may have local chapters. Local groups without a national affiliation are also very powerful in some communities. Second, IFAN members are asked to lend support when a controversy erupts in their community. Such support could take the form of a letter to the editor, attending a school or library board meeting, or even a supportive phone call to a colleague being challenged.

The OIF keeps the IFAN up-to-date by maintaining an electronic discussion list of members who receive information on controversies where assistance would be appreciated. IFAN members have been helpful in several local and statewide controversies involving book challenges, proposed changes in library policy and operation that would limit access to library materials, and state legislation that would restrict the availability of constitutionally protected expression.

The IFAN was formed as a "rapid response" force to counter the successful and widespread efforts of national censorship pressure groups to organize and mobilize local chapters working on the local level to restrict the availability of expressive materials with which they disagree or find offensive. Librarians being attacked by such groups were encountering an organizational level to which they could not, alone, respond. The IFAN works to address the need for support and eliminate the sense of isolation that so often plagues librarians who find themselves in the eye of the censorship storm.

All librarians and supporters of intellectual freedom should join the Action IFAN by contacting the OIF at oif@ala.org.

State Library Association
Intellectual Freedom Committees

Many other avenues of activism in support of intellectual freedom are open to ALA members on the state and local levels. The *Library Bill of Rights* calls on libraries to "cooperate with all persons and groups concerned with resisting abridgment of free expression and free access to ideas." Such groups and individuals exist in virtually every community, and very often it is the formal and informal ties established by individual ALA members that enable the ALA to cooperate with them.

Of special importance, of course, are the state library associations' intellectual freedom committees (www.ala.org/alaorg/oif/stateifc.html). The extent and nature of the activities of these committees vary from state to state. Some groups are more active than others. In some states, the committees have worked with other organizations to build impressive state coalitions in defense of intellectual and academic freedom. Elsewhere they have concentrated on compiling and developing state intellectual freedom manuals and continuing education materials. The relationship of the ALA, the IFC, and the OIF with the state committees is one of mutual cooperation and assistance. The OIF supports the work at the state level with information, coordination, and ideas. On their part, the state committees can be the OIF's "eyes and ears" at the local level. And, of course, when incidents or other controversies arise, it is very frequently the state library association's intellectual freedom committee that "mobilizes the troops" and, in cooperation with the ALA, provides embattled librarians with "on the spot" assistance.

Becoming involved and working together with colleagues and friends, librarians can fulfill their mission to confront censorship and protect access to the broadest range of information.

Intellectual Freedom Coalitions

Librarians who work for intellectual freedom know there is broad support for the concept among diverse constituencies. When would-be censors seek to deny access to library materials, a remarkable array of individuals and organizations can and do come to the library's defense. Many of these people are already active in defense of intellectual freedom elsewhere in society.

Article IV of the *Library Bill of Rights* states that "Libraries should cooperate with all persons and groups concerned with resisting abridgment of free expression and free access to ideas." To facilitate such cooperation, libraries, individual librarians, and state intellectual freedom committees have joined with booksellers, publishers, artists, civil libertarians, journalists, authors, musicians, and other groups and individuals with First Amendment concerns in local, state, and regional coalitions in defense of intellectual freedom.

Such coalitions are helpful for several reasons. It is, of course, simply common sense to know, so to speak, who your friends are and how to keep in touch. Beyond this, uniting with others in coalition permits greater coordination of effort and allows supporters of intellectual freedom to reach broader audiences. Coalitions also can benefit from an expanded financial base and from the collective prestige, resources, and contacts of the constituent groups. By uniting together, concerned organizations can pool resources to avoid duplications of effort and to concentrate limited funds and personnel where they are most needed. For example, groups concerned with intellectual freedom may collectively monitor legislative activity, or they may form a joint speakers' bureau.

The task of organizing a statewide coalition for intellectual freedom may at first seem intimidating. But coalitions differ greatly from each other. Some are highly structured, full-time organizations themselves. Others are closer to an informal network of communication and support. The same coalition that may, at times of crisis, function like a well-oiled machine, may at other moments be minimally active. In short, a coalition is what its members make it. There is no ideal model for a coalition. The level of organization and commitment should be appropriate to the needs of those involved and no more. If a coalition's needs can be met through a structure that simply facilitates regular contact and little more, this is also fine.

Everywhere there is a need for greater cooperation and more joint efforts by various supporters of intellectual freedom. The following suggestions will be useful to organize a coalition (www.ala.org/alaorg/oif/coalitions.html).

The first step in organizing a coalition is to identify those organizations in the state or region whose goals and objectives are consistent with the ALA's intellectual freedom principles. Consider inviting local and regional chapters of the American Civil Liberties

Union; booksellers' and publishers' groups; arts groups; religious organizations; civic groups; educational organizations, including the PTA, the National Education Association, the American Federation of Teachers, the National Council of Teachers of English, and groups of school administrators; lawyers' organizations; and societies of authors and journalists. Individuals also should be sought out and encouraged to participate, since they may be in the best position to do the kind of day-to-day coordination that will be necessary to keep the coalition functioning.

Develop a succinct letter of introduction to be sent to those invited to the organizational meeting. Spell out clearly your own conception of the proposed coalition, but make it clear that the final goals and objectives, as well as the structure of the group, are to be determined democratically.

At the first meeting, the coalition should draft a statement of its principles and, if desired, a constitution and bylaws. These can be more or less formal, depending on the desires of the constituent groups. Committees with concrete goals and specific projects should be organized immediately so the coalition does not become bogged down in sterile debate or bureaucratic busywork. Choose responsible officers who have the time and commitment to keep things going.

Possible projects for the coalition to take up include design of a public relations brochure, publication of a newsletter, legislative monitoring, organization of an information network to mobilize support during times of crisis, and organization of statewide conferences on intellectual freedom.

For an example of a highly successful coalition, see Mainstream Loudoun (http://loudoun.net/mainstream/Library/Internet.htm), which helped defeat an overly restrictive Internet policy and, for that effort, was awarded the 1999 John Phillip Immroth Memorial Award. In addition, see "Some Suggestions about Things You Can Do to Counter Censorship in Your Community" (www.ncac.org/action/suggestions.html), on the National Coalition Against Censorship's Web site.

Summary

Over several decades, the ALA and the library community as a whole have built an impressive network of support for intellectual freedom. The foundation of this network is the efforts of volunteer librarians, library trustees, and library users at the state and local levels. Such people have contributed and continue to contribute to the cause of intellectual freedom in many ways and through many organizational forms.

Combating censorship is a never-ending struggle. To cope with challenges to library materials, librarians and the general public interested in defending and preserving intellectual freedom must be able to deal effectively with the media and to communicate effectively with concerned parents and would-be censors, who may be well organized and well financed. The best line of defense is good preparation, effective policies, knowing where to go for help when necessary, and library advocacy. The promotion of intellectual freedom and the promotion of libraries are inseparable.

NOTES

1. "Intellectual freedom is the right of every individual to both seek and receive information from all points of view without restriction. It provides for free access to all expressions of ideas through which any and all sides of a question, cause or movement may be explored . . . Intellectual freedom encompasses the freedom to hold, receive and disseminate ideas" ("Intellectual Freedom and Censorship Q&A"; www.ala.org/alaorg/oif/intellectualfreedomandcensorship.html).

2. "The *Library Bill of Rights* is a policy statement adopted by the American Library Association to protect the right of all library users to choose for themselves what they wish to read or view. The policy is more than 60 years old and has been adopted voluntarily by most libraries as a way of ensuring the highest quality library service to their communities" ("Coping with Challenges: Strategies and Tips for Dealing with Challenges to Library Materials"; www.ala.org/alaorg/oif coping_inf.html).

3. See the *ALA Handbook of Organization*, 2000–2001, p. 18.

2

Lobbying
for Intellectual Freedom

CAROL C. HENDERSON
and the
ALA WASHINGTON OFFICE

Lobbying is the process through which citizens seek to persuade elected officials to a cause or to a particular course of action. In a democracy, lobbying is a legitimate and productive aspect of citizen participation, and helps keep democracy healthy and responsive. Lobbying for library interests must be ongoing, and is usually most effective when it involves the joint efforts of professional lobbyists and individual librarians and library supporters. In lobbying for intellectual freedom, supporters will find advice and guidelines for library advocacy and library lobbying from the ALA, its Office for Intellectual Freedom, its Washington Office, and its state chapters.

When lobbying on intellectual freedom issues raised by state or federal legislation, keep in mind that First Amendment and censorship issues tend to generate controversy and strong emotions. Lobbying in this arena requires special sensitivity and care in working with elected officials to develop policies supportive of intellectual freedom.

Library Lobbying Builds on Strengths

The library community enjoys a number of advantages in working productively with legislators at local, state, and national levels:

> Legislators respond to relevant factual and anecdotal information, succinctly presented; librarians are accustomed to marshaling information.

Legislators respond to numbers and to their own voting constituents; libraries and their supporters exist in every legislative district.

Libraries enjoy bipartisan support, and library legislative champions come from both sides of the aisle; library associations such as the ALA have worked well with representatives of both major political parties.

Librarians have many friends and allies, who are more numerous than themselves and weigh more heavily in the political scales. Many of these supporters are knowledgeable, well-connected politically, take an active interest in legislative issues, cultivate legislator contacts, and respond to action alerts.

Keep Informed
and Know the Issues

The first step in keeping informed on legislative issues is to follow regularly the printed and electronic sources of information from the ALA Office for Intellectual Freedom and the ALA Washington Office. The opportunity for timely and effective action is much greater through the use of electronic technologies. The ALA Washington Newsletter is issued monthly, but ALAWON, the ALA Washington Office Newsline (available to any individual or organization with e-mail capability), may be issued as often as once a day during periods of intense activity.

The ALA Office for Intellectual Freedom tracks state-level legislation through its relationship with Media Coalition (www.media-coalition.org). The Media Coalition is an association that defends the First Amendment right to produce and sell books, magazines, recordings, videotapes, and video games; it also defends the American public's First Amendment right to have access to the broadest possible range of opinion and entertainment. Other sources for news and action alerts regarding state-level activity include state library associations and school library media associations, and their legislation and intellectual freedom committees.

Organize Library and Intellectual Freedom Supporters

Work closely with your state library association's legislation committee and any lobbyists associated with the state library association. If the state association has a "federal relations coordinator" or a lobbyist or political consultant with ties to the congressional delegation, contact them. In any event, stay in touch with the ALA's Washington Office. Let them know who you are speaking with and what their response is. The state association may have a well-organized legislative network in place, with an active telephone tree or other communications structure to alert supporters when action is needed, or to activate the best contacts with particular legislators.

Intellectual freedom committees in the state should coordinate with and make use of these existing networks, which often include library trustees and Friends of libraries in strategic positions of influence. At the same time, be sure there is a core group of individuals knowledgeable about intellectual freedom issues who are willing and able to speak on short notice at hearings or to participate in key meetings.

Build Coalitions

The very nature and diversity of librarians' work both in libraries and in the communities, campuses, or organizations they serve make them highly capable coalition builders. Librarians can work with groups representing educators and educational institutions, for example, or with groups representing children or parents, or with scholars and news reporters, or with publishers and chambers of commerce, or with citizens' and public interest groups. At the national level, the ALA Washington Office has found that librarians are represented in almost every one of the numerous coalitions working on Internet issues. Library interests relating to the public's access to needed information cross over levels of education, industry concerns, and the many content-related issues of public interest groups.

Thus, a wide variety of groups either share library objectives or can be persuaded to do so. These groups may work with the library field on all issues of concern, or only on one measure. Some organizations or industry groups may join librarians on one bill, and be on the other side of the table on the next piece of legislation.

For the most part, American politics is coalition politics rather than confrontation politics. Candidates and elected officials strive to satisfy as many elements of their constituency as possible. It is helpful to demonstrate to legislators that many nonlibrary organizations support library efforts. If a library group takes a position on a bill, that position is strengthened if the statement is signed by many other organizations.

These coalition relationships must be seeded and nurtured. Library advocates should make contact with and keep in touch with the leadership and the legislative activists of organizations with similar objectives. Coalition building and nurturing should be organized to develop clear lines of communication and action, to avoid duplication of effort, and to avoid conflicting messages. Keep a current file of coalition contacts so they can be called upon to help when the need arises.

Use the Media

Public opinion should not be overlooked. In addition to letters to legislators, timely, concise, and cogent letters to the editor, as well as op-ed pieces, should be sent to newspapers and other publications. The public relations programs of individual libraries can be called on to good effect on legislative and regulatory issues. If an editorial or a columnist calls for lower government expenditures, a letter should point out the effects of a cutback on library users. If a pending bill is endorsed, or opposed, a letter should present the library position.

Try to develop a good working relationship with the publications and media outlets of greatest influence in the area. Don't wait until a time of desperate need. The ALA's "Library Advocacy Now!" materials and training packages provide excellent tips and advice on getting the library message across to both opinion molders and decision makers.

Know the Legislative Process

Learn how the state legislature works, when it is in session, what the committees are, where relevant legislation will be referred, and what steps a bill must go through to be enacted. Know who has power in the legislature, and who has influence on those with power. What are the priorities of the party in power? What other issues are on the agenda of the committee that has jurisdiction over library or intellectual freedom issues? Know the committee assignments of the state's congressional delegation.

Know the Legislators, and Know Who Knows Them

In general, only a few legislators will take a strong and detailed interest in library legislation—because they have a personal interest, or because of a concerned relative or friend, or because they are on a committee or subcommittee handling bills of this type.

Every member of Congress and U.S. senator has an office in the home district as well as in Washington. It is just as important to get to know local congressional staff as it is to know their staffs in Washington. Go to see these local staffs and invite them to your library for a program or a tour. Introduce them to your patrons, their boss' constituents, and brief them on matters important to your library.

Long before a library measure is being promoted, or before a crisis erupts, it's important to identify sympathetic individuals in the political structure. Keep a current file of library and intellectual freedom supporters in the legislature and a current file of knowledgeable library and intellectual freedom advocates in the community, and keep in touch with both. These friendly legislators and their staffs can become a source of information and advice regarding effective strategy and timing, positions to be taken in hearings, the nature of the testimony that will be most effective, the kinds of witnesses to be secured, and the sources of opposition to a particular measure.

Personal Contacts with Legislators Work Best

It is implicit in all that has been said thus far that considerable contact between library supporters and legislators is essential during this process. All persons who are active in legislative affairs will be seeing legislators frequently, and in time will know many of them well as individuals. The most useful visits are in the home district rather than at the state capital or in Washington. Become familiar with their home offices and staff. All members of Congress maintain at least one office in the home district, and the staff there will know when the legislator will be at that office and available to citizens.

To meet with a legislator, make an appointment, then leave little to chance. Plan what to say, be well-versed on the issue or bill being discussed, and provide a "leave-behind," a one or two-page memorandum or fact sheet covering the relevant points. A fact sheet on the local library and its services and users also would be valuable. During the meeting, the librarian should give the legislator ample opportunity for questions, ask which staff member to keep in touch with when the legislator is unavailable, and request to be kept informed on progress on the measure under discussion. Similarly, it's important to keep legislators informed of the library's activities, invite them to functions or special activities (particularly those with media presence), or ask them to join a board or advisory group if appropriate.

A small group visit to a legislator is particularly effective, especially if the group includes a trustee or Friend of the library, and representatives of community groups or of library user constituencies. A good way to gain experience in this type of lobbying is to participate in the annual Library Legislative Day of organized lobbying in the spring in Washington, D.C., organized by the ALA Washington Office and the D.C. Library Association. Library delegations from each state visit congressional offices in team visits, preceded by briefings and followed by a reception. Many state library associations also sponsor state legislative days or special events in the state capital.

Library supporters have discovered during their visits to Washington that often, twenty minutes with the key legislative assistant for the representative or senator may be more productive than five minutes with the legislator himself or herself. At the federal level, personal or committee staff draft bills, develop floor statements, brief the legislators, and convey constituent opinion to their bosses. Don't neglect legislative staff.

Meetings with legislators need not be frequent. Usually one meeting before a legislative session begins, preferably in the district, and perhaps one more during the legislative session when an important measure is at a decisive point, will be sufficient. Of course, new legislators should be visited early, even before they are elected, to ascertain their viewpoints, their interests, and their potential positions regarding library issues.

Follow Up with Letters

Personal contacts with legislators should precede letters and other less personal communications whenever possible. Letters, faxes, phone calls, and e-mail messages will be much more effective if the sender is a voting constituent known to the office, or the sender can refer to a recent visit or personal contact. Ideally, each legislator should have a flow of contacts with one or more library supporters from the home district or state, a number of letters each year, and at least one visit during each legislative session.

The ALA Washington Office has issued two sets of helpful tips—"Effective Ways to Communicate with Legislators" (http://www.ala.org/washoff/ways.html) and "How to Write a Letter to Your Legislator" (http://www.ala.org/washoff/letter. html). These suggestions apply just as well to state and local lawmakers. The main message is that frequently, a handful of thoughtful, factually persuasive letters have changed a member's mind or caused him or her to review an issue. Letters should be timely and constructive as well as accurate, brief, and clear.

Be Persuasive, Professional, and Persistent

Legislative strategies and tactics require adjustment to changing conditions. Don't neglect the minority party; they may be in power next year. Adjust to the style of a key legislator; facts and figures may work with one chair of a committee, while the sponsor in the other chamber may need homey library stories to recount to colleagues or in floor statements. Politics is called the art of the possible, and democratic politics is often the art of compromise. Progress must often come one step at a time. Library groups should not think in terms of "winning" or "losing," but of how to move forward, even if it involves three steps to the side first.

It's important to stay professional in demeanor with enemies as well as friends. Stay alert to the moral and philosophical attitudes of candidates and officeholders. Recognize that those on opposing sides may have legitimate concerns; sometimes those concerns can be addressed through other means without harmful effects on libraries or the First Amendment. Don't make the mistake of being as emotional as those who would censor. Make library concerns known early, and where possible, get commitments in support of intellectual freedom before controversy erupts.

Each step in the process of achieving rapport with legislators is simple in itself. The power of these efforts is in their cumulative impact and their multiplication when performed by many others. Each participant in the process and each step in the process is significant. There may be many decision points and calls for action on the way to enactment. There may also be a few times when the process falls short and must be started all over again. Once the ALA's Washington Office was established, it took ten years before the first federal library legislation was enacted. Persistence pays off, so keep at it!

APPENDIX I

CODE OF ETHICS

As members of the American Library Association, we recognize the importance of codifying and making known to the profession and to the general public the ethical principles that guide the work of librarians, other professionals providing information services, library trustees and library staffs.

Ethical dilemmas occur when values are in conflict. The American Library Association Code of Ethics states the values to which we are committed, and embodies the ethical responsibilities of the profession in this changing information environment.

We significantly influence or control the selection, organization, preservation, and dissemination of information. In a political system grounded in an informed citizenry, we are members of a profession explicitly committed to intellectual freedom and the freedom of access to information. We have a special obligation to ensure the free flow of information and ideas to present and future generations.

The principles of this Code are expressed in broad statements to guide ethical decision making. These statements provide a framework; they cannot and do not dictate conduct to cover particular situations.

I. We provide the highest level of service to all library users through appropriate and usefully organized resources; equitable service policies; equitable access; and accurate, unbiased, and courteous responses to all requests.

II. We uphold the principles of intellectual freedom and resist all efforts to censor library resources.

III. We protect each library user's right to privacy and confidentiality with respect to information sought or received and resources consulted, borrowed, acquired or transmitted.

IV.   We recognize and respect intellectual property rights.

V.   We treat co-workers and other colleagues with respect, fairness and good faith, and advocate conditions of employment that safeguard the rights and welfare of all employees of our institutions.

VI.   We do not advance private interests at the expense of library users, colleagues, or our employing institutions.

VII. We distinguish between our personal convictions and professional duties and do not allow our personal beliefs to interfere with fair representation of the aims of our institutions or the provision of access to their information resources.

VIII. We strive for excellence in the profession by maintaining and enhancing our own knowledge and skills, by encouraging the professional development of co-workers, and by fostering the aspirations of potential members of the profession.

Adopted by the ALA Council, June 28, 1995.

APPENDIX II

SELECTED BIBLIOGRAPHY

Bald, Margaret. *Banned Books: Literature Suppressed on Religious Grounds*. New York: Facts on File, 1998

Curtis, Michael Kent. *Free Speech, The People's Darling Privilege: Struggles for Freedom of Expression in American History*. Durham, N.C.: Duke University Press, 2001.

Davis, Charles N., and Sigman L. Splichal, eds. *Access Denied: Freedom of Information in the Information Age*. Ames: Iowa State University Press, 2000.

Dunham, Corydon B. *Fighting for the First Amendment: Stanton of CBS vs. Congress and the Nixon White House*. Westport, Conn.: Praeger Publishers, 1997.

Foerstel, Herbert. *Banned in the Media: A Reference Guide to Censorship in the Press, Motion Pictures, Broadcasting, and the Internet*. Westport, Conn.: Greenwood Press, 1998.

Foerstel, Herbert. *Free Expression and Censorship in America: An Encyclopedia*. Westport, Conn.: Greenwood Press, 1997.

Goldman, Roger, and David Gallen. *Justice William J. Brennan, Jr.: Freedom First*. New York: Carroll & Graf Publishers, 1994.

Hentoff, Nat. *Living the Bill of Rights: How to Be an Authentic American*. Berkeley: University of California Press, 1999.

Hit List: Frequently Challenged Books for Children. Rev. ed. Chicago: American Library Association, 2001.

Hit List: Frequently Challenged Books for Young Adults. Rev. ed. Chicago: American Library Association, 2001.

Hollingsworth, Peggie J., ed. *Unfettered Expression: Freedom in American Intellectual Life*. Ann Arbor: University of Michigan Press, 2000.

Jones, Barbara M. *Libraries, Access, and Intellectual Freedom: Developing Policies for Public and Academic Libraries*. Chicago: American Library Association, 1999.

Karolides, Nicholas J. *Banned Books: Literature Suppressed on Political Grounds.* New York: Facts on File, 1998.

Peck, Robert S. *Libraries, the First Amendment and Cyberspace: What You Need to Know.* Chicago: American Library Association, 2000.

Rabban, David M. *Free Speech in Its Forgotten Years.* Cambridge: Cambridge University Press, 1997.

Reichman, Henry. *Censorship and Selection: Issues and Answers for Schools.* 3rd ed. Chicago: American Library Association, American Assciation of School Administrators, 2001.

Robbins, Louise S. *Censorship and the American Library: The American Library Association's Response to Threats to Intellectual Freedom, 1939–1969.* Westport, Conn.: Greenwood Press, 1996.

Sova, Dawn B. *Banned Books: Literature Suppressed on Sexual Grounds.* New York: Facts on File, 1998.

Sova, Dawn B. *Banned Books: Literature Suppressed on Social Grounds.* New York: Facts on File, 1998.

Strossen, Nadine. *Defending Pornography: Free Speech, Sex, and the Fight for Women's Rights.* New York University Press, 2000.

Symons, Ann K., and Charles Harmon. *Protecting the Right to Read: A How-to-Do-It Manual for School and Public Libraries.* New York: Neal-Schuman Publishers, 1995.

Symons, Ann K., and Sally Gardner Reed, eds. *Speaking Out: Voices in Celebration of Intellectual Freedom.* Chicago: American Library Association, 1999.

INDEX

"100 Most Frequently Challenged Books," 389–90
"700+ Great Sites for Kids," 293, 310

A

AAP. *See* Association of American Publishers
AASL. *See* American Association of School Librarians
abortion counseling, 267
academic freedom, 46
academic libraries
  classes of users, 89
  exhibit spaces, 143
  intellectual freedom and, 46–49, 163–67
"Access for Children and Young People to Videotapes and Other Nonprint Formats" (interpretation)
  as access issue, 10
  history, 72–74, 78–79
  text, 75–77
"Access to Electronic Information, Services, and Networks" (interpretation)
  history, xvi, 71, 73, 94–96
  in Internet policy, 291
  questions and answers, 84–93
  text, 80–83
access to information
  economic barriers to, 128–35
  and filtering, 245–54
  and freedom of expression, 305–6
  handicapped users, 260–62
  as intellectual freedom issue, 4, 9–14
  for minors, 152–62
  public libraries as limited public fora for, 323–28

restrictions on, 176–83, 273–74
school library media centers, 44
"Access to Library Materials, Services and Facilities." Guidelines for . . .". *See* "Policies, Regulations and Procedures Affecting Access to Library Materials, Services and Facilities" (ALA policy statement)
"Access to Library Resources and Services regardless of Gender or Sexual Orientation" (interpretation)
  as access issue, 10
  history, 70, 73, 100–4
  text, 87–89
"Access to Resources and Services in the School Library Media Program" (interpretation). *See also* School libraries
  as access issue, 10
  history, 74, 107–11
  text (1986), 109–11
  text (2000), 105–6
"Access to the Use of Libraries and Information by Individuals with Physical or Mental Impairment" (ALA policy statement)
  history, 262
  text, 260–61
ACONDA (Activities Committee on New Directions), 21
ACRL. *See* Association of College and Research Libraries
Action Network. *See* Intellectual Freedom Action Network
Activities Committee on New Directions (ACONDA), 21
ad hoc censorship organizations, 368
adaptive technology, 89

administration of library and
    handling concerns, 280
"Administrative Policies and
    Procedures Affecting Access
    to Library Resources and
    Services," 158, 267
adolescents
    preconference on, 66
    suppression of reading of, 204
Adult Education Association, 283
"adults only" restrictions. *See*
    Restrictions on materials
Adventures of Huckleberry Finn, The,
    121, 371
"advocacy" vs. "neutrality," 23
    gay rights policies, 30
    and Gulf War, 29
    as intellectual freedom issue, 4
age-based restrictions on access,
    160–61. *See also* Barriers;
    Children; Minors
    defined, 265
    in Internet use policies, 310
    in *Library Bill of Rights,* 76, 155
agenda for challenge hearing, 342,
    344
Agnew, Spiro, 214
AIDS, 260–61, 262, 309
AIDS-related complex (ARC),
    260–61, 262
ALA. *See* American Library
    Association
ALA Committee on Legislation, 386
ALA Washington Office
    and lobbying efforts, 400
    and repressive legislation,
    390–91
ALA Web site, ix
ALAWON (Washington Office
    Newsline), 400
Alcohol, Tobacco, and Firearms
    Division, 238
Allain, Alex P., 154
American Association of School
    Librarians (AASL), 96, 107, 108,
    155, 338
American Association of University
    Professors, 46, 166, 206

American Association of University
    Women, 309
American Book Publishers Council
    (ABPC)
    "Freedom to Read" policy, 205,
    209, 215
    on resisting censorship, 283
American Booksellers Association
    "Freedom to Read" policy, 221
    and Office for Intellectual
    Freedom, 16, 388
American Booksellers Foundation
    for Free Expression, 206, 388
American Civil Liberties Union
    1928 civil liberties issue, 25
    in coalitions, 396–97
    and Communications Decency
    Act, xvi, 30
    and concerns about resources,
    281
    "Freedom to Read" policy, 221
    on labeling, 189
    and Office for Intellectual
    Freedom, 16
    on resisting censorship, 283, 285
American Civil Liberties Union v. *Janet
    Reno,* 307. *See also Reno* v. *ACLU*
American Educational Publishers
    Institute, 205–6
American Family Association, 35, 379
American Federation of Labor
    Librarians' Union, 5
American Federation of Teachers,
    AFL-CIO, 221, 397
American Legion, 64, 188
American Library Association (ALA)
    guidance to librarians, 41
    history, 3–32
    nefarious ultraliberal agenda of,
    373
    programs in intellectual freedom,
    385
    and social responsibilities, 24, 25
American Library Association v. *U.S.
    Department of Justice,* 30–31, 290,
    307. *See also Reno* v. *ACLU*
American Library Trustee
    Association, 156, 296

American Society of Journalists and Authors, 206

American Society of Newspaper Editors, 206

Americana (DeLillo), 22

Americans United for Separation of Church and State, 388

Amnesty International, 35

animal rights, 309

Annie on My Mind (Garden), 314–15

annoying behavior, 273

anonymous complaints, 341

anti-apartheid ordinance, 26–27

Anti-Defamation League of B'nai B'rith, 206, 221

antifamily accusations, 373

appeals for challenged materials, 340

  in policies and procedures, 265

  in selection policy, 336

  in writing, 342

appropriateness to level of user, 335

Aristophanes, 313

arts as target of censorship, 222

Association for Educational Communications and Technology, 44

Association for Library Service to Children, 157, 170, 296

Association of American Publishers (AAP)

  "Freedom to Read" statement, 206

  and Office for Intellectual Freedom, 16, 388

  report on boycotts, 28

  South Africa boycott, 196

Association of American University Presses, 206, 221

Association of College and Research Libraries (ACRL), 19, 96, 166

audience for intellectual freedom message, 356–57

Audio-Visual Board, 72

Audio-Visual Committee, 64

authenticity, 335

awards for intellectual freedom, 16–17

B

background, defined, 265

balance in collection. *See also* Collection development

  defined, 119

  as intellectual freedom issue, 8

  vs. diversity in collections, 125

Balzac, Honoré, 377

Banned Books Week, 359, 377

Banned Books Week Resource Kit, 15, 387

banning of publications and materials, 5–6, 61. *See also* Censorship

Bantam Books, Inc. v. Sullivan, 114, 312

barriers between patron and library materials

  and library policies, 263–64

  and restrictions on materials, 176–83

Bauer, Gary, 372–73

Bauer v. Kincaid, 321, 322

Becker, Beverley, 41–53, 331–46

bequests, restricted, 130

Berelson, Bernard, 209

Berninghausen, David K., 61, 238

best-sellers, 289, 336

Bethel School District No. 403 v. Fraser, 312–13

Beyond the Horizon (O'Neill), 7

Bill of Rights and privacy, 350–51

Black Panther Party, 214

Blackmun, Harry A., 267

blocking software. *See* Filtering software

Board of Education, Island Trees (New York) Union Free School District No. 26 v. Pico, 38, 302–3, 312, 314, 315, 316

Bodger, Joan, 18

body language, 364

Bolger v. Youngs Drug Products Corp., 318n2

bombings, threat of, 236, 347

Boston, Rob, 370–81

Bostwick, Arthur E., 6

Boundary Lines (film), 64

Bradshaw, Lillian, 19

breast cancer, 309
Brennan, William Joseph, Jr., 38
broadcast media, restrictions on, 308
Brotherhood of Man, The (film), 64
Brown and Williamson (tobacco
company), 13
Buckley Amendment, 319–22
bulletin boards
interpretations, 140–46
as limited public fora, 328
in publicly supported libraries,
263
Bureau of Independent Publishers
and Distributors, 221
Burress, Phil, 375–76

C

Cage aux Folles, La (film), 170
Campbell v. *St. Tammany Parish School
Board*, 314
campus computer network, 48–49
Carnegie libraries, 5
Carnovsky, Leon, 61
Case v. *Unified School District No. 233*,
314–15
Castagna, Edwin, 215
cataloging records
barriers in, 48
labeling in, 184
Catch-22 (Heller), 315
Cat's Cradle (Vonnegut), 315
cause, definition of, 23–24
Caywood, Carolyn, 222
CEE. *See* Citizens for Excellence in
Education
censors. *See also* Censorship
identifying potential, 357
motives and tactics, 366–81
censorship
contrasted with complaints, 43
definition, 116–17
expurgation as, 147
handling attempts at, 278–86
as intellectual freedom issue,
4–9
justifications for, 118, 201
labeling as, 184, 189
as tool of tyranny, 194

*Censorship and Selection: Issues and
Answers for Schools*, 387
censorship database, 389–90
censure of librarians, 86
Center for Democracy & Technology,
206
challenge hearings. *See* Complaints
"Challenged Materials" (interpretation)
history, 8, 113–17
text (1981), 116–17
text (1990), 112
"Challenged Materials, Resolution
on," 8, 114, 124
challenges to library materials,
331–46, 369
challenge hearing, 341–44
hearings, 342–43
Internet use policy, 344–46
materials selection policy, 332–38
procedures for handling complaints, 278–86, 331, 336,
338–41
by Religious Right, 371
sources of support, 388–89
and state library agencies, 52
change
and censors, 367
and legislators, 405–6
charges for library services. *See* Fees
Chaucer, Geoffrey, 313
Chicago Public Library Web site, 35
Child Online Protection Act, 316
child pornography
illegality of, 307
on Internet, 286
in Internet use policy, 292, 294
legal definition of, 288–89
children
access to information, 306
access to services, 105–11
and Internet, 34
and objectionable materials, 123
programs for, 170
rights of, 38–39, 291
"Children and the Internet:
Guidelines for Developing
Public Library Policy," 296

Children's Book Council, 150, 206, 221
Children's Online Privacy Protection
    Act, 40
Chmara, Theresa, 311–18
Christian Coalition, xv, 370, 371, 372,
    373
"Circulation of Motion Pictures and
    Video Productions," 78
circulation records. *See also* Confi-
    dentiality; Library records
    and age-based restrictions, 161
    in school libraries, 320–22
    special collections, 49
Citizen Issues Alert, 375–76
Citizen magazine, 371
Citizens for Excellence in Education
    (CEE), xv
civic organizations and handling
    concerns, 280
civil rights activities, 8, 256
Civilian Conservation Corps camps, 6
civility, 49
classes of users, 47, 89
    access for minors, 155
classics as object of weeding, 376–78
classified documents in federal
    libraries, 51
Cleaver, Eldridge, 314
Clift, David H., 237, 282
"closed shelf" materials. *See*
    Restrictions on materials
coalition building, 359, 396, 401–2
coalitions for intellectual freedom,
    395–97
code of conduct in Internet use
    policy, 310, 345
"Code of Ethics" (ALA)
    and confidentiality, 239
    and librarians' personal intellec-
        tual freedom, 14
    in privacy policy, 353
    text, 407–8
    as voluntary policy, 86
    vs. "Libraries: An American
        Value," 231
Code of Federal Regulations, 320
collection development
    in academic libraries, 163

diversity in, 118–27
    in school libraries, 44–45, 105
    specifications, 333–34
collection development policy. *See*
    Selection policy
collection evaluation, 136–39
collection maintenance in selection
    policy, 336
Committee on Book Selection in
    Defense of Liberty in Schools of
    a Democracy, 107–8
Committee on Intellectual Freedom,
    7. *See also* Intellectual Freedom
    Committee (IFC)
Commitee on the Status of Women
    in Librarianship, 68
communication skills, 280
Communications Decency Act
    (CDA), xvi, 30, 252, 290, 307–8,
    316
communications technologies, xvi
communist materials
    labeling of, 186
    suppression of, 8
    as target for censorship, 367
communist threat, responses to,
    21
community organizations, 369
community values, 309
complaints
    about exhibits, 141
    censorship distinguished from,
        43
    definition, 116
    as expression of rights, 340
    procedures for handling, 278–86,
        331, 336, 338–44
Computer Matching and Privacy
    Protection Act of 1988, 351n11
Conable, Gordon M., 42–43, 253
concern, expression of, 45, 116
Concerned Women for America
    (CWA), xv, 327–28, 375
Concerned Women for America v.
    Lafayette County, 328
confidentiality
    ALA defense of, 228
    current issues, 39–40

confidentiality (cont'd)
and electronic information access,
86–87
and government intimidation,
257, 258
history, 10–14
importance of, 347–50
as intellectual freedom issue, 4, 31
in interpretations, 81
legal basis of, 350–52
in public libraries, 42
school library records, 319–22
*Confidentiality in Libraries: An
Intellectual Freedom Modular
Education Program*, 350, 387
"Confidentiality of Library Records"
(ALA policy statement)
history, 10–11, 236–40, 348
in policies, 336, 353
procedural statement, 234–35
text (1971), 238–39
text (1986), 232–33
"Confidentiality of Personally
Identifiable Information about
Library Users" (ALA policy
statement)
history, 243–44, 350
text, 241–42
confidentiality policy
development of, 353–55
in Internet use policy, 292
in selection policy, 332
conservative supporters of library,
380–81
consortium agreements, 87–88
Conspiracy Act of 1968, 257
content-neutral criteria, 289
content of communication, 289
contracts, 81
controversial materials
in academic libraries, 46, 47, 163
and budget cuts, xvii
in collection evaluation, 136
on Internet, 83
in programs, 169
and restrictions on access, 176
and restrictions on children, 153
in selection policy, 336

controversies, dealing with, 362–64,
387–88. *See also* Challenges
"Coping with Challenges," 386
copyright law
and "Code of Ethics," 408
and electronic information, 93
expurgation as violation of, 148
cost in selection policy, 335
Couples, Fred, 309
court order and release of library
records, 239
courtesy, 338, 340
creative thought, 203
criminal investigations and library
records, 348
crisis communications. *See* Mass
media
crisis management plan, 362
criteria for protection in confidentiality policy, 353
criteria for selection, 335
current awareness on intellectual
freedom issues, 390–91, 394
current selection needs, 334
curriculum decisions, 303, 312,
313
CWA. *See* Concerned Women for
America (CWA)

D
"Dallas Resolution on Governmental
Intimidation," 256–57
database searches and confidential-
ity, 349
Day, J. Dennis, 170
"Dealing with Challenges to Books
and Other Library Materials,"
388–89
"Dealing with Complaints about
Resources," 286
"Dealing with Concerns about
Library Resources" (ALA proce-
dural statement), 386
guidelines for selection policy, 332
history, 282–86
text, 278–81
Dean, Frances C., 68, 143

Decatur Public Library v. *The District Attorney's Office of Wise County,* 12–13, 349n1

Decatur (Tex.) Public Library, 348–49

defamation as limit on free speech, 9

DeJohn, William, 215

DeLillo, Don, 22

democracy, 68–69
    and access to electronic information, 84–85
    ALA support of, 229
    and censorship, 4–9
    and confidentiality protections, 348
    education for, 39
    freedom to read, 203
    fundamental premise of, 201
    library's role in, 33, 92

Democratic National Convention (1968, Chicago), 214

depositions, 234

depository libraries, 51

depth of collection, 333

Des Moines Public Library, 59–60

deselection. *See* Weeding

designated public forum. *See* Limited public forum

disabled users
    and access to electronic information, 89
    ALA policy, 260–62

disarmament, ALA position on, 24–25

discrimination in 1961 *Library Bill of Rights,* 64

diversity
    as concept, 124–25
    in democracy, 203
    and freedom to read, 205
    in library exhibits, 140

"Diversity in Collection Development" (interpretation). *See also* Collection development
    in academic library policies, 48
    history, 120–27
    text (1982), 126–27
    text (1990), 118–19

diversity in collections
    as ALA policy, 228

and budget cuts, xvii

Dix, William S., 207, 209

Dobson, James C., 371, 372

Doctor Doolittle, 121

donors, restrictions imposed by, 46, 49, 133, 177

Douglas, William O., 350

Dudley, Margaret, 283

due process, 19
    in academic libraries, 164–65
    in Fourteenth Amendment, 350
    in policies and procedures, 264
    in user behavior policies, 276

"Dungeons and Dragons" game, 170

E

eBay, 309

"Economic Barriers to Information Access" (interpretation)
    as access issue, 10
    history, xvi, 70, 73, 132–35
    restriction of services, 89–90
    text, 128–31

economic conditions, impact of, xvii

editors, dealing with, 361

education about intellectual freedom, 356–65
    in academic libraries, 48
    during challenge attempts, 369
    Internet training (*See* Internet training)
    by Office for Intellectual Freedom, 387–90
    as preparation for hearing, 343
    as protection for children, 39
    in public libraries, 42
    school library media centers, 45–46
    for users, 81

Educational Film Library Association, 64

"Effective Ways to Communicate with Legislators," 405

electronic discussion lists
    ALAOIF, 390
    IFAN, 394
    intellectual freedom information on, 359

Electronic Frontier Foundation, 206
electronic information, preservation
    of, 83
electronic networks and confiden-
    tiality, 349
Eli M. Oboler Memorial Award, 17,
    393
Ennis, Bruce J., 301–4
environmental characteristics in
    selection policy, 333
Epaminondas and His Auntie, 178
ephemeral materials, 336
"Equal Access to Library Service"
    (ALA policy), 131
Equal Rights Amendment (ERA),
    ALA position on, 26
Ervin, Sam J., Jr., 237
Erzoznik v. City of Jacksonville, 38,
    318n2
"Especially for Children and Their
    Parents," 346
Establishment Clause
    and censorship attempts, xv
    and limits on meeting rooms,
        328
ethical practices in Program of Action,
    19. *See also* "Code of Ethics"
"Evaluating Library Collections"
    (interpretation)
    in academic library policies, 48
    history, 138–39
    restricted access, 177, 183
    text (1973), 138–39
    text (1981), 136–37
Evans, Luther, 207
Evergreen Review, 113–14
excellence as selection criterion, 289,
    335
exhibit spaces
    in academic libraries, 164
    and age-based restrictions, 161
    as limited public fora, 328
    in publicly supported libraries,
        263
    and services to gays, 99
"Exhibit Spaces and Bulletin
    Boards" (interpretation). *See also*
    Bulletin boards; Exhibit spaces

history, 142–46
    text, 140–41
expensive materials, 336
expression of concern, 116
expurgation, removal of labels as,
    185, 192
"Expurgation of Library Materials"
    (interpretation)
    history, 149–51
    and rating services, 76n
    text (1973), 150
    text (1981), 151
    text (1990), 147–48

F
facilities in public libraries, 42
fact sheet in legislative visits, 404
"factually correct" materials. *See
    also* "Sound factual authority"
    criterion
    in 1948 *Library Bill of Rights,* 63
    as intellectual freedom issue, 8
    and Internet content, 82
Fagan, Patrick, 370
fair employment practices, 19
fair warning measure, 265, 277
Falwell, Jerry, 371
Family Educational Rights and
    Privacy Act of 1974. *See* Buckley
    Amendment
Family Friendly Libraries, 374–75
Family Research Council (FRC),
    372–73, 376–78
family values as motive for censors,
    xv, 367
Farley, Judith, 133
FBI. *See* Federal Bureau of
    Investigation
FCC. *See* Federal Communications
    Commission
Federal Bureau of Investigation (FBI)
    Library Awareness Program,
        11–12, 243, 347, 350
Federal Communications
    Commission (FCC), 7
federal libraries, 49–52
federal relations coordinator, 401

fee-based information services
in academic libraries, 46
in interpretations, 82
fees
in academic libraries, 164
and age-based restrictions, 161
desirability of, 90
as economic barrier, 129
for electronic services, 95
for library programs, 169, 172
and meeting room use, 174
in public libraries, 42
as restriction on access, 176
Feminists for Free Expression, 206
FERPA. *See* Buckley Amendment
Fifth Amendment and privacy
rights, 350, 353
"fighting words" as limit on free
speech, 9
films
in 1948 *Library Bill of Rights*, 64
and clarification of *Library Bill of
Rights*, 72
in library programs, 170
filtering software, 34–35
in academic libraries, 164
defined, 248
effectiveness of, 289–90
for home use, 307, 308–9
liability for failure to install,
317
in *Library Bill of Rights* interpretations, 91–92
problems with, 248–50, 309
and Religious Right, 378–79
as restrictions on access, 176
in school libraries, 316
"Filtering Software, Statement on
Library Use of" (ALA policy
statement)
history, 252–54
in Internet policies, 291–92
text, 247–51
"Filtering Software in Libraries,
Resolution on the Use of"
history, 252–54
in Internet policy, 291–92
text, 245–46

financial aid in challenges, 393
financial deposit as restricted access,
176
"Financing of Libraries" (ALA
policy), 131
fines as economic barrier, 129
fingerprints, 243
First Amendment rights
in academic libraries, 46–47
and ALA policies, 228,
301–4
and blocking software, 291
in collection development
policies, 119
and community values, 91
expansion of, 213–14
and fees for service, 134
as foundation of intellectual
freedom, 289–91
and hostile work environment
complaints, 37
and Internet, 245–46, 247–48,
252
in *Kreimer* v. *Morristown*, 324
library's place in, 269
organizations supporting, 388
and privacy, 11–12, 241
professional practice, 9
and publicly supported libraries,
263, 264
and restrictions on access, 309
in school libraries, 311–18
in selection policy, 336
sensitivity of issue, 399
time, place, or manner restrictions (*See* Time, place, or
manner restrictions)
in view of censors, 368
Fleishman, Stanley, 154
Fletcher, Homer L., 178
Focus on the Family (FOF), xv, 371,
372, 376–78
FOIA. *See* Freedom of Information Act
foreign nationals, privacy rights of,
242
formats
age-based restrictions on, 161
in public libraries, 42

Fourteenth Amendment
  in policies and procedures, 264
  and privacy rights, 350, 353
Fourth Amendment and privacy,
  350, 351, 353
FRC. *See* Family Research Council
  (FRC)
"Free Access to Information" (ALA
  policy), 131, 133
"Free Access to Libraries for
  Minors" (interpretation). *See
  also* Children
  as access issue, 10
  history, 154–62
  in *Library Bill of Rights* interpreta-
    tions, 75–76
  restrictions on access, 177, 183
  rights of youth, 38–39
  text (1972), 156–57
  text (1981), 158–59
  text (1991), 152–53
free communication, importance of,
  202
"Free Flow of Information, The," 28,
  197. *See also* "Universal Right to
  Free Expression, The" (interpretation)
free materials, distribution of, 336
freedom of expression
  ALA defense of, 229
  as human right, 193–97, 194, 195
  on Internet, 308
  in interpretations, 81
Freedom of Information Act (FOIA)
  and confidentiality, 40
  in federal libraries, 50–51
Freedom of Information Center (U.
  of Missouri), 189, 221
Freedom of Information Day, 359
freedom of speech as basic right, xiii
"Freedom to Read, The" (ALA policy statement)
  on collection development,
    122–23
  history, 207–27
  in selection policy, 336
  text (1953), 209–13
  text (1972), 216–21

  text (2000), 201–6, 222–27
  vs. "Libraries: An American
    Value," 230
Freedom to Read Foundation
  "Freedom to Read" policy, 206, 221
  history, 13–14, 19–20
  on Internet use policies, 345
  and *Kreimer* v. *Morristown,* 324
  legal support, 391–92
Freidenberg, Edgar L., 154–55
Friends of the Library
  and pressure groups, 379
  as spokesperson, 358
  workshops for, 360
funding of libraries
  and censors, 368
  and economic barriers, 130–31
  and limits on selection, 306

G
Gaines, Ervin, 65, 154–55
Garden, Nancy, 314–15
Gay Liberation, Task Force on, 10
gay rights and ALA actions, 30
"Gay Rights and Materials,
  Resolution on," 101
gays and lesbians. *See also* "Access to
  Library Resources and Services
  regardless of Gender or Sexual
  Orientation"; Homosexuality
  and Religious Right
  exhibits, 142
  in interpretations, 97–99
gender discrimination. *See* "Access
  to Library Resources and
  Services regardless of Gender
  or Sexual Orientation"
  (interpretation)
gift books in selection policy, 59, 336
gifts, restricted, 130
global information access
  importance of, xiv
  in interpretations, 82
  and selection policies, 90–91
Godfather, The (film), 170
Gounaud, Karen Jo, 374–75, 378
governing body
  censorship by, 43

in complaint process, 339
and confidentiality policy, 354
and Internet use policy, 345–46
government information in electronic format, 92
government investigations
and confidentiality, 232–40
and library records, 241–44, 349–50
"Governmental Intimidation, Resolution on," 258–59
"Governmental Intimidation" (ALA policy statement).
See also Intimidation
history, xiv, 256–59
and privacy, 241
text, 255
Grapes of Wrath, The (Steinbeck), 7
Greenaway, Emerson, 283
Griswold v. Connecticut, 350n2, 351
"Guidelines and Considerations for Developing a Public Library Internet Use Policy." See "Internet Use Policy, Guidelines and Considerations for Developing a Public Library"
"Guidelines for the Development of Policies and Procedures regarding User Behavior and Library Usage." See "Policies and Procedures regarding User Behavior and Library Usage" (ALA policy statement)
"Guidelines for the Development . . . of Policies, Regulations and Procedures . . .". See "Policies, Regulations and Procedures Affecting Access to Library Materials, Services and Facilities" (ALA policy statement)
Gulf War, ALA response to, 29

H
hackers, 349
handicapped users, 260–62
harassment
and hate speech codes, 49

and Internet filtering, 36–37
and restrictions on speech, xvii
"harmful matter," labeling of, 189
"harmful to minors" statutes
definitions of, 288–89, 307
in Internet use policy, 292, 345
library response to, 294–95
and restrictions on access, 303
and state laws, 302
Harry Potter books, xv, 38, 376
hate speech
codes against, 49
on Internet, 95
Hazelwood School District v. Kuhlmeier, 312, 313
health and safety regulations and user behavior policies, 276
hearings
conducting, 341–44
requirement of, 112, 124
on school records, 319
Hefley, Sue, 107
Helfand, Esther, 154
Heller, Joseph, 315
Henderson, Carol C., 399–406
Henington, David, 26
Hentoff, Nat, 387
"high demand" materials. See Restrictions on materials
HIV (human immunodeficiency virus), 260–61, 262
Hodgin, T. Ellis, 21–22
Hoduski, Bernadine Abbott, 49–52
homosexuality and Religious Right, 374–75
homosexuals. See Gays and lesbians
Hopkins, Dianne McAfee, 43–46
Horn, Zoia, 256
hostile situations, dealing with, 363–64
hostile work environment
Freedom to Read Foundation memoranda, 392
as intellectual freedom issue, 31
and Internet filtering, 36–37
Houghton, Arthur A., 209

"How Libraries and Schools Can Resist Censorship," 282–83
"How Libraries Can Resist Censorship," 283–86
"How to Write a Letter to Your Legislator," 405
human rights, 194, 195
humanism and Religious Right, 379

I

IFC. *See* Intellectual Freedom Committee (IFC)
IFRT. *See* Intellectual Freedom Round Table
illegal materials on Internet, 292. *See also* Child pornography; Obscenity
Immroth Memorial. *See* John Phillip Immroth Memorial Award
In the Night Kitchen (Sendak), 149
inaccuracy in school records, 321–22
indecent materials, 290, 307
intellectual freedom
    basis of, xiii
    challenges to, xiv–xv
    and "Code of Ethics," 407
    federal libraries and, 49–52
    and First Amendment, 289–91, 305
    historical overview, 3–32
    librarians' personal intellectual freedom, 14–23
    meaning and scope, 287–89
    public libraries and, 42–43
    school library media centers, 43–46
    state library agencies and, 52–53
    weakening of supports for, 215
Intellectual Freedom Action Network
    functions, 15–16, 358
    history, 19–20
    purpose, 394
"Intellectual Freedom" (ALA policy), 131
Intellectual Freedom and the Teenager preconference, 66, 154–55

Intellectual Freedom Committee (IFC)
    fact-finding studies, 18–19
    function, 3, 386
    history, 7, 14
    state (*See* State library association intellectual freedom committees)
"Intellectual Freedom in the News," 391
"Intellectual Freedom Principles for Academic Libraries" (interpretation)
    history, 8–9, 166–67
    text, 163–65
Intellectual Freedom Round Table (IFRT)
    activities, 393–94
    history, 16–17
intellectual property. *See* Copyright law
interest level in selection policy, 335
interlibrary loan metaphor for Internet filtering, 293–94
interlibrary loans
    age-based restrictions on, 161
    confidentiality of, 11
    controversial materials, 48
Internal Revenue Service (IRS), 10–11, 236–38
International Conference of Police Associations, 120
International Reading Association, 44, 206
"International Relations" policy (ALA), 194
Internet
    and access to information, 306
    current issues, 34–36
    effect on global communications, xvi
    and privacy issues, 39–40, 349
    as protected medium, 308
    recommended sites, 292–93, 310
    and school libraries, 45, 315–17
Internet policy
    development of, 332, 344–46

specific provisions, 291–93
"Internet Toolkit," xvi, 386
Internet training, 35, 91, 250–51, 292, 310, 346
"Internet Use Policy, Guidelines and Considerations for Developing a Public Library"
and developing a policy, 345
history, 296–97
text, 287–95
intimidation
by government, 195
by pressure groups, 380
IRS. *See* Internal Revenue Service (IRS)
Island Trees. See Board of Education, Island Trees (New York) Union Free School District No. 26 v. Pico

J
Jackson (Miss.) incident, 214
Jefferson, Thomas, 84
Jenner & Block, 295, 392
Jennison, Peter, 215
John Phillip Immroth Memorial Award, 16–17, 393
Johnson, Lyndon B., 214
"Joint Statement on Access," 177
"Joint Statement on Faculty Status of College and University Librarians," 166–67
Jones, Barbara M., 46–49
judgmental language in intellectual freedom message, 357

K
Kathleen R. v. City of Livermore, 317
Katz v. United States, 351
Kennedy, David M., 237
Kennedy, Robert F., 214
Kent State incident, 214
"KidsClick!" Web site, 310
King, Martin Luther, Jr., 214
Kirsh, Robert, 154
Kleeman, Richard, 222
Kreimer v. Morristown, 268–69, 275–77, 323–28

Krug, Judith F., 3–32, 215, 305–10
Ku Klux Klan exhibit, 142

L
"Labeling, Statement on" (interpretation)
and collection development, 123
history, 8, 64, 186–92
and rating services, 76n
text (1951), 187–88
text (1981), 191
text (1990), 184–85
labeling campaigns, xv
labeling in "Freedom to Read" statement, 204
Lacy, Dan, 209, 215, 282–83
LAD. *See* Library Administration Division
Ladof, Nina S., 188–89
Lamont v. U.S. Postmaster General, 350
language of materials in collection development, 119
LAP. *See* Federal Bureau of Investigation (FBI) Library Awareness Program
Lasswell, Harold D., 209
"laundry list" problem, 100, 103
law enforcement authorities. *See also* Confidentiality
and confidentiality threats, 355
and patron behavior, 272
requests for records, 239, 241–44
lawyers in coalitions, 397
Layton, Jeanne, 22–23
legal counsel
in challenge attempts, 369
confidentiality issues, 232n, 234
legally dangerous actions against labeling, 191
legislation, tracking, 52–53, 280, 390–91
legislative process, 402–3
legislative staff, 403, 404
legislators, lobbying, 399–400, 403–5
Leigh, Robert D., 17
LeRoy C. Merritt Humanitarian Fund, 20, 393
lesbians. *See* Gays and lesbians

letters from pressure groups, 380
letters to the editor
  by censors, 368
  in controversies, 363
  and lobbying efforts, 401, 405
  and promotion of intellectual
      freedom, 358, 361
levels of services and user fees, 133
Lewis, Freeman, 215
libel actions against labeling,
  189
librarians
  attitude of, 3
  "Code of Ethics," 407–8
  commitment to intellectual free-
      dom, 14, 120–21
  confidentiality responsibility,
      352–53
  and freedom to read, 202–5, 208
  personal intellectual freedom, 4,
      14–23, 28
  responsibilities of, 230
Librarians' Union, American
  Federation of Labor, 5
"Libraries: An American Value"
  (ALA policy statement), 230–31,
  386
libraries, role of, xvii–xviii. See also
  Limited public forum; Mission
  and objectives
  and access to electronic informa-
      tion, 84–85
  in education of children, 39
  in social change, 23
  in view of censors, 367–68
"Libraries & the Internet Toolkit,"
  xvi, 386
Library Administration Division
  (LAD), 19
"Library Advocacy Now!", 401
Library Awareness Program. See
  Federal Bureau of Investigation
  (FBI) Library Awareness
  Program
Library Bill of Rights
  in collection development policy,
      44, 47–48, 336
  and filtering, 248, 254

and handling concerns, 281
in hearing preparation, 343
history, 8–9, 59–71
interpretations, 10, 72–74
and library standards, 52
observed in policies and proce-
    dures, 264–65
in privacy policy, 353
in review of complaints, 339
revision of, 100–1, 102
text (1948), 63
text (1961), 64–65
text (1967), 67
text (1980), 57–58
as voluntary policy, 86
library board president as spokes-
    person, 358
library cards, 155, 157, 160, 161
library director as spokesperson,
    358
"Library-Initiated Programs as a
    Resource" (interpretation)
  history, 73, 170–72
  text, 168–69
Library Legislative Day, 404
Library of Congress (LC)
  as federal library, 49
  fees for services, 132, 133
library records. See also
    Confidentiality
  and Freedom of Information Act
      requests, 40
  state law protection of, 352
"library-related" activities and meet-
    ing room restriction, 174
library service policy
  in academic libraries, 164
  and "Code of Ethics," 407
  development of, 333
  and response to concerns, 278
"Library Services for the Poor"
  (ALA policy), 131
library staff
  censorship by, 43
  in challenge attempts, 369
  and confidentiality, 349, 354–55
  and intellectual freedom
      message, 358

training in user behavior, 273, 276

workshops for, 360

library trustees, 160

and intellectual freedom message, 358

liability for labeling, 189

workshops for, 360

Library's Bill of Rights (1939).

See also Library Bill of Rights

access issues in, 10

history, 7–9, 8–9, 59–61

text, 59–60

licensing agreements

in academic libraries, 164

as economic barrier, 48

in interpretations, 81

and users' rights, 86

limited public forum

academic library as, 47

defined, 325

and Internet filtering, 37

public libraries as, 269, 289–91, 323–28

and user fees, 134

Lindsey, John R., 349

lines of communication with community, 280

linguistic barriers. *See* Multilingual communities

linguistic pluralism, 106, 111.

See also Multilingual communities

Lions Club, 188

listening to concerns, 280, 338, 364

Little Black Sambo, 120–21

"Little Mermaid," 375

lobbying, 399–406

local control of library, 35

"locked case" materials. *See* Restrictions on materials

"Lottery, The" (film), 313

Loudoun County (Va.) Library, 36, 375, 397. *See also Mainstream Loudoun* v. *Board of Trustees of Loudoun County Library*

low-cost alternatives in academic libraries, 164

"Loyalty Programs, Policy on" (ALA policy), 21

Lysistrata, 313

M

Madison, James, 41, 84

Magazine Publishers Association, 221

Mainstream Loudoun v. *Board of Trustees of Loudoun County Library,* 316

Marcus v. *Search Warrants,* 114

marketplace of ideas, collection support of, 334–35

Mars Exploration Web site, 35, 309

mass media

and handling concerns, 280

and intellectual freedom message, 359–60

and lobbying efforts, 402

and pressure groups, 380

in publicity for hearing, 342–43

working with, 360–62

materials selection policy. *See* Selection policy

McCarthy era

effects of, 107

and revision of "Freedom to Read" Policy, 214

McConnell, J. Michael, 18–19, 22

McMullin, Florence, 23

McNeal, Archie, 283

media. *See* Mass media; Nonprint media

Media Coalition, 388, 400

Media Institute, 206

media training, 358

meeting rooms

as access issue, 8, 10

and age-based restrictions, 161

in *Library's Bill of Rights,* 60

as limited public forums, 327–28

and services to gays, 99

"Meeting Rooms" (interpretation)

history (*See* "Exhibit Spaces and Bulletin Boards": history)

text, 173–75

mentally impaired users, 260–62
Merchant of Venice, The
    (Shakespeare), 121
Merritt Fund. *See* LeRoy C. Merritt
    Humanitarian Fund
message sheet, 357, 361
Miller, Henry, 282
Miller's Tale (Chaucer), 313
Milwaukee Public Library, 236
Minarcini v. *Strongsville City School
    District*, 315
minorities, portrayal of, 122
Minority Concerns Committee
    and 1988 *Library Bill of Rights*, 70
    and economic barriers, 132
    policy and procedures, 267
    and revisions of interpretations,
        73
minority rights as motive for censor-
    ship, 367
minors. *See also* Adolescents;
    Children
    access to electronic information,
        85, 88–89
    access to libraries, 27, 152–62
    confidentiality, 319–22
    restricted access, 181
    rights of, 30
mission and objectives
    and collection development pol-
        icy, 92, 152, 332
    in *Kreimer* v. *Morristown*, 325
    and restrictions on access, 265
    and user behavior policies,
        272
Molhollan, Daniel, 133
Monteiro v. *Temple Union High School
    District*, 318n5
Moral Majority, 371
moral support, 358
Morgan, Candace, 101, 102, 133,
    275
Morristown (N.J.) Public Library. *See*
    Kreimer v. *Morristown*
*Mother Goose Nursery Rhymes and
    Fairy Tales*, 121
Motion Picture Association of
    America (MPAA), 76, 221

motion pictures. *See* Films
motivation of censors
    and book removal, 303, 314–15
    Religious Right, 378–79
multilingual communities,
    168, 172. *See also* Linguistic
    pluralism
music as target of censorship, 222

N

NAACP (National Association for
    the Advancement of Colored
    People), 178
NAACP v. *Alabama*, 351
National Association of Christian
    Educators, xv
National Association of College
    Stores, 221
National Book Committee (NBC),
    215, 221, 283
National Coalition against
    Censorship, 206, 388, 397
National Council for Social Studies,
    44
National Council of Negro Women,
    221
National Council of Teachers of
    English, 44, 221, 281, 283, 285,
    397
National Education Association, 281,
    283, 285, 397
National Freedom Fund for
    Librarians (NFFL), 22
National Library Week Program,
    221
National PTA, 206, 397
national security, 242
National Security Archive (NSA), 12
negative language in intellectual
    freedom message, 357, 364
"NetFind for Kids," 310
netiquette classes, 35
network of local advocates, 358
neutrality. *See* "Advocacy" vs. "neu-
    trality"
New Jersey libraries, 186
New Jersey Library Association, 324
New York Times Company, 21

"News Sources for Information about Censorship . . .", 390

Newsletter on Intellectual Freedom, 15, 387

newspapers, xiii, 369. *See also* Mass media; School newspapers

NFFL. *See* National Freedom Fund for Librarians (NFFL)

Nixon, Richard, 214

"no comment" response, 361

nonlibrary supporters in lobbying efforts, 403

nonprint media
  in 1948 *Library Bill of Rights,* 63–64
  access for minors, 75–77
  censorship of, 7
  inclusion in *Library Bill of Rights,* 72

nonpublic forum, defined, 325

Nordstrom, Ursula, 149

NSA (National Security Archive), 12

O

objectionable materials
  discovery by censors, 368
  labeling of, 184
  and restricted access, 176–77

Oboler Award. *See* Eli M. Oboler Memorial Award

obscenity. *See also* Pornography; Sexually explicit materials
  attempts to restrict, xvi
  and concerns about resources, 281
  as defined by Religious Right, 374–75
  in "Freedom to Read" policy, 208
  on Internet, 286, 294
  in Internet use policy, 292, 345
  legal definition of, 113, 288–89, 307
  as limit on free speech, 9
  as screen for political objections, 367

occultism
  and "protect the children" campaigns, 38
  and Religious Right, xv, 376

"off the record" statements, 364

Office for Intellectual Freedom (OIF), 387–90
  challenge support, 281, 343, 369
  history, 14–16
  and lobbying efforts, 400
  modular education program, 350
  on selection policies, 338
  state-level lobbying, 400

Ogburn, William, 6

OIF. *See* Office for Intellectual Freedom (OIF)

O'Neill, Eugene, 7

op-ed pieces, 361, 401

open meetings laws, 342
  and Religious Right, 379

oral complaints, definition of, 116

origin, defined, 265

Osborne v. *Ohio,* 351

Owens, T. J., 178

Oxford (Miss.) Public Library, 327

P

P.E.N.–American Center, 221

Paine, Thomas, xiii

parental authority and responsibility
  and access for minors, 153, 160
  ALA defense of, 228
  guidelines on, 78
  and Internet use, 82, 249–50, 252, 291
  and Internet use policy, 345
  in *Library Bill of Rights* interpretations, 76
  methods of protecting children, 307
  preparation for diversity, 204
  and privacy rights of children, 349
  right to know, 319–22
  and school records, 319–22

parental permissions, 88–89, 161

Parents, Families and Friends of Lesbians and Gays, 206

"patently offensive" materials, 290, 307

patience in lobbying, 406

patron behavior, 271–77, 323–28

penalties for violation of Internet use
     policy, 345
"Pending Internet Legislation," 390
Penway, Anne Levinson, 319–22,
     323–28
People for the American Way, 206,
     388
Peoples of the U.S.S.R (film), 64
Peoria (Ill.) Public Library, 64, 72
performance measures, 52
Periodical and Book Association of
     America, 221
Perry Education Assn. v. *Perry Local
     Educators Assn.*, 318n4
personal attacks, 364
petition drives by censors, 368
photocopying charges, 135
physically impaired users, 260–62
*Pico. See Board of Education, Island
     Trees (New York) Union Free
     School District No. 26* v. *Pico*
Pierce, Dennis, 375
Pilpel, Harriet, 215
Pinnell-Stephens, June, 230
Playboy, 362
police officers. *See* Law enforcement
     authorities
"Policies, Regulations and
     Procedures Affecting Access
     to Library Materials, Services
     and Facilities" (ALA policy
     statement)
     history, 267–70
     text, 263–66
     use of, 386
policies and procedures. *See also
     specific policies*
     in academic libraries, 47
     on confidentiality, 232
     for electronic information access,
        88
     in federal libraries, 51
     guidelines for, 263–70
     harassment, 37
     on Internet use, 35–36, 250–51
     and responses to pressure
        groups, 380
     sample, from state library
        agencies, 52

     on use of exhibit areas, 140–41
     written, 331
"Policies and Procedures for
     Selection of Instructional
     Materials," 337
"Policies and Procedures regarding
     User Behavior and Library
     Usage" (ALA policy statement)
     guidelines, 271–74
     history, 275–77
     as response to *Kreimer* v.
        Morristown, 327
"Policy concerning Confidentiality
     of Personally Identifiable
     Information about Library
     Users." *See* "Confidentiality of
     Personally Identifiable
     Information about Library
     Users" (ALA policy statement)
"Policy Objectives" (ALA policy),
     131
"Policy on Confidentiality of Library
     Records." *See* "Confidentiality
     of Library Records" (ALA
     policy statement)
"Policy on Governmental
     Intimidation." *See* "Govern-
     mental Intimidation" (ALA
     policy statement)
"political correctness" campaigns, xv
political issues
     as motive for censorship, 121, 367
     and Religious Right, 372
     and role of libraries, 24
pornography. *See also* Obscenity;
     Sexually explicit materials
     as defined by Religious Right,
        374–75, 378
     in "Freedom to Read" policy, 208
     on Internet, 286
     as protected speech, 306–7
positive provision of opportunity
     and freedom to read, 205
practical concerns against labeling,
     187, 191
Pratt v. *Independent School District
     No. 831*, 313
preparation for controversies, 362–63
preparation for media contacts, 360

preservation and replacement
in academic libraries, 164
and restrictions on access, 177
"Preservation Policy," 177, 183
press releases, 361
pressure groups
and freedom to read, 204
responding to, 379–81
pressure toward conformity, 202
"Principles for the Development of
the National Information
Infrastructure," 94
printouts, charges for, 90
privacy. *See also* Confidentiality
in academic libraries, 48–49, 163
and "Code of Ethics," 407
current issues, 39–40
and First Amendment, 11–12
in Internet use policy, 292,
345
legal basis, 350–52
and physical environment, 87
school library records, 319–22
Privacy Act of 1974, 351, 353
privacy screens, 250
problem patrons, 268–69
procedures. *See* Policies and procedures; *specific issues*
professional practice
as intellectual freedom issue, 4,
27–30
in school libraries, 45
Program of Action for Mediation,
Arbitration, and Inquiry, 19
Program of Action in Support of the
Library Bill of Rights, 17–19
programming in library
and age-based restrictions, 161
family-friendly, 380
and intellectual freedom, 168–72
on intellectual freedom, 359–60
Promise of the First Freedom, The, 216
promptness of response, 380
"protect the children" campaigns,
xv, 38
psychological barriers, 176
public access catalog contract, 49
public attack, definition of, 116

public forum
defined, 324–25
Internet as, 95
public information programs, 280
public libraries. *See also* Limited
public forum; Publicly supported libraries
attacks by Religious Right, 373
classes of users, 89
intellectual freedom and, 42–43
Public Library Association, 96, 155,
296
public opinion, formation of, xiii
public relations
in controversies, 362
lobbying efforts, 401
in preparation for challenges,
369
in selection policy, 332
public schools, 373
publicity for hearing, 342
publicly supported libraries. *See also*
Limited public forum
academic libraries, 46–47
access to, 263–70
status under First Amendment,
309
publishers
in coalitions, 397
and freedom to read, 202–5, 208
as support in challenges, 369
purpose statement in Internet use
policy, 345

Q

Quantity of Copies of Books, A., v.
Kansas, 114

R

racist materials
and "protect the children" campaigns, 38
and removal of materials, 121,
122
Racketeer Influenced and Corrupt
Organizations (RICO) Act, xv
radio broadcasts, 7
Ramparts magazine, 188–89

rating services, 76–77, 290
rating systems as labeling, 184
reading, value of, 203–5. *See also*
      "Freedom to Read, The" (ALA
      policy statement)
reconsideration committee, 341–42
reconsideration of materials, 44
records. *See* Confidentiality; Library
      Records; School library records;
      School records
recriminations against librarians, 21
"Reevaluating Library Collections,"
      138–39
reference interview, 46
reference services and age-based
      restrictions, 161
"Regulations, Policies and
      Procedures Affecting Access to
      Library Resources and
      Services," 267, 270
religious groups
   and labeling, 186
   and meeting rooms, 141, 143–44,
      173, 327–28
Religious Right, 370–81
religious views as motive for censor-
      ship, 367
removal of labels, 185, 192
removal of materials from library,
      112
   court decisions, 302–3
   legality of, 303–4
   and objectionable materials, 123
Reno v. *ACLU*, 30–31, 34, 247, 290,
      292, 294, 316
reporters, dealing with, 360–61
"Reporting a Challenge," 389
repressive legislation, combating,
      390–91
request for reconsideration, 115
"Request for Reconsideration of
      Library Resources," 279, 339
request to examine, 234
"Resolution on Access to the Use of
      Libraries . . . by Individuals
      with Physical or Mental Impair-
      ment." *See* "Access to the Use of
      Libraries and Information by

Individuals with Physical or
      Mental Impairment" (ALA
      policy statement)
"Resolution on Challenged
      Materials," 8, 114, 124
"Resolution on Gay Rights and
      Materials," 101
"Resolution on Governmental
      Intimidation," 258–59
"Resolution on the Use of Filtering
      Software in Libraries." *See*
      "Filtering Software in Libraries,
      Resolution on the Use of"
resolutions of support, 343
responsibility
   in confidentiality policy, 353
   for selection, 335, 339
"Restricted Access to Library
      Materials" (interpretation)
   history, 74, 178–83
   objectionable materials,
      123–24
   text (1973), 179–81
   text (1981), 181–83
   text (2000), 176–77
restricted-use areas, 158, 160
restrictions on access
   attempts by censors, 368
   on basis of viewpoint, 302
   and Religious Right, 378
   as violation of First Amendment
      rights, 303
restrictions on materials
   and managerial concerns, 88
   as response to complaints, 43
reviews of policies and procedures,
      265, 272–73
   after complaint, 339–40
   selection policy, 331
Rexroth, Kenneth, 154
right to receive information, 319
right to vote, xiii
Robertson, Pat, 371, 372
Rogers, Rutherford D., 186
role of library. *See* Libraries, role of
Rom, Patricia, 256
Rowling, J. K., 376
Rust v. *Sullivan*, 267

S

St. Charles (Mo.) County Library,
    188–89
San Jose (Calif.) libraries, 178
sanctions policy, 17
SAR. *See* Sons of the American
    Revolution
Sarokin, H. Lee, 276, 324
satanism and library records, 347
school libraries
    access to, 105–11
    court decisions, 311–18
    exhibits, 142
    First Amendment rights in, 303
    intellectual freedom and, 43–46
    selection policy, 328, 335
School Library Bill of Rights, 108–9
school library media center. *See*
    School libraries
school library media specialists, role
    of, 43
school library records, 319–22
school newspapers, 312
school records, 319–22
SCMAI. *See* Staff Committee on
    Mediation, Arbitration, and
    Inquiry
Scott, Walter, 377
SCRIM. *See* Standing Committee on
    Review, Inquiry, and Mediation
scripts for speakers, 359
security concerns
    electronic records, 87
    in *Library Bill of Rights* interpreta-
        tions, 81, 82
selection aids, 335, 339
selection metaphor for Internet
    filtering, 293
selection policy. *See also* Collection
    development
    in academic libraries, 47–48
    and challenged materials, 115, 339
    development of, 332–38
    in federal libraries, 51
    as intellectual freedom issue, 8
    and Internet content, 82
    library-initiated programs, 169
    outline, 337

in preparation for challenges, 369
    and response to concerns, 278
self-censorship, xvi
    and services to minors, 153
    and suppression efforts, 202
self-incrimination, privilege against,
    and privacy rights, 350
Sendak, Maurice, 149
Sessions, William, 243
sex education materials, 98
"Sex Education Materials in
    Libraries" (ALA policy), 73, 104
Sex Information and Education
    Council of the U.S., 221
sex-linked language, 68
"Sexism, Racism, and Other -Isms in
    Library Materials," 121–22
sexist materials
    and "protect the children" cam-
        paigns, 38
    removal of materials, 121, 122
sexually explicit materials. *See also*
    Obscenity; Pornography
    challenges to, 113
    and filters, 290
    on Internet, 286
    as target for censors, 367
    as threat to values, 367
Shaevel, Evelyn, 3–32, 41–53
Slaughterhouse Five (Vonnegut),
    314
"smell" rule, 326, 327
Smith, W. Lester, 216
social issues and role of library, 23,
    24
Social Responsibilities Round Table
    (SRRT)
    government intimidation, 257
    South Africa boycott, 29, 196
    Task Force on Gay Liberation, 10
social tensions, xvii, 202
Society of American Archivists, 177
"Some Suggestions about Things
    You Can Do to Counter
    Censorship . . .", 397
Sons of the American Revolution
    (SAR), 186–87
Soul on Ice (Cleaver), 314

"sound bite," 357
"sound factual authority" criterion,
    121. *See also* "Factually correct"
    materials
South Africa, Republic of, 26–27,
    28–29, 196
Spaulding, Forrest, 59
speakers, controversial, 169, 170
speakers in support of intellectual
    freedom
    at hearings, 343, 344
    and Intellectual Freedom Action
        Network, 388
speaking engagements and educa-
    tion on intellectual freedom,
    359
special collections
    and age-based restrictions, 161
    confidentiality issues, 49
    restrictions on access, 177
    in selection policy, 336
Special Committee on Civil
    Liberties, 10, 64
special events for intellectual free-
    dom, 359
Spock, Benjamin, 188–89
spokespeople, 358, 363
sponsored materials, 336
SRRT. *See* Social Responsibilities
    Round Table (SRRT)
Staff Committee on Mediation,
    Arbitration, and Inquiry
    (SCMAI), 19
staff training
    in application of policies and
        procedures, 266
    on confidentiality policy, 49,
        355
    handling complaints, 278–79
standards, 52
Standing Committee on Review,
    Inquiry, and Mediation
    (SCRIM), 19
Stanley v. *Georgia*, 350–51
"Starvation of Young Black Minds,
    The," 28
State and Regional Achievement
    Award, 16, 393

state law
    "harmful to minors" statutes (*See*
        "Harmful to minors"
        statutes)
    protection of library records, 352,
        353
state library agencies, 52–53
    sample selection policies, 338
state library association intellectual
    freedom committees
    and lobbying, 401
    as resource for intellectual free-
        dom message, 361–62
    and state library agencies, 52
    as support during challenges,
        343, 369, 395
state library association legislation
    committee, 401
"Statement of Principles of
    Intellectual Freedom and
    Tenure for Librarians," 18
"Statement on Labeling." *See*
    "Labeling, Statement on"
    (interpretation)
"Statement on Library Use of
    Filtering Software." *See*
    "Filtering Software, Statement
    on Library Use of" (ALA policy
    statement)
statutes and ordinances
    and handling concerns, 280
    in policies and procedures, 264
    and user behavior policies, 272
Steig, William, 120–21
Steinbeck, John, 7
stereotypes about censors, 366
Stewart, Potter, xiii
Strange Fruit, 8
Strategic Lawsuits against Public
    Participation (SLAPPs), xv–xvi
Student Press Law Center, 206
students as speakers, 343
subject headings, 48
subpoena, response to, 232, 234
subversive materials
    and concerns about resources, 281
    in "Freedom to Read" policy, 208
    labeling of, 8, 186–87

and library records, 348
   as target for political censors, 367
"subversives," response to, 21
Sullivan, Richard, 215
supernatural themes, 376. *See also*
   Occultism
supporters of intellectual freedom,
   357, 394
suppression, attempts at, 201–2, 209
suppression of ideas, 201–2
Sylvester and the Magic Pebble (Steig),
   120–21
Symons, Ann K., 230, 253

T
Tabb, Winston, 133
talk shows, 360, 362, 363
talking points, 357
teachers
   and freedom to read, 204
   and threats to confidentiality,
      349
"TEENHoopla," 293
Telecommunications Reform Act of
   1996. *See* Communications
   Decency Act (CDA)
tenure issues, 18–19
Thackeray, William, 377
theft and mutilation protection and
   restricted access, 180, 182, 302
theft as method of censorship, 370,
   375
Thomas Jefferson Center for the
   Protection of Free Expression,
   206
threats against library staff, 235
Thrower, Randolph W., 237
time, place, or manner restrictions,
   88
   in exhibits, 141
   and First Amendment rights,
      289
   in Internet use policy, 292, 345
   in limited public fora, 325
   meeting rooms, 173
   on patron behavior, 90, 93, 272
   in policies and procedures, 264

time limits for hearing, 342
Tinker v. *Des Moines Independent
   Community School District*, 38,
   311–12
tobacco archive and confidentiality,
   13
totalitarian systems and freedom to
   read, 203
Tropic of Cancer (Miller), 282
Twain, Mark, 371, 377

U
Under Cover, 8
United States Constitution. *See also*
   First Amendment rights
   and access to electronic informa-
      tion, 84–85
   freedom to read in, 202
United States Department of
   Education, 319, 320
United States Supreme Court
   conservative appointments, 214
   definition of obscenity, 113,
      287–88
   on freedom of speech, 9
   human and civil rights decisions,
      213
   on Internet, xvi, 34–35, 245–46,
      247–48, 252, 292, 294, 308
   on privacy, 350–51
   on public and nonpublic fora,
      324–25
   on removal of materials, 302–3
   students' rights, 38, 311–12
   viewpoint-based discrimination,
      267–68
United States Treasury Department,
   236, 348. *See also* Alcohol,
   Tobacco, and Firearms Division;
   Internal Revenue Service
Universal Declaration of Human
   Rights, xiv, 27, 28, 193–94, 196
"Universal Right to Free Expression,
   The" (interpretation). *See also*
   Freedom of expression
   and global thinking, xiv
   history, 28, 73, 196–97
   text, 193–95

University of California at Berkeley, 142
University of California at San Francisco, 13
unreasonable search and seizure and privacy rights, 350
"User Behavior and Library Usage, Guidelines for . . .". *See* "Policies and Procedures regarding User Behavior and Library Usage" (ALA policy statement)
user groups in selection policy, 333
users
    behavior of, 271–77
    rights of and censors, 367–68
Utah Library Association, 21

V
vendors, 336
Vermouth, Paul, 222
Veterans of Foreign Wars, 188
videotapes, 75–77
Vietnam War, 214
    ALA response to, 8, 24
    and government intimidation, 256
viewpoint-based discrimination, 267–68
viewpoint-neutral restrictions, 315
    meeting rooms, 145, 174
violence
    effect on freedom of expression, 214
    and restrictions on speech, xvii
Virgil v. *School Board of Columbia County, Florida,* 313
Vonnegut, Kurt, 314, 315

W
Wall Street Journal, 21
Waller, Theodore, 215
warning labels on recordings, 192
warnings in Internet use policy, 345
Washington Library Association, 239

Washington Newsletter, 400
Washington Office Newsline (ALA-WON), 400
Weathermen group, 214
Web sites
    current issues, 34
    intellectual freedom information on, 359
    preselected, 292–93, 310
Webster Groves School District v. *Pulitzer Publishing Company,* 319
weeding, 138n, 289. *See also* Collection evaluation
Westchester Conference, 207
Wexner v. *Anderson,* 303–4
"What You Can Do," 389
Wise County. See Decatur Public Library v. *The District Attorney's Office of Wise County*
Women's National Book Association, 221
women's rights, 309
Wood, Don, 385–98
"Workbook for Selection Policy Writing," 338
workshops on intellectual freedom, 359–60
written complaints, 116, 341
written policies, 331
Wynn, Vivian, 222

Y
You and Machines (Ogburn), 6
Young, Diana, 52–53
Young Adult Services Division, 155–56, 157, 170
Young Women's Christian Association (YWCA), 221

Z
Zeran v. *AOL,* 317
Zola, Émile, 377
zoning laws, xvi